AF696808

Governance through Development

Governance through Development locates the Poverty Reduction Strategy Paper (PRSP) framework within the broader context of international law and global governance, exploring its impact on third world state engagement with the global political economy and the international regulatory norms and institutions which support it. The PRSP framework has replaced the controversial structural adjustment programmes as the primary mechanism through which official development financing is channelled to low-income developing countries. It has changed the regulatory landscape of international development financing, signalling a wider paradigmatic shift in the cartography of aid and, consequently, in the nature of north–south relations. *Governance through Development* documents and analyses this change within the legacy of postcolonial economic relations, revealing the wider legal, economic and geo-political significance of the PRSP framework. Celine Tan argues that the PRSP framework establishes a new regulatory regime that builds upon the disciplinary project of structural adjustment by embedding neoliberal economic conditionalities within a regime of domestic governance and public policy reform.

The book will be of interest to scholars, researchers and students of law, political science and international relations, sociology and development studies.

Celine Tan is Lecturer in Law at the University of Birmingham. Her research explores aspects of international economic law and regulation, focusing on the intersections between law, policy and governance, and the development impacts of global economic governance. She is co-editor with Julio Faundez of *International Law, Economic Globalization and Developing Countries.*

Law, development and globalization

Series Editor: Julio Faundez

University of Warwick

During the past decades, a substantial transformation of law and legal institutions in developing countries has taken place. Whether prompted by market-based policies or the international human rights movement, by the relentless advance of the process of globalization or the successive waves of democratization, no area of law has been left untouched. The aim of this series is to promote cross-disciplinary dialogue and cooperation among scholars and development practitioners interested in understanding the theoretical and practical implications of the momentous legal changes taking place in developing countries.

Titles in the series:

State Violence and Human Rights: State Officials in the South
Andrew M. Jefferson and Steffen Jensen (eds)

The Political Economy of Government Auditing: Financial Governance and the Rule of Law in Latin America and Beyond
Carlos Santiso

Global Perspectives on the Rule of Law
James J. Heckman, Robert L. Nelson and Lee Cabatingan (eds)

Marginalized Communities and Access to Justice
Yash Ghai and Jill Cottrell (eds)

Law in the Pursuit of Development: Principles into Practice?
Amanda Perry-Kessaris (ed.)

Forthcoming titles in the series:

Lawyers and the Construction of Transnational Justice
Yves Dezalay and Bryant Garth (eds) (2011)

Lawyers and the Rule of Law in an Era of Globalization
Yves Dezalay and Bryant Garth (eds) (2011)

Policing and Human Rights: The Meaning of Violence and Justice in the Everyday Policing of Johannesburg
Julia Hornberger (2011)

Social Movements, Law and the Politics of Land Reform
George Meszaros (2011)

Governance through Development

Poverty Reduction Strategies, International Law and the Disciplining of Third World States

Celine Tan

Routledge
Taylor & Francis Group
a GlassHouse book

First published 2011
by Routledge
2 Park Square, Milton Park, Abingdon, Oxon, OX14 4RN

Simultaneously published in the USA and Canada
by Routledge
270 Madison Avenue, New York, NY 10016

A GlassHouse book

Routledge is an imprint of the Taylor & Francis Group, an informa business

© 2011 Celine Tan

The right of Celine Tan to be identified as author of this work has been asserted by her in accordance with sections 77 and 78 of the Copyright, Designs and Patents Act 1988.

Typeset in Baskerville by Taylor & Francis Books
Printed and bound in Great Britain by CPI Antony Rowe, Chippenham, Wiltshire

All rights reserved. No part of this book may be reprinted or reproduced or utilised in any form or by any electronic, mechanical, or other means, now known or hereafter invented, including photocopying and recording, or in any information storage or retrieval system, without permission in writing from the publishers.

British Library Cataloguing in Publication Data
A catalogue record for this book is available from the British Library

Library of Congress Cataloguing in Publication Data
Tan, Celine.
Governance through development : poverty reduction strategies, international law and the disciplining of third world states / Celine Tan.
p. cm.
Includes bibliographical references.
1. Poverty–Government policy–Developing countries. 2. Economic assistance–Developing countries–Management. 3. Law and economic development. I. Title.
HC59.72.P6T36 2011
338.9009172'4–dc22
2010050841

ISBN13: 978-0-415-49554-7 (hbk)
ISBN13: 978-0-203-83458-9 (ebk)

For my parents, Helen and Philip, my husband, Paul, and my son, Isaac.

Contents

List of illustrations xi
Acknowledgements xii
A note on terminology xiv
List of abbreviations xvii

1 Introduction 1

1.1 Crisis and change in international economic lawmaking 1
1.2 A new 'social contract' 3
1.3 Scope of inquiry 5
1.4 Framework of analysis 9
1.4.1 Analysing the relationship between actors, principles and mechanisms of globalisation 9
1.4.2 Locating regulatory patterns within a wider analysis of power 12
1.4.3 Representational power and the discipline of discourse 14
1.4.4 Legal pluralism and the constitutive power of law 16
1.5 A note on methods 18
1.6 Cartography of the book 18

2 PRSPs in postcolonial international law and global governance 23

2.1 PRSPs in the international order: asymmetrical sovereignty and circumscription of state autonomy 24
2.1.1 Locating the PRSP project in the 'postcoloniality' of international law 25
2.1.2 Reproducing colonial asymmetries through postcolonial law 27
2.2 Institutions of postcolonial governance: the Bretton Woods system 31
2.2.1 Legacies of the colonial encounter 31
2.2.2 Aggravating asymmetry 33
2.2.3 Monopolising the forum 35

2.3 Managing the third world: the Bank and Fund in postcolonial governance 36
2.3.1 Bridging the dynamic of difference 37
2.3.2 Managing the terms of engagement 41
2.4 Continuities and consolidation of postcolonial law 50

3 PRSPs and the crisis of legitimacy in the international order 60

3.1 PRSPs as a response to the limitations of structural adjustment 61
3.1.1 The disciplinary rationale of adjustment lending 62
3.1.2 The failure to discipline 63
3.2 Postscripting the Washington Consensus 64
3.2.1 From adjustment to poverty reduction 65
3.2.2 Securing legitimacy through participation 66
3.2.3 Universal framework for disbursement 66
3.3 Competing agendas for change 68
3.3.1 The role of the epistemic coalition 69
3.3.2 The institutional response to the conceptual framework 72
3.3.3 Geo-strategic interests and the role of the NGO lobby 75
3.4 Missing pieces in the jigsaw: the absent south 80
3.5 PRSPs and the legacy of state fragmentation 82
3.5.1 Internationalisation of decision-making 82
3.5.2 The retreat of the state 84
3.6 Crisis and containment 86

4 'Ownership' as conditionality: PRSPs and the evolution of conditional financing 94

4.1 Deconstructing conditionality 95
4.1.1 Conditionality versus conditions for financing 96
4.1.2 IMF conditionality 98
4.1.3 World Bank conditionality 100
4.1.4 Policy regulation 101
4.2 Conditionality as a default regulatory instrument 102
4.2.1 Evolution of IMF conditionality 103
4.2.2 Conditionality and the Bank's new role 106
4.3 Conditionality as a mechanism for economic governance 110
4.3.1 Fund conditionality enshrined 110
4.3.2 Governance through resource dependency 113
4.4 A new jurisprudence 115
4.4.1 Discretionary control 116
4.4.2 Mission creep 117
4.4.3 Absence of external oversight 118

4.5 From coercion to consent 120
4.5.1 Carrots not sticks 120
4.5.2 From tranching to front-loading 123
4.5.3 Increasing institutional leverage 126
4.6 Conditionality, discipline and the new biopower 127

5 Reforming the nation state: PRSPs and rehabilitating the structurally adjusted state 134

5.1 Rehabilitation of the state 135
5.1.1 The good governance agenda: continuities and discontinuities 135
5.1.2 Reinventing the regulative capacity of the state 138
5.2 Modalities of state reconfiguration 142
5.2.1 Globalised development modelling 142
5.2.2 Standardising domestic governance 146
5.3 Ownership and the principle of country selectivity 150
5.3.1 Rewarding 'good' behaviour 150
5.3.2 The JSAN guidelines and biopolitical control 153
5.4 Donor interventions and the politics of partnership 156
5.4.1 Micro-management and diverted emphasis 156
5.4.2 Discipline of the bottom line 159
5.4.3 PRSPs and the aid harmonisation agenda 161
5.5 Control and constitutional mimicry 163

6 Redesigning the political project: discipline and legitimation through participatory policymaking 169

6.1 The liberal political project as an antidote to state autonomy 171
6.1.1 Responding to the 'democratic deficit' 171
6.1.2 Liberal legality and neocolonial representations 172
6.2 Participation, politics and policy accountability 175
6.2.1 PRSPs and participatory policymaking 175
6.2.2 The participation myth 177
6.3 Reconfiguring the political landscape: PRS processes in operation 178
6.3.1 The imported state 179
6.3.2 The politics of technocratic governance and the role of transnational advocates 184
6.3.3 The marginalisation of indigenous politics 189
6.4 The globalisation of political consensus 193
6.4.1 PRSPs and the lack of operational relevance 194
6.4.2 Dissonance between policies, practice and programmes 196
6.5 Remapping the political landscape 198

7 Consolidation and conclusion: PRSPs, transnational governance and globalised legal regimes 204

7.1 A new global compact 205
7.2 A new regulatory project 207
7.2.1 A global administrative space 208
7.2.2 Discursive discipline 210
7.2.3 The rise of network governance 211
7.3 Foreclosing international reform 213
7.3.1 Problematising the state 213
7.3.2 The nation state as a site of political struggle and redistribution 215
7.3.3 Subverting the 'right to development' 216
7.4 Biopower and the new technologies of discipline 218
7.4.1 A biopolitical global constitution 218
7.4.2 Resistance and 'globalisation from below' 221
7.5 Concluding remarks and directions for further research 222

Appendix 225
Bibliography 232
Index 250

List of illustrations

Figures

1 Relationship between the PRSP and financing instruments 226–227
2 World Bank financing structure 228–229
3 IMF financing structure 230–231

Box

4.1 Examples of programme conditionalities 97

Acknowledgements

This book has its roots in a doctoral dissertation submitted to the University of Warwick and owes a debt of gratitude to the many people who have supported me during the years it took to come to fruition, many of whom went more than the extra mile beyond the call of duty and friendship.

My thanks to my doctoral supervisors, Abdul Paliwala and Upendra Baxi, without whom much of this project would not have been possible. I am also grateful to Julio Faundez for his guidance and support. I would also like to thank Fiona Macmillan and Peter Muchlinski for casting a critical eye over the manuscript in its earlier manifestation.

Lee Bridges and the Warwick Law School facilitated the financial and institutional resources necessary to complete the research for the project. Former colleagues and friends at the Warwick Law School provided the logistical and emotional support during this long and often lonely journey of research and writing. I would like to thank Jennifer Mabbett in particular for her friendship and support over the years.

Many people took time to share information, insight and intellectual guidance over the course of my research. My appreciation goes out especially to Martin Khor, Goh Chien Yen, Yilmaz Akyuz, Tetteh Hormeku, Yao Graham and Roberto Bissio, without whose insights and support the book would have been impoverished. The team at the Third World Network furnished me with many opportunities for research and information gathering. Thanks also to Charles Abugre, Nancy Alexander, Jeff Powell, Rick Rowden and Alex Wilks.

I am grateful to my interviewees and contacts for sharing their thoughts and experiences with me, both officially and unofficially. To the officials from the World Bank and the International Monetary Fund who took time out from their busy schedules to explain their perspectives to me, this book may be a critique of Bretton Woods institutions but not a critique of your openness and honesty.

My friends and family have kept me grounded during the length and breadth of the project. I am grateful to you all for your love, encouragement and friendship. In particular, my gratitude goes out to my parents, brother Gareth and sister Kathleen.

And of course, my love and thanks always to my husband Paul, without whom this work would never have been completed. Your well of patience and love is infinite and this book is as much yours as mine.

Finally, this project was not just an intellectual and academic exercise. It was driven by a desire to study the instruments of power, deceit and iniquity in today's global economy, motivated by a need to make the wrongs right. The work would have been unnecessary without the suffering of those of whom the unequal international economic order has marginalised and failed. This book owes a debt – bigger than intellectual thirst – to those whom the institutions of global power have failed and for whom academic discourse and theory are indifferent and irrelevant to the impoverishment of their daily lives.

To these people, and to the often maligned and struggling policymakers in the third world who do what they can with limited resources and even more restrictive political space, I owe a special debt. I only hope this work is a small step to greater understanding and even greater justice.

A note on terminology

1 PRSP, PRS and PRSP framework

In this book, the term 'Poverty Reduction Strategy Paper' (PRSP) will be used to refer to the document which is the outcome of the 'Poverty Reduction Strategy' (PRS) process. The terms 'PRSP framework', 'PRSP project' or 'PRSP initiative' will be used to refer to the PRSP operational framework as a whole, including the PRS process, the PRSP evaluation, PRSP-related financing instruments, etc.

2 World Bank and IDA

The term 'World Bank' is commonly used to refer collectively to both the International Bank for Reconstruction and Development (IBRD), the original 'World Bank' set up in 1944 at the Bretton Woods conference in New Hampshire, as well as the International Development Association (IDA), the World Bank's concessional financing arm, established in 1960. Unless otherwise stated, the term will be similarly utilised here.

The World Bank Group consists of the IBRD, the IDA, the International Finance Corporation (IFC) (established in 1956), the Multilateral Investment Guarantee Agency (MIGA) (established in 1985) and the International Centre for the Settlement of Investment Disputes (ICSID) (set up in 1966).

3 Development financing and aid, donors and recipients

The term 'development financing' is generally used to refer to all forms of financing for economic development purposes, commercial or otherwise, and undertaken both by the private and the public sectors. This book uses the term 'development financing' to refer to what is commonly known as 'development aid' or formally classified as 'official development assistance' (ODA).

The OECD Development Assistance Committee (DAC) classifies ODA as transfers from donor countries to recipient countries or multilateral institutions, such as the World Bank or regional development banks or UN agencies. In order for transfers – financial or in the form of 'technical assistance' – to be classified as ODA, they must:

- be undertaken by the official sector;
- have economic development and welfare as their main objectives;
- be provided on a concessional basis, through outright grants, debt relief or loans with a 25 per cent grant element.

Sometimes, for the sake of brevity or in reference to an external source, the term 'aid' will be used instead of 'development financing', but I recognise the anachronism of the term and its connotations. It will normally be used to denote the asymmetrical nature of the financing relationship between the disbursers of aid ('donors' or 'financiers') and the parties in receipt of it ('recipients' or 'clients').

4 Third world, developing countries, north and south

While the term 'third world' has been characterised in various quarters as anachronistic in today's global context, and has been discarded in favour of the geographically attributed 'north/south' terminology, many scholars and activists from the developing countries have retained its usage as a continuing form of resistance to hegemonic attempts to disperse the collective voice and organising unity of third world states and third world peoples. As Chimni has argued, 'once the common history of subjection to colonialism, and/or the continuing underdevelopment and marginalization of countries in Asia, Africa and Latin America is attached sufficient significance the category "third world" assumes life' (Chimni, 2003: 49).

The term has particular resonance for third world legal scholars for whom the uniformity in application of international law has had the effect of aggregating the structural iniquities which continue to characterise the developing world's engagement with the international legal order (see discussion in Chapter 2). Again, as argued by Chimni, the category of the 'third world' is 'crucial to organizing and offering collective resistance to hegemonic policies' and 'reflects a level of unity imagined and constituted in ways which would enable resistance to a range of practices which systematically disadvantage and subordinate an otherwise diverse group of people' (ibid.).

In this book, the term 'third world' will be used interchangeably with the term 'developing countries' and with the occasional reference to the terms 'north' and 'south', but again recognising some negative associations of the use of such terms.

5 Low-income countries

Low-income countries are defined as countries with a per capita income of less than US$1,135 a year (as of 2010). These are the countries eligible to borrow from the IDA, the concessional lending arm of the World Bank. The term is used in this book technically rather than normatively.

6 Policy-based versus project financing

Policy-based lending is discussed in detail in Chapter 4, but, generally, policy-based or programmatic lending differs from 'investment lending' – financing for a specific project – in that it provides balance of payments support to countries in exchange for a programme of economic reform, either at the national or sectoral level.

List of abbreviations

AAA	Accra Agenda for Action
ADB	African Development Bank; Asian Development Bank
ADF	African Development Fund
Afrodad	African Forum and Network on Debt and Development
AML	anti-money laundering
APR	annual progress report (PRSP)
ARPP	Annual Report on Portfolio Performance
BWI	Bretton Woods institution
CAS	Country Assistance Strategy
CAS PR	Country Assistance Strategy Progress Report
CCJP	Catholic Commission for Justice and Peace
CDD	community-driven development
CDF	Comprehensive Development Framework
CFAA	Country Financial Accountability Assessment
CFT	countering the financing of terrorism
CG	Consultative Group
CNES	Citizens Network on Essential Services
CPA	Country Procurement Assessment
CPIA	Country Policy and Institutional Assessment
CSO	civil society organisation
DAC	Development Assistance Committee (OECD)
DBS	donor budget support
DFID	Department for International Development (UK)
DPL	Development Policy Loan
DSA	debt sustainability assessment
EBRP	Estrategia Boliviana de Reducción de la Pobreza (Bolivian PRSP)
EC	European Commission
ECF	Extended Credit Facility
ECOSOC	Economic and Social Council
EFF	Extended Fund Facility
ESAF	Enhanced Structural Adjustment Facility

ESF	Exogenous Shocks Facility
ESW	economic and sector work
EU	European Union
Eurodad	European Network on Debt and Development
FAO	Food and Agriculture Organisation
FCL	Flexible Credit Line
FDI	foreign direct investment
FFD	Financing for Development (UN)
FSAP	Financial Sector Assessment Programme
G7	Group of 7
G8	Group of 8
GAB	General Arrangements to Borrow
GAO	General Accounting Office (US)
GATS	General Agreement on Trade in Services
GPRS	Ghanaian Poverty Reduction Strategy
GRA	General Resources Account
GRC	governance-related conditionality
HIPC	Heavily Indebted Poor Countries Initiative
IBRD	International Bank for Reconstruction and Development
ICJ	International Court of Justice
ICSID	International Centre for the Settlement of Investment Disputes
IDA	International Development Association
IDB	Inter-American Development Bank
IDS	Institute of Development Studies
IEG	Independent Evaluation Group (World Bank)
IEO	Independent Evaluation Office (IMF)
IFC	International Finance Corporation
IFI	international financial institution
IMF	International Monetary Fund
IMFC	International Monetary and Financial Committee
INGO	international non-governmental organisation
I-PRSP	Interim Poverty Reduction Strategy Paper
ISN	Interim Strategy Note
JFA	Joint Financing Arrangement
JSA	Joint Staff Assessment
JSAN	Joint Staff Advisory Note
LDC	least-developed country
LDP	Letter of Development Policy
LICUS	low-income country under stress
LOI	Letter of Intent
MAI	Multilateral Agreement on Investment
MDB	multilateral development banks
MDBS	Multi-Donor Budget Support programme (Ghana)
MDG	Millennium Development Goal

MDRI	Multilateral Debt Relief Initiative
MEFP	Memorandum of Economic and Financial Policy
MEJN	Malawi Economic Justice Network
MIGA	Multilateral Investment Guarantee Agency
MOU	Memorandum of Understanding
MPRS	Malawian Poverty Reduction Strategy
MTEF	Medium-Term Expenditure Framework
NAB	New Arrangements to Borrow
NAFTA	North American Free Trade Agreement
NDPC	National Development Planning Commission (Ghana)
NGO	non-governmental organisation
NIEO	New International Economic Order
NSC	National Steering Committee
OBA	Output-based aid
ODA	official development assistance
ODI	Overseas Development Institute
OECD	Organisation for Economic Cooperation and Development
OED	Operations Evaluation Department (World Bank)
PAF	Performance Assessment Framework
PAP	Participation Action Plans
PBA	performance-based allocation
PDR	People's Democratic Republic; Policy Review and Development (World Bank)
PEAP	Poverty Eradication Action Plan
PEM	public expenditure management
PER	public expenditure review
PF	Partnership Framework
PFM	public financial management
PFP	Policy Framework Paper
PNoWB	Parliamentary Network on the World Bank
PPA	Participatory Poverty Assessment
PREM	Bank's Poverty Reduction and Economic Management (World Bank)
PRGF	Poverty Reduction and Growth Facility
PRGT	Poverty Reduction and Growth Trust
PRS	Poverty Reduction Strategy
PRSC	Poverty Reduction Strategy Credit
PRSP	Poverty Reduction Strategy Paper
PRSTF	Poverty Reduction Strategy Trust Fund
PSAC	programmatic structural adjustment credit
PSAL	programmatic structural adjustment loan
PSI	Policy Support Instrument
PSIA	Poverty and Social Impact Assessment
PTF	Poverty Task Force

RCF	Rapid Credit Facility
SAF	Structural Adjustment Facility
SAL	Structural Adjustment Loan
SAP	Structural Adjustment Programme
SAPRI	Structural Adjustment Participatory Review Initiative
SAPRIN	Structural Adjustment Participatory Review International Network
SBA	Stand-By Arrangement
SCF	Standby Credit Facility
SDR	Special Drawing Rights
SECAC	sectoral adjustment credit
SECAL	Sectoral Adjustment Loan
SEDP	Socio-Economic Development Program (Cambodia)
SIDA	Swedish International Development Cooperation Agency
SRF	Supplemental Reserve Facility
SSA	sub-Saharan Africa/African
TORs	terms of reference
TRM	Transitional Results Matrix
UMDF	Ugandan Multilateral Debt Fund
UN	United Nations
UNCTAD	United Nations Conference on Trade and Development
UNICEF	United Nations Fund for Children
UNDP	United Nations Development Programme
UK	United Kingdom
US	United States
WDR	*World Development Report* (World Bank)
WHO	World Health Organisation
WTO	World Trade Organisation

Chapter 1

Introduction

1.1 Crisis and change in international economic lawmaking

The late 1990s was a period of dislocation and change in development policymaking and in international economic governance. The street protests against the locus of international trade and financial law and policymaking in Seattle (World Trade Organisation), Cologne (G8) and Prague (World Bank and the International Monetary Fund) in 1999 capped the crescendo of public dissatisfaction brewing over the past two decades resultant from the globalisation of the economic policies advanced by the Washington Consensus[1] and pursued through national regulatory reforms overseen by global and regional governance institutions.[2]

A new discourse of development was taking place amidst the growing discontent with the processes and institutions driving the global economy. A decade and a half of structural adjustment policies imposed on third world countries by the World Bank and the International Monetary Fund (IMF) in exchange for badly needed financial resources had seen little or no improvement but had, in many cases, led to deterioration in the social and economic situation of the countries in receipt of such financing. Debt accumulation was starving many countries of the resources needed to fund basic goods and services, and countries were increasingly locked in a vicious cycle of aid leading to debt servicing leading to more aid.

In 1996, Jubilee 2000 was set up by a coalition of groups and individuals, including religious organisations and church groups, to campaign for a full cancellation of third world debt before the millennial year. In 1998, the coalition, enjoying broad-based support from organisations and individuals from the north and the south, mobilised 300,000 demonstrators in Birmingham at the site of the G7 summit, calling for greater and deeper debt relief than the existing measures offered, including those under the Heavily Indebted Poor Countries Initiative (HIPC).[3]

The Jubilee 2000 campaign was pivotal in fostering a new public consciousness in what is now termed the 'post-structural adjustment' era by explicitly linking the problem of sovereign debt with citizenry impoverishment in developing countries at the level of international policymaking. The coalition also exemplified the increasing political clout of non-state actors in the international normative order, notably that of a cadre of specialist non-governmental advocates and lobbyists in the form of international non-governmental organisations (INGOs). Unlike their predecessors, these new actors brought onto the world stage a professionalisation of traditional advocacy and lobbying roles and increasing sophistication in global policy analysis, not only creating an alternative tapestry of political and policy narratives but also forming an emerging constituency of civil society advocates at the global level.

While the existence of pressure groups in decision-making fora was not a new development, the role of debt campaigners as lobbyists *for governments* in the south rather than as lobbyists against the same governments[4] was a significant development in international law and policymaking. Bolstered by the support of this new political force, a new confidence was imbued in the weaker state actors involved in the negotiating structure of global economic governance. The effect was a powerful assault on the asymmetrical norms of international economic law and the global regulatory regimes which sustain them.

The collapse of the World Trade Organisation (WTO)'s third ministerial meeting in Seattle in 1999 demonstrated to the world the strength of political mobilisation on the part of weaker actors in the global system – the developing countries within the WTO who walked out of the unfair negotiating structure of the trade talks *and* the affected communities of individuals and groups outside on the streets who coalesced in numbers outside the institutional framework to make their voices heard.[5]

As protesters thronged the streets, the analytical and operational framework of international economic governance and international economic law, including the fundamental aspects of sovereign debt and development financing, was subject to re-examination within international policy circles. The collapse of the tiger economies in east and south-east Asia during the Asian financial crisis of 1997–98 and the subsequent social and economic upheavals accompanying IMF stabilisation programmes in countries such as Thailand, Indonesia and South Korea provided the catalyst for the financial community as a whole to reconsider the fundamental tenets of the global economy. While deriding the masses of 'anti-globalisation' protesters[6] for their railings against the international economic system, there were real concerns within the international financial community of the consequences of not addressing these issues relating to the state of the world economy.

It was in this political climate that the Poverty Reduction Strategy Papers (PRSPs) were introduced. The World Bank and IMF Board of Governors announced at their annual meetings in September 1999 that PRSPs would serve as the new framework for regulating access to debt relief and concessional financing[7] for low-income countries (World Bank and IMF, 1999). In terms of its relationship to the Bank and the Fund, the PRSPs replaced the Policy Framework Papers (PFPs) as prerequisites for financing from their concessional facilities (see pp. 3–5). The announcement of the PRSPs came quickly after the announcement by the G8 ministers in Cologne of a new enhanced debt relief package for developing countries – the enhanced HIPC (HIPC II) – which would be centred upon the PRSPs and be funded by bilateral and multilateral donors and from the proceeds of gold sales by the IMF.

Taken together, the PRSP framework and its attendant financing instruments represent a significant shift not only in the modalities of delivering development finance to low-income countries, but also in the form and substance of these countries' engagement in the international arena. For many countries dependent on external public financing, the PRSP framework would become central to the development of a 'new architecture of aid', governing not only their access to financial resources but also their engagement with the international community.

1.2 A new 'social contract'

A PRSP is primarily a document outlining a country's national economic policy with a focus on a programme for poverty reduction, developed nationally through a participatory process involving a cross-section of stakeholders. Aside from identifying the nature, sources and incidences of poverty in the country, a PRSP must detail how the country's resources – chiefly those provided through debt relief and concessional financing – will be disbursed to ameliorate these problems. Programme support from the World Bank and the IMF and debt relief – under HIPC II or the recently instituted Multilateral Debt Relief Initiative (MDRI) – is contingent upon the completion of a PRSP – or at least an Interim-PRSP (I-PRSP) – and the said PRSP being evaluated by the Bank and the Fund.

PRSPs have now become the focus for much of the policy dialogue and negotiations for financing between low-income countries, international financial institutions (IFIs), and bilateral and multilateral donors. PRSPs now provide the basis for the majority of World Bank and IMF financing to low-income countries, the facilities for which were also renamed in the PRSP changeover, with the IMF replacing its Enhanced Structural Adjustment Facility (ESAF) with the Poverty Reduction and Growth Facility (PRGF) and the World Bank introducing Poverty Reduction Strategy Credits (PRSCs) as new financing instruments for countries borrowing from the International Development Association (IDA). In 2009, the IMF further restructured its concessional lending architecture to create three distinct concessional facilities – the Extended Credit Facility (ECF), the Standby Credit Facility (SCF) and the Rapid Credit Facility (RCF) – under a newly constituted Poverty Reduction and Growth Trust (PRGT) (IMF, 2009: para. 6). While PRSPs are not mandatory for access to all facilities, PRSP documentation and the overarching 'poverty reduction' approach remain the mainstay for the bulk of negotiations under the reformed framework (ibid.: para. 12).

PRSPs also inform the World Bank's Country Assistance Strategies (CAS), the blueprint for all Bank financial operations in member states, and have regularly been instituted as prerequisites for bilateral donor financing and Paris Club debt restructuring negotiations for low-income countries. They are also becoming central to negotiations for multilateral and multi-donor financing programmes and are increasingly providing a convenient pivot for a plethora of development initiatives piloted by regional and multilateral institutions.

The PRSP framework consolidates the development agendas of the 1990s and has come to represent the new landscape of aid relations in the 'post'-Washington Consensus era. Operationally, the PRSP represents a bridge between the new conceptual framework of development financing, such as the principles enshrined in the World Bank's Comprehensive Development Framework (CDF)[8] or the United Nations-initiated Millennium Development Goals (MDGs),[9] and new financing instruments, outlined on p. 3, that would facilitate the disbursement of resources for meeting these objectives.

However, the PRSP approach goes beyond conceptual rhetoric and procedural documentation – it operationalises a framework which prescribes and institutionalises procedural and institutional reforms that PRSP countries have to undergo to facilitate their access to external financing from the IFIs and official donor agencies. For example, the World Bank distinguishes the PRSP from the CDF in terms of this attachment to resources and operations. According to the Bank, the CDF is 'a set of principles, processes or mechanisms rather than a programme of action', unlike the PRSP, which it describes as 'an instrument of policy implementation' to detail priorities, targets, indicators, costings and financing plans, and procedures for monitoring (World Bank, 2003a: 13).

Evaluation of countries' compliance with these criteria is conducted primarily by the Bank and the Fund through the Joint Staff Advisory Note (JSAN) process, which will assess the PRSP in relation to its suitability to form the basis of financial support from the Bank, Fund and other financiers[10] (World Bank and IMF, 2005a). A World Bank-led study described the PRSP approach as 'a new form of social contract' entered into by governments of low-income countries with official bilateral and multilateral financiers for the production of a 'credible framework' for concessional financing and debt relief (World Bank, 2003a: 13).

Each PRSP is required to be: (1) *nationally owned*, meaning the strategies outlined in the PRSP are generated by the constituencies it purports to serve and by the government of the country involved in the process; and (2) formulated in a *participatory* manner, involving a wide range of government and civil society actors, including representatives of 'the poor' whom these policies affect. This is institutionalised in a participatory Poverty Reduction Strategy (PRS) process, a mechanism through which intra-governmental, inter-governmental and non-governmental dialogue is established with a range of stakeholders and policy formulated via a process of representation, consultation and engagement between all parties.

From the point of view of PRSP proponents, this process rebalances the power asymmetries inherent in international development financing and injects a measure of agency and accountability into a previously opaque and hierarchical decision-making process. Cash-strapped countries now possess the operational framework through which social and economic priorities may be developed in a consultative manner with all segments of society and government, and subsequently presented to the official financing community as a plan for effective utilisation of financial assistance.

The implementation of the agreed economic reforms (in exchange for external financing) and appropriate utilisation of financial resources are subsequently policed through greater oversight of public expenditure management. Accordingly, the Bank and Fund view the PRS approach as one of 'balancing mutual accountabilities' – of client governments to domestic constituents and official financiers, and of official financiers to client governments – over the use of state economic resources (IMF and World Bank, 2005: para. 21).

Yet, herein lies the fundamental premise – and the fundamental problem – of the PRSP initiative: that is, the framework serves to a large extent as a regulatory restraint for the states subject to its discipline. It follows, from the conceptual principles and operational directives underpinning the PRSP approach, that the PRSP state, as the recipient of concessional financing and debt relief, must demonstrate its desire to be disciplined by a set of rules representing the universal normative framework for all state resource extraction, allocation and administration.

The PRSP framework involves a substantial reorganisation of state apparatuses in PRSP countries, facilitating not only the universalisation of national economic planning – the setting of uniform 'development' targets and common prioritisation of public policy – but also a globalisation of bureaucratic and political structures: the establishment of a template for public participatory policymaking and intra-governmental policy dialogue.

These extensive interventions belie the PRSP project's rhetoric of 'country ownership' inasmuch as it serves to establish compliance with the asymmetrical rules of the current international economic order. Conformity with the status quo is assured by excluding those states who fail to play by the rules, not through force but through the evaluation of their willingness to be subjected to 'universally' recognised policy objectives and the corresponding reforms to secure these objectives.

The impact of the PRSP framework has, over the years since its introduction, reverberated beyond its immediate utility as a means of aid disbursement. The conceptual principles underpinning the PRSP approach have been adopted as the default mode of crafting international development policy, organising aid relations and, progressively, informing other forms of international economic relations between developed countries, representing the majority of aid donors, bilateral creditors and contributors to multilateral finance, and developing countries, representing the recipients of aid and sovereign debtors.

1.3 Scope of inquiry

The objective of this book is to locate the PRSP framework within the broader framework of international law by exploring its impact on third world state engagement with the global political economy and the international regulatory norms and institutions which support it. This book thus situates the PRSP framework within the context of contemporary global governance, international relations[11] and postcolonial international law,[12] particularly, but not exclusively, in global economic governance and international economic law.

The book is a critique of the PRSP operational framework, the conceptual underpinnings of the project and the political and geo-strategic agenda driving its operationalisation. It is not about specific PRSP processes in individual countries, nor is it an examination of the substantive content of PRSPs and/or PRSP-related instruments.

There is a wealth of literature, including many empirical studies, on the different country processes and individual and comparative studies of PRSP documents (see, for example, Cling *et al.*, 2003; Christiansen with Hovland, 2003; Gould, 2005a, 2005b; Molenaers and Renard, 2002) many of which have also been carried out by non-governmental organisations (NGOs) participating in either the country processes or Washington, DC-based reviews (for example Chavez-Malaluan and Guttal, 2003, 2002; World Vision, 2005).[13] This book does not aim to duplicate the excellent work that has been done by these researchers but to conceptualise the phenomenon they describe in the context of its impact on international law and economic relations.

The book thus concentrates on examining the effect of this new approach to aid regulation and, consequently, its impact on international economic law-making and global governance, specifically third world engagement in these arenas. The epistemological objective here is to construct a theoretical understanding of the PRSP process and its attendant financing and policy instruments in the context of international law and global governance. This book aims to site the PRSP initiative within existing debates on globalisation, law and global governance by evaluating whether the PRSP framework constitutes an extension and/or an intensification of existing patterns of global regulation in the post-colonial period, particularly in the era of globalisation, and, if so, how and what implications do such changes have on the constitution of global economic governance and international law?

In seeking to answer these questions, the book juxtaposes an analysis of the operational aspects of the PRSP initiative, including its legal and policy components, with an examination of its conceptual framework and its political and economic drivers. This involves an examination of the PRSP project as both a *legal* and *political* phenomenon. For the PRSP to have a legal impact, it must affect the rights and duties of actors involved in the framework, and for it to be political, it must have an impact on the normative power of these actors, that is, the ability to set rules and to advance principles through normative mechanisms.

This book was born out of a discovery of the paucity of research on the *realpolitik* of the PRSP project in the context of international law and economic relations, locating the conceptual and operational underpinnings of the PRSP project and PRSP-related instruments within the discourse and historical context of international law and politics. While research into development policy and practice has traditionally straddled the disciplines of political economy, economics and sociology, there have been very few interdisciplinary analyses of the legal and non-legal normative framework regulating relationships between parties to development financing agreements, much less of the forms of power that structure these relationships.

Scholarship in this area is clearly bifurcated between positivistic accounts of the techno-legal aspects of development financing (see Gold, 1996; Shihata, 2000a, 2000b, 2000c)[14] and contextual political economy analyses of aid relationships and development policy, including the PRSP framework (see Craig and Porter, 2006, 2003; Helleiner, 2002; Wade, 2001; Woods, 2006). Legal scholars of international economic law, such as Lastra (2006), Lowenfeld (2008) and Qureshi and Zigler (2007), have contributed significantly to a substantive understanding of the legal framework of the World Bank and the IMF but have stopped short of an analysis of what these legal structures mean to the constitution of international law and global governance, and, less so, on how they impact on the dynamic of relationships between the actors involved in international legal and non-legal normative processes. Similarly, institutional approaches to the study of development financing and policy contribute to the understanding of the institutional context in which development financing takes place (see Miller-Adams, 1999; Pincus and Winters, 2002; Stone and Wright, 2007) but do not link these institutional processes to a wider normative context.

This book is therefore both a critique of the PRS process and its accompanying policy and financing mechanisms as well as a critique of the current epistemology of PRSPs in the context of development studies and approaches to international law and global governance. It considers, in particular, the PRSP initiative in relation to the Bretton Woods institutions (BWIs) and examines the framework in the context of the evolving mandates of these two organisations[15] over the decades since their inception. Specifically, it examines their centrality to the system of resources mobilisation and extraction and the roles they play in managing third world engagement in international law and economic relations.

However, the research here goes beyond an institutional analysis of the BWIs, either from an organisational theory perspective, an intellectual approach popularised in recent years (see Babb and Buira, 2004; Miller-Adams, 1999; Stone and Wright, 2007; Woods, 2006),[16] or from a standard political economy approach, which analyses the effect of Bank and Fund operations either from a conventional materialist perspective (see Cammack, 2001a, 2001b; Craig and Porter, 2006, 2003; Chossudovsky, 1997a, 1997b) or from a socio-anthropological perspective (see Abrahamsen, 2004, 2000; Gould, 2005a, 2005b; Harrison, 2005, 2001a, 2001b).

Although a focus on the organisational structure and culture of the World Bank and IMF – given that these institutions are large, hierarchical bureaucracies – is critical to understanding the driving imperatives behind the PRSP approach, such an approach can only partially explain the widespread acceptance of the process by their membership. The universalisation of the PRSP process can only be fully explained by entering into the realm of political economy, where political power at the international inter-state level structures, to a large extent, the policies that are conceived and implemented by financing institutions such as the Bank and the Fund.

Recourse to the theoretical categories established by international relations researchers, in particular in postcolonial research in this area, remains necessary to an attempt to answer the aforementioned research questions. In particular, it is necessary to question the existing methodologies of studying the PRSP phenomena in the context of development financing and international economic law.

Socio-legal research in this area is limited, and tends to be clustered around the epistemology of political economy and, occasionally, anthropology and sociology. Except for Anghie (2004, 2002, 2000), Chimni (2004, 2003) and, to a limited extent, Rajagopal (2003) and Pahuja (2004, 2000), few legal theorists have approached the subject of IFIs through the prism of postcolonial research, or have successfully adopted sociological and political economy approaches in their consideration of the substantive structural concerns of international law and power. Nonetheless, a comprehensive examination of the modalities of the PRSP framework and their implications for the structure of global governance and international law must include an exploration of the historical context that gave birth to the PRSPs, including their imperial heritage.

Moreover, given that law plays a constitutive role in shaping economic and social relations, there is also a need to examine the methodologies of research that feed into the policies of the PRSP framework and, ultimately, their normative consequences. Therefore, it is critical that research on PRSPs take into account the methodological narratives that shape research on PRSPs and development financing as a whole and take care not to reinforce (through adoption) methodological stereotypes.

A critique of methodology was thus an ongoing exercise during the course of research for this book. Like the authors in Cooke and Kothari's insightful compendium of research into participatory development approaches, this research aimed to move away from the 'methodological revisionism' that characterises the study of PRSPs towards addressing 'more directly how the discourse itself, and not just the practice, embodies the potential for an unjustified exercise of power' (Cooke and Kothari, 2002: 4).

At the same time, there is also a need to link the theoretical conceptualisations of three significant notions which have emerged in development policy and practice over the past three decades – law, globalisation and development – and examine the means by which these three spheres interact within the international policy and regulatory context. Here, the critical practice developed by some scholars of the 'law and development' doctrine – the broad conceptual umbrella encompassing scholarship examining the relationship between legal systems and development theory and practice (Trubek and Santos, 2006: 3–4) – is useful in orienting the scope of this book's inquiry. In particular, methodologies of examining law (and non-legal regulatory structures) as discursive *as well as* constitutive instruments for structuring societies and economies (see, for example, Rittich, 2006: 215) are constructive in developing new ways of analysing the modalities of development finance and their normative effects.

It is thus hoped that adopting a different approach to the study of PRSPs will lead to the excavation of the real dynamics of power that reside within the PRSP initiative and contribute to the unmasking of fissures that will serve as opportunities for real transformatory power in international law and economic relations.

1.4 Framework of analysis

This book approaches its subject matter from both a *structural materialist* perspective – examining the apparatus of the PRSP process, its underlying power constituents and its effects on the structure of global governance and international regulatory mechanisms – and a *discursive* perspective – examining the discourses that inhabit the PRSP process and the means by which these discourses contribute to the restructuring of the relationships between the actors involved in the process and their engagement with international law and institutions of global governance. In doing so, the book juxtaposes an empirical methodology for examining the normative linkages between the operational framework of the PRSP initiative and the actors who forward these norms with a critical analysis of the power dynamics underlying the relations between the subjects and objects of the framework.

To achieve this, the research borrows from the methodology adopted by Braithwaite and Drahos (2000) in their study of global business regulation and combines it with a materialist analysis of power at the global level. At the same time, it goes beyond the materialist critique and adopts a discursive method of analysing the mechanics of structural power by studying the conditions that give rise to the representational power of the PRSP discourse. Here, Foucault's analysis of power enables us to understand the technologies of power at play in international economic relations and the postcolonial structures of international law and global governance which regulate these relationships.

1.4.1 Analysing the relationship between actors, principles and mechanisms of globalisation

The 'new aid architecture' promulgated by the advent of the PRSP initiative may be viewed as a means of globalising not just aid relations but also other regulatory norms that underpin international economic and political relations. Thus, as a starting point, it is necessary to draw the links between the empirical reality of PRSPs and the contribution of the PRSP framework to international law and global governance by drawing on the techniques utilised by Braithwaite and Drahos to understand the trends in the globalisation of regulation.

Braithwaite and Drahos view the process of globalisation as best conceptualised in terms of the relationships between actors, mechanisms and principles, with understanding conflicts of principles as key to understanding regulatory globalisation (Braithwaite and Drahos, 2000: 15). Adopting the approach to social scientific study from Elster (1989),[17] Braithwaite and Drahos use mechanisms as a means of explaining the causal link between events in regulatory globalisation,[18] identifying mechanisms of globalisation as 'processes that increase the extent to which patterns of regulation in one part of the world are similar, or linked, to patterns of regulation in other parts', with these processes involving 'one or more actors (state and non-state) in a series of actions (and reactions) that are linked to the goals and desires of the actors' (Braithwaite and Drahos, 2000: 15, 17). Mechanisms such as economic or military coercion, modelling and capacity building are used by actors within the global economic system to effect change in their favour through the advocacy of principles such as 'transparency', 'reciprocity' and 'national treatment'.

Braithwaite and Drahos found in their study of global business regulation 'that actors involved in the processes of globalization articulate, support and seek to entrench principles in regulatory systems in different ways' and that, 'in the contest of principles, actors use mechanisms to give weight to some principles over others' (Braithwaite and Drahos, 2000: 18–19). Principles are defined as norms, which may or may not be juridical in nature, that inform the construction of rules in the globalisation of business regulation (ibid.: 18–20). The authors view the examination of this contest of principles as crucial:

> Understanding the conflict of principles is integral to understanding the globalization of business regulation. The successful weighting of one principle over another has consequences at both the level of conduct and for regulatory change.
>
> (Braithwaite and Drahos, 2000: 18)

As a policy instrument that is applied to all countries seeking bilateral and multilateral debt relief as well as concessional financing from the Bank, Fund and other aid agencies, the PRSP may be categorised as a 'mechanism of globalization' as defined by Braithwaite and Drahos. When examining the impact of the PRSP approach on the constitution of international law and global governance, it is necessary to consider how the PRSP framework promotes the universalisation of regulatory norms that further the interests of actors engaged in the process. Approaching the PRSP framework from this perspective enables us to consider the contest of principles between actors that exists in the wider sphere of global economic governance and to locate the PRSP framework within this contest.

The relationship between these principles and the actors who advance the principles sheds light on how the PRSP framework is conceived and constructed, and, more importantly, highlights the means by which the PRSP initiative serves a larger governance purpose outside the regulation of development financing. Principles, according to Braithwaite and Drahos, serve as 'abstract prescriptions that precede rule complexity' (Braithwaite and Drahos, 2000: 15). Consequently, it is possible to analyse the principles that underlie the PRSP framework as the prescriptive instruments upon which regulatory mechanisms, such the PRSP process and PRSP-related policy and financing instruments, are based.

A complementary methodology is used by Jayasuriya in analysing the phenomenon of globalisation. Jayasuriya adopts an epistemological approach to studying the changes in the globalised economy that is premised on understanding the means by which globalisation and 'its new ensemble of governance institutions' work towards changing 'the internal architecture of the state' (Jayasuriya, 2001a: 5). He argues that the 'key issue' for understanding the way in which globalisation is reshaping domestic and global governance is understanding the modalities of producing and reproducing 'economic order' locally and globally, and that such analysis should be directed at examining the 'production of "order" in the global economy' rather than focused on 'the significance of trade and capital market transformations in the global economy' (ibid.: 4–5).

In other words, Jayasuriya provides an inverse but complementary approach to studying the globalisation of regulation to that of Braithwaite and Drahos, contending that an examination of how the state is being transformed internally through external pressures will enable us to better understand how regulatory norms are translated and homogenised across jurisdictions (Jayasuriya, 2001a). Through an examination of this 're-engineering' of the state, we can understand how state forms are embedded within a larger global framework of regulation and how these global institutions and the hegemonic actors which shape them correspondingly embed these norms within domestic state structures (Jayasuriya, 2001a, 2001b). The modalities of state reconfiguration taking place under the PRSP initiative may therefore be seen as part of wider shifts in the technologies and modalities of governance at the global level.

These shifts may also be reflective of the practice of 'forum shifting' by the hegemonic actors seeking to forward favoured principles in the different regulatory regimes. Braithwaite and Drahos define 'forum shifting' as the means by which powerful actors in global regulatory regimes, usually states, most notably the United States, shift the regulatory agenda away from a particular forum to another forum or abandon the forum when the forum proves inconvenient for advancing its interests (Braithwaite and Drahos, 2000: 564). The reason for shifting forums, the authors argue, is to prevent defeat at the hands of negotiating opponents:

> Forum shifting is a form of optimizing behaviour. An actor avoids a suboptimal outcome by shifting to a new game in which it has a better shot at an optimal outcome.
>
> (Braithwaite and Drahos, 2000: 564)

Here, the PRSP framework may be regarded as a form of 'forum shifting' by the dominant states in the global economy seeking to maintain the legitimacy and operational status quo of the regulatory norms and practices under attack from the resistance against neoliberal globalisation.[19] In the contest of principles, only powerful actors have the capacity to utilise this mechanism, inasmuch as they have the capacity to redraw the disciplinary landscape of international economic law and the institutions of global governance.

1.4.2 Locating regulatory patterns within a wider analysis of power

In considering the contest of principles in the wider global governance forum, it is necessary to locate these principles within a larger theoretical and methodological framework. It is in this critical assessment of the PRSP operations that the limitations of Braithwaite and Drahos' methodology become clear and a need to have recourse to an alternative method of critique becomes apparent. While the authors identify key principles that underlie the processes of globalisation through their empirical research and provide a methodological link between the advocacy of principles, actors' interests and mechanisms used to advance these principles, they do not enter into a debate about the power structures that underlie this contest of principles.

Similarly, while scholars of international relations such as Jayasuriya seek to construct an understanding of the operational impact of regulatory structures, either through an analysis of the impact of globalisation on internal structures or from the internationalisation of state structures, such analyses often fall short of providing a contextual account of the nature of the power relationships behind these changes. Accordingly, while it is imperative that we study the impact of the PRSP framework on the structures of international law and global governance, including examining its impact on third world engagement with the same, it is also crucial that we unmask the modalities and dynamics of power which underpin the framework.

This book therefore relies on Foucault's methodology of analysing power and representation to investigate both the contested terrain in which the principles that underlie the PRSP project are constructed and their effect on international law and global governance. Specifically, Foucault's methodology of studying the manifestations of power through understanding *power relations* rather than studying the effects of *powerful institutions* (or entities)[20] enables us to map the transition by means of which this power is manifested or, rather, the means through which discipline is enforced over the objects of power (see Foucault, 1994; 340–345; 1991: 261–266).

For Foucault, power is immanent to the object it regulates; it is reproductive rather than hierarchical, to be appropriated by individuals, institutions or states when they exercise control over another individual, institution or state (Foucault, 1994: 340–343). Accordingly, a Foucauldian theory of power rests upon understanding power as the sum of power relations: 'Power exists only as exercised by some on others, only when it is put into action' (ibid.: 340). When analysing the impact of the PRSP framework on the globalisation of regulation and the constitution of international law, therefore, it is necessary to understand the dynamics between the parties to the framework and their relationship to each other and the discipline to which they are subjected.

According to Foucault:

> A power relationship … can only be articulated on the basis of two elements that are indispensable … : that the 'other' (the one over whom power is exercised) is recognized and maintained to the very end as a subject who acts and that, faced with a relationship of power, a whole field of responses, reactions, results and possible inventions may open up.
>
> (Foucault, 1994: 340)

The exercise of power is therefore 'a management of possibilities' (ibid.: 341), and to understand the operations of power is to understand how these possibilities are administered over the object of the power relations, either inciting, inducing or seducing the object to be disciplined or making things easier or more difficult for it, releasing or contriving, making more or less probable and, 'in the extreme', constraining or forbidding absolutely (ibid.).

For Foucault, it is the exercise of such power over the process of economic production and reproduction that constitutes the mode of action called 'government' (ibid.: 341). Consequently, the process of 'governmentality' thus involves an ensemble of institutional apparatuses and strategies 'that allow the exercise of this very specific albeit complex form of power' and 'the development of a whole complex of knowledges' to manage the objects of this power (ibid.: 219–220). Murray Li interprets this as 'the attempt to shape human conduct by calculated means', operating through the education of 'desires' and the configuration of 'habits, aspirations and beliefs' so that power is dispersed across its target population (Murray Li, 2007: 5). The distance of the source of power from its objects renders the question of consent difficult to ascertain as consent is secured through covert rather than overt means (ibid.).

Foucault's methodology enables us to consider the historical conditions that gave rise to the principles that underlie the PRSP project and to locate them in the context of the PRSP as a mechanism of globalisation as well as an instrument of governance. In unmasking the dynamics of power inherent in the framework, we can excavate the objectifying narratives of its underlying disciplinary norms and critically assess their wider impact on the construction of other regulatory norms and normative networks. Scheurich terms this 'policy archaeology' – the deconstruction of a priori assumptions about a problematic that contributes to policy research and the 'powerful "grids" or networks of regularities' that determine the problematising of key concepts within policy studies (Scheurich, 1997: 94–118).

Using this methodology also enables us to examine how power is exercised through various regulatory instruments at the global level, including how the PRSP framework represents a shift in the modalities of global power and global governance. Specifically, this book considers how the PRSP framework constitutes an evolution from what Foucault terms the 'technologies of domination' to 'technologies of self', the two poles from which 'the organisation of power over life' is deployed or, in other words, the movement from a 'disciplinary society' to a 'society of control' (see Foucault, 1994: 220–221; 1991: 261–263). Here, the movement is away from the disciplinary supervision of societies (or, in our case, third world states) – that is, through establishing normative frameworks for behaviour and the exclusion/penalisation of departures from such norms – towards the establishment of a 'biopolitical' power in which the objects of power (societies or states) reproduce these norms and seek to insert themselves into the very relationship of power (ibid.).

This dovetails with Braithwaite and Drahos' analysis of the processual shifts in global business regulation today, which sees the movement away from remunerative and coercive webs of influence towards the use of dialogic webs in securing both adoption of and compliance with norms in the aforementioned contest of principles.

According to Braithwaite and Drahos:

> Dialogic webs also heighten the probability that the norms established by means of the web will be internalized by actors who are part of the web. Dialogic commitments to a regime bring fidelity to norms that webs of coercion do not. Obtaining a fidelity to norms means that compliance with the norms is more likely to be robust.
>
> (Braithwaite and Drahos, 2000: 563)

Although Braithwaite and Drahos do not subscribe to postmodern analyses of discourse, their analysis of dialogic regulatory sequences resonates with Foucault's conception of power, inasmuch as it resonates with Foucault's discourse politics and the power of discursive technologies (see following section). As Braithwaite and Drahos contend: 'Hegemony means that within dialogic webs there is more reason to hear the voices of those with a capacity to escalate webs of reward and coercion' (ibid.: 551).

Thus, insofar as dialogic webs remain dominated by powerful actors within the regulatory fora, compliance with the norms advanced by these actors by weaker actors in the system through such mechanisms of dialogue indicate the reproductive nature of the power inasmuch as it demonstrates continuity with the overt disciplinary force of power.

1.4.3 Representational power and the discipline of discourse

Fidelity to the norms advanced by powerful constituencies is also an indication of the discursive strength of their dialogic webs, indicating the persuasiveness of their representations. Consequently, adopting a discursive methodology in studying the representational power of concepts articulated in the PRSP project enables us to understand not only the conditions under which such concepts are problematised but also the normative impact flowing from this problematisation. This contributes to our understanding of the relationship between the principles of the PRSP project, the actors who advance these principles and the mechanism by which these principles are advanced, namely the PRSP framework.

A Foucauldian analysis of the development discourse has been applied in recent years by authors mapping the evolution of development thinking. In particular, Escobar has examined the role of development discourse in constructing the current reality of development policy and practice through the 'colonization of reality', that is, 'how certain representations become dominant and shape indelibly the ways in which reality is imagined and acted upon' (Escobar, 1995: 5; see also Chapter 2, section 2.1).

A team of researchers at the Institute of Development Studies (IDS) has utilised this approach to examine the policy processes that impact upon poverty policy. For McGee and Brock, viewing 'policy as a discourse' is useful in illuminating some of the processes through which certain policies and research methodologies that feed into policymaking gain hegemony, particularly 'through their attachment to particular narratives of cause and effect' (McGee and Brock, 2001: 6). This requires an analytical approach that can account for how particular versions of policy triggers and solutions 'are taken up and embedded and ... locate the emergence and shaping of these versions in particular social and historical contexts' (Brock *et al.*, 2001: 4).

This approach to the study of development policy and practice – in this case, the policies and institutional practices regulating access to development financing – offers what Crush terms the 'conceptual space' for exploring 'the links between the discursive and the non-discursive; between the words, the practices and the institutional expressions of development; between the relations of power and domination that order the world and the words and images that represent those worlds' (Crush, 1995: 6).

Some legal theorists have similarly applied discursive analysis to the study of law as a culturally productive force, that is, understanding law and legal regimes as systems of symbols and signification normalising or delegitimising images and representations of social, political and economic relationships (see Rittich, 2006: 215; Merry, 1992: 358–361; Santos, 2002). This form of legal anthropology evaluates the ways in which 'legal institutions and actors create meanings, the impact of those meanings on surrounding social relationships, and the effect of the cultural framework on the nature of legal procedures themselves' (Merry, 1992: 360).

Braithwaite and Drahos do not preclude the possibility of subjecting their methodology to further theoretical scrutiny, acknowledging that there is opportunity within their methodological framework to consider theories of globalisation that are 'more reductive or structural in orientation' (Braithwaite and Drahos, 2000: 15).

However, at the same time, the authors reject structuralist Marxist critiques and critical 'postmodernist' approaches, including discursive techniques, to explaining the phenomena of globalisation. They argue that their method reveals 'little support' for a 'more sophisticated structuralist Marxist explanation which subordinates purposive action to the reproduction of systemic inevitability', at the same time as postmodernist theory fails to take into account the dominating forces of military and financial coercion when prioritising discourse in the construction of social reality (Braithwaite and Drahos, 2000: 601).

This book argues to the contrary and demonstrates the epistemic advantage of combining a positivist methodology of conceptualising legal and political phenomena, such as that adopted by Braithwaite and Drahos, and a critical methodology that aims to unmask the power relations behind the processual shifts and their representational impact.

In examining an institutional framework such as the PRSP and PRSP-related instruments, it is necessary to adopt a structuralist perspective 'that sees certain phenomena as having a function, without implying that it is completely purposive, still less conspiratorial', but at the same time conforming to an unalterable system (Biel, 2000: 231). While not necessarily adopting the structuralist explanation as to the systemic inevitability in the contest of principles and power relations among actors, employing a structuralist materialist approach to studying globalisation is necessary to identify the structure and forms of dominance, in this case in conceptualising the powerful interests behind the PRSP approach. At the same time, a discursive approach to the study of the PRSP framework enables us to unravel the narratives reflecting these hegemonic interests that feed into the policy and lawmaking exercise associated with the PRSP initiative and the new aid architecture.

Therefore, in answering the research questions posed at the outset of this book, it is necessary to view the PRSP framework as both: (1) *an institutional process* – locating the general PRSP process within the historical and contemporary context and examining the structures of power that inhabit this process; and (2) *a textual foundation of knowledge production* – examining the discourse of the PRSP process as embodied in PRSP documentation and in ideas, concepts and epistemic rules that emerge from the PRSP process through actors connected with the process. Only in this way can we construct an epistemology around the PRSP framework as a regulatory mechanism and/or a new disciplinary framework, and, following this, construct an understanding of its impact on law and governance in a globalised society.

1.4.4 Legal pluralism and the constitutive power of law

The disciplinary power of the PRSP framework, as discussed previously, is manifested in its impact on countries' engagement with its external and internal constituencies. In their relationship with the exterior, states under the discipline of the new aid architecture negotiate their interactions with other actors (state and non-state) within the international legal system subject to the constraints placed upon it by the PRSP framework. Meanwhile, in their relationship with internal constituents, states also have to manage the competing interests and conflicts of municipal legal entities within the confines of the regulatory and policy dictates of the aid framework they have been conscripted to.

Consequently, in analysing the wider normative effects of the PRSP framework, we need to identify the scope of these normative orders. This book assumes a legally pluralistic understanding of law, and hence the normative orders in question go beyond what we conventionally understand as law and legal regimes. It is not the place here to reinvestigate the definitional multiplicities associated with the concept of legal pluralism. Instead, the book adopts the view that, despite past contestations, it is now widely accepted that the concept of legal pluralism refers to the coexistence of formalised legal regimes (conventionally referred to as 'state law') with a wide and varied range of constitutive orders (or 'non-state law').

The first category of laws is what Szablowski describes as 'a normative regime that is generated from (or recognised by) a formal institutional context and is intended to be enforced by a bureaucratic coercive apparatus' (Szablowski, 2007: 11–12; see also Tamanaha, 1995). The second category refers to a constellation of regimes which regulate social conduct and economic relations (sometimes popularly described as 'soft law'), or what Merry terms 'informal ordering systems' (Merry, 1992: 358). Legal pluralism focuses on considering the 'dialectic, mutually constitutive relations' between the two normative regimes, including how 'state law' affects other normative orders and vice versa, how non-state regulatory regimes either resist, capture or appropriate state legal orders (ibid.).The intersection between legal and non-legal normative orders has important resonances for our study on the impact of PRSPs on international law and global governance, particularly in terms of evaluating their significance to the two functions of law: *regulation* and *legitimation.*

A focus on analysing the dynamics of power inherent in the global law- and policymaking processes must also include an examination of how legal and non-legal normative orders construct and deconstruct power relations. According to Merry, law is no longer perceived only as 'a mode of social control' but as 'a constitutive system that creates conceptions of order and enforces them' (ibid.: 361). In other words, law does not merely regulate behaviour, it also legitimises and sanctions certain codes of conduct, thus contributing to a restructuring of social, economic and political relationships in the image of those who control its narratives. In this manner, law is seen as 'more than a system of meanings' and, at its most adverse, can also constitute 'a form of violence endowed with the legitimacy of a constituted authority' (ibid.; see also Mattei and Nader, 2008: 1–3).

In seeking to understand the normative impact of the PRSP framework, it is therefore essential that this constitutive function of law be taken into account, particularly in relation to how it restructures the engagement of third world states in the international order. The policy narratives of the PRSP process are thus important to restructuring states' interactions with their domestic constituents inasmuch as they reorganise states' encounters with external actors, including the conscription of states into new legal and non-legal regulatory disciplines, with ramifications for the constitution of global governance.

1.5 A note on methods

As previously mentioned, this book aims to conceptualise the PRSP process and its implications for international law and global governance. Much of the research for the book therefore involved theoretical and contextual analysis of existing reports and documentation on the PRSP processes in different countries and reviews of the overarching operational framework of the initiative and its associated financing instruments, encompassing primary and secondary documentary material sourced from libraries and organisational archives.

The documentary research entailed consultation and analysis of a range of official and unofficial documentation on the PRSP framework, PRSP processes and PRSP-related instruments, such as the PRGF and PRSCs. These documents were drawn from a myriad of official BWI and non-BWI documents – most of them now freely available on the World Bank and IMF websites – as well as legal agreements and some confidential policy documents obtained from first-hand sources. Qualitative assessments of specific documents were undertaken in line with the methodologies outlined previously.

This review of PRSP and PRSP-associated literature was supplemented by qualitative interviews and informal conversations with a sample of policymakers, activists and campaigners, politicians and institution bureaucrats, including some of the key players in the PRSP process, as well as observations from attendance at a number of consultative meetings and internal discussions with campaigners and activists. The field research was carried out mostly during the period of a year from April 2004 to April 2005. As some of the information obtained through such interviews, conversations and observational engagements is highly confidential and/or controversial if ascribed to particular sources, some sources have asked to remain anonymous or have non-attributed quotations. These interviews have supplemented, expanded upon or clarified data drawn from the aforementioned literature and documentation.

1.6 Cartography of the book

This book aims to draw a conceptual and methodological map of the PRSP framework and its impact on the constitution of global governance and postcolonial international law.

Following this introductory chapter, Chapter 2 situates the PRSP framework within the wider context of postcolonial international law, locating this initiative within the legacy of circumscribed sovereignty which characterises third world state engagement with the exterior. Establishing the theoretical frame of reference for the book, this chapter examines how the PRSP framework has been inserted into the dynamic of postcolonial relationships and how the

World Bank and the IMF emerged as central institutions in the management of the third world, particularly states' engagement with the international economy.

Chapter 3 proceeds to examine how the pivotal roles played by the Bretton Woods institutions in the postcolonial international order established them as key institutions for managing the crisis of legitimacy in the international order in the late 1990s. This chapter seeks to understand how the temporal convergence between the shifting institutional agendas of the Bank and Fund and the geostrategic imperatives of their major shareholders – the industrialised countries that form the metropolitan centres of the postcolonial global economy – to quell the rising tide of dissent against the dislocations of neoliberal economic reforms resulted in the formation of the disciplinary framework of the PRSP project.

Chapter 4 begins the examination of the disciplinary power of the PRSP framework through an analysis of how the reforms of the PRSP architecture reshape the modalities of states' engagement with the external economy and, notably, with its external financiers. This chapter will demonstrate how the changes in the technologies of aid regulation reflect the shifting forms of power at the global level, with particular reference to the evolution of the doctrine of 'conditionality' as a pivotal regulatory instrument.

Chapter 5 continues with the analysis of the PRSP framework's disciplinary power over third world states by examining the impact of the PRSP framework on the internal constitution of states, particularly through the efforts at capturing domestic *policy space*. It considers how the paradoxical incentivising and disciplining of the states subject to the PRSP initiative – together with their domestic constituents and external sympathisers[21] – has been operationalised through a framework which engenders the utilisation of new modalities of discipline highlighted in the previous chapter.

Chapter 6 follows on from the analysis in the preceding chapter, examining the participatory process mandated under the PRSP framework, locating these socio-political reforms within the overarching effort to rehabilitate the state apparatus under the PRSP framework. Where Chapter 5 examines how discipline is maintained through the internalisation of policy and institutional reform by states, this chapter seeks to examine how these reforms are legitimated through the *capture of political space* – the mobilisation of domestic political consensus in support of such reforms.

Chapter 7 consolidates the findings of the book within a wider examination of the dynamics of power in the international arena and considers the implications of the reforms on the constitution of global governance and international law. This chapter considers whether the forms of intervention in sovereign nations necessitated by the PRSP project are deeper and greater than previous forms of control, and considers the potential of the PRSP project in subverting or rekindling the possibilities for engaged collective action among the state actors in resistance to the inequities of the current globalised economy.

Notes

1 The 'Washington Consensus' is a term often misrepresented and misunderstood. The term itself was coined by US economist John Williamson, who first used it in a background paper for a conference on Latin American structural adjustment to refer to a set of ten economic reforms that he considered were necessary in order to redress the economic problems faced by Latin America in the 1980s. The paper, entitled 'What Washington Means by Policy Reform', identifies the ten policy instruments – including fiscal austerity, trade and financial liberalisation, deregulation and privatisation – which Williamson felt could be deployed in these countries with 'a reasonable degree of consensus' in Washington, the 'Washington' being 'both the political Washington of Congress and senior members of the administration and the technocratic Washington of the international financial institutions, the economic agencies of the US government, the Federal Reserve Board and the think tanks' (Williamson, 2004: 2; 2002). The term has been used since as a catch-all phrase to encompass the policies espoused by Williamson (see discussion in Chapter 3).

2 The key to the 'politics of globalisation', articulated in part through what Higgott (2000) terms the 'combative politics' of the late 1990s, is this correlation between globalisation and poverty as exemplified by the growth in income disparity between the world's richest and the world's poorest, demarcated usually along geographical lines. Higgott argues that, independently of whether the two are causally related, this perceived relationship between inequality and the policies of economic globalisation, combined with 'the degree to which the existing institutions [are seen] to underwrite the *status quo* rather than work for its eradication', has led to the challenges heaped on these institutions by their detractors (Higgott, 2000: 137; see also discussion of this point in Chapter 3, section 3.1).

3 The HIPC initiative was introduced in 1996 to grant debt relief to a ring-fenced set of countries who were deemed to have 'unsustainable debt burdens' and included for the first time relief from debt owed to multilateral institutions such as the IMF and the World Bank.

4 This was in contrast to what was (and still is) the case with areas such as human rights and environmental safeguards.

5 For detailed analysis of the collapse of the talks, see Khor (1999a) and the documents in 'Africa Policy E-Journal on Africa: Seattle Aftermath' at http://www.africaaction.org/docs99/wto9912.htm.

6 The term 'anti-globalisation', often used as an adjective to describe the social movements opposed to the globalisation of Washington Consensus-type economic reforms, was initially coined by the financial press. It is another term that is commonly misused and is misrepresentative of the majority of these non-governmental organisations and social movements as well as supporters of their campaigns who are not opposed to the concept of 'globalisation' on principle but are critical of the modalities of certain types of economic globalisation. Campaigners have sought to reclaim the terrain of terminology by substituting their own nomenclature. For example, the term 'economic justice movement' is now widely used to denote the coalition of civil society groups and individuals fighting to reform the structural inequities of the current global economy.

7 Concessional financing is typically financing extended to countries who cannot afford market-based lending and is used here to denote all or any of concessional lending (loans provided on an interest-free basis with generous repayment periods); grant financing; or debt relief (see Note on terminology, p. xv).

8 See Chapter 3, section 3.3 for details on the CDF.

9 The MDGs refer to the eight development goals to be achieved by 2015 by state signatories to the Millennium Declaration (adopted in September 2000 by 189 nations and signed by 147 governments at the UN Millennium Summit). These goals include the eradication of poverty, the achievement of universal primary education, the reduction of child mortality and improvement in maternal health and the promotion of gender equity). See: http://www.un.org/millenniumgoals/.

10 The JSAN replaced the Joint Staff Assessment (JSA) in November 2004, primarily to dispense with the received notion that the JSA represented a 'Washington sign-off' and to enable Bank and Fund staff to exercise greater frankness and candour in their evaluations (World Bank and IMF, 2005a: para. 2; see Chapter 5 for a detailed discussion of this shift).

11 Although some scholars do not place importance on distinguishing between the use of the terms 'global governance' and 'international relations', this book believes that the distinction between them should be noted. 'International relations' is a subset of 'global governance', referring to relations between sovereign states. 'Global governance' would refer to the system of governing global relations, including relations between states but not exclusively so. It also involves the establishment of institutions of governance at the global and international level to regulate international relations, political, economic or social. Most of such institutions remain *international* rather than *global* in nature as representations are still primarily made by state actors which remain primary subjects of *international* law and which constitute the primary legal personalities under constitutions of global governance organisations. However, the increasing jurisdiction of these institutions in what were previously sovereign territorial concerns under the delegated authority conferred on these institutions has morphed many of such 'international organisations' into 'global governance agencies' tasked with specific administrative duties over their members (see Scholte, 2000: 22, 132–134).

12 The term 'postcolonial international law' is used here to distinguish the set of rules, doctrines and institutions which form the normative and operational framework of the international legal order in the postcolonial era from those which served to order the conduct between imperial powers and between colonial states and their dominions. The term 'postcolonial' is used here temporally and distinguished from its use to denote a specific epistemological practice, that is, the scholarship of 'postcolonialism', although the book is sympathetic to the theoretical concerns of postcolonialism.

13 In this regard, the PRSP framework has significantly changed the landscape of research on subjects of this nature, in particular the involvement of a broader range of actors – notably civil society organisations (CSOs) in the research and hence a change in the type of research produced – as well as a shift towards more advocacy-type research. While NGOs have been involved in empirical research before, the difficulty in obtaining documents had deterred many from undertaking research on the impacts of development finance on the constituencies they represent or work with. The PRSP framework, while still marred by lack of transparency in many areas, has at least enabled the publication of essential documents as part of the consultation process, and hence facilitated research on the substantive content of PRSPs. Engagement with governments, and the IFIs, in the process of policy formulation has also led to a rise in anecdotal literature on the process of development financing and enabled more first-hand experienced critique of the process.

14 The late Joseph Gold and late Ibrahim Shihata were former general-counsels of the IMF and the World Bank Group, respectively.

15 The World Bank and International Monetary Fund.

16 The adoption of methodologies from organisational studies and management research in the study of international organisations, notably the World Bank, has become

increasingly popular over the years, as researchers begin to recognise the limitations of relying on a single approach to social-political research on these organisations and their impact on their constituents. In particular, phenomenological approaches to organisation theory depicting organisational structures as legitimating myths have been utilised by World Bank researchers to explain the Bank's rationalisation of its policies and the constraints the bureaucracy of the Bank places on its own operations. This has followed on from the popularity of socio-organisational approaches in economic sociology – pioneered by Karl Polanyi and popularised by organisational theorists such as Mark Granovetter and Paul DiMaggio – that have applied sociological models of analysis to economic phenomena (see Zukin and DiMaggio, 1990).

17 Elster approaches the study of social phenomena through 'explanation by mechanisms', using a causal mechanism to explain the link between two events in order to build a 'temporal snapshot' of events to construct a factual account of social reality (Elster, 1989: 3).

18 Braithwaite and Drahos define the globalisation of regulation (or regulatory globalisation) as the replication of regulatory norms, standards, principles across different regulatory jurisdictions (see, for example, Braithwaite and Drahos, 2000: 3–10).

19 The term 'neoliberal globalisation' is used to denote the globalisation of regulation facilitated by adherence to the Washington Consensus model of economic organisation and to contrast between other forms of social, cultural and economic forms of globalisation (see note 1 for a definition of the 'Washington Consensus').

20 For Foucault, analysing power by analysing specific institutional manifestations of such power, without its grounding within the social nexus from which it is drawn, risks masking the real source of power in pursuit of analysing the bureaucratic imperatives which drive the institutional agenda, and risks giving the institutions and their attendant regulations 'an exaggerated privilege in the relations of power and, hence, seeing in the latter, only modulations of law and coercion' (Foucault, 1994: 342–343).

21 This term is used to refer to the coalition of citizenry groups from the third world and their metropolitan centres (that is, the south and north) which provided the external support to groups fighting the domestic manifestations of structural adjustment.

Chapter 2

PRSPs in postcolonial international law and global governance

> The international legal system is a powerful site for contestation ... Because law has the constitutive power to universalize certain knowledges and to disqualify others, the ability to speak and to influence law-making processes is a critical determinant of access to power.
>
> (Otto, 1996: 359)

Poverty Reduction Strategy Papers have been hailed as the greatest change in development financing since the introduction of structural adjustment lending in the early 1980s, reflecting not only a change in the structure of concessional financing but also a shift in the discourse of development policy and practice. Crucially, the framework signals a larger paradigmatic shift in the cartography of aid and, consequently, in the constitution of north–south relations, of which aid relations form a pivotal strand. For many third world states whose relationships with the exterior have been primarily characterised by such relationships of resource dependency, the PRSP framework has fundamental implications for their engagement, both individually and collectively, in international lawmaking and multilateral governance institutions.

The reorganising of the form and substance of negotiations between developing countries and international financial institutions as well as other official financiers impacts critically on the relationships these countries maintain in other areas of significance, notably in the realm of international economic law and global financial and economic governance. In this manner, PRSPs are not only restructuring the modalities of financing but also reframing fundamental tenets of international law and mechanisms of global governance, implemented through a series of strategic interventions in target countries.

The extensive state interventions brought about through the PRSP framework are, however, only possible where the sovereignty of the states in question is circumscribed through their initial insertion into the international order and the continued existence of international institutions that facilitate the extension of this imperial character of international relations. Accordingly, there is a need to situate the PRSP approach and its attendant institutional framework – notably its organisational drivers, World Bank and the IMF – within the structure of postcolonial international law as well as within contemporary structures of global governance.

This chapter seeks to explore the ways in which third world states were originally incorporated into the international legal order to explain how the PRSP framework and other interventions of the postcolonial period can and have been effected and legitimised despite incongruence with conventional understandings of international law. Locating third world engagement with international law in the 'colonial encounter' (Anghie, 2004; Otto, 1996), in the logic of modern legal mythology (Fitzpatrick, 1992; Tarullo, 1985) and in contemporary politics of patronage (Badie, 2000), including the central facilitating role played by the Bretton Woods institutions, will enable us to better situate the PRSP framework within the current framework of economic globalisation and contemporary international relations.

This will demonstrate that, rather than being inimical to the project of international law, the PRSP framework forms a vital and cohesive part of international law, specifically international economic law and the attendant institutions of global economic governance, so constituted in the postcolonial era. Crucially, the disentanglement of the PRSP approach and its attendant discourses from the self-validating narratives of universalism, enfranchisement and empowerment is key to understanding the role it plays in perpetuating inequalities at the international level.

Consequently, it is argued here that the PRSP framework represents a continuation, if not an exacerbation, of the asymmetrical sovereignty characterising postcolonial 'international' law and the imperial nature of the 'development' project which has sustained the logic of this relationship. In arguing thus, this chapter demonstrates, in a similar vein to Anghie's analysis of the 'good governance' project which preceded the PRSP framework, that the insertion of the PRSP framework into sovereign lending operations masks 'the imperial character' of international law 'even when it is being reproduced in a way that powerfully shapes contemporary international relations' (Anghie, 2004: 250). Understanding this legacy is central to developing a theory about the role of the PRSP framework in the context of globalisation and contemporary global governance.

2.1 PRSPs in the international order: asymmetrical sovereignty and circumscription of state autonomy

The PRSP framework may be regarded as an affront to the principles of sovereign equality and non-intervention, the pillars of the postwar international legal order enshrined by the norms established in the Charter of the United Nations, 1947. The extensive domestic interventions of the PRSP approach and its reorganisation of the socio-political fabric of PRSP countries represent a clear circumscription of the principles of state sovereignty, non-discrimination and self-determination constituting the lynchpins of international law in the postcolonial period.

Yet, the near universal implementation of such an intrusive, institutionalised instrument of state reorganisation in the third world has gone virtually unchallenged in the international arena. On the contrary, the introduction of such a process of 'participatory' policymaking and 'consultative' decision-making, linked to the disbursement of much needed external financing, has been welcomed, if not celebrated, by previous detractors of the BWIs and the current aid architecture on the grounds of its inclusiveness and its promotion of 'country ownership'. Where there has been criticism of the PRSP approach, such critiques have centred on the disjuncture between the rhetoric of the PRSP principles and their operational implementation rather than on the impact or potential impact of such an interventionist mechanism in international law.

This can be partially explained by the practice of epistemic delineation and/or disciplinary incoherence in analysis of the PRSP framework, notably in the absence of legal critique on an issue that is viewed primarily as a subject of international political economy or international relations or under the rubric of 'development studies'.

More significantly, however, this failure to critically contextualise the PRSP framework in international law can be attributed to the perception that the PRSP approach is appropriately constituted within international law – international economic law in particular – in that the framework rehabilitates, albeit incrementally, the unequal nature of international economic relations. In this manner, the PRSP framework is viewed as reforming the iniquities associated with the circumscription of autonomy under structural adjustment. At the same time, its spotlight on poverty reduction rescues the focus of international economic law from a mandate premised on the project of modernity that accompanied postcolonial economic governance.

These conceptualisations, and, consequently, the operational efficacy of the PRSP framework, could only have taken place within a legacy of state asymmetry in international law into which postcolonial third world states have been inserted. The wholesale revision of the modalities of PRSP countries' engagement with the international community – through the rules regulating access to aid, concessional financing and debt relief – exemplifies the current international legal order, in which third world states remain primarily *objects* of international law rather than its *subjects*. The interventions facilitated by the PRSP approach may thus be regarded as being both *legitimised by* and *facilitative of* the imperial character of international law, exemplifying what Pahuja (2005) terms 'the postcoloniality of international law'.[1]

2.1.1 Locating the PRSP project in the 'postcoloniality' of international law

Fundamental to the constitution of this 'postcoloniality' in international law is its sustenance of the 'dynamic of difference' (Anghie, 2004: 4) as reflected in (1) the construction of European/western/occidental identity in opposition to a self-constructed, alternative representation of what it is not or, in Fitzpatrick's words, 'an identity in negation' (Fitzpatrick, 2001: 147); and (2) the ceaseless creation of an 'Other' – a reduction of non-European identity to the characteristics which this definitive 'Self' rejects[2] (Anghie, 2004; Fitzpatrick, 2001; Pahuja, 2005; Said, 2003).[3] This process creates the 'gap between two cultures, demarcating one as "universal" and civilized and the other as "particular" and uncivilized' (Anghie, 2004: 4), in which the constitution of the 'universal' avoids the fixity of definition by positing itself 'in an irredeemable opposition' to savagery, which constitutes the 'particular' (Fitzpatrick, 2001: 147).

The European or occidental identity therefore reserves for itself the characterisation of the 'universal' and of 'civilisation' not through the design of rules for what it should *include* but by reference to what it should *exclude*, that is, anything the west abrogates, abhors or declares aberrant. It is this underlying delineation which defines the function of postcolonial international law not as creating order among sovereign states but as seeking containment of this 'cultural difference' among states (Anghie, 2004, 2002). It is also this binary between 'civilisation' and 'primitivity' that distinguishes between first and third world engagement with international law, a distinction which also underlines the logic of the PRSP approach and inserts this framework within the current context of international law.

First, the 'dynamic of difference' ensured the universalisation of 'a single system of international law with explicitly European origins' (Anghie, 2002: 516) – a process forged during the colonial era and intensified during the period of decolonisation – and the unquestioning assumption of newly independent and non-European societies into the pre-existing community of nations and their subjection to norms which these new entities had played no part in designing (Anghie, 2004, 2002; Fitzpatrick, 2001; Pahuja, 2005). As a consequence, asymmetrical relationships were established in the international legal order between the 'subjects' of international law, the former colonial powers for whom international law pre-decolonisation regulated their access to and use of *terra nullius*, and the 'objects' of international law – former colonies and other non-European states whose inclusion in the sovereign realm was governed by their accession to the aforementioned established 'universal' norms (Anghie, 2004: 100–104).[4]

The force of the corpus of rules, doctrines, practices and institutions which make up international law thus has differing applications for the differing states party to them. Whereas for first world states international law served, and still serves, the function of ordering relations among sovereign states, for third world states the question was one of 'acquisition of sovereignty', because the concept of sovereignty was aligned, as it were, 'with European ideas of social order, political organization, progress and development' (Anghie, 2004: 102–103). This has resulted in what Badie calls 'the juridical fiction of sovereignty' in which the 'international system can be constituted only of sovereign states whose juridical identity reflects that of Western states' (Badie, 2000: 78).

Formal sovereignty acquired in its juridical form in the postcolonial period therefore did not accord postcolonial states substantive equality in their engagement with international law because the doctrine of sovereignty itself was 'improvised out of the colonial encounter' when applied to new recruits to the international legal order, rendering third world sovereignty distinct in its vulnerability and dependence from first world sovereignty (Anghie, 2004: 6).

Consequently, and second, because international law is constituted based on the idea of civilisation, a 'civilisation' that is premised on the redemption of 'the backward, aberrant, violent, oppressed and underdeveloped people of the non-European world' (Anghie, 2004: 3), international law and international institutions sought to bridge the aforementioned gap between cultures through the development of techniques to confront and contain this difference and to achieve 'uniformity and universality' among states (ibid.: 4; Anghie, 2002: 516–520). This became imperative in the aftermath of the decolonisation process, which necessitated 'a new form of containment' of the 'Other', the newly established states brought 'into an even more proximate relation with the West' (Pahuja, 2005: 465).

The technologies and institutions of postcolonial international law provide the instruments for such containment inasmuch as they provide the mechanisms to frustrate anything less than an orderly entry of these new states into the international legal order, and anything less than a full acquiescence to the terms and conditions, through, *inter alia*, the withholding of commensurable rights and privileges associated with such entry. The legitimacy of interventions on the part of the 'international community' via 'international' institutions was secured through the maintenance of the aforementioned 'dynamic of difference', enabling the 'application of sanctions' and necessitating internal interventions in communities which failed to comply with the universal norms established by the international community, in the same way that imperial conquest had been legitimised by the 'civilizing mission' to transform 'backward and primitive' societies' (Anghie, 2004: 3–4; 2002: 519; Pahuja, 2005: 465).

For Anghie, the development of new international institutions – beginning with the Mandate System of the League of Nations[5] and culminating with the birth of the international financial institutions – was crucial to the foundation of the postwar legal order, enabling the development and implementation of new technologies to rehabilitate the state in aberration of 'universal' values (Anghie, 2004, 2002). Subsequently, the circumscribed nature of third world sovereignty and the colonial legacy of international law enabled international law and institutions of global governance to intervene in the domestic sphere and 'to administer civilizing therapy' to these newly 'sovereign' states (Anghie, 2002: 547).

2.1.2 Reproducing colonial asymmetries through postcolonial law

The imperial heritage of international law juxtaposed with the invention of 'developmentalism' has produced a powerful body of rules, doctrines, institutions and regimes of knowledge which has governed third world engagement in the international arena in the postcolonial era. For Escobar, the systems of discourse and representation associated with the advent of 'development' as 'a domain of thought and action'[6] in the immediate postwar period went beyond the creation of knowledge about the third world and instead organised postcolonial states into a social Darwinistic model of progress, enabling the successful deployment of 'a regime of government' over the third world, the one half of a bifurcated reality between 'developed' and 'underdeveloped' (Escobar, 1995: 9–10).

Accordingly, while the justification for the interventionist restructuring of sovereign third world states was reframed from one based on biological hierarchies to one delimited by cultural polarities, the object of the 'civilising mission' remains the same. The replacement of 'biological racism with an equally pernicious form of cultural racism' through which Eurocentric ideas of socio-political and economic organisation became superior (Tucker, 1999: 5) thus became an important instrument in the consolidation of the postcolonial world economy. 'Development' became a 'historically singular experience, the creation of a domain of thought and action' (Escobar, 1995: 10) which served to contain and discipline not only the internal productive capacities of postcolonial states but also the liberatory potential and political autonomy of their new-found sovereignty.

The recognition of third world states and the legitimacy of third world claims under international law then became premised on (1) their capacity to demonstrate adherence to the norms established by the 'international' legal order; and (2) in their failure to demonstrate the aforementioned, their willingness to be rehabilitated and accept interventions for reform in order that they might be restructured into compliance. In this manner, colonialism gives way to a 'new legal imperialism' which operates not through direct colonialism by singularly powerful nation states but through the control and manipulation by these states of a community of nations – the 'internationalisation' of colonial power through new 'contractual modes of domination' or voluntary accession to the institutions of the global political economy (see Fitzpatrick, 2001: 212–213).

International law and the institutions sustaining it therefore became not only the means through which first world states determined third world accession to the global political and economic order, but also a means by which third world participation in these international domains is continually disciplined through a constant revision of the terms and conditions of their engagement. The modernist discourse of difference which underpinned the development of the postwar international legal order – whereby 'decolonization was only available on narrow terms, to entities that resembled the European nation-state' (Otto, 1996: 343) – continue to serve as exclusionary devices in current international relations (ibid.: 338).

Hence, the translation of what Tarullo terms 'the myth of normalcy' – the sanctifying of a singular image of what is 'normal' for states participating in the international economy[7] – into international economic law constrains the third world's participation in and contribution to the development of its organising principles (Tarullo, 1985: 547–548, 550).[8] The institutionalising of this logic of normalcy in international economic relations between states not only naturalises and perpetuates the aforementioned categories of representation in international legal discourse; it also confines negotiations and resolution of disputes to the reproduction of these 'images of sameness where they do not already exist' and the 'eradication of communities of difference' where they do exist (Tarullo, 1985: 550–552). These 'myths' inherent in international economic relations 'teach difference as a departure, often temporary, from normal' and aberrations which necessitate the intervention of the international community, such as IMF conditionalities to redress the financial imbalances of an indebted state (Tarullo, 1985: 546–547).

At the heart of these attempts at 'containment' are both the need to ration the transfer of capital from the north to the south and the need to maintain access to the resources of the south by the north, in keeping with the geo-strategic and economic imperatives of maintaining the status quo of colonial economic relations in the postcolonial period. This regulation of capital flows to the south – in terms of monitoring the volume of resource transfers as well as the utilisation of such resources domestically – is driven by the necessity of maintaining what Hopkins and Wallerstein term the 'core–periphery zonal organization of world production' (Hopkins and Wallerstein, 1996: 4),[9] characteristic of the postcolonial international financial and trade architecture.[10]

Accordingly, the sustenance of the systemic 'peripheralisation' of the world economy – maintaining developing countries within the lower echelons of the global commodity chains pivoted around organising centres in the north (Hudson, 2003: 186) – necessitates that development occurs only within the tightly controlled terms established by the metropolitan states and that the 'political and social conditions for the global accumulation system are maintained' (Biel, 2000: 87). In other words, in maintaining the imperial relationships of dependency in the postcolonial period, the flow of capital to postcolonial states needed 'to be regulated to prevent the South from using the resources to catch up with the centre' (ibid.: 86).

This logic of unequal exchange still characterises the relationship between third world states and their former imperial powers today. The continued dependence of postcolonial states on the political and financial patronage of the metropolitan centre necessitates the constitutional mimicry by these states that facilitates the reproduction of the aforementioned norms (Badie, 2000: 24–27, 77–78).This is mediated through the financial flows from the north to the south – either in the form of private capital investment (foreign direct investment (FDI) or technology transfer), publicly guaranteed debt (bond issues, development financing loans) or concessional resource transfers (bilateral or multilateral aid or debt relief) – which remain contingent upon the adoption of reforms contractually obliged by such transfers.

These reforms are subsequently legitimised through the enrolment of the discursive and constitutive powers of law and legal ideology. Most notably, the translation of contemporary 'rule of law' and 'good governance' ideologies into development policy and practice – through the export of European law and the process of administrative, legislative and judicial reform in third world states (see further discussion in section 2.3) – has provided the institutional framework for legalising and legitimising the structural economic reforms to be embedded within postcolonial states. This has led authors Mattei and Nader to consider law as an instrument of 'plunder' – defined as 'the inequitable distribution of resources by the strong at the expense of the weak' – and the 'rule of law' ideology as providing continuity with rather than acting as an interruption in colonial practice (Mattei and Nader, 2008: 3, 11).

Thus, the fact of juridical sovereignty is incommensurate with the act of self-determination, which in itself remains a normative value for many third world states, divested of economic resources and dispossessed of political and territorial authority, in the postcolonial era. This leads to the paradoxical legitimating of interventions aimed at redressing this 'sovereignty gap', a justification that is also increasingly advanced in the discourse accompanying the PRSP-led 'new architecture of aid'. The circumscribed nature of third world sovereignty, along with the uneven integration of states into the postcolonial international economy, has resulted in the creation of a discourse of 'quasi states' or 'negative sovereignty' (see Jackson, 1990; Williams, 2000) to describe the condition of postcolonial statehood, including that of many PRSP states, in accordance with the binary representations of difference discussed on pp. 25–27.

Here, states which depart from the norms of statehood are considered to have 'failed to fulfil the purposes of state sovereignty' (Williams, 2000: 567) by failing 'to meet the basic prerequisites of a sovereign government', thereby necessitating the imposition of 'state-building' exercises from the exterior to close the gap between their *de jure* and *de facto* sovereignty (Ghani *et al.*, 2005: 4). Badie argues that this paradox of sovereignty is encouraged by the metropolitan states because of the benefits they accrue from such practice (Badie, 2000: 79). The maintenance of the 'non-West' in the condition of Jackson's 'negative sovereignty' worsens the relationship of dependency between the core and peripheral states by weakening the authority of the peripheral state (ibid.: 80). The need to maintain the aforementioned juridical fiction of statehood thereby legitimises interventions to negate this fragmentation of the peripheral state as a result of failure of either resources or political cohesion.

The rehabilitation of states under the PRSP framework, organised around dependence on external resources, resonates with the logic of asymmetrical sovereignty and the embedded paternalism of 'international cooperation' therein. The conceptual premise and operational framework of the PRSP approach therefore reflect a continuity with the legacy of international law as forged in the colonial confrontation and represent the most recent example of how Anghie's 'dynamic of difference', as manifested contemporarily in Tarullo's 'myth of normalcy', continue to serve as mechanisms for revising third world engagement with international law.

2.2 Institutions of postcolonial governance: the Bretton Woods system

The binary constructions of 'order' and 'disorder' and 'positive'/'negative' sovereignty in international law necessitated, as previously discussed, the establishment of institutional structures to support the management of third world states' entry into and participation in the international legal order, including the maintenance of the aforementioned systems of representation. The birth of the Bretton Woods institutions must therefore be located in the context of this 'unique relationship' between international institutions and the third world (Anghie, 2002: 625), requiring the development of technologies aimed at 'developing, refining, reinforcing, reproducing and managing' the specific model of statehood and sovereignty discussed previously (Anghie, 2000: 289).

Consequently, it follows that the efficacy of the PRSP framework in managing the participation of postcolonial states in the global economy is centred upon the historical influence of the World Bank and the IMF on third world states. The evolutionary (but not necessarily linear) progression of modalities of development financing towards the PRSP approach must therefore be situated within the postcolonial political economy of aid and the centrality of the BWIs to this system of resource mobilisation and transfer.

Since their inception in 1947, the World Bank and the IMF have served as pivotal institutions mediating postcolonial states' engagement with the international economy and with the international legal mechanisms sustaining such engagement. Both the Bank and the Fund have, particularly in the last three decades, served as powerful intermediaries between postcolonial states and their imperial metropolis.[11] Due to their formidable institutional leverage, the BWIs have, crucially, acted as conduits for the transmission of the aforementioned narratives of normalcy, seeking to contain and manage the difference located between the oppositional representations of the two worlds and, at the same time, providing the organisational framework through which these narratives might be transformed into operational norms and institutions.

2.2.1 Legacies of the colonial encounter

The force of the World Bank and the IMF resides in their unique governance structure, which remains fundamentally different and separate from that of the United Nations and other UN specialised agencies, even though the institutions are formally incorporated as 'specialised agencies' under the Charter of the United Nations.[12] Reflecting the geo-strategic and economic imperatives of the immediate postwar period, the current governance structure of the Bank and the Fund continues to operate on an anachronistic decision-making framework favouring the powerful former imperial powers and marginalising the economically weak and politically peripheral postcolonial states. While both institutions justify their autonomy from the UN system on the grounds that each of them is 'required to function as, an independent organization',[13] neither of these institutions is truly 'independent' or 'international' in character.

Although there is a limited equalising provision in the decision-making structures of the World Bank and the IMF in which each member state is allocated a basic share of votes, the voting power of each member is contingent primarily upon how much economic weight the country carries in the world economy (Buira, 2005; Woods, 2006: 22–24).[14] This relative economic weight is then reflected in assigned quotas for each member at the IMF, which is then translated into 'a share of contributions and votes (and in the IMF, access to resources)',[15] resulting in the US possessing the largest share of votes (and effective veto power), followed by four other G7 countries, Japan, Germany, France and the UK (IBRD, 2009; IDA, 2009; IMF, 2009b, 2009c; Woods, 2006: 22).[16]

The controlling influence of these countries at the BWIs is reinforced by the representation structure of the Bank and Fund Executive Boards, the main decision-making organ of the BWIs,[17] in which only the largest five countries (plus China, Russia and Saudi Arabia) are represented individually by a single executive director appointed by their countries. Other members are grouped into 16 constituencies reflecting the relative strength of their members and elect an executive director between them. Consequently, the countries most subject to Bank and Fund interventions, including, especially, the low-income countries subject to the PRSP framework, have the least voice. Sub-Saharan African (SSA) countries, representing 25 per cent of the membership and making up the majority of PRSP countries, are particularly marginalised. Forty-four SSA countries are represented by only two executive directors and wield a mere total of 4.4 per cent of the total voting power in the IMF and slightly under 2 per cent at the Bank (IMF, 2009b; World Bank, 2009a).

The disenfranchisement of developing countries at the BWIs is further magnified by the asymmetrical manner in which countries are represented by the executive directors. Employed as officials of the Bank and the Fund and funded by the two institutions, executive directors are theoretically responsible to their institutions and not to individual member states and are not obliged 'to defer to the view of [their] member states nor cast votes in accordance with their instructions'[18] (Brown, 1992: 105–107; Shihata, 2000a: 653–656). In practice, the system favours single-country constituencies, where executive directors are *appointed* by countries they represent and are most likely to take instructions from their capitals.[19] Executive directors *elected* in group constituencies on the other hand are not able to split the votes in their constituency to reflect the differing views of member states (ibid.: 656). This particularly marginalises developing countries in mixed constituencies, where the executive director is likely to be from an industrialised member country.

Moreover, in spite of this complicated voting structure decisions at the Bank and the Fund do not involve a formal tally of votes. Instead, they are made through an ascertainment of 'the sense of the [Board] meeting' by the Bank president or the IMF's managing director as chairs of the respective Executive Boards, although this 'sense' must be a position that 'is supported by Executive Directors having sufficient votes' (Van Houtven, 2002: 23; see also Shihata, 2000a). Consequently, both the chair of the Board and sufficiently influential executive directors can – and frequently do – have a significant impact on the decisions taken at the Executive Board (see Van Houtven, 2002: 24), more so when BWI convention dictates that the Bank president is appointed by the US and the IMF managing director by the European members, once again reflecting anachronistic postwar alliances.

The porousness of the Bank and Fund's governance structure to political pressure is reflected in the policy shifts of the institutions over the years, including the decision to implement the PRSP framework.[20] As will be discussed in Chapter 3, the impetus for the PRSP initiative came not from the south but from a constellation of political and economic forces in the north, and the decision to operationalise the framework was adopted in spite of opposition by representatives of the low-income countries affected on the Bank and Fund Executive Boards (see Chapter 3, section 3.4).

2.2.2 *Aggravating asymmetry*

Over the six decades since their inception, the governance asymmetry at the World Bank and the IMF has been exacerbated through a series of manoeuvres by the powerful states to strengthen their influence at the BWIs and to block institutional reforms called for by developing country members. These interventions have also resulted in the *de facto* cartelisation of development financing by the Bank and the Fund as financier countries chose to channel multilateral financing through the institutions over which they had greater leverage.

First, the limited voice and vote of developing country members have been further eroded through unbalanced quota reviews over the years, and proposals for reform of the system initiated in 2008 at the IMF will result only in marginal changes to the decision-making structures.[21] Quota increases at the Fund have not reflected the increasing economic strength of developing countries, particularly emerging market economies, in the world economy – exacerbating comparative voting anomalies so that, for example, Brazil's quota is two-thirds that of Belgium, and China's quota until recently was smaller than Italy's and remains smaller than the UK's (IMF, 2009b). Previous quota reviews have also failed to revise the number of basic votes, resulting in the decline of basic votes relative to total votes from 11.3 per cent in the 1970s to 2.1 per cent in the 2000s (Buira, 2005: 9; Van Houtven, 2004: 19; 2002: 6).

Efforts underway to increase the 'voice and vote' of developing country members at the IMF will contribute little to reforming this system of representation based on economic strength. The reforms will see a tripling of basic votes from 250 to 750 votes and an indexing of basic votes to 5.5 per cent of the overall quota levels as well as ad-hoc quota increases for a number of countries whose shares were previously underrepresented (IMF, 2009b, 2008b). The quota increases will be based on a new quota formula, and constituencies with 19 members or more (the two African constituencies) will be allocated an additional alternate executive director to assist with the workload (ibid.). However, critics have pointed out that these reforms do not go far enough to redress the asymmetries in governance, particularly as the total size of quotas will only be increased by an overall 11.5 per cent and the increase in voting rights has also been marginal (still below the original level of 12 per cent), and comprehensive reform of Executive Board composition remains off the table (Chowla, 2008).

The second issue aggravating asymmetries at the BWIs has been the creeping bilateralism at the BWIs, which has undermined the initial objectives of multilateralism, however circumscribed. Central to this development has been the introduction of donor-driven concessional windows at the Bank and the Fund, primarily the IDA and the ESAF, now the PRGF, the operations of which centre around the PRSP framework. Although the original financing structure of the BWIs – notably through market-based lending at the Bank[22] and capital subscriptions at the Fund – rendered them relatively immune to political pressure (Woods, 2006: 23), the establishment of these concessional windows has drastically eroded this financial autonomy. The periodic replenishment requirements of these concessional facilities has enabled the major shareholding countries of the Bank and Fund to exert leverage over the policies of the Bank and the Fund outside the formally constituted decision-making framework, allowing the bilateral interests of these financiers to be cloaked in the veneer of multilateral policymaking.

The creation of the IDA, with its short three-year replenishment cycle, in particular, has enabled the US to significantly influence not only the policies of the Association but also those of the World Bank Group as a whole (Kapur, 2003: 7; Shihata, 2000a: 564; Woods, 2006: 28–29). Substantial expansion of the Bank's mandate has come about as a result of IDA replenishment negotiations carried out by the 'IDA Deputies', representatives of creditor (or Part 1) countries involved in replenishment discussions, bypassing formal channels of decision-making and thereby excluding representatives of developing countries.[23] The US has repeatedly 'used threats to reduce or withhold contributions to the IDA in order to demand changes in policy' at the World Bank (Woods, 2006: 28), a policy which has now been imitated by other IDA creditor governments, albeit to a lesser degree. Such operational policy reforms impact upon the relationship between the World Bank and its borrowers and are often reflected in more onerous conditions for financing.

Bilateral influence at the World Bank has also further increased as a consequence of the Bank's use of co-financing instruments and trust funds which are managed and administered by the Bank in collaboration with an external donor,[24] as well as the creation of debt relief trusts, notably the HIPC and the new MDRI Trusts. The introduction of the ESAF Trust, subsequently the PRGF Trust and now the PRGT, and the equivalent debt relief trust funds – the PRGF-HIPC and

PRGF-MDRI Trusts – at the IMF also create a corresponding problem of bilateralism at the Fund in that resources for such funds must be mobilised elsewhere but conditions attached to financing from these trusts are implemented by the IMF in IMF member states.[25]

Consequently, and third, the leverage exerted bilaterally by their most powerful members has resulted in the influence of the Bretton Woods institutions being extended into areas outside their original constitutional remit. Significant institutional reforms have been formulated during the IDA replenishments as a result of donors making such changes a prerequisite for IDA contributions. Most notably, since the Ninth Replenishment, issues of institutional policy, including Bank operational policies and management of Bank activities, have 'become a fundamental element' in the IDA replenishment negotiations[26] (IDA, 2001a: para. 13; Kapur, 2003: 2–3), including policies which led to the inception of the PRSP framework. This 'mission creep'[27] has correspondingly increased the institutions' leverage over third world states and has progressively bolstered the role of the IMF and the World Bank in facilitating north–south financial flows, notably but not exclusively that of official financial transfers.

Moreover, as financing for PRSP countries is drawn exclusively from the IDA, the PRGF and the relevant debt relief trusts, many of the operational decisions affecting these countries are likely to be made in these bilateral forums with little or no input from the countries affected by such policy shifts. For example, the structure of the Bank's MDRI Trust, which remains premised on the IDA replenishment model – that is, that the debt relief allocated to eligible countries is contingent upon periodic donor contributions (IDA, 2006: para. 42)[28] – ensures that the terms of financing for debt relief-eligible countries will remain contingent upon negotiations between the IDA Deputies rather than discussions at the Executive Board level.

2.2.3 Monopolising the forum

The decision to retain the organisational independence of the Bretton Woods institutions from the UN system[29] and the maintenance of the aforementioned governance structure favouring a small cartel of industrialised countries has had significant implications for global economic policymaking and international economic and financial regulation. The increasing encroachment of the Bank and Fund into areas outside their traditional remit has meant the emergence of the Bank and the Fund as the primary global institutions for social and economic development and regulation, with the treatment of their additional mandates subject to the political and economic interests of their major shareholders.

At the same time, the influence of the UN economic agencies has been progressively weakened, with these organisations' capacity in economic research, policy formulation and international economic negotiations eroded through financial and other pressures brought to bear on these agencies and their personnel by industrialised countries (South Centre, 1996). The coinciding of the expansion of the BWIs' work programmes with the reduction in the UN's role in economic policy agenda setting represented a slow but sure 'transfer of power' from the UN agencies to the World Bank and the IMF (ibid.: ch. 8), who are shielded from the UN's relatively more representative governance structure by virtue of their specific Relationship Agreements (see section 2.2.1).

According to the South Centre,[30] the policy positions adopted by northern countries vis-à-vis these agencies have been driven by more than budgetary concerns and represented 'consistent efforts to discourage and diminish the South's collective action, and to limit key economic activities and initiatives within the UN system', thereby 'eroding and weakening those organizations which were *not fully under the major powers' control*' (South Centre, 1996: ch. 2, emphasis added). As a result, the UN agencies, including other specialised agencies which have comparative advantage over economic research and social and development policies and in poverty reduction and humanitarian relief, such as the Food and Agriculture Organisation (FAO), the United Nations Conference on Trade and Development (UNCTAD), the United Nations Development Programme (UNDP) and the World Health Organisation (WHO), have been increasingly sidelined in the shift of these issues to the Bank and the Fund.

More importantly, there has been a concerted effort on the part of northern states to undermine the regulatory powers of the UN, particularly in extinguishing efforts to develop regimes for transnational economic regulation within the ambit of the UN system. The stalled attempts at mobilising a New International Economic Order (NIEO)[31] in the late 1970s and early 1980s and the collapse of the international commodity agreements – coordinated under the auspices of UNCTAD – in the 1980s are illustrative of efforts by the industrialised countries to reassert hegemony over postcolonial states by shifting the regulatory forum for negotiations on international economic issues.

This progressive undermining of more democratic and inclusive regulatory forums cognisant of the needs and interests of postcolonial states, particularly in the last 30 years, and the corresponding rise of the Bank and Fund as institutions of governance, as opposed to merely financial institutions, is reflective of the significant 'forum shift'[32] of the northern states towards regulatory regimes favourable to the interests of not only metropolitan capital but global capitalism in itself. The centrality of the BWIs under the 'new architecture of aid' – in terms of administering the PRSP framework and debt relief mechanisms as well as providing concessional finance – has further marginalised the UN economic agencies, notably UNCTAD and the UNDP, from key roles in the social and economic organisation of these countries.

2.3 Managing the third world: the Bank and Fund in postcolonial governance

The asymmetrical governance framework of the World Bank and the IMF, replicating colonial power relations and privileging the industrialised countries of the north, has resulted in the creation of a formidable apparatus of governance and management of the third world. The role played by the World Bank and the IMF in sustaining the imperial character of postcolonial international law has been twofold.

First, the institutions have intervened to rehabilitate, internally, the postcolonial state in the process of bridging or normalising the 'difference' among states and thereby sustaining the logic of 'normalcy' in international relations. Second, the BWIs have served to manage the third world's engagement in the international order by organising the terms of their participation in the global economy and administrating their economic relationships with the north, both official and commercial. Not only have the Bank and Fund established themselves as repositories of knowledge about the third world, with increased regulatory powers, these two institutions have effectively marshalled this knowledge into controlling the participation of developing countries in the international system.

2.3.1 Bridging the dynamic of difference

One of the key mandates of the World Bank and the IMF in developing countries in the postcolonial period has been the containment of 'difference' between states and the modernising imperatives to efface structures of socio-political and economic organisation incommensurate with the logic of postcolonial economic relations and, in the past three decades, with the logic of neoliberal globalisation. The transformation of these societies and the erasure of different systems of social and economic organisation were critical to the sustenance of the postcolonial international relationships in pursuit of neocolonial economic expansion.

a) Problematising poverty

As discussed in section 2.1, the problematisation of poverty in the postcolonial period created new regimes of representation in which racialised constructions of identities of 'Self' and 'Other' forged in the colonial confrontation have been recast in the modernist discourse of development. These powerful regimes of representation, defined by Doty as 'the ways in which the South has been discursively represented by policymakers, scholars, journalists and others in the North' (Doty, 1996: 2), are central to the development of techniques of discipline and incorporation in the postcolonial period.

This 'body of theory and practice' – Said's 'Orientalism' – sustained through generations of 'considerable material investment' and systemised into 'an accepted grid for filtering through the Orient into Western consciousness' (Said, 2003: 6), has been effectively deployed in the postcolonial era to maintain exploitative relationships between the north and south. The problematisation of 'poverty' and 'underdevelopment' in postcolonial states therefore necessitated the production of a 'science' of 'developmentalism' which, translated into policy and practice, legitimises certain interventions in the third world aimed ostensibly at the eradication of poverty (Escobar, 1995: 21–24).

The BWIs have been instrumental in advancing this 'science' of development and in sustaining such practices of representation through the organisation and dissemination of particularised and essentialised knowledge and meanings about the developing world and about the structure of the global economy. Over the years, the Bank and the Fund have progressively reserved for themselves the task of gathering, disseminating and, most importantly, gatekeeping the information about and for developing countries. This includes naturalising knowledge about certain types of socio-economic development and political organisation, and classifying countries' involvement in the international arena in accordance with the adherence to such naturalised understandings of the domestic and international economy and the role of developing countries within it.[33]

And while the organisation of such knowledge was primarily linked with the disbursement of financial resources by the institutions themselves in their early period, the emergence of the BWIs as 'development agencies' since the 1970s has extended the discursive reach of the Bank's and Fund's narratives on development and financial and economic organisation. In other words, where previously the generation of financial and economic knowledge about their borrowers was confined to what was necessary for institutional fiduciary assessments of project loans (for the Bank) and for access to counter-cyclical financing (for the Fund),[34] the expanded mandates of the two institutions have resulted in a wider and much more influential role for the production of such information and generated an expansion in the coverage of the information gathered and disseminated.

b) Banking on knowledge

The Bank's role in knowledge production and dissemination is as extensive as it is intensive, encompassing a wide range of research work, analytic and advisory services and capacity building programmes. This knowledge dissemination role is critical to developing the Bank's reputation as a development agency, more so than its financing operations. The ideas generated by the Bank in this capacity, along with information emanating from the Fund, are extremely influential in shaping the development trajectories of its borrowing members as they are often 'vital in providing roadmaps for policymakers contemplating change' (Woods, 2006: 4) as well as providing key signalling to other official financiers and private markets.[35]

The unparalleled access of the Bank to a 'rare, privileged and sensitive cache of country level information' on its diverse areas of work (Guttal, 2004: 5) not only lends legitimacy to its narratives but also gives it an enormous advantage over alternative discourses. Diagnostic economic and sector work (ESW) instruments work in powerful ways to contain the aforementioned dynamic of difference by establishing the threshold of the 'norm' and by reviewing the extent of countries' departure from such 'norms' in order that such 'aberrations' may be confronted and redressed. These analytical tools, constituting wide-ranging assessments and reviews of a country's economic, financial and governance systems,[36] not only generate an enormous amount of data on the Bank's borrowing members, but also evaluate countries' social, political and economic systems in accordance with the criteria established by the Bank and the geo-strategic and economic interests which underpin these criteria.

This process of reproducing the discursive dichotomies of difference is reinforced by the Bank's technical assistance and capacity building work to promote the internalisation of the aforementioned norms of social and economic organisation. As Stone and Wright note:

> Part of the mission of the World Bank is to conduct research and produce new ideas to inform policy, as well as to spread knowledge about best practices and persuade client countries and other stakeholders of the validity of such knowledge.
>
> (Stone and Wright, 2007: 9)

c) Policing the financial system

Although the IMF's role in such knowledge production is much less extensive than the Bank's, the information generated by the Fund is much more influential. However limited in comparison, there remains significant competition for the ideas generated by the Bank's vast knowledge machinery from other multilateral development organisations, such as regional development banks and the UN development agencies, and from bilateral development agencies, think tanks and research institutions. There remains little counterweight to the specialised information collated and generated by the IMF, particularly in its capacity as supervisor of the international financial architecture. Furthermore, like the World Bank, the Fund is privy to highly sensitive and confidential financial information of its member states, particularly the developing country members which draw on its resources, and its analysis of the domestic policies of these members is often a key determinant in these countries' access to official and private financing.[37]

Central to the discursive power of the IMF is its surveillance work under Article IV of its Articles of Agreement,[38] which gains the institution entry to key financial and policy records of member states and accords it the power to translate the harvested data into the 'technical' knowledge by which these countries are represented in the world economy. Consequently, like the Bank, the Fund uses its privileged access to information about its members to construct representations about these countries and reproduce entrenched meanings about the structure of the world economy and the role of these countries within it.

The organisation of such information by the Fund rearticulates the dichotomies of 'civilisation' and 'primordialism' by classifying countries in accordance with their adherence to the strictures of the neoliberal postcolonial economy. The Fund's oversight responsibilities, and consequently the amount of data it generates and the meanings it reproduces, have expanded greatly in the last decade, encompassing not only issues under its original mandate of surveillance but also assessments of countries' compliance with other international regulatory norms. The institution's work on standards and codes, evaluating countries' compliance with international regulatory standards,[39] is particularly illustrative of the contribution of the IMF's discursive role in maintaining the 'myth of normalcy' – premised on adherence to fundamental principles of capitalist regulation – in the international financial system.

The Bank and Fund's near-monopoly on information on critical aspects of social and economic development and financial issues has led to a crowding out of alternative voices on many issues of critical import to its developing country members, particularly those from low-income countries for whom other sources of information remain either prohibitively expensive or linguistically inaccessible. As Guttal observes, these institutions, backed up by 'immense financial resources', create a 'giant "knowledge monopoly", edging out competition from alternative perspectives, analyses and ideas' (Guttal, 2004: 12). The 'epistemic' role of the Bretton Woods institutions is reinforced by their leverage as 'lenders of last resort', providing financing and technical advice in times of crisis (Woods, 2006: 68).

This institutional foray into new areas of work has been driven by a combination of deference to the politically motivated demands of their major shareholders (see section 2.2.1) and the BWIs' own bureaucratic imperative to maintain institutional relevance and legitimacy in the world economy. Therefore, while the impetus to reproduce the dichotomous images of modernity and primordialism may be largely driven by the geo-strategic and economic interests of their industrialised country members, a significant part of this effort may be attributed to the Bank and the Fund's organisational instinct for survival (see Woods, 2006: 4–5; also Tan, 2006a).

The maintenance of the aforementioned embedded distinctions between states thus provides political and institutional justification for the continued interventions of both institutions in developing countries. Accordingly, while the technical work undertaken by the Bank and the Fund is used extensively in support of their policy interventions, these financial data sets and 'academic' prescriptions of social and economic development have often been found to be 'based neither on clear evidence nor on pure expert analysis or predictions' but instead to reflect bureaucrats trying to square political pressures and institutional constraints (Woods, 2006: 4).

Additionally, due to their conflicting interests as financiers and technical advisors to member states, much of the 'knowledge' generated by these two institutions has been produced to justify lending practices and changes in operational policies due to shifting political interests (see Guttal, 2004: 5; Woods, 2006: 4). In an external evaluation of the Bank's research from 1998 to 2005, for example, auditors criticised the Bank's use of its internally generated research 'to proselytize on behalf of Bank policy, often without taking a balanced view of the evidence, and without expressing appropriate skepticism', adding that 'research that was favorable to Bank positions was given great prominence, and unfavorable research ignored' (Banerjee *et al.*, 2006: 6).

2.3.2 Managing the terms of engagement

Having constructed the discursive regime within which postcolonial states need to operate, the BWIs have proceeded to act as interlocutors between these countries and the international community, particularly with respect to their insertion into the global economy and the public and private international law which sustains it. The management of postcolonial states' entry into and engagement in the international economic and financial system is a critical aspect of the work of the World Bank and the IMF, providing the institutional framework through which the disciplinary technologies sustaining the postcolonial international economy may be applied to states subject to their jurisdiction. As discussed previously, the legitimacy of these interventions stems from the regimes of representation which naturalise certain ideas of progress, the lack of which in third world states requires the intercession of the 'international' community as embodied by these two multilateral organisations.

Given the institutions' juxtaposed mandates as financiers in and regulators of the global economy, these institutions have provided the ideal institutional framework for the management of such postcolonial economic structures and relationships. First, the Bank and the Fund have supplied or facilitated access to the necessary financial resources – both catalytic and compensatory – for the internal reorganisation or rehabilitation of third world states to accommodate the project of development and, consequently, the exigencies of neoliberal globalisation. Second, the institutions have served to manage the conditions of entry and participation of these states in the international economy, not only rationing their access to external economic resources but also organising the terms of such transfers to and from these economies.

a) Financing the postcolonial economy

Implicit in the constitutional mandates of the World Bank and the IMF is acknowledgement of the inherent instability of the international economy and system of social, economic and political organisation into which the institutions were born. The failure of capital markets and the private sector to finance the provision of global public goods and to stimulate developing economies as well as the intrinsic fragility of financial markets prone to cycles of expansion and depression have long served as rationales of official multilateral lending (see Akyüz, 2006), and the imperative to mitigate the effects of unfettered private capital markets was fundamental to the decision to establish the BWIs in 1947.

While originally aimed at regulating postwar economic relations between industrialised countries to prevent a recurrence of the economic depression and destructive adjustment policies during the interwar period,[40] the World Bank and the IMF quickly evolved into institutions aimed at managing the insertion of the former colonies of these industrialised countries into the international economy. The inability of the newly independent states to raise sufficient capital for the process of modernisation and incorporation into the international economy necessitated the facilitation of financing for these countries, but on terms that would subject them to the discipline of international capital markets and within the carefully controlled parameters of BWI supervision. At the same time, the fragile dependence of these newly integrated economies into the international financial architecture also required the existence of some form of safety net to cushion the effects of market volatility in these states and on private capital.

CATALYSING GROWTH

The catalytic role of BWI financing has been realised through the provision of loans (and later grants) by the IBRD, and subsequently the IDA and, to a limited extent, the IMF through its concessional facilities, for capital investment in social and economic sectors, as well as through the facilitation of private capital flows. World Bank financing therefore plays a dual role in catalysing market-led growth in postcolonial states – first, by directly financing development and economic restructuring projects in developing countries and, second, by creating a conducive environment for private investment through the conditions of its loans and grants. World Bank financing is also aimed at catalysing private capital flows by promoting market discipline among its borrowing members.

The financing of specific projects for 'reconstruction and development' enables the Bank, on behalf of the US and other major shareholders, to channel financial resources into sectors of the economy which are conducive to the maintenance of the aforementioned demarcated world economy and to control the conditions under which third world states can organise their economies. Financing large-scale infrastructure and agricultural development projects, including extractive industries and cash crop production, alongside investment in transport and financial service sectors, has enabled the World Bank to assist countries in reorienting their economies towards export-oriented commodity production aimed at servicing northern-based transnational commodity chains at the expense of domestic industrialisation and food security.[41] Meanwhile, the shift from project lending to policy-based lending in the late 1970s and early 1980s enabled the Bank to finance extensive restructuring of third world economies to better facilitate their insertion and integration into the globalised world economy (see Chapter 3; also section 2.3.2(b)).

The regulation of borrowing country economies by Bank financing is further reinforced through the terms of such financing. For example, the prohibition against financing local expenditures[42] has, for many years, meant that borrowers can only use Bank resources for *purchasing goods and services from abroad* if circumstances warrant such financing, preventing the endogenous development of local industries and maximising the utility of local capacity (see Hudson, 2003: 190–191; World Bank, 2004a: paras 18–22).[43]

Although this policy has now been relaxed – in terms of allowing greater latitude for financing local expenditures – the Bank remains prudent in authorising such financing, citing macroeconomic considerations, such as inflationary pressures (see ibid.: paras 18–22). Additionally, loan or grant resources from the Bank are not directly transferred to the borrower but only disbursed against authorised expenditures from a central disbursement account 'following a very rigid procedure under the strict supervision and control of the World Bank' (Agarwal, 2000: 7; Article II, IBRD General Conditions for Loans; Article II, IDA General Conditions for Credits and Grants).

Additionally, World Bank financing is viewed as a stimulus for private capital flows through the fostering of financial discipline in respective borrowing countries and the accrual of investment ratings for individual countries through their continued debt servicing to the Bank. Hence, although the IBRD extends financing to countries which do not have the requisite financial standing to borrow from international capital markets,[44] these loans are provided under market or near-market conditions.

While the IBRD Articles of Agreement state that loans should be provided to members on 'reasonable' terms (Article III, Section 4(ii)), with such terms remaining unspecified,[45] the Bank has consistently applied market-based interest rates to its loans[46] (World Bank, 2003b: paras 1, 4). Furthermore, as IBRD loans are to facilitate the 'investment of capital for productive purposes' only (Article I (i), IBRD Articles of Agreement), such loans must be 'capable of generating a financial surplus to amortize the loan and pay interest upon it in a definable time span' (Hudson, 2003: 191).

Meanwhile, although the IDA was established to provide similar financing on concessional terms to developing countries ineligible for IBRD lending, the IDA Articles of Agreement stipulate that such financing should not be extended if members can obtain similar resources either from the IBRD or 'from private sources on terms which are reasonable for the recipient' (Article V, Section 1(c)). Both the IBRD and IDA constitutions also stress the supplementary function of World Bank financing, that is, Bank financing should only be ancillary to or supportive of private capital flows and such financing should be aimed ultimately at facilitating country access to private sources of financing (see Article I (ii), IBRD Articles of Agreement; Article V, Section 1(c), IDA Articles of Agreement; Shihata, 2000b: 75–76).

The creation of the International Finance Corporation (IFC) in 1957 and the Multilateral Investment Guarantee Agency (MIGA) in 1988 to stimulate the private sector in developing countries further cements this mandate of the World Bank Group. The IFC provides loans and advisory services to private companies investing or operating in developing countries, while MIGA provides investment guarantees to commercial entities doing the same in developing countries.

COMPENSATING LOSSES

In addition to their catalytic financing function, the Bank and the Fund also play an important role in moderating the excesses of the global capitalist system, primarily in financing the fallout from financial crises, in terms of cushioning the effects of such crises on affected member states, but also, more importantly in recent years, in mitigating the effects of such crises on northern private capital and the credibility of the globalised financial architecture.

By providing counter-cyclical financing – that is, providing resources during periods when private capital is unwilling or unable to extend finance – the Bank and the Fund operate to shore up the existing financial system by underwriting the risks associated with reliance on private markets. Such financing, available through IMF drawings and the World Bank's policy-based lending, enables these institutions to compensate for financial difficulties faced by member states as a result of their integration into the global economy. However, while some proportion of the resources disbursed for such purposes may serve as social and economic safety nets in affected countries, the primary objective of such financing is to militate against any moves to radically change the fundamental premise of the postcolonial world economy or the international financial architecture.

Crisis financing by the IMF – through its Stand-By Arrangements (SBAs), Flexible Credit Line (FCL),[47] Extended Fund Facility (EFF) or through its concessional lending facilities (see Chapter 3) – enables members experiencing balance of payments difficulties, arising from what the Fund classifies either as short-term, temporary or cyclical causes or longer-term structural problems, respectively, to draw on the IMF's collective pool of resources to meet its external financial obligations. Originally aimed at providing financing to support domestic economic activity and stimulate local productive capacities in times of global capital market failures, even this mandate of the Fund has evolved over the years to a more retrogressive function of maintaining countries' currency on debt repayments.[48]

Accordingly, the IMF's interventions in financial crises now primarily involve 'ad hoc financial bailout operations designed to keep countries current on their debt repayments to private creditors, to maintain capital account convertibility and to prevent default' (Akyüz, 2005: 27). Often, this also involves governments assuming the financial liabilities of the local private sector to foreign investors, converting private debt into public debt and, ironically, undermining the true market discipline by encouraging imprudent lending by private investors and creating what economists term 'moral hazard' (ibid.: 30). In other words, the IMF's 'overdraft facility' – replenishing government reserves through its own resources and facilitating bilateral lines of credit – 'constitutes a convenient "social safety net" for the institutional speculator' (Chossudovsky, 1997b).

This pattern was once again repeated in the 'global' response to the international financial crisis of 2008–2009, which clearly illustrated the centrality of the BWIs to the postcolonial economic order. Prior to the advent of the financial crisis, the Bank and Fund were themselves institutions in crisis. Lacking in credibility and seeking to redefine their roles in the wake of declining revenue streams, waning global influence and perennial public critique, the institutions had become increasingly marginalised in the global economy.[49] The onset of the global economic recession, however, led to a resurgence of interest in the Bank and Fund, driven mainly by the politically motivated demands of their major shareholders (the G7), which sought to channel crisis financing through institutions that they controlled.

Due to renewed public and private funding of the institutions, the IMF regained its place as the lender of last resort for countries facing financial crises and the World Bank significantly expanded its financing portfolio and technical assistance toolkit to accommodate new imperatives in public financing in the wake of the crisis, such as the establishment of social safety nets and financing for climate change in developing countries.[50] The institutions have also positioned themselves as pivotal repositories of information and technical knowledge about the financial crisis and its resolution.

Nonetheless, aside from such financing, there was little discussion on reforming the international financial regulatory system to curb the financial excesses and combat the financial instability which had contributed to the crisis. The crisis was, once again, viewed as an aberration rather than a systemic condition of a globalised capitalist economy.

Mitigating financial crises and balance of payments difficulties associated with the volatile global economy through policy-based lending therefore enables the BWIs and their major shareholders to recast the negative consequences of iniquitous international economic law and financial rules as domestic problems caused by endemic internal institutional or policy failures which require 'structural adjustment' rather than as systemic failures requiring a radical revision of the rules of global finance and international trade. Consequently, the provision of much needed financing during periods of crisis by the Bank and the Fund obscures what Biel terms 'NIEO-style-demands to change the system itself', reducing policy solutions to a question of adaptation of domestic institutions to the global system, providing 'pre-emptive' financing to compensate local political elites for the economic fallout of the crises and mitigating 'the poverty which encouraged revolution' against the system (Biel, 2000: 233).

b) Managing participation in the postcolonial economy and international legal order

One of the most significant outcomes of the third world's reliance on financing from the Bretton Woods institutions and from BWI-linked resources, as will be alluded to throughout this book, has been the appropriation of domestic policy space by these two institutions, including the circumscription of state regulatory authority. A corollary of such a requisition has been the curtailment and/or containment of states' autonomy in managing their external relations with other members of the international community. As previously discussed, the discursive regime established by the World Bank and the IMF and the accompanying conditions of resource dependency create a powerful regulatory forum through which the major shareholders of the institutions – the northern, metropolitan states – can oversee the insertion of these economies into the international economy and hence supervise their relationships with northern capital.

These interventions have been facilitated by the consolidation of the use of 'conditionality' as a default regulatory instrument between the BWIs and their borrower, a development which has accorded the Bank and Fund, and, by extension, their most powerful shareholders, greater authority over borrowing countries and which has progressively entrenched the BWIs as regulatory domains as opposed to them functioning purely as financial institutions (see Chapter 4).

ADJUSTMENT CONDITIONALITIES

The terms of structural adjustment or policy-based lending – and to a large extent the conditions of crisis financing[51] – have enabled the World Bank and the IMF to facilitate the internal regulatory reforms necessary for states' integration with other international regulatory fora, notably in international trade and finance. The extensive restructuring of domestic institutions and regulatory policy through structural and sectoral adjustment conditionalities has resulted in the Bank and Fund's effective management of borrowing countries' external trade and financial policies. The impact of these reforms has been a collective undermining of developing countries' negotiating strength within the multilateral (and some bilateral) fora as a result of concessions undertaken unilaterally by these countries under the auspices of Bank and Fund adjustment programmes.

Two important reforms wrought by structural/sectoral adjustment and/or economic stabilisation programmes by the Bank and the Fund on developing countries in the past three decades have been the progressive liberalisation of the domestic trade and financial regimes to facilitate greater integration of countries into the global economy. In particular, the drastic reduction and elimination of trade barriers and the removal of controls on capital flows in countries subject to economic reform programmes of the Bank and the Fund have meant that the pace and sequencing of these countries' entry into the international trading and financial system has been determined less by national economic geo-strategic needs than by the dictates of financing conditionalities and the imperatives of global capital. The BWIs thus mediate the engagement of their borrowing members in the world economy by determining the conditions under which these countries can and should engage in cross-border movement of trade and financial capital.

This development has had two major impacts on affected countries. First, the rationalisation of trade and finance regimes under structural adjustment has created what Chimni has referred to as 'a *functional unified global economic space* for the operation of transnational capital' through the 'prescription of uniform global standards' (Chimni, 2004: 6–7, 9). In presiding over the economic restructuring of countries undergoing structural or sectoral adjustment programmes, the Bank and the Fund have been able to harmonise trade and financial rules across a large cross-section of the third world. For example, Stewart points out that the BWIs, notably the IMF through its lending conditionalities and technical assistance work, have been at the forefront of what she terms the 'mass production of tax reform' in developing countries, modelling fiscal policies after tax regimes in industrialised countries which favour private investors and the home countries of foreign capital (Stewart, 2003).

Often, these reforms have paved the way for formalised entry into binding bilateral agreements, such as bilateral tax or investment treaties, international or regional regulatory regimes, such as the WTO or the North American Free Trade Agreement (NAFTA), or accession of 'soft' regulatory norms, such as the Basel Committee's standards of banking supervision. This has included, in some cases, specific conditionalities requiring countries to bring domestic legislation into conformity with international regulatory norms, such as establishing intellectual property rights, and implement financial codes and standards, such as central bank accounting procedures, without the countries involved necessarily having negotiated for themselves within the said regulatory forum.

Second, by obliging countries to undertake unilateral liberalisation measures or, in some cases, privatisation reforms, Bank and Fund conditionalities have undermined these countries' negotiating positions in other regulatory fora and enabled, in many cases, unilateral concessions made under structural adjustment to be 'locked in' by binding legal obligations in other forums[52] (Rowden, 2001; Tan, 2001). Developing countries which enter into talks with low applied tariffs or with many more sectors of their economies liberalised under structural adjustment lose their bargaining position as a result of such unilateral liberalisation.

Conditionalities requiring countries to reduce or eliminate applied tariff rates, for example, impact on these countries' ability to negotiate for higher bound tariff rates during bilateral or multilateral trade talks, such as at the WTO, as these countries would be hard pressed by trading partners, usually the powerful industrialised countries which also represent the BWIs' major shareholders, to justify a higher bound tariff rate in view of existing tariff structures[53] (see Khor, 2005). Additionally, countries which have unilaterally liberalised their financial services sectors or privatised public service sectors under structural adjustment may be pressured by the same trading partners in the WTO to bind such commitments under the General Agreement on Trade in Services (GATS).

The problematic application of conditionalities in the context of developing countries' engagement with the international economy is further compounded by the significant influence of private commercial interests in the design and terms of Bank and Fund financial arrangements. As discussed in previous sections, the advent of concessional windows at the BWIs has rendered the institutions susceptible to the bilateral influence of individual official creditors and donors. The proliferation of the Bank's trust fund portfolio has also enabled private donors, such as charitable foundations, to influence the direction and content of development financing emanating from the World Bank Group. At the same time, the IMF's crisis financing has become increasingly porous to the influence of private financial institutions which serve as 'supplementary financiers' to IMF lending (Gould, 2003: 552) These financiers, who have been playing a larger role over the years in supplementing IMF financing to countries facing balance of payments problems, have been able to 'alter the terms of Fund conditionality arrangements systematically' due to their considerable financial leverage over the Fund in providing additional financing to Fund borrowers (ibid.: 555, 581). Favourable conditions include prioritising payments to private financiers under the IMF arrangement and the implementation of bank-friendly regulatory reforms in countries subject to the IMF arrangement outside conventional channels of law and policymaking.

COERCION OF INDEBTEDNESS

The undermining of third world capacity to negotiate in the international arena is compounded by the roles that the World Bank and the IMF play in gate-keeping financial resource flows to these countries, including the management of sovereign debt. While not the largest providers of global development financing, the Bank and Fund exercise enormous influence over borrowing countries because of the sequencing and significance of such financing. Aside from the fact that 'the timing of their loans gives them considerable leverage because they lend at times when governments have few alternative sources of finance' (Woods, 2006: 71), the *signalling* function of these loans to other official donors and private creditors reinforces countries' dependency on the Bretton Woods institutions, particularly in times of financial crisis and prolonged sovereign indebtedness.

Over the years, and especially since the onset of the debt crises in Latin America and Africa in the 1980s, the Bank and Fund have emerged as important interlocutors between indebted third world states and their creditors/donors, defining the means and methods by which these countries engage with the international financial community. This function both contributes to and is a result of the 'preferred creditor' status of the World Bank and the IMF, which situates the two institutions at the top of the pecking order when it comes to debt repayment from debtor countries (Woods, 2006: 164). Furthermore, the vast technical arsenal of the two institutions and their privileged access to country data also places them, especially the IMF, at the helm of any coordinated financing effort, rendering financial flows contingent upon Bank and Fund accreditation, such as the commonly utilised IMF macroeconomic 'stamp of approval'.[54]

The IMF, in particular, is at the heart of managing third world debt, both in terms of facilitating financial 'rescue packages' for middle-income countries in crisis – mobilising resources from bilateral creditors and donors in addition to its own financing (see Akyüz, 2005: 27) – as well as administrating debt relief and debt rescheduling negotiations for low-income countries. Not only does the Fund coordinate countries' relations with their creditors, it also establishes conditions for debt relief or terms for debt rescheduling.

Most notable is the prominent role it plays at the Paris Club[55] negotiations, the first port of call for countries seeking to reschedule sovereign debt or seek debt relief. Not only are countries required to prepare a PRSP – coordinated and evaluated by the Bank and Fund – as well as implement an IMF-supported programme as prerequisites for Paris Club negotiations (Vilanova and Martin, 2001: 2), but assessments of a country's 'debt sustainability' and hence its eligibility under various debt rescheduling and debt relief schemes are also determined by the IMF. Callaghy contends that 'debt sustainability' is often 'a highly ambiguous and manipulatable [sic] [and] political, notion', determined in many cases through consideration of political rather than economic or technical factors (Callaghy, 2003: 212–213).

Additionally, the IMF also sits on, and often chairs, alongside the World Bank, the various country or regional Consultative Groups of donors and creditors which negotiate at the national level with country authorities on issues of debt and official development financing. This cooperative of donors and creditors forms an intimidating pre-emptive bloc to indebted countries, often undermining their capacity to negotiate bilaterally with creditors on more favourable terms or seek to bargain collectively as a group or on multilateral terms. Paris Club negotiations are conducted on a country-by-country basis between the organisation of creditor country representatives and a delegation from the country seeking debt rescheduling, resulting in bilateral agreements between the creditor and debtor countries giving weight to the multilaterally agreed minutes of the negotiations (Callaghy, 2003: 202).

The cartelisation of debt management ensures that countries' debt strategies are managed in accordance with the interests of the OECD countries and private capital rather than on the basis of the country's national interests. The individualisation of debt negotiations precludes collective bargaining by debtor states, even though these states often accumulate debts to the same creditors and are subject to the same debt regime,[56] and the effect of such 'case-by-case' negotiations has been 'to institutionalize huge asymmetries in bargaining power in debt negotiations' (Fogarty, 2003: 237). This enables creditor countries to extract the greatest concessions from debtors to maximise their share under the association's burden-sharing framework.

Like the lead role of the BWIs in consultative donor/creditor groups for development financing – which have become increasingly widespread under the new architecture of aid with the shift from project to programme aid and budget support systems (see Chapter 3) – the linking of debt negotiations with BWI assessments and implementation of Bank and Fund programmes severely circumscribes indebted countries' ability to obtain alternative sources of financing and has contributed to the unpredictability of resource flows to these countries. As Biel contends, the absence of competition among sources of development finance makes it difficult 'for the South to bargain for better terms in funding' and debt relief and enables creditor countries to 'present a united front to developing countries' with demands that approval by the BWIs 'is a necessary condition for investment' (Biel, 2000: 241).

2.4 Continuities and consolidation of postcolonial law

The insertion of postcolonial states into the international legal order was premised on the sustenance of colonial economic relationships and the national geo-strategic interests of the postwar planners of the international governance architecture. This chapter has demonstrated that, despite formal bequests of sovereignty and constructions of state autonomy in the postcolonial era, third world states remain conscripted into a straitjacket of interlocking economic and political strictures as a result of the asymmetrical international order and system of global governance they were initially inserted into. These iniquitous relationships are continually validated by the evolving discursive regimes of representation deployed to legitimise the interventions of the former and new (read: United States) imperial powers in the ostensibly sovereign states of the postcolonial international order.

The symbols of the new 'international community' have since been harnessed to recast the colonial 'civilising mission' as the logic of 'reconstruction', 'development' and 'cooperation', the acquiescence of postcolonial states to the intercessions of this new 'community of nations' acquired through the perceived need of recently sovereign states to constitutionally mimic the socio-economic, political and juridical structures of the metropolitan states to maintain access to the economic resources and geo-strategic alliances resulting from their continued relationships of dependency. Consequently, as Badie observes:

> Western international law had become universalized, accepted and recognized by non-Western partners as the procedure for regulating international relations', with 'the conditions of inequality and dependence [having been] softened symbolically by the fact that they appeared to result from the voluntary consent of the contracting parties, hence from their sovereignty.
>
> (Badie, 2000: 77)

Conceptualising the new north–south relations in terms of representational practice enables us to situate current interventions of the international juridical and economic order within this series of historical encounters, which Doty terms 'imperial encounters' – 'the idea of asymmetrical encounters in which one entity [the west/north/Anglo-European world] has been able to construct "realities" that were taken seriously and acted upon and the other entity [the non-west/south/non-European world] has been denied equal degrees or kinds of agency' (Doty, 1996: 3). The continued constructions of identities of peoples, societies, states and regions in binary terms – the abstract oppositions between 'developed' and 'underdeveloped', 'modern' and 'traditional', 'rich' and 'poor' – creates the 'dynamic of difference' that justifies the reconstructions of postcolonial societies and economies by institutions of the new international legal order.

The creation of the Bretton Woods institutions and the progressive enlargement of their mandate in the years following their inception was premised upon this fundamental demarcation between the north and the south, and the need to efface the difference between the west and non-western world to better facilitate the project of the new international economy based on what Badie calls 'the logic of universalization' (Badie, 2000: 77). These institutions have been cast as the face of the 'international community', the source of multilateral economic engagement, serving to create 'the international system [that] was unified around a center that the West intended to occupy' (ibid.), thereby universalising the laws and principles of social and economic organisation which the west pioneered and which serves the geo-strategic interests of the northern states and the economic imperatives of transnational capital.

This is validated by the regimes of representations which continue to characterise and regulate international relationships. The birth of international financial institutions has been pivotal to sustaining this postcolonial order and based on the need to mediate the engagements of these countries in the governance of the global economy. At the same time, this mandate, corresponding with the design of the postcolonial system of aid, was suffused with the very real objective of rationing capital transfers to the south, effectively preventing the endogenous development of southern countries, which may threaten the relationship of dependence upon which the postcolonial world order was premised (see Biel, 2000: 87). This necessitated the development of disciplinary instruments – the 'science' of developmentalism and aid management – to mediate the engagements between the south and the north and between the south and northern private capital.

The existence of a regime of knowledge production and dissemination, embedded within particular 'myths' of social, economic and political organisation, therefore sustains, as much as it is sustained by, a corresponding regulatory regime disciplining the detractors of such conventional wisdom. In other words, unless there are punitive repercussions, real or perceived, resulting from normative departures or disengagement from the established order, the efficacy of this discursive framework in containing the cultural difference so feared by the former colonial states of their newly sovereign colleagues (or, in the case of the most recent postcolonial period, the endogenous economic strength of the newly industrialising countries) is circumscribed. The process of subordinating peripheral economies to the dictates of imperial capital through certain social transformations – including the restructuring of indigenous patterns of socio-economic organisation – not by direct coercion or military force but by new means of indirect control (through development financing modalities, for example) has, according to Wood, 'been a major function of capitalist imperialism since its inception' (E.M. Wood, 2005: 21).

The asymmetrical governance structure of the BWIs and their tentacular reach into the interior of third world member states over the years have furnished powerful imperial states with the ideal institutional framework through which such disciplinary power may be exercised. The PRSP framework, located within this imperial legacy of international law and international institutions, may therefore be viewed as part of the evolution of disciplinary instruments – regulatory norms and discourse – central to the governance of the postcolonial world order, characterised today by patterns of neoliberal globalisation. Understanding the way in which third world states were originally incorporated into the international legal order will go far in explaining how these and other interventions of the postcolonial period can and have been effected and legitimised in spite of their apparent incongruence with fundamental principles of international law.

At the same time, the changes in the world economy and the shifting geo-politics of the international order over the period of decolonisation have necessitated corresponding changes in the means by which these structures, ideologies and disciplinary techniques are deployed to further the aforementioned entrenched economic and geo-strategic interests. The shifting locus of global power – and, correspondingly, global authority – has shifted the foundations of the immediate postcolonial order premised on the Westphalian model of postcolonial international law and governance. In particular, the emergence of a transnational capitalist class as well as what Cutler terms as the new 'mercatocracy' – 'an elite association of public and private organizations engaged in the unification and globalization of transnational merchant law' (Cutler, 2003: 180–181) – has challenged not only the traditional instrumentalities of regulatory discipline on a global level, but also the ontology of global governance in the postcolonial period.

These new developments, along with exhortations about the demise of the state, necessitate an examination of the new modalities of control and configurations of power, including those which the PRSP framework and its attendant forces represent. Therefore, where the instruments of postcolonial governance resonate with the technologies of imperialism, the reconfigurations of global power, particularly in the past three decades, and the new patterns (and sophistication) of resource transfers require a more nuanced analysis of how postcolonial international law and the institutions of postcolonial economic governance – notably the Bretton Woods institutions – have evolved to reinforce the patterns of influence in the postcolonial period. In this regard, the PRSP framework forms a pivotal part of this new disciplinary global constitution, and the following chapters will explore the framework's role in this wider shift in the regulatory framework of global governance.

Notes

1 Pahuja uses this term to refer to how international law 'both sustains and contains within it what we might call the condition of the postcolonial' (Pahuja, 2005: 460).

2 This analysis viewing the constitution of reality as a complex intersection between domains of recognition and relational experiences – the formation of self-identity residing in the modality of that identity's relation to others (or the 'modality of relation to the self' or 'technologies of self') bolstered by a series of discursive practices – was pioneered by Foucault (see, for example, 'Preface to the History of Sexuality, Volume II' in Foucault, 1991: 336–339; and Foucault, 1972) and applied to the construction of knowledge about non-European societies by Said in 1972 in his germinal work on *Orientalism* (see Said, 2003) and, later, to the practices and institutions of 'development' by Escobar (1995).

3 The bulk of such scholarship on postcolonial representational practices has drawn heavily upon Said's aforementioned work on the Orientalist discourse – the phenomenon of 'Orientalism' – in which the production of ideas about the non-west is bound up with the complex hegemonic relationships of power and domination between the Occident and the Orient (see Said, 2003).

4 An exception to this development has been the diverging economic trajectories of the countries of the Communist bloc during the Cold War, as well as Cuba and China prior to the liberalisation of the Chinese economy in the late twentieth and early twenty-first century. However, the economic reforms which then followed the Eastern European and ex-Soviet Union countries' and China's (and, to a lesser extent, India's) accession into the current global economy post-Cold War reiterate the application of this norm.

5 The Mandate System was an international regime created by the League of Nations in the aftermath of the First World War for the purpose of governing the territories annexed or colonized by Germany and the Ottoman empire, the two great powers defeated in the war, placing these territories 'under a system of international tutelage' rather than distributing them 'among the victorious powers as spoils of war' (Anghie, 2004: 116). The Mandate System marked a shift from an endorsement of conquest in international law to an attempt to include previously exploited and colonised peoples in the international system and 'promote self-government' in accordance with the norms of the 'international' community (ibid.).

6 Escobar views the process of 'development' as constituting a part of the 'anthropology of modernity', a historically contingent phenomenon premised upon the elevation of one system of knowledge – the 'modern', industrialised west – and the 'marginalization and disqualification of non-Western knowledge systems' (Escobar, 1995: 13). Escobar attributes the possibility of this epistemological approach to the development of tools of analysis in the 1960s and 1970s, notably those found in Foucault's work on discourse, which 'produces permissible modes of being and thinking while disqualifying and even making others impossible' (Escobar, 1995: 5; see Chapter 1, section 1.4, for a discussion on Foucault's theory of discursive power).

7 In this respect, Tarullo adopts the Escobarian definition of developmentalism – and its critique of the modernist categorisation of 'development' as a societal graduation from agrarian to industrial (ibid.) – less as a normative interpretation of international economic relations, such as Escobar *et al.* give, than as a heuristic device for understanding the logic of international economic law, which has at its core the 'myth of normalcy' as its organising principle (Tarullo, 1985). Oppositional interpretations are viewed not as generating alternative systems of knowledge or practice but as departures from the norm for which rehabilitation is necessary.

8 See also Pahuja's exploration of Tarullo's 'myth of normalcy' (Pahuja, 2000: 792–793).

9 As 'world-systems' theorists, Hopkins and Wallerstein's approach to understanding the postcolonial world economy and its impact on socio-political relations is premised

upon an analysis of the systemic changes in the forms and structures of the inter-state system and world production – 'evolving institutional domains' they term 'vectors' of the world system which have served to organise people's activities in the period following the end of the Second World War. According to Hopkins and Wallerstein, 'the modern world system' has developed six 'distinguishable but not separable vectors': 'the interstate system, the structure of world production, the structure of the world labour force, the patterns of human welfare, the social cohesion of states and the structures of knowledge' (Hopkins and Wallerstein, 1996: 2). Hopkins and Wallerstein, while acknowledging the role of hegemonic state power under the inter-state system, place greater emphasis on the dominating impact of the world production structure in organising social relations worldwide (ibid.: 2–5). Specifically, the process of capital accumulation on a world scale, which saw 'the establishment of commodity chains of production extending backwards from the organizing centres', continually maintains the 'core' countries in a position of privilege by virtue of their capture of the means of production and the countries in the 'periphery' in a position constantly subject to the exigencies of the centres of production (ibid.). Nonetheless, 'world-systems' theorists generally reject the theories of dependency or neo-imperialism as they argue that 'core-periphery zonal organization' could occur within third world states and that it is not confined to state accumulation on a global scale.

10 As Hudson argues, the narrow preoccupation of the northern architects of the postwar world economy was centred on the development of 'export enclaves' in the south 'to produce raw materials needed by North American and European industry, at prices satisfactory to the user countries' (Hudson, 2003: 186).

11 While not explicit at the outset, this role has expanded over time. Since the collapse of the Berlin Wall in 1989, the BWIs have also assumed the key responsibility for mediating the rehabilitation of ex-Communist bloc countries, notably in Eastern Europe, into the neoliberal economic order as well.

12 Article 57 of the UN Charter 1945 provides that inter-governmental organisations having responsibilities in 'economic, social, cultural, education, health and related areas' may be brought into a relationship with the UN under Article 63 of the Charter. Article 63 authorises the Economic and Social Council (ECOSOC) to enter into agreements with these agencies and coordinate the activities of these agencies in consultation with the General Assembly and UN members (Agreement between the UN and the IMF and the Agreement between the UN and the International Bank for Reconstruction and Development (IBRD) 1947, hereinafter known as the 'Relationship Agreements'). Agreements between the UN and other members of the World Bank Group, such as the International Finance Corporation (IFC) in 1956 and the IDA in 1961, are governed by similar provisions to that of the UN–IBRD agreement.

13 Articles 1(2) of the Agreement between the UN and the IBRD 1947 and the Agreement between the UN and the IMF 1947.

14 See Article V, Section 3(a), of the IBRD Articles of Agreement and Article XXII, Section 5 (a), of the IMF Articles of Agreement. The IDA has a slightly different voting structure, in which members are accorded 500 membership votes plus an additional vote for every US $5,000 of their initial subscription. Subscriptions other than initial subscriptions of original members have voting rights as determined by the Board of Governors (Article Vi, Section 3(a), IDA Articles of Agreement). The discretionary voting rights were reviewed during the Third Replenishment negotiations and voting rights now take into account the cumulative financial contributions of IDA creditor (known as Part 1) countries, although the basic votes of borrower (or Part II) countries are maintained through an increase in subscriptions at a nominal rate (IDA, 2001a: para. 11; Shihata, 2000a: 585–589).

15 In the IMF, each member receives, in addition to the fixed basic votes, one vote for every US$100,000 (or subsequently for every SDR 100,000) of quota, while in the

Bank, each member receives an additional vote for each share of stock (valued at US $120,635 per share) held by the country on top of its basic votes (Woods, 2006: 22–24; see also Buira, 2005: 9). In 2008, the IMF's Board of Governors proposed to amend the IMF's Articles of Agreement to triple the basic votes allocation of 250 votes (IMF, 2008a; see the discussion in section 2.2.2).

16 The US currently holds 16.77 per cent of the total voting power in the Fund and 16.36 per cent in the IBRD – followed by Japan (6.02/7.85 per cent), Germany (5.88/4.48 per cent), France (4.85/4.3 per cent) and the UK (4.85/4.3 per cent) (IMF, 2009a; IBRD, 2009). G7 countries collectively hold around 45 per cent of the total votes in both institutions and the combined share of the European Union countries stands as high as 32 per cent, while African countries as a whole only wield slightly less than 6 per cent of the overall total (ibid.). At the IDA, Part 1 countries (the majority of historical donors) hold 55.93 per cent of the votes, with the US holding the greatest share, at 11.72 per cent, followed by Japan at 9.18 per cent, Germany at 6.07 per cent, the UK at 5.18 per cent and France at 3.9 per cent (IDA, 2009).

17 Constitutionally, the highest decision-making bodies at the Bank and the Fund are the respective Boards of Governors, comprised of the finance ministers, central bank governors or other high-ranking government official of all member states. However, the governors may (and have) delegate the exercise of their powers to the respective Executive Boards, except those powers reserved exclusively for the Board of Governors (Article V, Section 2(b), IBRD Articles of Agreement; Article VI, Section 2(b), IDA Articles of Agreement; Article XII, Section 2(b), IMF Articles of Agreement). Two committees of governors have also been created in each institution, the Development Committee for the Bank and the International Monetary and Financial Committee (IMFC) (previously the Interim Committee) for the Fund, with a similar composition to that of the respective Executive Boards, to provide greater political oversight of the institutions.

18 According to Brown, the Bank's (and, by extension, the Fund's) Articles of Agreement can be interpreted as providing that 'it is the members who have the voting power but it is the Governors and/or the EDs [executive directors] who are actually entitled to cast the votes of those members' (Brown, 1992: 107).

19 The United States ED's office in particular acts almost like an arm of the US government, with US federal law entitling such executive directors to all benefits accruing to US civil servants (ibid.: 108), and the US Treasury oversees and vets all decisions taken by the US executive director. US executive directors at multilateral development banks (MDBs) are also bound by Congressional legislation to vote in accordance with the relevant legislative provisions in pursuit of US political and economic interests, for example opposing financing by the MDBs 'if it will establish or expand production for export of certain agricultural commodities … and thereby cause injury to US producers of the same or competing products' (ibid.: 204–205).

20 The PRSP initiative may also be viewed as part of a larger UK government-driven – or, more specifically, UK Treasury-driven – campaign on Africa, particularly in relation to debt relief and aid, operationalised at the Bank and the Fund largely as a result of then UK chancellor Gordon Brown's chairmanship of the IMFC, the political oversight committee of the Fund. Meanwhile, the Bush administration's policy stamp at the World Bank was clearly marked by former Bank president Paul Wolfowitz's push for governance and anti-corruption measures to be instituted as part of the operational policy of the World Bank Group.

21 As IBRD and IFC voting rights are also linked to IMF quota subscriptions, quota reviews also affect the voice and vote of countries at the World Bank Group.

22 Founded by the paid-in capital subscriptions of its members, the IBRD raises financial resources from investments on the international capital markets, drawing upon the

callable capital of its members (representing 90 per cent of capital subscriptions) as guarantees, as well as through retained earnings and loan repayments, while the IMF relies on the capital subscriptions of its members and the General Arrangements to Borrow (GAB) and the New Arrangements to Borrow (NAB), which enable the Fund to borrow from select members to finance drawings from other members (see Woods, 2006: 24, 31).

23 The extent to which the IDA Deputies now control policymaking at the Bank has been criticised by its former Bank general counsel, the late Ibrahim Shihata. He argued that attaching policy conditions to IDA replenishments circumvents official governance arrangements by allowing policy decisions to be 'practically predetermined by IDA Deputies' – who 'are not an organ of the IDA in any formal sense' – instead of being freely considered by executive directors who are duly appointed or elected by members (Shihata, 2000a: 567–568). The High-Level Commission on the Modernisation of the World Bank Group Governance chaired by Ernesto Zedillo also criticised the role of the IDA Deputies in IDA decision-making and leveraging IDA contributions to influence IBRD policies, calling the system 'opaque' and stating that it created 'an accountability gap' (World Bank, 2009b).

24 These co-financing arrangements and trust funds give donors 'much more direct control over the resources used' (Woods, 2006: 29) and undermine cohesive policy-making at the Bank.

25 For example, the locus of the HIPC initiative and the MDRI was at the G7 summits of 1999 and 2005 but the modalities for these instruments were developed at the Fund (see Chapter 3).

26 This includes the incorporation of environmental safeguards in IDA (and subsequently IBRD, IFC and the Multilateral Investment Guarantee Agency (MIGA)) operations (Ninth and Tenth Replenishments) as well as the inclusion of governance-related conditionalities (GRCs) which were pushed through by donors during the Twelfth IDA replenishment in 1998 (IDA, 2001a: paras 14–17; Kapur and Webb, 2000: 3).

27 The concept of 'mission creep' is often used to describe the progression of the World Bank and IMF activities over the years. Babb and Buira define 'mission creep' as 'the systematic shifting of organizational activities away from original mandates' (Babb and Buira, 2004: 2).

28 According to IDA, 'additional resources for financing the costs under the MDRI will be added to IDA's resources broadly following the established procedures for regular IDA replenishments. Donors will contribute the additional resources under Instruments of Commitments, which will be amended over time to reflect updated cost estimates as well as additional donor financing commitments as these become available' (IDA, 2006: para. 42). The crucial factor here is that the resources allocated for cancelling an eligible country's debt service for any given year will be deducted from the country's total allocated IDA allocation for the year and any additional donor resources will be allocated to countries according to their performance under the IDA performance-based allocation (PBA) system (ibid.: para. 31; see also Chapter 4 for further details on the PBA system), making future financing contingent upon the implementation of 'performance criteria' set by the IDA, primarily through the IDA replenishment negotiations.

29 And hence from the more rigorous scrutiny of the more representative UN General Assembly.

30 The South Centre is an inter-governmental organisation established by developing countries following on from the work of the South Commission, to mobilise expertise, policy support and collective action for southern states at the international level. See South Centre website at http://www.southcentre.org/ASouthIGO.htm.

31 The NIEO or 'New International Economic Order' represented a concerted effort by the newly independent states to assert their rights for a more equitable and redistributive global economy which dispenses with the pre-existing framework of colonial extraction and exploitation of the developing world. See discussion in Chapter 3, section 3.1.1.
32 See Chapter 1, section 1.4, for a description of 'forum shifting'.
33 According to Doty, the rhetorical strategies of 'naturalisation' and 'classification' are central to the disciplinary power of discursive practice – where 'naturalisation' serves to construct a presupposed reality, creating 'background knowledge that is taken to be true', the strategy of 'classification' establishes hierarchies of belonging in accordance with observance of such naturalised conduct, often serving 'to naturalize by placing human beings into the categories in which they "naturally" belong' (Doty, 1996: 10).
34 For more on the expansion of the Bank and Fund's original mandate, see Chapter 4 and detailed accounts in Akyüz (2004) and Tan (2006a).
35 A Bretton Woods Project report, for example, cites a World Bank 1999 report highlighting the widespread reach of the Bank's analytic work: 84 per cent of 271 high-level policymakers in 36 developing countries and transition economies surveyed said they used the Bank's analytical reports and rated the Bank as 'the most important information source of a list of domestic and international organisations' (Wilks, 2000: 1). According to the Bank itself, the institution delivered 437 economic and sector work and 545 technical assistance activities in 2009 (World Bank, 2009c: 61), and an external evaluation of the Bank's research noted that the institution's researchers and consultants produced over 4,000 reports and papers between 1998 and 2005 (Banerjee *et al.*, 2006: 3).
36 Such as poverty and social impact assessments (PSIAs), public expenditure reviews (PERs) and country financial accountability assessments (CFAAs). These instruments focus, respectively, on reviewing countries' poverty policies, evaluating public expenditure management and reviewing the regulatory framework of public and private sector financial management. See the World Bank website on ESW at http://go.worldbank.org/Q6PGVPEMV1.
37 As will be discussed in following chapters, this gatekeeping role extends even to World Bank financing, which is contingent upon a satisfactory macroeconomic assessment from the Fund.
38 Article IV provides that each member of the IMF 'undertakes to collaborate with the Fund and other members to assure orderly exchange arrangements and to promote a stable system of exchange rates', including, *inter alia,* directing its economic and financial policies towards securing orderly economic growth, international monetary stability avoiding manipulation of exchange rates (section 1). It also mandates the IMF to 'oversee the international monetary system in order to ensure its effective operation' and 'to oversee the compliance of each member with its obligations under Section 1', and places an obligation on each member to supply the requisite information as requested by the Fund to carry out these duties (section 3). The Fund's bilateral surveillance function includes assessments of countries' exchange rate, fiscal and monetary policies; financial sector issues, including reviews under the Financial Sector Assessment Programme (FSAP); risks and vulnerabilities arising from the countries' exposure to international capital flows; and domestic institutional and structural policies (IMF, 2007).
39 The Fund conducts regular assessments of countries' compliance with any one of 12 areas and associated standards which it considers useful for its and the Bank's operational work, including areas such as banking supervision, fiscal transparency, insolvency and creditor rights, insurance supervision and even anti-money laundering and countering the financing of terrorism (AML/CFT) (introduced in November 2002) (IMF, 2003a: 8, Box 1).

40 This included the prevention of what is commonly known as the 'beggar-thy-neighbour' policies, in which countries facing balance of payments problems unilaterally undertake deflationary adjustments in their fiscal policies and adopt trade and exchange rate restrictions which result in negative externalities affecting other countries (see Akyüz, 2006), raising the propensity for military conflict as happened in the period preceding the Second World War.

41 The political economy of these projects and the adverse social and economic impacts of such projects have been well documented (see, for example, Chossudovsky, 1997a, 1997b; George and Sabelli, 1994; Sender, 2002).

42 Unless justified under 'exceptional' (for IBRD lending) or 'special' (for IDA lending) circumstances, World Bank loans are denominated in *foreign currencies* to meet the *foreign costs* of the project financed (Article IV, Section 3, IBRD Articles of Agreement; Article V, Section 2, IDA Articles of Agreement).

43 Hudson, and others like him, have argued that while such currency restrictions have had the positive effect of maintaining financial prudence in borrowing countries – that is, making countries commit substantial amounts of their own resources towards financing domestic expenditure for development projects – they have precluded the development of local industries since capital has to be imported from abroad, such as financing only aspects of agricultural technology that could be imported from more advanced nations (Hudson, 2003: 191).

44 Article III, Section 4(ii), of the IBRD Articles of Agreement provides that IBRD loans or guarantees may be extended if '[t]he Bank is satisfied that in the *prevailing market conditions* the borrower would be unable otherwise to obtain the loan under conditions which in the opinion of the Bank are *reasonable* for the borrower' (emphasis added).

45 Except for the provision that the rates, charges and repayment schedule should be 'appropriate to the project' (Article III, Section 4(iv), IBRD Articles of Agreement).

46 Although repayment terms may vary with the per capita income of the borrower (World Bank, 2003b: paras 1, 30–33).

47 This facility was introduced in 2009 following the global financial crisis of 2008–2009 to provide more flexible financing to IMF members with 'very strong fundamentals, policies, and track records of policy implementation'. Unlike traditional SBAs (see Chapter 4), FCL arrangements are approved for countries meeting pre-set qualification criteria and disbursements are made upfront rather than phased (see IMF, 2009d).

48 As Shihata observed, in relation to the financial crises of the 1980s, '[t]he inability of many middle-income countries to service their commercial bank debt posed a systemic threat to the banking systems of the major developed countries' and necessitated 'a continuous flow of new money to debtor countries in order to ensure that they remained current on their interest payments' (Shihata, 2000b: 362).

49 In particular, the institutions were facing revenue shortfalls as developing country borrowers gained greater creditworthiness and sought financing from other sources. The IMF's conventional revenue streams, for example, dried up following the prepayment of loans by its major clients, including Argentina, Brazil, Indonesia, Philippines and Uruguay in the two years preceding the crisis. Repaying the institution ahead of schedule meant that these countries not only avoided further interest payments but also exited from the Fund's economic control. At the same time, the Bank was facing significant competition from private and larger developing countries emerging as new official creditors, such as China and Brazil, to whom many of their traditional concessional and non-concessional clients were turning for alternative sources of credit (Tan, 2007a, 2007b).

50 In 2009, the World Bank Group committed over US$60 billion in loans and grants (mainly loans) to developing countries, a 54 per cent increase on the previous year and a record high for the institution (World Bank, 2009d).

51 See Chapter 4 for a detailed discussion on the difference between Bank and Fund financing in this regard.

52 And, as shall be discussed in following chapters, despite some rhetoric to the contrary, these economic reforms have not changed with the advent of the PRSPs.

53 Bound tariff rates are maximum rates which countries have contracted to be bound by under the WTO – countries may, however, choose not to apply tariffs up to the bound tariff rate and frequently do so, so that applied tariffs are usually lower than bound tariffs. However, many developing countries choose to bind their tariffs at a higher rate in order to provide for exigencies, such as responding with the imposition of higher import duties to instances of import surges whereby the local market is flooded by imported products as a result of low or non-existent barriers. Unilateral liberalisation makes it difficult for such countries to justify imposition of higher bound tariffs when their applied tariffs are significantly lower.

54 Due to the absence of any other agency with comparable capacity, IMF accreditation is used as the default assessment of a country's macroeconomic framework for almost all bilateral and multilateral donors and a number of private investors.

55 The Paris Club was founded in 1956 as 'an informal group of creditor countries with no permanent members', established originally 'to provide debt relief to debtor countries with temporary liquidity problems, with the aim of preventing imminent defaults' (Vilanova and Martin, 2001: 1). Since the 1980s, the organisation (which derives its name from its permanent secretariat based in Paris) has primarily functioned as a debt rescheduling institution not only aimed at preventing further liquidity problems but also at alleviating debt burdens of heavily indebted countries. The Club functions to ensure 'unanimity' of rescheduling terms to debtor countries and 'equal burden sharing' among its creditor members (ibid.). In other words, the Paris Club acts as a cartel for creditor countries to ensure that none loses out in rescheduling debtor country debt.

56 A reform of this format of debt negotiations was sought by third world states as a key demand in their calls for an NIEO but this faltered alongside the other demands of the NIEO lobby (Callaghy, 2001, cited in Fogarty, 2003: 237).

Chapter 3

PRSPs and the crisis of legitimacy in the international order

> The way poverty is framed clearly has an important influence on the ways in which poverty reduction policies come to be shaped ... these narratives establish the frames of reference that define and bound what forms of knowledge count, and whose versions, claims and interests are legitimate.
>
> (Brock *et al.*, 2001: 8)

The Poverty Reduction Strategy Paper framework departs conceptually and operationally from previous modalities for development financing, forming a central pillar in the 'new architecture of aid', the collective term ascribed to the constellation of new financing initiatives and regulatory instruments that have emerged in the 'post-structural adjustment'[1] era. However, far from being just a policy instrument, the PRSP framework represents a larger ambitious attempt to harmonise aid regulation, hitherto a fragmented web of overlapping yet dispersed network of policy and practice.

Chapter 2's situation of the PRSP approach outside the immediacy of its operational function as an instrument for delivering development finance and within the larger framework of international relations and global governance enabled us to conceive of the role of PRSPs in advancing wider objectives in the international legal and political order. In this manner, the PRSP framework seeks not only to consolidate the diffused network of actors in these processes but also to shape the normative content of these actors' engagements in the aforementioned regulatory and quasi-regulatory webs.

Consequently, an examination of the historical context that gave birth to the PRSPs is necessary in order to locate the sites of dominance and influence in which the conceptual and operational underpinnings of the framework emerged. This is an important exercise as conventional narratives of the PRSP framework often fail to locate the birth of the PRSP project within a specific temporal and geo-political space. This has limited the analysis of how the framework sits within the shifting constitution of postcolonial power relations, particularly within the dynamics of inter-state and *inter*-national engagement in the era of globalisation.

This chapter argues that while aspects of the PRSP approach reflect the evolving agendas of and changing dynamics between institutional actors in the international development community[2] in the period preceding its inception, the framework itself and its relationship to the wider new architecture of aid can be specifically foregrounded in the aftermath of *a crisis of legitimacy* in the international economic order in the late 1990s and the failure of conventional disciplinary mechanisms – notably structural adjustment programmes (SAPs) – to contain this crisis.

The operationalising of a framework, such as the PRSP, linking a political and social governance agenda to disbursement of financial resources was primarily catalysed by an imperative to restore relevance to existing structures of multilateral trade and finance, notably to third world states, and to mitigate the groundswell of public dissent to the free-wheeling policies of the globalised Washington Consensus bankrolled by the international financial institutions.[3]

Accordingly, this chapter will demonstrate that the principles which subsequently formed the conceptual and operational basis of the PRSP framework had been framed amidst a contested terrain of policy narratives and regulatory objectives, the outcome of which was the result of privileging certain voices and excluding others, notably the very constituency – the third world – upon whom the framework impacts. At the same time, the paradox of the PRSP process is illustrated by its implementation within a disciplinary framework established through the precedents of SAPs and the opportunities afforded by the attendant regulatory vacuum left by their economic reorganisation.

3.1 PRSPs as a response to the limitations of structural adjustment

The reorientation of international development policy vis-à-vis low-income countries in the decade preceding the inception of the PRSP framework was clearly a response to a carefully couched problematic: the economic reforms of neoliberal globalisation were leading to a deterioration in the social and economic condition of communities in countries undergoing such change, and development financing, delivered through conventional mechanisms, notably SAPs, has failed to contain the dislocations and mitigate the pressures associated with these reforms.

As in Higgott's (2000) analysis of the political impact of the correlation between globalisation and inequality,[4] it is argued here that for the purposes of understanding the context in which the PRSP approach was developed, the causal relationship between these economic reforms (pursued through SAPs or other mechanisms) and impoverishment need not necessarily be verified for it to form what Higgott terms 'a political issue of [the] utmost importance' (Higgott, 2000: 136) for the actors involved.

The mere correlation between structural adjustment and poverty necessitated the corresponding revision of institutional policy and regulatory practice in response, the distinction residing in the differing desired outcomes of the actors involved. Accordingly, the interaction of the various actors engaged in the formulation of the PRSP process with this problematic has been, as we will see in section 3.3, dependent on their political, institutional and geo-strategic objectives. The PRSP framework may be viewed as a reflection of the contested heritage of the principles fought for at this level. For the hegemonic state actors involved, this impetus was driven largely by the aforementioned failure of SAPs to contain the disruptive potential of the fallout from neoliberal globalisation.

3.1.1 The disciplinary rationale of adjustment lending

Locating the PRSP framework within the wider political economy of neoliberal globalisation, we may therefore trace the genesis of the project to the failure of SAPs to respond to the challenges in the world economy preceding the inception of PRSPs. As discussed in Chapter 2, adjustment financing enabled hegemonic states, operating through the aegis of the Bretton Woods institutions, to manage third world participation in the postcolonial international economic system through the prescription of specific policy conditionalities tied to the disbursement of aid.

The motivations for the introduction of SAPs were themselves primarily rooted in another crisis of legitimacy in the international political economy in the late 1970s and early 1980s. The emergence of policy-based lending in the 1980s originated largely from an imperative to stem the rising tide of economic nationalism among developing countries, using conditionality as a tool for reforming the nationalist economic policies that were taking shape in these countries (see Mosley *et al.*, 1991: 3–4).[5] As the period of mass decolonisation drew to a close, the industrialised countries in the west faced a new third world rebellion in the form of the movement for a New International Economic Order.

The NIEO movement challenged the fundamentals of the international economic system, which, in spite of decolonisation, remained premised upon the exploitative relationship of the colonial period and linked the notion of economic sovereignty with political independence. Developing countries began to address issues of ownership and control over their natural resources, questioning the concentration of economic power in northern-based transnational entities, and many embarked on a process of delinking from the patterns of colonial ownership in their national plans (Biel, 2000: 124; Mosley *et al.*, 1991: 3–4).

The demands of the developing countries vis-à-vis western capital culminated in the United Nations General Assembly Resolution of 12 December 1974 on the Charter of Economic Rights and Duties of States[6] and the adoption of a manifesto on the 'Declaration and Program of Action of the New International Order'.[7] The NIEO demands threatened to undermine the rationing of capital from the north to the south that was carefully regulated through existing aid policy and trade agreements that mirrored former colonial relationships.

As discussed in Chapter 2, the role of administering the ration was vested by the industrialised powers in the World Bank and the IMF, enabling these institutions to act not only as conduits for financing to the south but also as monitors of public and private capital flows from the north to the south (see Chapter 2, sections 2.2 and 2.3; Biel, 2000: 86–87, 232–233). Structural adjustment programmes were consequently the response to these increasing threats to the hegemony of western capital. Through SAPs, the industrialised countries, via the Bank and the Fund, were able to substitute their definition of 'structural problems', interpreting them as internal macroeconomic disequilibria which had to be corrected and unnecessary state intervention into markets which had to be removed. This new discourse, argues Biel, 'completely rejected the NIEO-style demands to change the system itself', reducing policy solutions to 'a question of "adapting" a country in the South to fit into the system by creating local conditions' conducive to foreign capital (Biel, 2000: 233) and, increasingly, the globalised economy.[8]

3.1.2 The failure to discipline

The resurgence of economic liberalism that accompanied the rise to power of Ronald Reagan and Margaret Thatcher on both sides of the Atlantic in the 1980s had set the conceptual framework for foreign policy objectives of the industrialised countries during the period of structural adjustment and, along with the geo-strategic imperatives of the Cold War, heightened the political imperatives to stem the rising tide of economic nationalism in the developing world that was cresting on the NIEO wave. The Washington Consensus model of socio-economic organisation, premised on the geo-strategic imperative to promote an ideological shift during the period of its inception, has been described by Brock *et al.* as 'the basic policy instrument of the neoliberal resurgence' (Brock *et al.*, 2001: 13).

Under this conceptual approach, economic growth led by market forces became the new economic rationale and the potential for development and poverty reduction lay in ensuring fiscal and monetary austerity in the developing economies and creating an enabling environment for economic activity, which included trade and financial liberalisation, investment deregulation, privatisation of publicly owned enterprises, including public services, and the creation of an enabling environment for private capital, both domestic and foreign (SAPRIN, 2004: 1–4).

Consequently, the policies driving development financing were premised on facilitating the universal adoption of the Washington Consensus model of economic policymaking, operationalised primarily through the introduction of policy-based loans at the World Bank and the introduction of structural economic conditions for lending from the IMF. Among other things, this has led to the now-universal critique of SAPs as the 'one-size-fits-all' blueprint or boilerplate for economic planning[9] (see Craig and Porter, 2006: 2–5; Stiglitz, 2002: 34, 47).

Financing agreements under SAPs were drawn up based on assessments by staff at the World Bank and the IMF, and loan conditionalities were drawn from economic policies designed at the Bank and Fund headquarters in Washington,

DC with little or no input from the local communities and civil society and marginal input from country policymakers and legislators. While wide-sweeping reforms were introduced in domestic regulatory policy, public expenditure, fiscal and trade policy, very little consultation took place nationally (between civil society, the public and the government) and bilaterally (between the government and the international financial institutions) prior to the entry into force of each agreement.

Towards the end of the 1990s, however, evidence began surfacing of the limitations of SAPs in mitigating the pressures associated with the economic reforms they sought to implement. In spite of the promises of economic growth and prospects for a raised standard of living under SAPs, poverty, even by the World Bank's and IMF's own accounts, rose in most countries that underwent structural adjustment. According to Bank and Fund figures, the number of people living below the poverty line (delineated at US$1 a day) in most parts of the world rose between 1990 and 2000, in many cases in countries where SAPs were introduced in the 1980s (World Bank and IMF, 2004 and World Bank, 2003 in World Bank, 2004b: Figure 1.1). Economic growth for least-developed countries (LDCs) from 1990 to 1996 was recorded at an average of 2 per cent[10] per annum (UNCTAD, 2002a: 3). Meanwhile, the burden of external debt was crippling many countries across the developing world, particularly in sub-Saharan Africa, where governments can spend from one-third to half of their national budgets on debt servicing (Vandermoortele, 2003: 16).

This extensive criticism of the Washington Consensus – the conceptual approach underpinning adjustment financing – coupled with a series of crises in the international financial system (see section 3.2), began to strain the capacity of SAPs to provide this disciplinary framework, necessitating a new institutional and *geo-political* response to the incipient crisis of legitimacy in the global economy.

3.2 Postscripting the Washington Consensus

PRSPs sought to redress the economic relativism of structural adjustment programmes by framing a conceptual approach to development financing that went beyond the fiscal and monetary straitjacket of SAPs and, at the same time, redressed the democratic deficits inherent in the process of accessing financing by enabling a more inclusive framework to socio-economic policymaking. In this manner, PRSPs reflect what Higgott describes as the 'mood swing' in the global political economy at the time from the Washington Consensus to the post-Washington Consensus, driven by the recognition in policy and academic circles, as we shall see later, 'that globalization has to be *politically* legitimized, democratized and socialized if the gains of the *economic* liberalization process are not to be lost to its beneficiaries' (Higgott, 2000: 134).

The post-Washington Consensus does not, however, see the rolling back of the policies of liberalisation, deregulation and privatisation which underpinned the modalities of SAPs or other regulatory reforms of globalisation in the 1980s and 1990s, but seeks rather to 'develop a political institutional framework to *embed* the structural adjustment policies of the Washington Consensus' (Jayasuriya, 2001a: 1, emphasis added; see also section 3.2.1). Encapsulating the post-Washington Consensus' core of 'anti-politics' by substituting 'the politics of procedure for the politics of bargaining' (ibid.), PRSPs therefore represent a conceptual departure from the previous modalities of regulating development financing – that is, under structural adjustment – in three critical areas: the *substantive emphasis on social mitigation*; the *broadening of constituents in policy formulation*; and the *mechanisms for delivery of financing*.

3.2.1 From adjustment to poverty reduction

First, PRSPs move away from a reductionist approach to economic policy-making by placing an emphasis on poverty reduction and, to a limited degree, on wider development priorities. The premise of structural adjustment – to correct the disequilibrium in a country's domestic balance of payments – focused largely on imposing fiscal and monetary discipline on the recipient country through IMF stabilisation programmes and on restructuring of the domestic economy targeted at attracting private and foreign capital through the liberalisation of key economic sectors, such as trade and public utilities (SAPRIN, 2004: 1–2) in the hope that these reforms would generate a 'trickle down' effect to the general population, alleviating poverty as the economy corrected itself.

The PRSP approach, on the other hand, prioritises poverty reduction in the economic planning of countries in receipt of PRSP-related financing, in terms of both assessing poverty impacts of economic policies and prioritising social sector expenditure in national budgets. The discourse of the PRSP also focuses on longer-term objectives, such as developing education and health sectors, and ensuring sustainability of development programmes, as opposed to short-term stabilisation measures under SAPs.[11]

This departure was particularly momentous for the IMF as, along with the changeover from the ESAF to the PRGF, it marked the first time the institution had explicitly adopted 'poverty reduction as a formal objective of its activities'[12] (IMF, 2004a: 26; Whaites, 2002: 12). In particular, this shift cemented the IMF's transition from a crisis lender financing temporary balance of payments deficits to a 'lender of first resort'[13] providing longer-term development financing to low-income countries.

The PRSP approach also paved the way for reform of the World Bank's programmatic or policy-based lending operations, culminating in the replacement of 'adjustment lending' programmes with 'development policy lending' operations under the new Operational Policy 8.60 (OP 8.60) on 'Development Policy Lending'. This new policy framework replaces the Operational Directive 8.60 (OD8.60) on 'Adjustment Lending Policy' and unifies all previous adjustment financing instruments under one umbrella (World Bank, 2004c: para. 20).

The plethora of acronymed policy-based loans, such as structural and sectoral adjustment loans and credits (SALs/SECALs/SECACs) and programmatic structural adjustment loans and credits (PSALs/PSACs) have been 'retired' and replaced by a single lending instrument – the development policy loan (DPL), although PRSCs retain their name 'to maintain continuity with this well-established approach' (ibid.).[14]

3.2.2 *Securing legitimacy through participation*

Second, PRSPs reinstate, at least nominally, the concept of *agency* in development financing policy and practice by institutionalising the requirements of participation and partnership in the financing operations of the Bank and Fund and other multilateral and bilateral donors. This represents a significant departure from the PRSP predecessor, the Policy Framework Paper, which has been described as 'a document drafted by the Fund and agreed by the Bank and the borrowing governments' (Mosley *et al.*, 1991: 53).

Mosley, Toye and Harrigan's extensive study of the World Bank's policy-based lending observed that the introduction of the PFP had significantly curtailed the borrowing country's ability to develop its own economic development agenda, effectively restricting 'room for independent manoeuvre' and creating 'a managed duopoly of policy advice' in which client countries – particularly 'poor, indebted countries where conditionality already bites the hardest' – find it difficult to challenge the policy decisions of the Bank and Fund once they have been taken (Mosley *et al.*, 1991: 55).

PRSPs have therefore been designed to alleviate the hostility associated with this centralisation of control. They are instead geared towards facilitating the engagement of a broad-based constituency of stakeholders in the formulation of domestic policy objectives, although not necessarily policy formulation (IMF and World Bank, 1999: para. 19; see also Chapter 5). Unlike SAPs, economic planning under PRSPs should reflect the development objectives and expenditure priorities of the countries in receipt of financing, as well as the citizens of those countries. This concept of *ownership* of development programmes represents a key shift in the discourse of development policy and practice brought about by the PRSP and the larger 'new architecture of aid' by shifting the emphasis from 'conditionality' to partnerships as the cornerstone of donor–recipient negotiations in aid relationships.[15]

3.2.3 *Universal framework for disbursement*

Finally, PRSPs consolidate the shift that began with SAPs from project- to policy-based financing which links aid efficacy with the reorganisation of the recipient institutions, and marks the movement from what Hall and de la Motte term 'tied aid' to 'globalised aid' (Hall and de la Motte, 2004: 3), whereby financing is increasingly funnelled through multilateral channels and through a single policy instrument to reduce transaction costs. This harmonisation is at the heart of the PRSP framework and underpins the wider 'new architecture of aid'.

While the policies driving the different operational frameworks may have changed, the essence of a policy-driven model of engagement between the donor community and the client countries remains the same. The terms of financing are inherently tied to a policy brief subscribed to by the donor policymakers, and engagement takes the form of 'policy dialogue', described by Cassen *et al.* as 'exchanges between aid donors and recipients about the domestic policy framework' and using the influence of 'aid transfer' to restructure domestic economies (Cassen *et al.*, 1986: 69). The difference is that the policy dialogue is now expected to take place in a more coordinated manner under the PRSP umbrella.

Prior to the PRSP approach, aid policy harmonisation had taken place on an ad-hoc basis or through country-specific mechanisms, such as the Bank- and Fund-led Consultative Groups or debt rescheduling meetings under the auspices of the Paris Club. These meetings were usually secretive, donor-controlled and centred on aid distribution and allocation from a lender's perspective as opposed to the recipient's (Degnbol-Martinussen and Engberg-Pedersen, 2003: 191).

The new financing modalities, such as the PRSCs and other general budget support instruments, which have developed alongside the PRSP framework have been designed to take into account this conceptual shift towards an allegedly more transparent and cohesive multilateralisation of aid.[16] According to Hall and de la Motte:

> This shift from micro to macro levels takes a number of forms through shifting aid from project support to more general budget and policy support, through the 'pooling' of donor aid from different countries behind common policy conditions or the use of regional aid instruments.
>
> (Hall and de la Motte, 2004: 4)

The PRSP was expected to form the backbone of this new aid agenda, acting as the common instrument through which bilateral and multilateral donors align their support to low-income countries.

On paper at least, these conceptual changes to the policy framework governing access to development financing appear to be wrought in favour of the communities in need of such financing, framed by a response to the failure of pre-existing modalities of financing to deliver on wider developmental objectives, including that of political franchise. However, as the following sections reveal, the aforementioned conceptual discourse of the PRSP was shaped and framed by imperatives which go beyond technicalities of aid and management of development finance. As such, the reforms of the PRSP project were brought about as a result of pressures brought to bear on the IFIs and the G8 countries that represent the major disbursers of development financing and took root within an inherently asymmetrical relationship between the parties to the new initiative.

3.3 Competing agendas for change

The 'new architecture of aid' developed in the 1990s is a product of what Brock, Cornwall and Gaventa term 'a process of hybridisation' by which 'dominant narratives of development policy and practice are constantly reshaped by their absorption of elements of counter-narratives', giving rise to 'the articulation of new variants that appear to offer a convergence of competing agendas, recasting old elements of older approaches in evocative new storylines' (Brock *et al.*, 2001: 8).[17] This is evidenced by the process in which the new problematic of the PRSP is framed and articulated and later transformed into policy, practice and regulatory norms.

Callaghy (2001), in his analysis of the shift in the regulatory norms of the international debt regime from the Paris Club restructuring to the multilateral debt relief programme under the HIPC in 1996 and the HIPC II in 1999, sites the locus of change outside the state-to-state bargaining system of the international economic regulatory fora. Instead, he identifies a 'triple helix' of relationships and connections, comprising 'the institutions of the international debt regime, the NGO debt networks, and the epistemic community', that, having been confronted with a 'central structural dilemma of the international political economy', reacted in different ways towards the resolution of the problem (Callaghy, 2001: 116–117).

Having identified the 'structural dilemma' (or what I term the 'new problematic') – the existence of a group of 'weak' states and economies which pose the potential for conflict in the international political economy due to their inability to 'benefit as easily or quickly from economic reform and democratization as those elsewhere in the world' – Callaghy considers how the disparate groups have responded to the problem. Change in the international debt regime to respond to the identified structural dilemma came as a result of 'the synergy between these various forms of power, knowledge and discourse as they interacted with the underlying structural dilemma' (Callaghy, 2001: 116–118).

Similarly, in mapping the evolution of SAPs to the PRSP framework, it is clear that the impetus for reform can be traced to three separate but interrelated clusters of actors and processes, each with distinct but interlinked objectives for reforming the system for delivering development financing to low-income countries. These developments serve to clear the ground for a convergence of policy, practice and politics at the critical moment – I call it the 'tipping point'[18] – in which the PRSP was introduced.

In each of the three instances – academic, institutional and geo-strategic – the objectives of the dominant actors and dominant discourses within the processes set the parameters for engagement with the problematic and, as a consequence, shaped the responses to the problematic accordingly. The PRSP and related financing mechanisms are the result of the convergence of these policy and political responses to the problematic and the extent to which they corresponded with the strategic objectives of the dominant actors. Linking these three clusters of actors and events is the crucial role played by civil society organisations, in particular a cadre of specialist NGOs which formed advocacy coalitions and moved in between the three clusters, pitching their cause according to the strategic interests of each cluster of actors.

3.3.1 The role of the epistemic coalition

First, PRSPs and the new financing modalities accompanying this initiative may be viewed as the outcome of a convergence of thinking in academia and policymaking circles on the effectiveness of aid and the impact of structural adjustment policies in the late 1980s and early 1990s. This 'epistemic coalition' played a crucial role in the formulation of the conceptual and operational principles that underlie the PRSP framework, helping to shape not only a consensus around identifying and framing the problematic, but also its policy solutions.[19] For Masood Ahmed, a key player in the design of the PRSP framework,[20] the initiative is a prime example of the results to be achieved when epistemic shifts in development policy*thinking* coincided with the political and institutional shifts in development policy*making* (Ahmed, 2004).

a) Epistemic shifts

For this epistemic coalition, what was important was the shaping of a new discourse of development policy and practice. This meant framing the problematic and proposed solutions within an acceptable policy narrative – the process of 'hybridisation' – palatable to the key institutional and political actors with the power to change the regulatory regime. The power of this epistemic coalition was what Ahmed alludes to as the 'multiplier effect' of a body of multi-disciplinary research with similar conclusions which led to the formation of a set of policy recommendations transmitted into policy narratives by key 'policy translators' in both the research and policy communities (Ahmed, 2004).

This body of research may be categorised into three key areas: (1) empirical economic research into the impacts of SAPs and the effect of the debt overhang in low-income countries; (2) research into the methodologies of aid assessment and aid delivery; and (3) scholarship on civil society participants and participation in policymaking. The third category is important as the increasing influence of civil society groups on international development policymaking has both corresponded with and often precipitated the increase in academic scholarship on these developments.

Each of the three categories of research contributed to the development and final articulation of the fundamental tenets governing the PRSP project. Empirical research on SAPs provided the foundational body of data to support policy change, while research into the methodologies of aid assessment and financing modalities suggested the problems with the existing system and proposed solutions for a new framework which were, in turn, supported by studies into incorporating new actors – civil society – into the policymaking process.

First of all, developments in the scholarship on poverty and welfare dimensions of structural adjustment and debt marked a shift away from the economic rationalism that characterised the SAPs. Catalysed by studies such as Cornia, Jolly and Stewart's influential report *Adjustment with a Human Face*[21] in 1987, the concept of 'poverty' was being redefined away from a purely economistic definition of income per capita towards encompassing issues of exclusion from social, political and economic services; of vulnerability by virtue of gender, class or race within communities of poor people; and of access to political structures, accountability and democratic participation in decision-making processes (Brock *et al.*, 2001: 15–16; Christiansen with Hovland, 2003: 10).[22]

Conceptualising poverty as both a socio-political and an economic construct required the construction of policy prescriptions which take into account the processes of policy formulation as well as issues of accountability and transparency in resource allocation, a key factor in determining the agency of poor people and in fostering empowerment. As such, policy prescriptions advocated by members of the epistemic community who took this view of the problematic focused on developing participatory methods in development assessment and planning (see, for example, Sen, 2001; Stiglitz, 2001) and on addressing the issue of governance within the recipient state to ensure transparency of aid allocation and disbursement.

Questions of ownership of economic reforms surfaced as NGOs increasingly lobbied the Bank and the Fund for greater access to the policymaking process. It was this criticism of donor-dictated policymaking associated with SAPs that began to find favour with donor technocrats who viewed the limits of policy conditionality from a technical perspective of aid efficacy. The limitations of structural adjustment as an instrument for policy leverage were highlighted by key studies which linked the failure of policy reform in SAP countries with the lack of political ownership in the design of adjustment programmes.

Mosley *et al.*, for example, argued that the lack of policy uptake in recipient countries was due to both the political nature of SAP conditions and the non-inclusive nature of programme formulation (Mosley *et al.*, 1991: 128). Implicit in Mosley *et al.*'s conclusions was the need to incorporate the political elites of recipient countries into the process of programme policy design in order to ensure greater adherence to the policy prescriptions set by the Bank and the Fund under economic reform programmes (ibid.: 129).

The findings from this study were supported by two influential World Bank research papers by Burnside and Dollar (1997) and Dollar and Svensson (1998) which linked the problem of aid effectiveness with the problem of institutional deficiencies within the recipient countries. Their contention that development aid was not having an impact on countries because of the countries' capacity to absorb and implement aid in an effective manner (Sender, 2002: 193) resonated with policymakers in the financier community who 'were keen to demonstrate a more rational basis for allocating their funds' (Ahmed, 2004). This discourse on aid effectiveness has widely been regarded as the overarching impetus for reform of the regulatory regime governing access to development financing.[23]

b) From research to policy change

One of the key epistemic components in creating the impetus for change from structural adjustment to the PRSP framework was the ESAF review. Commissioned by the IMF in 1996 to evaluate its concessional lending facility, the ESAF review was a first on many levels, including being the first IMF review to include an external evaluation. The external reviewers concluded that country studies indicated that 'ownership' was a necessary condition of successful policy reform and 'program implementation', and recommended that 'ownership' be strengthened at country level through the formulation of a national medium- to long-term strategy around which a body of national consensus can be built prior to negotiations with the Fund (IMF, 1998: 21).

The impact of ESAF reviews demonstrates the effect of the epistemic convergence in forging the conceptual framework for the PRSP approach. While the reviewers of the ESAF, both internally and externally, were mainstream economists, some of whom were committed to the Washington Consensus economic ideology, the views of the ESAF reviewers nonetheless resonated with other external researchers, and some researchers within the Bank, who subscribed to a more comprehensive view of development models and means of achieving development objectives. At the same time, the ESAF reviews reinforced what the policymakers in Washington, DC had already been aware of for some time – that the PFPs were failing to generate results and creating deeper resentment in the relationships between the IFIs and the recipient countries (interview: Plant, 2004).

The discourse of aid effectiveness also had particular resonance with the decision-makers at the IFIs, namely the Bank president and the Fund managing director[24] and major shareholding governments on the Executive Boards, in considering operational changes to the development financing regime. The policy consensus emerging from mainstream discourses on aid effectiveness and the efficacy of conditionality provided policymakers with, in effect, an escape clause from architectural reform of the aid system. Policy conclusions that 'there was no need to change fundamentally the policy prescriptions associated with aid' but rather that 'aid should be directed only to those countries that have already demonstrated the capacity to adopt good policies' (Sender, 2002: 193)[25] enabled the Bank and the Fund to absorb the alternative conceptual approaches to development financing without rocking the foundations of its substantive content.

This episode demonstrates the centrality of epistemic coalitions to changes in public policy, notably global public policy. Engagements with the external research community reinforce internal knowledge shifts within policy institutions, but such changes are operationalised only when there are political pressures to build convergence between the two. According to former World Bank senior economist Ravi Kanbur[26] (whose resignation from the World Bank over the furore relating to the *WDR 2000/01* marked the first of a series of high-profile departures from the institution), more often than not the epistemic community was called upon to provide the intellectual response to external demands on the Bank and Fund created by developments in the global context (interview: Kanbur, 2004).

In other words, more than the 'agenda-setting' role of epistemic networks, academic research, within and outside the policy environment, often becomes 'a source of institutional legitimacy for chosen development paths' (Stone and Wright, 2007: 9). Therefore, the 'tipping point' for the shift from SAPs to the PRSP framework took place not only in the convergence within the epistemic coalition but also in a convergence between the interests of the *advocates for reform* and *the politics of reform*. In Ahmed's words, 'the time was right, the politics was right' (Ahmed, 2004).

3.3.2 The institutional response to the conceptual framework

Under pressure from both the public lobby and their political masters to reform the aid delivery system in the face of the incipient systemic crisis and the backlash against the IFIs in the late 1990s, the World Bank and the IMF, and, to a lesser extent, bilateral aid agencies such as the UK's DFID, were confronted with the impetus to provide a sustained organisational solution to the problematic. The institutional processes that shifted the political ground for the inception of PRSPs are distinguished from the role played by the institutional policymakers who formed a part of the aforementioned epistemic community. These institutional advocates for reform relied upon the organisational impetus to respond to external pressure by translating the narratives for reform into policy solutions to the problematic, drawing upon the support of the wider epistemic community to legitimise their own strategies for reform.

a) The Wolfensohn legacy

A key political development in the 1990s that led to the PRSP framework was the appointment of former banker James Wolfensohn as president of the World Bank Group in June 1995. Wolfensohn's appointment has been widely regarded as a turning point for World Bank operational policies and, consequently, for those of most other bilateral and multilateral donors who regard the Bank as the 'leader' in development policy thinking. Wolfensohn was under pressure from the

US administration and from other major Bank shareholders to address the rising tide of criticism of the Bank, particularly from a coalition of Anglo-American NGOs and its domestic supporters.

Wolfensohn's appointment was, to all intents and purposes, deliberately orchestrated to reinvent the Bank in the face of mounting criticism and to rehabilitate the Bank in the interests of US foreign policy. Vice-president Al Gore was said to be keen to revitalise the Bank's role in what was seen to be 'security areas' neglected during the Cold War, such as poverty, disease, etc. (Mallaby, 2004). According to veteran environmental campaigner Bruce Rich,[27] the Bank at the time when Wolfensohn took over was faced with a serious crisis of credibility, threatened with marginalisation in the international arena due to its inability not only to 'move money' to developing countries but also to construct 'coherent, believable approaches' to resolving 'the economic and social quandaries of poorer parts of the world' (Rich, 2002: 28).

Wolfensohn was particularly mindful of the fact that he had inherited an institution in crisis, riddled with bureaucratic inertia and faced with external credibility issues. Not only were the protests against Bank projects becoming more public, but internal reports such as the critical *Wapenhans Report*[28] in 1992 confirmed that the Bank senior management was deeply steeped in a 'culture of loan approval' which was overriding performance and efficacy considerations in Bank operations, a practice that the incumbent president had pledged to change on taking office (Rich, 2002: 26–27).

Part of Wolfensohn's brief was to create greater legitimacy for Bank interventions in the developing world, both for the benefit of external critics such as advocacy groups and NGOs and for detractors within the US Congress, particularly a group of hard-core Republican politicians who viewed the Bank as an unnecessary tax on the US public. In the face of the congressional Meltzer Commission, established in 1998 to examine the role of the BWIs, and its unfavourable report,[29] Wolfensohn's plan was to engage the critics head on. One such strategy was to engage in a dialogue with NGOs (see section 3.3.3), setting a precedent for the Bank administration.

Joseph Stiglitz,[30] appointed as the Bank's chief economist in February 1997, supplemented Wolfensohn's reforms by supplying the intellectual counterpart to Wolfensohn's political strategies. Stiglitz's time at the Bank marked the demarcation in the policy discourse of the Bank between the top-down monetarist approach of the SAPs and the more inclusive, holistic approach of the post-structural adjustment era (Chang, 2001: 1–4; Pender, 2001: 402–408; interview: Guerrero, 2004). Indeed, Stiglitz's ideas formed the basis of much of the new post-Washington Consensus ideology, triangulating the link between the neoliberalism of the structural adjustment era and what Hatcher terms the 'neo-institutionalism' of the post-structural adjustment era, and helping the Bank shape what she calls the 'integrated development model', which sought to 'implement new forms of governance in order to lock-in market-enabling policies' in client countries (Hatcher, 2006).

Stiglitz, in many ways, served as the link between the shifts in the conceptual framework of development policy and the political imperatives that drove institutional policy.[31] For some researchers at the Bank, Stiglitz paved the way for the articulation of alternative policies and provided the intellectual cover under which these policies might be developed and operationalised. In Chang's opinion, Stiglitz's criticism of the Washington Consensus came at a critical period, coinciding, as it were, 'with rising intellectual criticism and a renewed political resistance from the developing countries towards the neo-liberal world order' (Chang, 2001: 2).[32]

In 1995, the financial crisis hit Mexico and the contagion subsequently spread to East Asia in 1996–1997. The collapse of key East Asian economies – Thailand, Indonesia, South Korea, Malaysia – in the financial crisis of 1996–1997 served as a wake-up call to the financial community, and the ensuing political unrest that accompanied the IMF stabilisation programmes in countries such as Thailand and Indonesia highlighted the social and political consequences of an economic programme based on fiscal austerity that neglected the social welfare dimension. Advocacy groups, including debt campaigners, seized on the opportunity of the East Asian financial crisis to call for a change in the global economic order, using the effects of the financial crisis and the negative impacts of IMF stabilisation programmes, including rising fuel prices, as an indicator of the fallout from unbridled capitalism and trade and financial liberalisation.

Stiglitz's ideas were ideally placed to counteract charges that the IFIs were not responding to global events and to form the foundation upon which an alternative policy framework could be conceptualised and operationalised.[33] This alternative framework was ultimately set out by Wolfensohn in his Comprehensive Development Framework, the conceptual treatise that would form the theoretical framework for the PRSP project.

b) Political currency of change

The institutional change at the World Bank was encouraged by the success of the Labour Party in the 1997 UK parliamentary elections and the subsequent appointment of then UK Chancellor of the Exchequer Gordon Brown to the chair of the International Monetary and Financial Committee. Coming in after almost two decades in the political wilderness on a platform of third way reformism, this new British government's entry into international development policy circles provided valuable support to the post-structural adjustment Stiglitz–Wolfensohn reforms in Washington and the conceptual framework for reform set by the epistemic coalition discussed on pp. 70–72.[34]

The CDF was also, in many ways, shaped by the Ugandan success story. The Uganda story has been cited as a successful story of participation in poverty reduction and an important example of policy success that shifted the discourse of development financing from conditionality to partnership and participation. Uganda's economic planning model, developed under President Yoweri

Museveni in the late 1990s, was premised on a programme of participatory politics centred around a series of consultations with local communities and NGOs, chiefly branches of transnational development NGOs – Oxfam International and ActionAid – that resulted in the Poverty Eradication Action Plan (PEAP) in 1997.

This document later formed the basis upon which negotiations between the Ugandan government and the IFIs were conducted. This included negotiations under the Ugandan Multilateral Debt Fund (UMDF), which was proposed by the Ugandan government and acted as a vehicle through which debt negotiations would take place (Callaghy, 2001: 128–131; Christiansen with Hovland, 2003: 21–23; Mallaby, 2004: 217–229). The Ugandan model was subsequently taken up by Bank designers of the PRSP framework and later supported by the British government, largely because of the revolving door of policymakers within the Ugandan policymaking processes at the time and NGOs such as Oxfam, debt campaign groups such as Jubilee 2000 and DFID, whereby the same persons who were instrumental in formulating Uganda's policies were later posted to London or Washington, DC (interviews: various).

The Washington CDF compact and the Ugandan debt and development model also provided a useful conceptual base upon which the conditions for debt relief under the HIPC could be drawn. These conditions would later be translated into concrete policies upon which the PRSP framework would be operationalised. The debt campaign was a critical step in the evolution of the PRSP from principles in a conceptual framework into conditions that would be attached to development financing, and this development was the result of the institutional response by the IFIs and donor countries to the demands of the debt campaigners and other advocacy groups.

The translation of CDF principles into a regulatory framework for accessing development financing was therefore an institutional response to the external pressures on the Bank, Fund and the G8 countries which had subscribed to the enhanced HIPC initiative. Debt campaigners, such as the Jubilee 2000 coalition, in their demands for greater and deeper debt relief for impoverished countries, had been denouncing the original HIPC initiative set up in 1996 as inconsequential due its limited impact on poverty reduction in the affected countries (see Christiansen with Hovland, 2003: 25–27; Callaghy, 2001, 131–139). As a result, their campaign for an enhanced HIPC initiative included calls for an alignment of debt relief with plans to reduce poverty in the indebted countries. NGOs campaigning for debt relief had demanded that the money that was to be saved from debt reduction should be spent by the country in receipt of such relief, on expenditure earmarked for poverty eradication.

3.3.3 Geo-strategic interests and the role of the NGO lobby

The Jubilee 2000 debt campaign demonstrated the strength of public opinion in mobilising support amongst institutional players for a change in the status quo and opened the space for the participation of a new coalition of actors in international development policymaking – that of the specialised NGO advocate. These developments served to widen the range of actors in international development policymaking and normalised the participation of non-state actors in the process of policy formulation, regulatory governance and international lawmaking.

a) The new non-state actors

Fogarty (2003) and Callaghy (2001) both view 'regime change' in the international debt regime from the ad-hoc Paris Club system to the multilateralised agenda of the HIPC regime as resulting from, in the absence of any other explanation, the pressures brought to bear upon the G7 governments by the debt campaign lobby. Fogarty observes:

> The LDCs' debt relationships through the mid-1990s were managed in a closed, secretive and rigid process among rich-country creditors, but since 1996, these relationships have become embedded in a more open, consultative and flexible process in which sovereign and multilateral creditors have ceded a greater voice to the LDCs and their NGO advocates. *In the absence of a major impetus to change from other relevant factors, the role of the NGOs seems to have been the key reason for this change.*
>
> (Fogarty, 2003: 230, emphasis added)

This observation is accurate to a certain extent, for while NGOs certainly contributed to the creation of political space in which the discourse of debt relief and poverty reduction could be articulated, framed and acted upon, the real political impetus for reform came less from the direct advocacy power of NGOs and social movements than from the discursive fallout of such pressure. While, arguably, some northern-based NGOs, such as Oxfam International, have claimed the credit for restructuring the debt regime, and consequently for the initiation of the PRSP framework,[35] their advocacy role in promoting this shift has not been as significant as the geo-strategic consequences of their 'profoundly *political* act of critique and mobilization' (Fogarty, 2003: 230). In other words, the political alliances built as a result of the NGOs' debt campaign created the impetus for the industrialised countries to act, through their majority voice in the decision-making processes of the international financial governance institutions, to retain their geo-political hegemony in these areas.

While protests against the multilateral banks and financial institutions have been ongoing since the 1980s, the movement in the 1990s shifted gears politically at the geo-strategic level as a result of the alliances built between advocacy groups in the north and governments of the south. In the 1980s, advocacy groups were largely campaigning against the environmental and social impacts of projects on affected communities in the south. In many of these campaigns, criticism was directed at the IFIs, the multilateral and bilateral donors and the governments of the recipient countries themselves.

With the advent of structural adjustment and the move away from project lending, the NGO lobby began to link the economics with the environment and campaigns began to be built around the general injustice of the global economic system as opposed to singling out a particular issue. According to Fox and Brown, '[a]s the social, geographic, and institutional base of the campaigns broadened, anti-poverty concerns and structural adjustment became growing priorities on the [multilateral development bank] agenda' (Fox and Brown, 1998: 6).

This was encouraged, albeit to a limited extent, by the Wolfensohn presidency of the World Bank. In 1996, a coalition of NGOs from the north and south formed the Structural Adjustment Participatory Review International Network (SAPRIN) in response to the incoming Wolfensohn's challenge to civil society groups to engage in a joint Bank and civil society 'multi-country, participatory investigation' into the impacts of structural adjustment policies. The five-year project, conducted through wide-ranging empirical research by grassroots organisations in 10 countries, culminated in the SAPRI report, which revealed damning evidence against SAPs (SAPRIN, 2004: 1–35). While the Bank subsequently disengaged from the project and sought to distance itself from the findings (ibid.: 31–35), the impact of the initiative had already been felt through the galvanising of political voices against the institutional agenda of SAPs.[36]

One crucial difference in the NGO campaigns around SAPs was that, unlike the environmental campaigns, the concerns about structural inequality and the welfare dimensions of sovereign debt and fiscal austerity required campaigners, despite their reservations, to work with the governments of indebted and low-income countries. This brought about a critical shift in the public lobby against the financial institutions and posed a more immediate and more potent geo-strategic threat to the G8 countries than the environmental campaigns that had focused solely on the complicity of the IFIs and the recipient governments. The campaigns against structural adjustment marked the beginning of an often uneasy and wary relationship between NGOs and governments of low-income countries. In this respect, NGOs soon began to work with governments in the south as opposed to working against them.

At the same time, the raft of regulatory reforms pushed through neoliberal reforms embedded in structural adjustment programmes and through increasingly powerful multilateral institutions such as the WTO were increasingly incurring resistance from developing countries. The campaign against the Multilateral Agreement on Investment (MAI) cemented the relationship between campaign groups in the north and the governments in the south – the proposal for a draft MAI was first obtained through government leaks by a Canadian environmental NGO, which circulated the information to the rest of the NGO community.

The strength of the international protests took many western governments by surprise in the late 1990s, with the large demonstrations of force outside key inter-governmental summits (G8, WTO, World Bank and IMF meetings) and corporate meetings (such as the annual World Economic Forum in Davos, Switzerland) forcing heads of state to confront the reality of the global order. Globalisation was creating, in Stiglitz's own words, 'its discontents' (Stiglitz, 2002). The famous 'Battle of Seattle' at the site of the aborted WTO ministerial meeting in 1999 exemplified the force of this new political alliance, and although the significance of this event is contested, it did, at its minimum, bring together a disparate network of dissenting voices restive for change and, in Higgott's analysis, set into motion 'a series of trigger points on the road to a changing international intellectual and policy agenda' (Higgott, 2000: 136).

b) Quelling the disruption

The international citizenry protests bolstered the 'renewed political resistance' (Chang, 2001: 2) of developing countries against the disadvantageous economic policies that were being enforced in their jurisdictions through iniquitous regulatory processes such as structural adjustment, and uneven economic forums such as the WTO, NAFTA and conditions attached to debt restructuring. After the OECD was forced to retract plans for the MAI as a result of the refusal of developing countries to subscribe to 'the discussion of what they saw as a highly biased agenda' (Chang, 2001: 3), the renewed political force of a united 'third world' became clear, as did the new political leverage of the transnational social movement.

The social and economic dislocations of the aforementioned 1997–1998 financial crisis and socio-economic fallout from their accompanying adjustment programmes heightened the global loss of faith in the international economy, precipitating a series of third world rebellions in the global governance arena, from the collective ministerial walkout of Seattle to the unilateral dismissal of IMF interventions in Mahathir-led Malaysia,[37] which held the threat of an incipient mass third world revolt against the rapaciousness of the neoliberal postcolonial world economy.

These geo-strategic imperatives were important in framing the objectives and, later, the regulatory agenda of the PRSP framework. The necessity of controlling the resistance – the 'prose of counter-insurgency', in the words of Pahuja (2000: 797) – was a very real geo-political factor in the conceptualisation of the PRSP framework. Like the introduction of its predecessor framework, SAPs, the origins of the PRSP initiative are located within the percolating incipient crisis of faith in and threats to the status quo of the international economy of its times.

Here, the impetus was driven by the concern within the international financial community – by this, I refer to the community of sovereign donors, IFIs and the international corporate community – that the political resistance by the developing countries within the global economic system, bolstered by the support of an increasingly powerful transnational social movement with networks of citizenry support spanning both north and south, posed a real danger to the functioning of the existing international economy and the global juridical order which sustains it. Pahuja speaks of a 'fear of exit' that poses an eternal spectre in the participation of the third world states in the international legal order:

> The effect of the eternal presence of the spectre of the Third World primordialism means that implicit in the articulation of the fear of entry and the risk of systemic breakdown immanent in that entry, is the *fear of exit*, or the desire to prevent nations in financial difficulties from dropping out of the international system altogether.
>
> (Pahuja, 2000: 797, emphasis added)

This 'fear of exit' is accompanied by the aforementioned 'fear of entry': the potentially disruptive potential of inclusion in the international legal and economic order of 'developing' states, whose juridical systems have not attained the corresponding safety level of 'governance' and institutional sophistication of the 'developed' world and whose limitations as such pose a real challenge to the maintenance of the geo-strategic hegemony of the industrialised nations (Pahuja, 2000: 785–788).

In this respect, the PRSP framework may be seen as a means of quelling this potential danger of 'exit' by the low-income countries from the international economic system and, at the same time, tackling the danger of 'primordialism' that accompanies these countries' inclusion in this system. This is evidenced by the conceptual and operational emphasis on country ownership of financing programmes and the provisions for debt relief to tackle the problem of 'exit' by providing incentives to countries to remain in the system, and by instituting process requirements such as poverty reduction strategies and monitoring systems to provide the necessary governance conditions to regulate the countries' continued participation in the economic legal order.

Conversation with a Bank staffer illustrates this point. This staff member admits that regulating the recipient countries' use of aid and debt relief (provided in response to the pressures of the NGOs and internal advocates for reform) was a particular concern of the industrialised country Board members in the changeover from structural adjustment to PRSP-initiated financing modalities, such as the budget support PRSC, who demanded, in many cases, that these countries adopt the fiscal accountability regimes set by their own domestic jurisdictions. According to this senior researcher, the G8 governments often refuse to give consent to economic policies which accord the recipient countries blanket autonomy unless 'these countries can show that they meet standards, and not only standards, but the highest and most demanding standards (*sic*)' available (interview: 2004).

The PRSP framework, with its set of operational parameters, provided the opportunity to arrest the dissonance within the international political economy.

While the PRSP only extends to the peripheral nations of the international financial system, mostly located in sub-Saharan Africa – as opposed to the politically powerful Asian and Latin American middle-income countries – the importance of maintaining this bloc of countries within the global capitalist system is as much an exercise of discourse as one of utility, the offsetting of the loss of faith in the policies of globalisation. The PRSP framework thus becomes the new regulatory framework for containing the threat of revolt, replacing the outmoded discipline of SAPs.

3.4 Missing pieces in the jigsaw: the absent south

One very clear conclusion that can be drawn from the genealogical discussion of the PRSP framework above is that the impetus for change from structural adjustment to this new approach of development financing came from outside the communities and countries which the PRSPs are designed to affect. The planning, design and implementation of the PRSP approach were consolidated in Washington, DC, London, Brussels and Paris with little input from the participants of the framework. The imperatives for these conceptual and operational shifts in the delivery of development financing lie outside the state-to-state negotiating structure and outside the democratic apparatus of accountability and transparency within the jurisdictions in which the framework is supposed to operate.

Christiansen and Hovland's study of the historical narrative of the PRSP project and its role in multilateral policy change found that there was little southern government input into the process of formulating the PRSP framework. They conclude:

> Other than some limited discussion at Executive Director level of the World Bank and IMF, the contribution of Southern governments was largely indirect, through the demonstration effect of poverty reduction programmes in practice. Countries named in this respect were Mozambique, Tanzania, Bolivia, and especially Uganda.
>
> (Christiansen with Hovland, 2003: 21)

The overarching framework of the PRSP was thus designed and executed in the OECD countries, in consultation with northern-based NGOs, driven by organisational and political imperatives of the north. Even where the 'contribution' of southern governments has been recognised as a precipitating factor, this process was largely driven by large transnational NGOs.[38] In Uganda for example, as noted in section 3.3.2, international NGOs played a key role in drafting the conceptual and operational framework for the PEAP. According to Christiansen and Hovland, it was Oxfam and the Ugandan government which initiated Uganda's first Participatory Poverty Assessment (PPA), which formed the backdrop for the PEAP process (ibid.: 22–23).

The absence of genuine southern participation in the PRSP project's inception is significant when analysing the impact of the framework as a regulatory mechanism and as a mechanism for globalisation. The lack of input from communities and states within this structure belies the true nature of the rhetoric behind the PRSPs that the framework is premised on notions of *ownership*, *participation* and *poverty reduction*. While the framework responds to some of the notions alluded to within its stated objectives, the origins of the PRSP approach not only impact significantly on the pursuit of these goals, but also question the authenticity of its stated objectives.

Ironically, the means through which the PRSP framework was conceived, negotiated and approved by the shareholding governments of the Bretton Woods institutions and subsequently adopted by these governments in their bilateral relationships with PRSP countries demonstrate the continued subservience of third world states and their communities to the political constituencies of the north. They also highlight the fundamental asymmetries of the decision-making structures of the World Bank and the IMF, as discussed in Chapter 2, in that the weighted voting structure of the institutions enabled reforms to be approved in spite of significant opposition from those countries to be affected by the changes and 'muted the voice of those members that knew most about the issue' (Rustomjee, 2005: 26).

Cyrus Rustomjee, former executive director for a constituency of sub-Saharan African countries at the IMF, reveals that the decision to operationalise the PRSP was taken by the Executive Boards of the Bank and Fund 'during a key board meeting in December 1999' in spite of significant objections from developing country members, notably SSA countries, on the form and substance of the PRSP approach and the capacity of resource-strapped client governments to implement such an ambitious project (Rustomjee, 2005: 26). According to Rustomjee:

> Relevant and legitimate issues were raised regarding the pacing and phasing of the PRSPs, the need for different approaches to PRSP preparation, the lack of domestic capacity to prepare PRSPs in many countries, the lack of fiscal resources to give effect to the recommendations which PRSPs were likely to generate; diversion of policy-maker's efforts from other crucial activities, including their macroeconomic reform efforts and their efforts to secure bilateral and multilateral debt relief. Only a few of these objections were translated into amendments to the framework's inception.
>
> (Rustomjee, 2005: 26)

The absence of third world voices from the construction of the PRSP project highlights the colonial legacy not just of this particular policy instrument and its attendant regulatory framework but also of the larger architecture of aid, the impact of which continues to resonate in the implementation of PRSPs and their financing instruments. It highlights what southern constituencies have criticised as a northern preoccupation with the technocratic nature of development and the aid architecture, a sense of 'tweaking' the systematic components rather than redressing the systemic flaws in the political and economic relations that underlie the aid system (Menocal and Rogerson, 2006: 7).

The framing of the PRSP project in this context therefore demonstrates the extent to which third world states and communities in the south continue to be the *objects*, as opposed to the *subjects*, of the project of development (and consequently of international law and global governance). This is exacerbated, as we shall see below, by the legacy of state fragmentation left by structural adjustment in ex-SAP/current PRSP countries and the precedents established by adjustment reforms which legitimise the interventions of the actors central to the PRSP initiative.

3.5 PRSPs and the legacy of state fragmentation

The imposition of the PRSP, with its significant interventions in target countries and implemented in a policymaking process that is set, by and large, by actors external to the country, is indicative of the destructive legacy of structural adjustment policies on the constitution of the state in SAP countries and the resultant marginalisation of domestic structures of decision-making in the context of national planning and regulation and international engagement of these states.

A critical impact of the disciplinary force of structural adjustment was the creation of a domestic political space that enabled the imposition of PRSP reforms. Efforts at restructuring the state that were pivotal to structural adjustment policies have resulted in the dispersal of state autonomy, which has paved the way for the successful insertion of the PRSP framework in these countries. In particular, the negative governance externalities of SAPs provided the impetus for interventions and, as the disciplinary framework, provided the regulatory precedents for interventions.

Two significant consequences of structural adjustment therefore have been, first, the concession of national regulatory authority to the international arena, resulting from the merging of domestic and international governance structures, and, second, and consequently, the fragmentation of state capacity, in terms of both economic reproduction and regulation, resulting from this shift in regulatory power. The 'successful' implementation of the PRSP framework is therefore a corollary to the 'successful' implementation of adjustment policies, a paradoxical heritage that is rarely represented in the discourse on the post-Washington Consensus architecture of aid.

3.5.1 Internationalisation of decision-making

Structural adjustment, as alluded to in Chapter 2 and in sections 3.1 and 3.2, legitimised policy reform as an objective of resource transfer and as a subject of financing. The introduction of 'policy-based' financing under SAPs – based on a programme of structural reform in recipient countries as opposed to financing an earmarked project under traditional 'investment' financing – marked a shift not only in the substance of development financing but also in the process of policymaking in recipient countries.

The design of structural adjustment had enabled the IFIs to permeate internal structures of recipient countries in ways that were not possible before. Where Bank and Fund bureaucrats previously possessed only the autonomy to dispense technical advice on (1) project implementation (in the case of the Bank) and (2) the domestic monetary and fiscal policy insofar as they impact on domestic economic stability and international financial cooperation, SAPs endowed these institutions with the political capital to capture key policymaking spaces within the domestic economy.

In doing so, SAPs created a transnational regulatory regime which has fragmented the internal sovereignty of states subject to its discipline and created what Jayasuriya terms 'polycentric legal orders' by internationalising specific state agencies and institutions – notably finance ministries, central banks and national financial regulatory authorities – which engage with the Bretton Woods institutions and which oversee domestic regulatory compliance autonomously from other institutions of domestic governance (Jayasuriya, 1999: 438–441).

The importance of Bank and Fund signalling to external resource mobilisation for many countries has resulted in the creation of 'islands of sovereignty' (Jayasuriya, 1999: 439) within a state as the aforementioned state agencies linked into the larger global financial architecture begin to (and are encouraged to) operate autonomously from other parts of the government machinery in order to facilitate more effective policy dialogue with these institutions and enforce greater regulatory compliance with their policy prescriptions. This has created the development of 'transnationalized sectors' of the economy which operate in accordance with 'regulatory logics' imposed by external financial institutions and respond to the disciplinary imperatives of these institutions (Santos, 2006: 50), resulting in relocation of regulatory accountability to international rather than domestic governance structures.

This reality is compounded, as we will see in section 3.5.2, by the internal fragmentation of state authority caused by the SAP reforms, notably the increasing reliance on external resources, financial and personnel, to carry out basic state functions. SAP policies to cut government expenditure (see the discussion in section 3.5.2) has meant that many low-income countries are now dependent on aid to plug not only the fiscal gap in government but also the human resources gap, leaving many countries dependent on aid to fund civil service personnel. Consequently, in many SAP countries donor influence is significant in public administration, with expatriate personnel, usually funded or seconded from bilateral aid agencies, occupying, and often heading, key ministerial positions in government departments.[39]

One of the implications of such dependence has been the integration of donor policies, or what Harrison terms 'the international orthodoxy of reform', in domestic governance (Harrison, 2001b: 670; see Chapter 5), thereby translating aid dependency into policy leverage.[40] Another important consequence has been the emergence of non-traditional actors in the policymaking processes in SAP countries, including non-state actors and donors, as key players in the process of state reconfiguration, legitimised at the international level through their links with the institutions of global governance (see sections 3.3.3 and 3.5.2).

Accordingly, it is not surprising that the reforms advocated by the constellation of actors responsible for the PRSP initiative have not been significantly challenged by the domestic constituencies they affect. Where the regulatory authority has been shifted to an external body and where domestic institutions are enmeshed in chains of resource dependency, the capacity for opposing a new disciplinary structure, initiated as it were within a discourse of political franchise, is geo-strategically and economically limited.

3.5.2 The retreat of the state

The PRSP approach has taken root in a political and economic vacuum in states where the apparatuses of governance and the functions of government have been weakened by successive onslaughts of structural adjustment reforms and where this vacuum has been partially filled by private entities and agencies, most of them linked operationally to organisations external to the countries in which they operate. It follows, then, that the restructuring of state apparatuses under the PRSP framework reflects the interests and strategic locations of the parties which have gained ascendancy in political and policy circles as a result of the regulatory driving seat being vacated by the state under structural adjustment.

Reforms under SAPs were premised on the rationale that state intervention in the markets caused economic growth to stagnate and created inefficiencies and distortions in the production and delivery of goods and services, and that the potential for development lay in the retreat of the state from economic activity through the deregulation, privatisation and liberalisation of economic sectors and the removal of government support for domestic productive sectors. Meanwhile, the fiscal austerity of financial stabilisation programmes, with their ceilings on public expenditure and curbs on domestic monetary supply,[41] and the non-negotiable debt service conditions led to a reduction in the resources that could be generated and spent by the government.[42]

The imposition of such policies on developing countries has led to a steady erosion of the function of government in these countries. Removing the state from economic activity and curtailing government regulation of domestic economic sectors has served to circumscribe the role of government, leaving little left for governments – including those democratically elected to serve the interests of the electorate – to do except enforce policies set for them by external parties and create an enabling environment in which foreign capital is free to operate. The SAPRIN report concluded that many of the negative social, economic and ecological impacts of SAPs were directly correlated with the declining role of the state in national policymaking, particularly in the undermining of the state's productive, redistributional and regulatory roles (SAPRIN, 2004: 222–223).

This sentiment is echoed by Ghanaian economist and veteran activist Charles Abugre, who contends that the neoliberal policies of structural adjustment programmes have precipitated what he calls 'a new crisis of the state' in countries affected by these policies, particularly those in sub-Saharan Africa, whereby the functions of government have been gradually eroded by successful adjustment programmes to the extent that there is no effective state left. He argues: 'As a result of the policies of structural adjustment, you have a situation in Africa now where there are good, active *governments* but hardly any space for *governance*' (Abugre, 2005a).

This undermining of state capacity in countries under structural adjustment is worsened by the policies of decentralisation and accompanying reform of the public services sectors that have been pursued by the Bank and the Fund in recent years through SAPs and other lending instruments, such as community-driven development (CDD) projects and output-based aid (OBA).[43] The bypassing of central government under these circumstances further erodes the fiscal autonomy of the state and weakens the administration of national government as a whole. The undermining of national budgetary and other administrative processes though policies of decentralisation not only results in inconsistent spending allocations and uneven coverage of public services and other state functions but also weakens political accountability and creates opportunities for interventions by other parties in the political affairs of the state.

The replacement of government with private entities, such as NGOs and corporations, weakens the compact between the state and its citizens and creates the opportunity for the proliferating private, profit and non-profit sector to capture key policymaking spaces.[44] Many non-governmental, non-corporate entities working in the delivery of basic services in low-income countries are branches of large, northern-based INGOs who have, on the basis of the scale of their operations, demanded a larger voice in the policymaking process, both in the local communities and national governments and at the locus of decision-making in the north.

The influential role played by the NGO lobby in the formulation of the PRSP initiative, as highlighted in section 3.3, is significantly due to this increasingly prominent role they played in the development sector in developing countries in the period preceding the PRSP inception, notably through their increased presence at the grassroots as substitute providers of goods and services that governments were unable, due to the aforementioned constraints of SAPs to provide.

International development NGOs in particular, such as Oxfam, World Vision, Save the Children and ActionAid, which have traditionally focused on discrete and disparate project work in developing countries, soon recognised the importance of shifting policy perspectives to engender greater changes, and have increasingly used their leverage to push for policy and operational reform at higher policymaking levels. As observed by Gould and Ojanen:

> A novel feature of the PRS is the extent to which a certain category of private, non-state actors have succeeded in legitimizing demands for inclusion in the direct exercise of decision-making power.
>
> (Gould and Ojanen, 2003: 49)

3.6 Crisis and containment

PRSPs emerged in the fallout from structural adjustment programmes. In many ways, PRSPs can be viewed as mechanisms for the containment of the political and economic pressures that were building up as a result of the negative impact of SAPs in the 1980s and early 1990s, and as a response to the backlash against the neoliberal resurgence and western unilateralism that characterised international development policy and international law regulating access to development financing in the 1980s. These pressures were leading to a 'structural dilemma' of economic stagnation and negative impacts on social welfare in large tracts of the developing world, and to the potential geo-strategic consequences that would follow in the event that such pressures were not addressed and managed.

The temporal convergence between the institutional agendas of the Bretton Woods institutions and the geo-strategic need on the part of the northern countries – the 'rule-makers'[45] of the international economy and underwriters of concessional finance – to quell disquiet in the international economic order resulted in widespread support within the development financing community of the PRSP and its attendant financing instruments. At the same time, the opportunities for operationalising the disciplinary framework of the PRSP project has also been facilitated by the state reorganisation that took place under structural adjustment.

This chapter has demonstrated that while the PRSP approach shifted the conceptual approach of the multilateral development financing community, the conceptual changes that were brought about in response to the operational and political pressures faced by the dominant actors in the process, namely the institutional players – the World Bank and the IMF, and the G8 countries – were developed in collaboration with a cadre of transnational NGO advocates.[46] These NGO actors have secured a space within the international development policymaking arena through their role in linking the epistemic coalition to the larger political platform, giving a voice to the discourses that need to be articulated. However, whether in doing so this particular group of advocates have excluded necessary voices in their desire to privilege their own is a question that will be considered in later chapters.

This chapter has further shown how the dominant actors within the development financing community have been able to absorb the narratives and counter-narratives and reshape the conceptual framework of their operations to maintain their institutional and geo-political hegemony within the international economic and legal order. Organisational theorist Miller-Adams, who studied the World Bank's shifting agendas in the 1990s, observes that 'one of the primary strategies of an organization is to "buffer" its technical core from disturbances in the environment' and considers the appropriation of outside agendas and the cooptation of outside elements as one of these strategies (Miller-Adams, 1999: 17, 74). She argues that, '[b]y incorporating alien and sometimes hostile elements into their decision-making structure, organizations are able to defuse external opposition to their activities' (Miller-Adams, 1999: 74).

In this regard, the conceptual changes wrought by the PRSP framework in relation to the operational and regulatory framework of international development financing may be viewed as a means of organisational survival, a necessary systemic change to ensure the maintenance of the status quo. Consequently, as other observers have suggested, this incorporation 'reflects a conscious political containment strategy' (Pincus and Winters, 2002: 1) by an institution famous for its periodic invention (the World Bank) and an institution forced to incorporate the political demands of its major shareholders in the face of external pressures (the IMF).

This in turn was driven by the impetus to control potentially insurgent nation states in the south in the face of dissonance within the international political economy and the diminished capacity of existing disciplinary instruments, such as structural adjustment programmes, to contain an incipient revolt. At the same time, the PRSP framework tackles the danger of 'primordialism' that accompanies these countries' insertion into the system – the potentially disruptive force of an inclusion into the international economic order of countries whose domestic regulatory apparatuses lack the maturity and sophistication to perform the disciplinary and redistributive functions of a state that are imperative to governing and mitigating the effects of an integrated market economy.

The conceptual and operational emphasis on 'country ownership', 'partnership', 'participation' and 'poverty reduction' of the PRSP framework serves a dual purpose in providing the incentive for southern states to remain in the international system and instituting the requisite discipline to regulate this continued participation by providing the framework for states to diffuse internal opposition and alleviate the social and economic dislocations of economic globalisation.

However, far from reflecting a break with the relationships of power and control that underpinned the structural adjustment programmes, the PRSP framework represents instead continuity with the dynamics of difference that characterised the conceptual and operational policies under structural adjustment. The need to reconstruct the state through the imposition of a participatory process of policymaking that engages the government in discussion with the citizenry and the reassertion of state autonomy through the representational practice of 'ownership' of development policy can only be evidence of how state authority, state autonomy and state activity have been curtailed by the policies of structural adjustment and the practice of control exerted by the IFIs in pursuit of these policies.

Locating the genesis of the PRSP framework within this crisis of legitimacy in the international economic and political order enables us to critically consider how the project that ostensibly represents a progressive agenda for change – in the rhetoric of 'poverty reduction', 'participation' and 'partnership' – is conversely retrogressive in its disciplinary force. It enables us to situate the framework within its wider objectives of enforcing multilateral discipline on terms of engagement established by hegemonic state and non-state actors in the post-colonial world economy and how such a framework revises the rules of international economic law.

This evolution in the mechanisms of discipline in development financing is illustrated more starkly when examining the shift in the modalities of regulation under structural adjustment to the new disciplinary framework of the PRSPs, notably through the PRSP approach's impact on one of the most significant regulatory impacts of structural adjustment – the emergence of policy conditionality as a regulatory instrument and its development as a mechanism of economic governance. Chapter 4 considers how the disciplinary force of the PRSP initiative is translated through a corresponding revision of the modalities of conditionality for development financing.

Notes

1 The term 'post-structural adjustment', like the term 'postcolonial', is utilised in this book nomenclaturally rather than substantively or normatively. It is used to denote the temporal period of development financing in the retirement of the conceptual and operational use of 'structural adjustment' by the 'international development' community, notably the World Bank and the IMF. It does not assume that the substance of 'structural adjustment' policies has been replaced by more heterodox policy prescriptions in the facilities which succeeded such financing programmes.

2 The term 'international development community' is used here as a means of describing a particular set of actors who work on issues relating to the social and economic policies in developing countries. Most of these actors are based in the north, comprising unaffiliated individuals and individuals in international organisations such as UN agencies, the Bretton Woods institutions, INGOs, such as Actionaid, Oxfam International and World Vision, in academia and within donor organisations. In no way is the word 'international' meant to convey any notion of a truly global community in terms of inclusiveness of voices from all corners of the globe. This is not the case, as governments in the south and most civil society actors outside the key policymaking capitals of Washington, DC, Brussels and London have little input into the policy outcomes affecting development models and options.

3 This is not to say that all actors involved in this process have such deliberate intentions individually; nor are the institutional apparatuses of the Bank, Fund and bilateral donors homogeneous in their outlook or beholden to these precepts and

ambitions, but the nature of the capital and its resulting systemic power is such that these twin aims appear to be consistently recurrent in conversations and documentation over the course of this research. While they are driven by different imperatives, there is a reluctance to address or assume personal responsibility for the consequences of the policies recommended or, at best, a failure to recognise the consequences of their individual or organisational actions in a larger scheme of operations. See Biel's elucidation of structuralism, which 'sees certain phenomena as having a function, without implying that it is completely purposive' (Biel, 2000: 231). Just as '[t]he World Bank does not necessarily start from a subjective desire to promote exploitation', so the individual technocrats within the Bank and Fund and within donor agencies do not possess a desire to control, but that control is part of a systemic desire, 'so one can only conform as best as possible to it', and this system is 'driven by capital accumulation' (ibid.).

4 See Chapter 1, note 2. Higgott argues that regardless of whether there is a causal relationship between globalisation and income inequality, either within or between states, 'the identification of the correlation' is sufficient to cause 'the dispossessed to believe that globalization is the source of their plight' (Higgott, 2000: 136). Correspondingly, I argue that regardless of whether certain institutional actors central to this process of globalisation, of which SAPs form a part, believe in the veracity of this correlation, the fact that it exists necessitates an appropriate technical and/or political response.

5 There are a couple of caveats which must be stressed with regard to the work by Mosley *et al.* in this respect. First, while the authors did conduct a wide-ranging study of the World Bank's policy-based lending, their research findings are largely empirical and the authors do not attempt a larger theoretical understanding of the Bank's structural role. Second, while the authors state that the objectives of their study are to assess 'aid and power', their study is limited to an instrumental assessment of such power. The authors concentrate on assessing the power exerted by international organisations, namely the World Bank and the IMF, over the policy autonomy of developing countries (Mosley *et al.*, 1991: 3) but do not question the role played by the Bank and Fund as institutional instruments of leverage by the industrialised countries which control the institutions.

6 General Assembly Resolution 3281 (XXIX), 12 December 1974.

7 The Charter reasserted, *inter alia*, the rights of states to full sovereignty over their natural resources, authority over foreign investment, including the right not to give preferential treatment to foreign investors, the right to regulate and supervise the activities of transnational corporations and the right to expropriate and nationalise foreign property with due compensation determined by the domestic law of the nationalising state (ibid., Article 2, Chapter II).

8 Indeed, Boughton's institutional biography of the IMF, which charts the evolution of the Fund from 1979 to 1989 – the years during which SAPs were widely introduced and implemented – is revealing in its analysis of the central role played by the IMF (and, to an analogous extent, the World Bank) in restructuring the framework of international economic relations during that period and of the motivations of the actors primarily responsible for instigating these reforms (Boughton, 2001). Boughton conceives the changes wrought through structural adjustment programmes as amounting to a *Silent Revolution* (the title of his publication), one that effected 'a shift in the prevailing paradigm for international and political relations, away from tendencies toward *autarky, insularism, mercantilism, and governmental planning and control over economic activity*; and toward a common set of beliefs and policies based on open international trade and finance, competitive pricing and production decisions, and cooperation between countries' (Boughton, 2001: 3, emphasis added).

9 Former Bank chief economist Joseph Stiglitz describes as standard, for example, the IMF practice of preparing a draft report known as the 'boilerplate' in full prior to visiting a client country, in which 'whole paragraphs' had been 'borrowed from the report of one country and inserted into another' (Stiglitz, 2002: 47; see section 3.3 for a discussion of Stiglitz's influence on the Bank).

10 This figure excludes Bangladesh, which accounts for one-quarter of the economic size of the group of LDCs profiled. With the inclusion of Bangladesh, this figure rises to 2.8 per cent (UNCTAD, 2002a: 3). In sub-Saharan Africa, the poverty 'headcount' rose from 47 per cent to 49 per cent, with a corresponding zero rate of economic growth in the same period (World Bank, 2004b: 1–2).

11 It must be noted, however, that these objectives remain underpinned by objectives of overall economic growth as '[t]he policy and institutional underpinnings for rapid sustained growth and poverty reduction – including goals for poverty reduction, institutional and structural reforms, sectoral strategies and specific anti-poverty programs, and the associated domestic and external financing needs – should all be integrated into a consistent macroeconomic framework over a three-year horizon' (IMF and World Bank, 1999: para. 15).

12 Whether or not the adoption of the 'poverty' work programme is desirable or appropriate in the context of the Fund's legal and institutional jurisdiction remains subject to contestation (see Chapter 4).

13 See discussion in Chapter 2, sections 2.2 and 2.3; also in Akyüz, 2005, 2004.

14 PRSCs differ from regular development policy loans as they are normally disbursed in a series of three or four single tranches based on countries fulfilling a set of prior actions under a medium-term framework as opposed to a multi-tranche financing operation in which each subsequent disbursement is contingent upon fulfilment of a set of *ex-ante* conditions (see World Bank, 2005b: paras 9 –12; Box 1 and Annex II; see also discussion in Chapter 4).

15 See Chapter 4 for a detailed discussion of this shift in conditionality.

16 It must be stressed at this point, however, that the multilateralisation of aid is aimed primarily at harmonising aid outside the UN agencies as the UN itself represents a form of multilateralised aid that had been in place long before the PRSP approach was conceptualised.

17 As mentioned in Chapter 1, Brock *et al.* adopt a Foucauldian analysis of development policy, viewing the evolution of development policy, including 'international' development policy and poverty policy, as the result of certain voices being privileged in the process of policy formulation and of dominant discourses setting the framework through which the 'problem' of poverty is framed, constructed and resolved (Brock *et al.*, 2001).

18 Sociologist Malcolm Gladwell conceptualises this phenomenon as the 'tipping point' of social epidemics – '[t]he name given to the one dramatic moment in an epidemic where everything can change all at once' (Gladwell, 2000: 9). In the case of the PRSP, the tipping point would be the event which consolidated developments of the 1990s and served to create a catalytic shift in the policy towards aid and concessional lending to low-income countries and, consequently, a shift in the regulatory regime governing financial and economic transactions between the north and the south.

19 However, it is important to note here that while the framing of this problematic and its policy prescriptions reflect in some way the heterogeneous nature of this coalition, the overarching consensus within the coalition furnishes evidence of what Kapur terms the 'crony intellectualism' (Kapur, 2003: 12) characteristic of networks of this nature. Stone and Wright describe this predisposition as 'an in-breeding tendency within intellectual networks to contact, consult and invite to conferences those who speak the same technocratic language or come from similar academic backgrounds'

(Stone and Wright, 2007: 14). Like all knowledge networks, the contest of knowledge within this particular epistemic coalition took place within limited parameters and privileged certain mainstream voices over other more radical voices. The nature of engagement also precluded the involvement of more critical researchers who have not been invited either because they do not speak the same technocratic language as the policy advocates or because they have chosen not to engage in what they view as a flawed process.

20 Ahmed has been credited as being a key player in moving the PRSP forward as an institutional advocate of the proposed framework within the Bank as vice-president of the Bank's Poverty Reduction and Economic Management (PREM) department, and within the Fund, working specifically on the PRGF, as deputy director of its Policy Review and Development (PDR) department (interview: Whaites, 2004; see also IMF, 2000). Ahmed left the Bank shortly after the inception of the PRSPs in 1999 for its sister institution after a falling out with Bank president James Wolfensohn (Mallaby, 2004: 256–257). At the time of making the aforementioned speech, he was policy director at the UK's Department for International Development (DFID). At time of writing, he is the IMF's director of external relations. Ahmed's career itself exemplifies the effect of the revolving door characteristic of employment practice at the level of international development policymaking.

21 The study, commissioned by the United Nations Children Fund (Unicef), concluded that SAP reforms were affecting children adversely and called for 'alternative approaches to adjustment … to tackle the rising problem of debt, poverty, and social strain' (Cornia *et al.*, 1987: 3). Unicef's *Human Face* campaign, which followed on from that report, was one of the first examples in this narrative of the 'hybridisation' policy, leading to the introduction of 'social safety nets' within adjustment programmes (Brock *et al.*, 2001: 14; Whaites, 2002: 11).

22 This distinct conceptual shift in the discourse of poverty within development circles can be bracketed by two issues of the World Bank's annual flagship publication, the *World Development Report (WDR)*, the first being the *WDR 1990* on *Poverty*, which first emphasised the centrality of poverty in development policy and practice in line with the stance taken by UN agencies, such as the United Nations Development Fund (UNDP) through its *Human Development Reports*. The second *WDR 2000/01*, entitled *Attacking Poverty*, broadened this approach by addressing issues of empowerment, security and opportunity for poor people, taking a wider construction of poverty in the context of larger development objectives (see Maxwell, 2003: 8–9). The *WDRs* are influential in shaping the conceptual approaches to development policy in the international arena due to the sheer scale of their dissemination from – estimated at a minimum print run of 50,000 copies and 50,000 produced in seven other languages – and their origins in the World Bank's large research department, which lends them 'considerable weight and legitimacy' in many quarters (Mawdsley and Rigg, 2002: 5–6).

23 See further discussion in Chapter 5.

24 Who were, respectively at the time, the charismatic James Wolfensohn (see discussion in section 3.3.2) and Michel Cammedessus, a conservative bureaucrat who was fairly unconvinced of the need to incorporate larger development priorities into structural adjustment and stabilisation programmes.

25 Ahmed himself admits the negative impact the discourse on aid effectiveness has had by advocating cutbacks to the countries with 'poor' policies (Ahmed, 2004; see also discussion on 'selectivity' in Chapter 5, section 5.2, and Chapter 6, section 6.3).

26 Kanbur was also responsible for coordinating the *WDR 2000/01* on *Attacking Poverty* and resigned in the later stages of the project when Bank senior management insisted on rewriting parts of the report, eliminating some of the report's more critical elements, although the Bank has stated that it believed Kanbur's reservations to be 'unfounded' (see Bretton Woods Project, 2000).

27 A lawyer by profession, Rich was at the time head of the Washington-based lobby group Environmental Defense's international programme, examining the social and ecological impacts of the US's aid policy and the activities of multilateral development banks on developing countries.
28 Officially known as the *Effective Implementation, Key to Development Impact: Report of the World Bank's Portfolio Task Force*, the report was christened the *Wapenhans Report* after Willi Wapenhans, the Bank vice-president who oversaw the study.
29 The final report advocated, *inter alia*, severely reduced roles for the World Bank and the IMF, calling for an end to long-term lending for poverty reduction by the IMF and limited assistance from the Bank, utilising regional development banks where possible and replacing loans with grants and subsidising privately funded public goods (US Congress, 2000).
30 A former economics lecturer and economics advisor to US president Bill Clinton, Stiglitz was to become, and remains today, one of the most vociferous mainstream critics of the neoliberal economic policies set by the Washington Consensus and promulgated through the Bretton Woods institutions. Although Stiglitz's most strident criticisms were reserved for the IMF – his famous book, *Globalization and Its Discontents* (Stiglitz, 2002), created a very public spat between Stiglitz and the IMF bureaucracy in which senior IMF staff raced to the defence of the institution by denigrating the substance of the book and through personal attacks on Stiglitz himself (see Dawson, 2002) – his wide-ranging views on development policy extended to the approach adopted by the World Bank (Chang, 2001: 2).
31 In the series of papers published during his tenure at the Bank, including those that make up the volume alluded to here, Stiglitz openly attacked the narrow conception of development offered by the Washington Consensus and operationalised through the policies of the international financial institutions, including the IMF and the World Bank, and called for a more comprehensive view of economic policy which took into account the role of institutions, people and regulatory mechanisms (see Chang, 2001: 4–15).
32 Paradoxically, these counter-ideas and Stiglitz's increasingly vitriolic criticisms of the IMF orthodoxy led ultimately to his high-profile resignation from the World Bank in November 1999. Stiglitz himself has said that his resignation came as a result of increasing disillusionment with the policies of the World Bank, which were not leading to timely policy responses, and with working for reform 'from the inside' (Ambrose, 2000).
33 The political currency of Stiglitz's ideas may be demonstrated by his retention by Wolfensohn as 'special advisor to the president' after his resignation as chief economist, although pressure from the US administration later made it too difficult for the Bank to continue defending Stiglitz's attacks on the IMF and he was subsequently dropped altogether.
34 The UK government, along with the Nordic countries, was the most committed to the framework of development policy envisioned by Wolfensohn and Stiglitz in the post-structural adjustment era. On paper at least, the UK's DFID, created under the new Labour government in 1997, remains committed to channelling most of its development assistance through the PRSP framework and using budget support mechanisms (see DFID, 2009, 2004). Both Labour prime ministers, Tony Blair and Gordon Brown, also sought to capitalise politically on their support for low-income countries, particularly those in Africa through various campaigns, including the large-scale Make Poverty History campaign. Brown, in particular, had tacked his prime ministerial ambitions onto his international work and many activists viewed his encouragement of various debt relief initiatives as part of his larger political platform, responding to NGO demands that the Bretton Woods institutions be made more accountable and inclusive.

35 Callaghy provides a descriptive account of these events (see Callaghy, 2001: 140).
36 For more details on the SAPRI controversy and the findings, see SAPRIN (2004).
37 Former Malaysian prime minister Mahathir Mohammad, already a vocal critic of western dominance in the global regulatory arena, vociferously criticised the IMF and western capital for the Asian financial crisis and proceeded instead to adopt policy measures which ran contrary to the received wisdom of the IMF and the western financial establishment (see Khor, 2001 for a discussion of the Malaysian policy response to the Asian financial crisis).
38 The role of these INGOs in the PRSP framework is considered in greater detail in Chapter 6.
39 Harrison notes, for example, that the Danish donor agency DANIDA had 22 'advisors of one kind or another' within Uganda in 1998 and that numerous expatriate 'technical advisors' held significant positions within the decision-making structures of the Ugandan and Tanzanian governments during the 1990s (Harrison, 2001b: 670–671).
40 'Technical assistance' therefore has often been used as an instrument of such leverage. A common practice is to finance the travel costs of recipient government officials to attend international negotiations in exchange for the presence of a member of staff from the bilateral aid agency within the delegation, or to fund the employment of a full-time consultant from the agency within the civil service of the recipient government. This enables the aid agency to intervene and to be privy to information at the heart of policymaking within the aid recipient state.
41 This included caps on budget deficits and freezes or reductions in government expenditure levels, curbs on monetary supply in the domestic economy, including limits on domestic resource mobilisation through taxes, and the devaluation of national currencies (Rowden, 2004: 11; SAPRIN, 2004: 176).
42 For a detailed critique of the IMF's low-inflation targets and their impact on social sector spending, see Rowden, 2004.
43 This development sees the locus of decision-making and financing for development projects, particularly for infrastructure development and service delivery, being transferred from national governments to the private sector, with resources being transferred directly from aid agencies and financial institutions to sub-national governments and local communities and private entities. At the same time, sub-national governments are supposed to develop fiscal self-sufficiency and national governments are to refrain from transferring central government resources to such devolved entities or 'bailing out' insolvent or indebted sub-national governments (Alexander, 2003).
44 Harrison, for example, highlights that in the mid-1990s NGOs contributed 64 per cent of the running costs of health services in Uganda (Harrison, 2001b: 668).
45 As opposed to the 'rule-takers', states who do not have the power to underwrite the norms of the international political economy and the legal rules which bind them (see Higgott, 2000: 142).
46 The role of these INGOs will be considered in detail in Chapter 6.

Chapter 4

'Ownership' as conditionality

PRSPs and the evolution of conditional financing

> The chief function of the disciplinary power is to 'train', rather than to select and to levy; or no doubt, to train in order to levy and select all the more … The success of disciplinary power derives no doubt from the use of simple instruments: hierarchical observation, normalizing judgment, and their combination in a procedure that is specific to it – the examination.
>
> (Foucault, 1991: 188)

'Country ownership' is a key pillar of the Poverty Reduction Strategy Paper framework. This prioritisation of 'country-owned' strategies in the negotiations for development financing – including engendering a broad-based participatory policymaking process – is considered a hallmark of the PRSP approach, distinguishing it from previous modalities of financing and signifying part of a wider conceptual shift in development policy and practice.

In this respect, the principle of 'ownership' is regarded as the opposite of the doctrine of 'conditionality' – as a conceptually and operationally divergent mechanism for regulating relationships between the disbursers of development financing, notably the World Bank and the IMF, and their client states. 'Ownership' is perceived of as a departure from the practice of 'conditionality' associated with structural adjustment financing, in which the behaviour of states – with particular reference to national economic policymaking and development planning – is governed by the financing terms set by the financiers.

Conventional critiques of the PRSP approach, including reviews by Bank and Fund evaluation offices, have therefore often centred on considerations of the tension between the conceptual objectives of the PRSP framework – the engendering of ownership of national policies – and the restraining instrument of conditionality. These conflicts, along with evidence demonstrating the clear disjuncture between the policies articulated in PRSP documents and the financing instruments that these documents inform, lead to the conclusion that the PRSP framework – inserted as it is into the dynamics of an unequal relationship between parties to the initiative – does not reflect a genuine shift in the *modus operandi* of the financing institutions and the international aid regime.

This chapter contends that the PRSP framework *does* represent a marked shift in the mechanisms of aid regulation, but, conversely, it does so in terms of the impact it has had in entrenching conditionality as a mechanism for regulation. In examining this shift, I argue that the principle of 'ownership' must be situated within the continuum of the conditionality doctrine rather than being perceived of as a break in the evolution of this regulatory instrument. Locating the concept of 'ownership' within the evolutionary history of conditionality enables us to examine the significance of the PRSP approach within the constitution of global governance and international law through an analysis of its impact on one of the most important regulatory mechanisms of the postcolonial era.

This chapter argues that the principle of 'ownership' as articulated under the PRSP framework and the accompanying 'new architecture of aid' must not be conflated with the principle of policy autonomy, which is clearly conceptually divergent from the doctrine of conditionality. Rather, 'ownership' should be viewed as an extension and refinement of the doctrine of conditionality, which, over the decades since the inception of the Bretton Woods institutions, has evolved not only to alter the relationships between the Bank and Fund and their borrowing members, but also to reshape these members' engagement in the wider global economy. The progressive entrenchment of conditionality as a regulatory instrument thus facilitated the emergence of the BWIs as the powerful institutions of postcolonial economic governance alluded to in Chapter 2.

The emergence of the principle of 'ownership' within the framework of the PRSPs and the new modalities of development financing therefore reflects the refinement of a specific instrument of disciplinary control over postcolonial economies that has evolved in tandem with the economic and geo-strategic imperatives in the international order. It is argued here that the fundamental *objectives* of conditionality as it has developed have not changed with the introduction of the PRSP approach. Instead, the *modalities* of conditionality have substantially altered, representing a deeper and more intrusive form of disciplinary control that has produced new mechanisms for controlling and restructuring state apparatuses in the third world.

4.1 Deconstructing conditionality

'Conditionality' represents the regulatory aspect of the relationship between parties involved in international development financing, most notably between the World Bank and the IMF and their client states. While the doctrine of conditionality shares similar characteristics with other contractual instruments, the nature and practical application of conditionality are largely peculiar to the relationship it regulates and to the type of financing that is being regulated. The disciplinary force of conditionality does not derive exclusively (and often not primarily) from standard contractual sanctions but from the wider economic and geo-political impact of non-compliance.

Conditionality polices what Degnbol-Martinussen and Engberg-Pedersen term 'the interface between normative and operational activities' (Degnbol-Martinussen and Engberg-Pedersen, 2003: 96), providing the framework to ensure that financed projects and programmes in recipient countries meet the normative objectives of the bilateral or multilateral donor or official creditor, notably the objectives of policy and institutional reform. It is the combination of fiduciary, political and policy elements of conditionality which makes this instrument particularly suited to regulating the relationship between the financiers and clients in receipt of development finance.

4.1.1 Conditionality versus conditions for financing

Like other contractual financing obligations, the principle of conditionality contains a fiduciary component requiring the performance of due diligence on the part of the financing institutions to minimise the risk of a debt default or a departure from agreed financing objectives. However, the scope and scale of this exercise under the doctrine of conditionality are far greater and much more intrusive than when undertaken in standard contractual or fiduciary relationships.

This reflects not only the disproportionate gap in bargaining power involved between the donor/lender and the client/borrower, but also the disciplinary objective of development financing as a whole, that is, to compel the client state to undertake domestic reforms in pursuit of objectives – social, economic or political – of the financier state or financing institution. The World Bank itself acknowledges conditionality's disciplinary force, admitting that conditionality 'is involved whenever the donor has the right to halt the flow of resources if the recipient country does not meet certain conditions' (World Bank, 2005c: 2). This link between the disbursement of funds and 'the implementation of a desired action of policy' (World Bank, 2005b: para. 1) is often the only sanction for non-compliance given the ambiguous legal nature of conditionality (see the discussion on p. 98).

'Conditionality' must be distinguished from 'conditions of financing' in the context of development financing agreements. 'Conditionality' refers to conditions which regulate the aspect of the economic programme or specific institutional or structural reforms that is being financed by the financing agency or institution, at either the national or sectoral level. Such programme or policy conditionalities are not specified in the legal agreements for financing but are, instead, incorporated by reference in such contracts (see the discussion below; also Tan, 2006b: 14, Box 2). These may include prior actions and tranche release conditions for the Bank and quantitative performance criteria and programme reviews for the Fund (see Box 4.1).

In contrast, 'conditions for financing' are comprised of the terms of the legal agreement between the financing entity and the client state, including financial conditions pertaining to the repayment period, loan charges, interest rate, procedures for loan withdrawals and policies on cancellation and dispute settlement

Box 4.1: Examples of programme conditionalities

The form and substance of conditionality varies from institution to institution, but the following are examples of what the World Bank and IMF consider core programme conditionalities. These conditionalities are incorporated by reference in the legal agreement (for all Bank loans) or financing arrangement (for IMF drawings):

- *Prior actions*: policy actions or measures to be adopted by the client government before approval of a loan or financing arrangement by the Bank or Fund Executive Boards or, in the case of the IMF, before the completion of a programme review.
- *Tranche release conditions*: policy actions which must be implemented before disbursement of each tranche of a standard multi-tranche loan by the World Bank. The Bank Executive Board may grant a waiver of conditions subject to circumstances.
- *Performance criteria*: the IMF's equivalent of a tranche release condition. An IMF programme may be suspended (or go 'off track') if performance criteria are not met. Compliance with performance criteria may be waived by the IMF Executive Board under certain circumstances.
- *Programme reviews*: the IMF conducts regular reviews of adjustment programmes it finances to assess if the programme is on track, taking into account the member's observance of other conditionalities. Conditionalities may be modified or new policy actions imposed as an outcome of a programme review.

In addition to the binding conditionalities above, the Bank and Fund also impose other conditions on their clients. These are not formally classified as 'conditionalities' as they may not be loan-specific and/or are not formally determinative of disbursements. They are:

- *Triggers*: triggers are what the Bank considers policy 'expectations' which inform the Bank's decision to lend. Implementation of Country Assistance Strategy (CAS) triggers informs the Bank's lending portfolio to a particular country, while triggers in programmatic operations, along with *outcome conditions*, form the basis of the Bank's decision to proceed with the second loan in the series and can form the prior actions for the second loan.
- *Benchmarks*: benchmark measures are 'milestones' or standards against which a country's performance under a programmatic operation is measured at the Bank. Like triggers, they are not tied to disbursements but can be used to inform future lending decisions and form prior actions for the next loan. *Structural benchmarks* are used in IMF programmes to assess country's compliance with policy actions in programme reviews, along with *indicative targets*.

Source: IMF (2009e); World Bank (2005c).

provisions (Agarwal, 2000: 1–9; Tan, 2006b: 18). In policy-based loans, this will also include a covenant referring to the 'programme' of policy reform or stabilisation that is being financed and an undertaking by the client state that it shall implement such a programme in exchange for financing[1] (Tan, 2006b: 14, Box 2).

Failure to comply with such policy or programme conditionality will not necessarily mean a breach of a legal covenant but may be considered evidence of such a breach if the financing institution deems it fundamental to the agreement (see, for example, Shihata, 2000a: 14–21). From a legal perspective, therefore, a borrower does not usually breach a legal obligation should it fail to comply with policy conditionalities. Instead, the penalty would be the non-disbursement of funds under the agreement (World Bank, 2005d: 1, para. 1). Failure of compliance can also have other financial repercussions for the defaulting state due to the 'signalling role' performed by the Bretton Woods institutions, notably the IMF, vis-à-vis other sources of finance (see section 4.1.4).

4.1.2 IMF conditionality

IMF conditionality applies to all its financing arrangements. While the use of conditionality is not unique to Fund operations, the IMF may be regarded as the originator of conditionality as we know it today. This is ironic given that the link between the policies of a Fund member and access to its resources was rejected at its founding conference at Bretton Woods in 1944 for fear of jeopardising members' access to financial resources. The idea that a member state seeking financial assistance from the cooperative monetary union of the IMF would be subjected to conditions requiring domestic policy and regulatory reforms engendered much discord among its founding members. While the UK – concerned that conditional financing would not just jeopardise access to resources but also impinge upon national sovereignty – sought unconditional access to IMF reserves subject to quota limitations, the US (as the Fund's largest shareholder) rejected the idea of automatic financing and insisted that conditions be applied to drawings to safeguard the institution's resources[2] (Akyüz, 2006: 490; Woods, 2006: 25; Vreeland, 2007: 21–22).

The result was an ambiguous compromise in the Articles of Agreement of the IMF which provided – under the original Article V, Section 3 – that each member could draw on the resources of the Fund when the member needed to, subject to the member representing to the Fund that such drawings were both necessary and consistent with the provisions of the Articles of Agreement (Akyüz, 2006: 491; 2004: 13; Lowenfeld, 2008: 611). In 1947, the IMF's Executive Board authorised the institution to challenge representations by members if there was reason to believe that such drawings were not needed or that the payments would be inconsistent with the Articles of Agreement (Akyüz, 2006: 492).

Consequently, in spite of its initial rejection, the process of ratcheting up conditionality started soon after the conclusion of negotiations (Akyüz, 2004: 19;

Woods, 2006: 25). The principle of conditionality was adopted by the IMF's Executive Board on 13 February 1952, which, while reiterating that resources should not be denied to members in 'temporary' financial difficulties, stated for the first time that in disbursing the resources 'the Fund should pay attention to a member's *general creditworthiness*, particularly *its record with the Fund*' (IMF, 1952, emphasis added).[3]

In their consideration of this aspect of conditionality, Mosley *et al.* conceive of conditionality as 'a side condition designed to ensure the execution of a *contract*', the contract being that of a lending agreement between the financing party and the financee (Mosley *et al.*, 1991: 66). The authors contend that, unlike conventional financing contracts, in this case the international financial institution involved in lending to sovereign states does not have much in a way of guarantee in the event of debt default because there is no practice of collateral lending in international finance. Conditionality therefore serves as 'a substitute for collateral' by 'increasing the likelihood of loan repayment' through policy reform and monitoring of compliance with such reforms, thereby 'giving the lender an early warning of potential repayment difficulties' (ibid.).

The 1952 provisions were extended and codified in the Fund's constitution by the First Amendment to the Articles of Agreement in 1969.[4] Notably, Article V was amended to *constitutionally mandate* the use of conditionality in Fund financing. It now reads:

> Section 3. Conditions governing use of the Fund's general resources
>
> (*a*) The Fund shall adopt policies on the use of its general resources … that will assist members to solve their balance of payments problems in a manner consistent with the provisions of this Agreement and that will establish *adequate safeguards* for the temporary use of the general resources of the Fund.
>
> (IMF Articles of Agreement, Article V, Section 3(a), emphasis added)

The IMF membership has since interpreted this provision as one delegating authority to the institution to implement its own policies to ensure that funds are disbursed in accordance with its fiduciary objectives under the Articles of Agreement. The Fund has subsequently implemented this through the issuance of guidelines on the modalities and practice of conditionality in general, such as the Guidelines on Conditionality and the conditions established under the special disbursement instruments, such as the Poverty Reduction and Growth Facility (PRGF) Trust Instrument.

The IMF's revised Guidelines on Conditionality 2002 reaffirmed that the purpose of conditionality is to ensure that Fund resources provided to members needing financial assistance are utilised 'in a manner that is consistent with the Fund's Articles and that establishes *adequate safeguards* for the temporary use of the Fund's resources' (IMF, 2002a: para. 1, emphasis added). As such, a member's application for Fund assistance 'will be *approved only if* the Fund is satisfied that the *member's program is consistent with the Fund's provisions and policies* and that it will be carried out, and in particular that the *member is sufficiently committed to implement the programme*' (IMF, 2002a: para. 5, emphasis added).

The exercise of conditionality is therefore governed by the provisos contained in these documents and in Executive Board decisions on financing arrangements for individual countries rather than by the constitutional provisions of the Fund's Articles of Agreement. Over the years, this discretionary authority has been strengthened, in tandem with the increasing power asymmetries at the Fund (see Chapter 2, section 2.2.2), to the extent that constitutional oversight is limited, if not non-existent, in the practice of conditionality, contrary to the initial objectives of conditionality.

4.1.3 World Bank conditionality

For the World Bank, conditionality is synonymous with policy-based lending as it is through this form of financing that conditionality was first introduced at the institution (see World Bank, 2005d: para. 5). The advent of structural adjustment lending changed the landscape of development financing by disbursing credit for policy reform ('adjustment') in the borrowing states as opposed to lending to fund specific development projects (see section 4.2.2; also World Bank, 2005d: para. 5).

Approval of financing in the form of structural adjustment loans – now known as development policy loans – hinged on two preconditions: (1) the country was anticipating or experiencing balance of payments problems, necessitating 'rapidly disbursing' external financing; and (2) the country's government would agree to a programme of policy reform or 'adjustment' in return for financing (Shihata, 2000a: 377; World Bank, 2005d: paras 1–2). Conditionality was brought into play to monitor country compliance with the latter programme of reform.

Mosley *et al.* distinguish World Bank conditionality from the IMF's rationale for conditionality on this basis. The authors argue that unlike the IMF's basis for administering conditionality – serving as a collateral substitute – the purpose of conditionality in the Bank's policy-based lending is not to increase the likelihood of loan repayment but rather is a means of administering reforms to remove 'policy-induced obstacles' to wider developmental objectives, notably economic growth (Mosley *et al.*, 1991: 66–67). Although this objective has been revised in the switchover from adjustment lending to development policy lending to encompass goals such as 'poverty reduction', the core purpose of policy-based loans remains the same, that is, to 'support a program of policy and institutional actions' (World Bank, 2004d: para. 2).

This is reflected in the Bank's operational policy on policy-based loans today. The new Operational Policy on Development Lending (OP 8.60) restated the provisions in the substituted Operational Directive on Adjustment Lending (OD 8.60), which enables the Bank to specify 'which policy and institutional actions by the country are critical for the implementation and expected results of the program supported by the development policy loan' (World Bank, 2004d: para. 13). While reiterating that there is 'no formal definition of "conditionality"' in the institution's legal framework or operational policy or procedures, the Bank's legal department has adopted the three requirements stipulated in OP 8.60 as 'essential conditions' for loan disbursements that are 'appropriately reflected in the legal agreement for these operations' (World Bank, 2005d: para. 9).

The OP 8.60 states that disbursements of policy-based loans are contingent upon: (1) the maintenance of an adequate macroeconomic policy framework;[5] (2) implementation of the overall programme in a manner satisfactory to the Bank; and (3) compliance with critical policy and institutional actions (World Bank, 2004d: para. 13). In this manner, conditionality serves as a 'trigger' for financial disbursements from the Bank, non-compliance with which will halt such transfers. In single-tranche loans (such as PRSCs), funds are made available when the borrower complies with all the necessary conditions for disbursement, while in multi-tranche operations, disbursements are made in stages 'as successive program conditions are met' (ibid.: para. 11–13).

4.1.4 Policy regulation

Conditionality is primarily a means of regulating the behaviour of the party in receipt of financing through the terms of credit disbursement, including the securing of compliance with certain performance criteria, and/or a programme of measures prior to or after the disbursement of funds from the financing party (Buira, 2003: 3; Kalderimis, 2004: 103). Some of these criteria and policies may be relevant to the technical exercise of due diligence on the part of the financing institutions or agencies, but, as this and following chapters demonstrate, most of the requirements set in these arrangements go beyond standard financial obligations to include changes in government policy and reform of state institutions.

The penalty for non-adherence to these terms of financing is the withdrawal of financing and/or ineligibility for further financing, as well as the attendant consequences of this withdrawal of support, including the effect this has on the borrower's credit rating in the international capital markets and/or with other bilateral and multilateral development financiers resulting from the signalling role of the IMF and World Bank (see Chapter 2; also Babb and Buira, 2004: 14). Conditionality therefore acts as a mechanism for policy leverage, 'a tool by which a country is made to adopt specific policies or to undertake certain reforms that it would not have undertaken, in exchange for support' (Buira, 2003: 3).

The combination of the policy reform content of conditionality and the link between such policy prescriptions and financial resources has lead Kalderimis to conclude that the practice of conditionality is a form of 'regulation by appropriation' (Kalderimis, 2004: 105). Here, regulatory norms are inserted into a jurisdiction – in this case, within a country subject to conditionality – through the terms of their financing arrangements and outside conventional arenas of norm-creation (ibid.). Accordingly, Braithwaite and Drahos view 'conditionality' as 'an enabling principle' – an operationalising mechanism through which 'states which are subject to it have to accept and institutionalize other principles … in a range of regulatory domains'[6] (Braithwaite and Drahos, 2000: 525).

It is this wide regulatory impact – the impact of conditions of lending outside the subject of the loans – which not only differentiates the doctrine of conditionality from conventional contractual principles but also represents the source of contention with conditionality. For Braithwaite and Drahos, as 'global regulatory norms [tend to] follow self-regulatory practice', the instrument of conditionality may therefore be viewed as activating the globalisation of regulatory norms through promoting the operation of such norms or principles in the countries under its jurisdiction (Braithwaite and Drahos, 2000: 491, 525). Accordingly, conditionality functions as an instrument of economic coercion deployed by the Bank and the Fund, on behalf of its powerful members, to pursue the globalisation of economic regulation by tying financial disbursement to compliance with prescribed regulatory business norms (ibid.: 525–535).[7]

The intensification of this regulatory role and the BWIs' progressive encroachment into areas outside their original mandate through the use of conditionality are central to contemporary critiques of conditionality. Over the years, conditionality has evolved into an important means of facilitating the roles of the Bank and Fund as intermediaries between third world states and the international arena, emerging not only as a default mechanism for regulating the relationship between the BWIs and their borrowers, but also as an instrument of international economic governance.

4.2 Conditionality as a default regulatory instrument

The emergence of conditionality as a default mechanism for regulating the relationship between the BWIs and their clients stems largely from the Bank and Fund's reluctance to employ full – or, in the case of the IMF, *any* – contractual force in their policy-based financing arrangements with members. While the rationale for this reluctance and its operational effect differ between the two institutions, the outcome has been the progressive intensification of conditionality as a mode of regulation and a corresponding expansion of the regulatory scope of conditionality.

The consequence of these developments has been the construction of a highly discretionary regime of financing, relying on the supervision of client states by an army of trained and expert staff with correspondingly few fixed rules of guidance (Woods, 2006: 25–26) and fewer constitutional limitations on the decision-making powers conferred on Bank and Fund bureaucrats. For Woods, this discretion accorded to the Bank and the Fund not only gave the US, as the major shareholder, a measure of influence over the financing policies of the institution; 'it also cast a large role' for the technocrats at the institutions in their advisory role to the Executive Boards in determining how and what conditions are imposed on borrowing countries (Woods, 2006: 27) without the necessary checks and balances on such discretion.

4.2.1 Evolution of IMF conditionality

a) From automaticity to conditional financing

The use of conditionality as a mechanism for regulating the relationship between the IMF and its borrowing member states intensified largely as a result of the IMF's traditional refusal to classify Fund arrangements – notably funding from the General Resources Account (GRA)[8] – as conventional contracts, in partial deference to its founders' original design for an international credit union and in recognition of the source of such financing and the Fund's constitutional obligation under Article 1 (v) to provide counter-cyclical financing to members facing financial difficulties (IMF, 2001b: 8, 19–21; see also the discussion in section 4.1.2).

Funds in the GRA are drawn from a repository of members' currencies lodged with the Fund through quota subscriptions or via standby credit arrangements with members' central banks,[9] and, as such, drawing upon Fund resources by member countries to meet balance of payments deficits can therefore be construed as akin to asserting a *right* as an IMF member to draw upon funds to which it contributed under the terms of the IMF's constitutional charter. The 'language of credit' is therefore absent in the construction of IMF agreements as a result of the founding ethos of the institution to treat as a right this automaticity of financing under the Articles of Agreement (Akyüz, 2004: 13).

The revised Guidelines on Conditionality 2002 thus reaffirmed the decision made in the original Guidelines on the Use of the IMF's General Resources and Stand-By Arrangements 1979, stating that:

> A Fund arrangement is a *decision of the Executive Board* by which a member is assured that it will be able to make purchases or receive disbursements from the Fund in accordance with the terms of the decision during a specified period and up to a specified amount. Fund arrangements are not international agreements and therefore language having contractual connotation will be *avoided* in arrangements and in program documents.
>
> (IMF, 2002a: para. 9, emphasis added)

Accordingly, a member's use of Fund's resources should be governed by the provisions of its constitution so as to represent its obligations to the membership of states that the institution represents, rather than by contractual terms entered into between itself and the institution as a bureaucracy. However, as suggested by former IMF general counsel Joseph Gold, it is this difficulty with defining breaches and administering penalties for breaches of the Fund's Articles of

Agreement that has led to the creation of facilities such as the SBAs and the resulting mechanism of conditionality to regulate the behaviour of members and meet the institution's fiduciary obligations under the charter without recourse to contractual terminology (Gold, 1996: 343–355; see the following discussion).

Although the IMF's Articles of Agreement enable the IMF to limit or suspend members' access to its general resources under Article V, Section 5 (for using funds 'in a manner contrary to the purposes of the Fund'), Article VI, Section 1 (for using funds to meet a large or sustained outflow of capital), or under Article XXVI, Section 2(a) (for failure to fulfil any obligations in the charter), there is ambiguity as to the interpretation of these provisions. Here, the difficulty in prescribing uniform criteria for establishing what measures are adequate to constitute fulfilment of a member's obligations under the respective provisions – such as what constitutes appropriate use under Article V, Section 5 – has led to reluctance on the part of Fund members to consider failure to comply with financing conditions as a breach of a member's constitutional obligations (Gold, 1996: 345).

Regulation of a member's economic policies vis-à-vis its obligation to the Fund and its constitution therefore turned to a less legalistic regime of conditionality as a mechanism was needed to act as fiduciary instrument. This instrument had to ensure that resources from the Fund are utilised in accordance with its mandate but without the penalty of a constitutional violation should this obligation not be fulfilled. The aforementioned 1952 Executive Board decision adopting the principle of conditionality thus also established Stand-By Arrangements as the operational modality for drawings from the GRA. As a line of credit extended by the IMF to a member facing balance of payments problems, an SBA assures a requesting member that it will be able to draw from the GRA in accordance with agreed terms (IMF Articles of Agreement, Article XXX(b)). In other words, SBAs were introduced so that a programme of economic adjustment could be designed prior to disbursement of resources and that disbursement was made contingent upon the fulfilment of the conditions of the programme design.

Countries who wish to borrow from the Fund beyond their reserve tranche[10] would have to submit a Letter of Intent (LOI) and/or a Memorandum of Economic and Financial Policy (MEFP) stipulating policy measures the country authorities would undertake in return for financial assistance (IMF, 2002a: para. 10; see Figure 3 on pp. 230–1).[11] Once approved, this programme of economic adjustment constitutes the basis for considering the country's eligibility to draw from the Fund, with the measures contained in the programme serving as the conditions for the financial assistance. Policy reforms are then implemented through an Executive Board decision approving the SBA or Extended Arrangement constituting the financing arrangement, with conditionality serving as the means of enforcing compliance.

Consequently, the practice of conditionality has gradually eroded the automaticity of Fund financing over time. The introduction of phased drawings in 1956 and the use of performance criteria, policy actions that must be implemented before each tranche of the financial package is released (see Box 4.1), further cemented the move away from automatic drawings. Commentators have suggested that this extensive use of conditionality policies as a regulatory mechanism has curtailed any real sense of *entitlement* of an IMF member country to draw beyond its reserve tranche, with the focus shifting progressively towards the *content* of conditionality policies rather than the *role* of conditionality (Kalderimis, 2004: 115; see also Akyüz, 2004: 19–21). As Kalderimis notes, 'most of the debate now centres on the meaning of "adequate safeguards" in Article 1(v)/ Article V (3)(a)', reserving the right of the IMF to require conditions for use of its credit and to determine what those conditions should be (Kalderimis, 2004: 115).

b) Trust funds and concessional financing

The evolution from automatic to conditional financing at the IMF was reinforced by the introduction of concessional financing via trust funds in the late 1970s (see section 4.3.1). The Second Amendment of the Articles of Agreement in 1979 conferred upon the IMF the power to grant concessional loans to low-income countries under Article V, Section 2 (b), which provides that: 'If requested, the Fund may decide to perform financial and technical services, including the administration of resources contributed by members, that are consistent with the purposes of the Fund'[12] (IMF Articles of Agreement; see also Gold, 1996: 368–369).

A significant distinction between financing under the IMF's General Resources Account and financing under the concessional lending trusts is the treatment of the legal status by the Fund of the financing agreement between the IMF and the borrowing member states under the two types of financing. In contrast to SBAs and other arrangements to borrow from the general resources, financing from the trust funds – such as the Poverty Reduction and Growth Trust – is clearly defined as 'loans'. For example, Section 1(1) of the Instrument to Establish the PRGF Trust states: 'The Trust shall assist in fulfilling the purposes of the Fund by providing *loans* on concessional terms ... to low-income developing members that qualify for assistance' (IMF, 1999, emphasis added).

The language of credit in these financing instruments has, once again, roots in the nature and source of such financing. Unlike financing from the general resources, financing from the IMF trust funds involves drawing on funds that have not been contributed by the borrowers themselves but rather are 'loans' from other sources, the interest rate on which is subsidised by the respective trusts.[13] The language of constitutional obligation and cooperative purpose that characterises the SBAs does not seem to apply to PRGT financing.[14] Funds from the PRGF are clearly earmarked for countries who meet the eligibility criteria for assistance from better-off members, and disbursement of these funds is clearly contingent upon compliance with Fund policy conditionalities.

As trustee, the IMF is also under a fiduciary duty to ensure that the terms and conditions of the trust instrument are complied with, but the Fund is generally accorded wide powers of discretion to determine the terms of eligibility and conditions for financial assistance to eligible members. Again, for example, Sections II (1)(b) and (bb) of the Instrument to Establish the PRGF Trust provide that assistance should be given to a qualifying member upon approval by the Fund of a three-year macroeconomic and structural adjustment programme, with disbursements contingent upon reviews of the country's performance under the programme, including compliance with key structural reform policies (IMF, 1999: Sections I–II).

However, the instrument is silent on the content of the structural adjustment programme to be undertaken and on the criteria for determining compliance with the conditions for policy reform in the borrowing member state. Under the respective trust instruments, it is left to the trustee – the IMF – to determine the phasing of loan disbursements and the conditions attached to such disbursements 'in the context of a review of the program with the member' (see IMF, 1999: Section II, para. 1(bb)). Once again, this leaves the IMF with broad discretionary authority to determine the content of loan conditions and when and if those conditions are met by borrowers. As discussed on pp. 103–105, there is a reluctance on the part of the Fund to declare members ineligible under Article V, Section 5, for failure to comply with the conditions of their loans. Similarly here, conditionality offers a less punitive mechanism for disciplining errant borrowers which still enables the Fund to link policy compliance with the disbursement of resources.

Therefore, it may be argued that the difference between financing from the GRA and from specially administered accounts, such as those under the PRGT, does not substantially alter the nature of IMF conditionality with respect to individual facilities. Conditionality remains the primary mechanism by which the relationship between the Fund and its members is regulated, the preference for such 'soft law' stemming from a reluctance to both confer on members or hold members accountable to obligations under formal IMF law, that is, those originating from its Articles of Agreement or from its formal trust instruments.

4.2.2 Conditionality and the Bank's new role

a) From projects to policy reform

The doctrine of conditionality under policy-based lending has shifted the Bank's fiduciary role from a purely technical focus – adherence to the technical obligations of traditional development financing (project documentation) – to an increasingly political role of monitoring policy reform as a means of contractual compliance. As discussed on pp. 100–101, conditionality under World Bank structural adjustment was primarily focused on achieving influence over the levers of government policy, viewed as an end in itself as opposed to a means to an end to prevent debt default, as is the purpose of Fund conditionality.

This distinction stems in part from the difference in legal construction of the Bank's lending versus the Fund's. Financing instruments of the World Bank are clearly regarded as loans and give rise to contractual obligations (World Bank, 2001a: paras 8–9; interview: Zerabruk and Braka, 2004). Bank loan agreements are classified as international treaties between the borrowing member state and the World Bank and are registered as such with the secretary-general of the United Nations pursuant of Article 102 of the United Nations Charter.[15]

Therefore, unlike the Fund, where the relationship between the organisation and its members is defined by their constitutional obligations under the founding treaty, the Bank operates very much like a financial institution, in which the principal legal instrument that regulates the relationship between itself and a borrower is that of a contractual legal agreement for financing. This includes agreements for policy-based loans even though the Bank admits that such operations sit uneasily with the Bank's traditional contractual framework because there is no specific 'project' for the borrower to 'carry out' in exchange for financing (World Bank, 2005d: para. 36).

However, the Bank has traditionally adopted a broad interpretation of the term 'project', to encompass 'development programs' as a whole[16] (Shihata, 2000a: 177). Former Bank general counsel Ibrahim Shihata notes that 'the practice of the Bank has consistently upheld a broad definition of the term "project" which covered "programs" where specific goods and/or services were allocated for well-defined purposes' (Shihata, 2000a: 178). This programme of economic policy and institutional reform therefore constitutes the *object* of the agreement between the Bank and the borrowing country and it follows that obligations of the parties involved would still be governed by the terms and conditions of a standard Bank agreement.[17] In project or investment operations, loan agreements 'describe the project objectives and components', but in policy-based loans, the agreements refer to the borrower's programme that the loan supports (World Bank, 2005d: para. 35; 2001a: paras 12, 16).

b) Circumventing constitutional limitations

The classification of a policy-based loan as constituting a 'project' for all legal intents and purposes also enables the Bank to resolve one of the most pressing constitutional questions that has arisen since the introduction of such lending – that is, whether such loans constitute a violation of the Bank's constitutional charter, which stipulates that the Bank should be primarily involved in 'project' lending.

Article III, Section 4 (vii) of the IBRD's Articles of Agreement states: 'Loans made or guaranteed by the Bank, shall, except in *special circumstances*, be for the *specific projects* of reconstruction and development' (emphasis added). A corresponding provision in the Articles of Agreement of the IDA states:

> Financing provided by the Association shall be for purposes which in the opinion of the Association are of high developmental priority in the light of the needs of the area or areas concerned and, except in *special circumstances*, shall be for *specific projects*.
>
> (IDA Articles of Agreement, Article V, Section 1(b), emphasis added)

The Bank has traditionally relied upon the 'special circumstances' exception[18] in the Bank charters to justify their disbursement of policy-based loans. Although the definition of and criteria for accessing what constitutes a 'special circumstance' were left to be 'determined on a case by case basis', Shihata has contended that these circumstances must be assessed in accordance with the Bank's constitutionally mandated purposes under Article I of the IBRD (and, by extension, IDA) Articles of Agreement:[19] 'If a Bank loan therefore does not directly finance a specific productive purpose, it must aim at serving other Bank purposes' (Shihata, 2000a: 379).

As a result of Shihata's authoritative legal opinions on this issue, the World Bank has been circumspect about the volume of its policy-based lending compared with its investment or project loans. The old OD 8.60 (see p. 100) set a guideline ceiling that the share of adjustment lending should not normally exceed 25 per cent of the total IBRD and IDA commitments over three years (World Bank, 2002a: para. 17). However, with the exception increasingly becoming the norm over the years – the combined share of such lending from the IBRD and IDA has reached or exceeded the one-third threshold since 1998 (ibid.; World Bank, 2009e: 1, para. 3) – the Bank has progressively disregarded this legal constraint and reinterpreted the constitutional provision to suit the evolving circumstances.

The new OP 8.60 dispensed with the quota on such lending, providing instead that the volume or share of development policy lending for a borrower be established on a case-by-case basis, determined in the context of the country's Country Assistance Strategy (see pp. 113–114) and that each policy-based operation must be approved by the executive directors as meeting the 'special circumstances' justification under the Articles of Agreement (World Bank, 2004c: paras 3, 4, 8; see also World Bank, 2002a: para. 17). The 25 per cent ceiling was replaced by an annual report by Bank management on the anticipated Bank-wide share of development policy lending in total lending, and on the basis of this report executive directors would issue guidelines for the average annual share of development policy lending on a rolling three-year basis[20] (World Bank, 2009e: 1, fn. 2).

Conditionality thus became increasingly important as a means of justifying policy-based loans under the aforementioned constitutional exception by linking the conditions of the reform programme with the constitutional objectives of the World Bank and meeting Shihata's 'productive purposes' criteria. The Bank's legal department notes that conditionalities perform a corresponding function in policy-based lending as the 'specific legal covenants' found in investment/project lending which 'require the borrower to carry out a project ... with due diligence and efficiency' (World Bank, 2005d: para. 31). It states that: 'Conditionality serves the role of a *useful navigational aid* to keep the borrower's development program *on course* to ensure its productive outcomes and objectives are achieved' (World Bank, 2005d: para. 31, emphasis added).

In contrast to an agreement for investment/project lending whereby the borrower is under a 'legal obligation to carry out a specific project', the World Bank does not regard the borrowing country's 'commitment to execute its program' as contractually enforceable for two reasons: (1) it could impinge upon the sovereign prerogative to determine policy and institutional actions to insist on compliance; and (2) 'treating a borrower's failure to implement a policy action as a breach of a legal obligation owed to the Bank could create significant financial repercussions for the country', including loss of other donor support and the borrower's standing in international financial markets[21] (World Bank, 2005d: paras 38–39).

Consequently, it is argued here that the emergence of conditionality as a regulatory instrument in Bank policy-based lending – in spite of these loans' differing legal status to Fund financing – was also driven primarily by a reluctance to impose full contractual force on policy conditions in light of both constitutional ambiguity regarding the mandate of the Bank to finance such programmes *and* the political ramifications of subjecting such financing to the rigour of conventional contractual enforcement. Bank counsels such as Shihata have routinely advised Bank staff that while there should be explicit and precise documentation of disbursement conditions in loan agreements, such agreements have to be structured '*to avoid covenanted legal obligations*' (Shihata, 2000a: 382–383).

Accordingly, policy-based lending arrangements at the World Bank have adopted a similar regulatory structure to that of the Fund, placing policy conditionalities within separate programme documents established prior to the financing agreement – the Letter of Development Policy (LDP) and/or a Medium-Term Expenditure Framework (MTEF) – detailing a programme of actions, objectives and policies and incorporated by reference into the loan agreements (World Bank, 2001a: para. 16). Financing is made contingent upon the borrower's implementation of the programme 'in a manner satisfactory to the Bank' (World Bank, 2004c: para. 13; see also Republic of Mauritania, 1987, Preamble: para. (A); Republic of Uganda, 2001, Preamble: para. (B)), thereby reinforcing the discretionary power of the Bank to stipulate conditions for financing.

Although non-compliance with programme conditions may not constitute a breach of a contractual obligation, the General Conditions for IBRD and IDA lending stipulate that the Bank may suspend financial transfers under the loan agreement if the borrower fails to perform its debt service or *any other obligation* under the agreement (IBRD General Conditions for Loans, 1 July 2005 (amended 12 February 2008), section 7.02; IDA General Conditions for Credits and Grants, 1 July 2005, section 6.02).The borrower is also under an obligation to consult the Bank 'on any proposed action' that would have the effect of 'materially reversing' the programme's objectives or 'any actions taken under it', including tranche release conditions, both during and after disbursements (World Bank, 2005d: paras 41, 46).

This means that failure to comply with a condition of a World Bank programme will not necessarily mean a breach of a legal covenant but it may be considered evidence of a violation of the terms of the lending agreement if the Bank deems it fundamental to the agreement. Countries may risk violating their financing terms if they fail to implement the policies contained in the agreed programme in a manner acceptable to the Bank. Determination of this, as the discussion below highlights, rests largely with Bank staff, its management and the Executive Board, and involves reviews of critical policy actions and institutional decisions of its clients, reaffirming the discretionary power of the Bank over constitutional oversight.

4.3 Conditionality as a mechanism for economic governance

The progressive entrenchment of conditionality as a default instrument for regulating the relationship between the BWIs and their client states has contributed significantly to the development of conditionality as a mechanism for economic governance. Chapter 2 demonstrated that the disciplinary power of the Bank and the Fund is derived not only from their role as financiers but also from their constitution as economic governance institutions and the legitimacy they derive from the 'multilateral' nature of their constituencies.

The increasingly discretionary nature of conditionality, coupled with the asymmetrical decision-making structure of the World Bank and the IMF, has led to its emergence as a mechanism through which the major shareholders of the Bank and Fund have progressively embedded policy reforms in developing member states. Accordingly, conditionalities imposed by the institutions on client states now represent more than fiduciary instruments. Instead, the doctrine of conditionality has developed as a key mechanism for organising, harmonising and enforcing regulatory norms across different jurisdictions in the developing world.

4.3.1 Fund conditionality enshrined

The watershed in the evolution of IMF conditionality occurred in the late 1970s, at the time of the Second Amendment to the IMF Articles of Agreement, which not only cemented the legal and political developments occurring at the Fund but also marked a turning point in international financial law and policy. By 1974, the fixed exchange rate regime (or 'par value' system) under the original Bretton Woods agreements had collapsed and led to the IMF adopting this pivotal amendment in 1979. This led to two major changes within the IMF which cemented the IMF's shift away from its original mandate and altered the nature of conditionality for good.

a) Collapse of the Bretton Woods system

First, the Second Amendment shifted the IMF's role away from ensuring stability through a fixed exchange rate system towards focusing on the soundness of domestic economic and financial policy as important factors in maintaining such stability. The amended Article IV, Section 2(b), now enabled IMF member states to choose their own exchange rate arrangements as opposed to adhering to the par value[22] under the original system. At the same time, the revised Article IV, Section 1 obligated members to undertake domestic economic and financial policies that would not produce disruptions in the global economy and Article IV, Section 3 further conferred upon the IMF a corresponding authority to exercise 'surveillance' over the international monetary system, including members' exchange rate policies, both bilaterally and multilaterally.[23]

Under this new regulatory regime, threats to the international financial system were perceived as stemming from errant domestic policies undertaken by countries rather than from inherent systemic problems with the governance of the global economy or from the destructive policies of other member states. International financial regulation was no longer influenced by an understanding of the need for rules-based, multilateral cooperation as the basis of international financial stability but would be based rather on creating the appropriate domestic framework within countries to prevent international financial crisis (Khor, 2001: 4–5; Pahuja, 2000: 778–779). Financing for countries facing balance of payments problems then became increasingly conditional upon their willingness to undertake 'appropriate' domestic policies to redress the economic instability.

At the same time, the changing clientele of the IMF borrowers – from states which provided the bulk of usable currency through their subscriptions, to states which relied upon the pool of *other* states' usable currencies as a source of finance – changed the discourse of Fund financing from one of entitlement to draw to one of conditional financing, compounded by the fact that the former category of members was industrialised countries and the latter was made up of developing states. The doctrine of conditionality soon became largely a north–south debate (Lowenfeld, 2008). Conditionality, working as 'an enforcement mechanism with selective effect', thus enhanced the asymmetrical nature of the north and south 'as subjects of IMF law' (Pahuja, 2000: 780), cementing the demarcated roles of the *rule-makers* and the *rule-takers* within the IMF's membership.

b) Foray into concessional financing

This asymmetry is further reinforced by the second major development in the role of the IMF in the late 1970s: the Fund's foray into development financing through its concessional lending window. The shift to development financing not only changed the nature of Fund financing and cemented the use of conditionality, it also altered the role of the Fund from that of an organisation for multilateral financial discipline focused on short-term, counter-cyclical lending to that of a development agency engaged in long-term economic rehabilitation. In doing so, the mandate of the Fund and, correspondingly, the remit of conditionality, was expanded to encompass broader structural economic reforms in client countries.[24] These conditions were (and continue to be), in turn, driven by the regulatory priorities established by the major donors to the PRGF trusts as part of its establishment or periodic replenishment processes (see discussion in Chapter 2, section 2.2).

Gold contends that the contractual terminology associated with concessional lending (see the discussion in section 4.2.1) is a result of these concessional loans departing from two basic principles that underpinned the IMF's Articles of Agreement: (1) the total resources of the IMF should not be reduced by its transactions with members; and, more importantly for our purposes, (2) *the member need not lose self-respect when soliciting assistance by the Fund* (Gold, 1996: 367–368, emphasis added). According to Gold, the abandonment by the IMF of 'these niceties of law and diplomacy' not only reflected the economic realities of the relationship between the IMF and borrowing countries but also helped develop the concept of conditionality as a modality of regulating this relationship (ibid.).

Thus, the nature of conditionality and the basis of conditionality shifted from ones premised on cooperation and respect for national sovereignty to ones premised on control and discretionary governance. When one set of members is subject to IMF surveillance and policy purview resulting from resource dependency while another set of members (with more than a 60 per cent share of the voting power) is not, the flexibility associated with conditionality as a regulatory mechanism acquires a radically different form. Here, it increases the number of legitimate interventions (conditions) in a borrowing member state under correspondingly selective criteria without a comparative safeguard mechanism for adjudicating disputes. Conditionality, due to its flexibility and discretionary character, therefore began to serve as an increasingly effective instrument in fulfilling the IMF's expanded disciplinary function over third world economies.

The significance of the IMF's financing reforms to the changes in the scope of its regulatory authority in the wake of the collapse of the par value system cannot be overstated. The IMF's new lending instruments emerged as the new means of international financial regulation under the amended Articles of Agreement. Without explicit authority to enforce fixed exchange rate policies at the supranational level, the IMF could only supervise members states' domestic policies as a means of fulfilling its role of overseeing the international financial system. Any reform necessitated could only be enforced through the terms of credit disbursement as the only regulatory tools left to the institution, soon resulting in the emergence of conditionality as a mechanism of global financial governance.

4.3.2 Governance through resource dependency

Unlike the IMF, the World Bank was not established as a regulatory body. It was not endowed with a governance mandate such as that established under the Fund's Articles of Agreement with regard to multilateral financial discipline. The primary function of the Bank was to provide resources for the reconstruction and development of developing countries or, in the case of IDA countries, to facilitate poverty reduction and generate economic growth. However, since the introduction of policy-based loans, the combination of financing and policy reform has led to the progressive embedding of a governance function in which regulatory norms across jurisdictions are harmonised through the Bank's credit process.

The Bank's expanding regulatory role has been facilitated by the fact that its criteria for financing as well as the content of its financing conditionality have been progressively established outside individual loan negotiation processes. Instead, many of these conditions have been predetermined through the Bank's increasingly political process of portfolio allocation that is contingent upon the interests of its major shareholders. This has led to increasing politicisation of Bank financing, since such financing, unlike the original practice of the Fund, is neither automatic nor based exclusively on a needs assessment of the country but instead is based on whether the countries meet Bank conditions for financial assistance and demonstrate a willingness to execute the policy reforms associated with such assistance.

a) Country Assistance Strategies

First, the allocation of funds to borrowing member states is based on the Bank's assessment of the country under the CAS, a document prepared by the Bank staff in dialogue with country governments and which serves as 'the central tool' which the Bank uses to 'review and guide' its support to its member countries (World Bank, 2005e: para. 1). The CAS sets out 'a four-year strategy of support for the country's own priorities, a Bank program of activities, and a results framework for managing and reporting on impact', providing 'an active and flexible roadmap for the Bank's engagement with a client country' (World Bank, 2009f: para. 12). This includes the Bank's 'diagnosis of [a] country's development situation and a selective program of planned Bank Group support' in the context of a country's national development strategy, 'the Bank's ongoing portfolio, and the activities of other development partners' (World Bank, 2005e: para. 2).

Through a CAS, the volume and composition of financial (and other) assistance extended by the Bank to its clients is determined by what the Bank considers appropriate for the country given its evaluation of, *inter alia*, the country's economic situation, governance, environmental/natural resource management, and poverty and social aspects. As of July 2002, CASs of countries with a completed PRSP must be based on the PRSP, and there has been a shift since 2005 towards greater ownership of a CAS, but the CAS itself remains a primarily non-negotiated document.[25] Differences in a country's own plans and the Bank's strategy are highlighted in the CAS document (World Bank, 2005e: para. 2) but the Bank itself admits that there remain tensions 'between alignment with country demand and priorities and the desire to reflect the Bank's sectoral and corporate priorities' within the CAS (World Bank, 2009f: ii–iii, para. 9).

Since 2005, a country's CAS must also incorporate a results-based framework highlighting 'the outcomes that are expected from Bank support during the implementation period' of the CAS (World Bank, 2005e: para. 2). This is implemented through an 'explicit results matrix' which links Bank activities to development outcomes through a set of monitoring milestones (World Bank, 2009f: iii, para. 9). Each lending operation – be it an investment project, a development policy loan or technical assistance – must be located within this framework and project, or programme documents must outline 'how the proposed operation derives from the results framework' of the CAS or its associated documents[26] (ibid.: para. 14). In other words, Bank operations must demonstrate alignment with the roadmap for development outcomes established through the CAS and this would, in turn, influence the content of conditionality associated with each operation as policy and regulatory reforms are prescribed in the context of meeting CAS indicators.

b) IDA allocation criteria

Second, for low-income countries financing is also determined by the IDA allocation criteria, which include allocation based on the country's policy and institutional performance and IDA replenishment conditions. IDA's resources are allocated to member countries through a combination of: (1) basic allocations;[27] (2) performance-based allocations; and (3) IDA replenishment conditions. The complexity of these criteria highlights, in some ways, how the Bank as an institution is trying to manage conditionality as a mechanism for regulatory change pursued by its major shareholders, developing complex techniques to administer and justify politically motivated reforms.

The PBA is centred on the Bank's Country Policy and Institutional Assessment (CPIA) – which 'assesses a country's present policy and institutional framework for fostering poverty reduction, sustainable growth and the effective use of development assistance' – and guided by the Bank's Annual Report on Portfolio Performance (ARPP), which is 'used to determine a score for each country's implementation performance' (IDA, 2003, paras 2–3). A complex scorecard is then determined using indicators from CPIA and ARPP assessments, including calculations of a 'governance rating' derived from a cluster of scores under the CPIA's section on 'public sector management and institutions' to obtain a country's performance rating (IDA, 2008: Annex 1, para. 3).

In this respect, the political dimensions of Bank conditionality cannot be overstated, particularly in relation to its increasingly disproportionate emphasis on governance as a criterion for determining individual country portfolios of financing. Not only has the focus on a country's policy and institutional performance in allocating IDA funds been a result of the emphasis placed on the IDA replenishment process – donors in the 14th IDA replenishment highlighted that the 'key aspect' of IDA's financial support to poor countries must be 'the strong and transparent link to country performance on economic policies, governance and poverty reduction efforts' (World Bank, 2005f) – but the operational procedure for determining IDA allocation has also been criticised for its subjectivity and lack of transparency. An external expert panel evaluating the CPIA and related IDA allocation criteria in 2004 criticised the procedure as 'highly non-transparent' given that 'the very large weight given to the governance factor is not obvious from the complex formula' (ibid.: para. 15). The panel had found the emphasis on governance 'excessive' and questioned the basis of the weighting, particularly that of the CPIA, which it felt did 'not find empirical support in available literature' (ibid.: para. 16).

Further, there has been extensive criticism of the Bank's use of the CPIA, with concerns over the capacity of Bank staff to assess inherently subjective areas of a country's domestic policy and institutional framework and ascribe a numerical rating to each criterion for the purposes of allocating funds under the CPIA. The CPIA scores countries on an extensive range of institutional and policy actions, basing these scores on 'actual policies not on promises or intentions' (World Bank, 2004f: para. 11). The 16 actions assessed are then grouped into four clusters – economic management, structural policies, policies for social inclusion/equity, and public sector management and institutions – with each cluster forming a 25 per cent weighting in the overall rating (ibid.: Box 1 and para. 15). The scores, determined from consideration of 'a variety of indicators, observations and judgments', including 'country knowledge originat[ing] from the Bank, analytic work or policy dialogue, or work done by parameters, and relevant publicly available indicators' (ibid.: para. 11), have been criticised by some as a 'composite of subjective judgments' of Bank staff on these issues (Alexander, 2004), while others have expressed concern over the lack of empirical evidence and analytic work supporting the ratings given in each cluster (see Van Waeyenberge, 2006; Bretton Woods Project, 2006).

4.4 A new jurisprudence

The examination of the development of the doctrine of conditionality within the World Bank and the IMF above has demonstrated that the logic that underpinned the inception of conditionality as a mechanism for regulating the relationship between subjects of international development finance – the flexibility, deference for the notion of sovereign equality and sovereign autonomy, and the discourse of the right to development and international development and economic cooperation – has been subverted over the years to take on a conversely regressive role between the parties to the financing, reflective of the developments in the international political economy and the corresponding necessity to respond to the geo-strategic governance imperatives of the major shareholders of the Bank and Fund. The development of conditionality as an instrument for regulating the relationship between the BWIs and their borrowing member states and its consequent emergence as a mechanism for economic governance has, consequently, had significant implications for third world states' engagement in the global economy.

4.4.1 Discretionary control

First, the progressive entrenchment of conditionality as a quasi-legal mechanism in World Bank and IMF financial transactions in lieu of formal legal arrangements has accorded the Bank and the Fund significant autonomy and wide discretionary powers vis-à-vis the nature and substance of their financial and policy interactions with their borrowing member states. This has shifted the domain of regulation from what legal scholars term 'hard' to 'soft' law, or, in other words, from a regime of fixed, binding juridical norms to one operating on a network of non-binding regulatory principles and standards.[28]

In this regard, the disciplinary characteristic of conditionality has not been derived from an express constitutional power of the institutions concerned but, rather, from the evolution of Bank and Fund practice. Conditionality has enabled regulation to be conducted, not through formal means of norm-construction, but through precedents set by the behaviour and conduct of the parties. Under regulation through the mechanism of conditionality, the legal relationship of the parties to the financing is based on the outcomes of individual processes of negotiation and bartering rather than on fixed contractual or other legal principles derived from a higher source of law.

This characteristic of conditionality has led the commentators Mosley *et al.* (on the Bank) and Sgard (on the Fund) to conceive of the process of conditionality as a negotiating game between the institutions and the borrowing member in which the 'two parties have (at least partly) opposed interests which they pursue by taking note of each other's likely behaviour, and in which the outcome depends on the strategies pursued by each party' (Mosley *et al.*, 1991: 67–68), thereby shaping 'a framework within which the actors interact, where successive moves take place and where, hopefully, credibility will accumulate' (Sgard, 2004: 17).[29]

Accordingly, the regulatory framework which governs the actors' behaviour in this process is derived from an accumulation of seemingly bureaucratic steps on the part of the Fund, with 'considerable rule-making activity' being invested by the institution in 'framing the sequential interaction with countries under [its] programme', such as prior actions, tranche release reviews, negotiations for waivers on performance criteria, and a host of programme evaluations (Sgard, 2004: 17). A similar process operates within the Bank in which conflict between the Bank's interests and the borrower's are resolved not through predetermined rules but by 'the outcome of strategy and external circumstance' (Mosley *et al.*, 1991: 69).

Sgard regards the conferment of wide discretionary powers on the institutions as a necessary component of this bargaining process that characterises the practice of conditionality (Sgard, 2004: 17). Consequently, the use of conditionality has increasingly consolidated more discretionary power in the hands of the institutions and the non-borrowing member states. Given the governance structure of the Bank and the Fund, this shift has had an adverse impact on the policy autonomy and negotiating strength of less powerful member states and, as we will see in Chapter 5, on the internal constitution of the borrowing states.

Mosley *et al.*'s analysis of the bargaining process of conditionality concluded that power relations between the institutions and the borrowing states play a substantial role in determining the outcome of negotiations and the rules of engagement between the parties vis-à-vis financing: 'the less the donor needs the recipient – either as an outlet or as political ally – the more the recipient needs the donor [and] the less room for manoeuvre the recipient has in those negotiations' (Mosley *et al.*, 1991: 74). As noted in Chapter 2, this interplay between the institutions' significant powers of discretion and the inherent power asymmetries within their membership renders the institutions extremely susceptible to strategic influence of their dominant member states.

Studies by Broz and Hawes (2006), Gould (2003) and Oatley and Yackee (2004) have all highlighted the link between the pursuit of US foreign policy and financial interests and IMF lending decisions resulting from the porousness of the IMF's governance structure to US executive and legislative influence. Gould's study of the influence of supplementary financiers – 'private and official financiers who supplement the Fund's loans to borrowers' – and IMF conditionality, for example, reveals that these financiers have been instrumental in expanding the scope and content of IMF programme conditions (Gould, 2003). Meanwhile, Oatley and Yackee's analysis of US interests and IMF lending suggests that 'American policymakers regularly shape the specific content of IMF conditionality agreements', extending their influence beyond input into 'the broad orientation of Fund policy' and into shaping the content of 'the Fund's single most important policy instrument'[30] (Oatley and Yackee, 2004: 425–426). The US General Accounting Office (GAO) itself reports that there exists a formal process to 'systematically promote' US interests – notably congressional mandates – at the Fund through an internal task force established by the US Treasury to facilitate coordination between the US Treasury and the US executive director and 'to identify early opportunities to influence decisions regarding Fund members' programs and economic reviews' (GAO, 2001: 9).

4.4.2 Mission creep

Over the years, the remit of conditionality has extended beyond purely fiduciary objectives, with the focus of conditionality shifting towards restructuring the institutional framework of the country through policy reform as an end in itself rather than as a means to an end, that is, fiscal stability (for the IMF) and economic growth (for the World Bank). Conditionality is no longer solely about maintaining debtor discipline in order to protect the 'revolving character' of Fund and Bank resources[31] or to meet fiduciary obligations under their institutional mandates. In fact, conversely, conditionality has enabled the BWIs to circumvent constitutional limitations on their roles as international financial institutions.

This shift in the focus of conditionality reforms is both a result of and a contribution to the intensification of conditionality as a regulatory instrument. The highly discretionary nature of conditionality has enabled it to be exercised as policy leverage, while at the same time it has contributed to the increasing use of the instrument for such purposes. Conditionality is a convenient means of regulating the relationship between the financing agency and the borrowing country as it is flexible and does not give rise to binding legal obligations. The lack of precise criteria for establishing non-compliance not amounting to a breach of a contractual obligation accords the financing agency – the World Bank and the IMF – the power not only to adjudicate disputes but also to determine when non-compliance constitutes a breach.

Consequently, as Mosley *et al.* argue, 'it is the power-relationship between donor and recipient, rather than the severity of the economic "disease" from which a country is suffering, which principally determines the nature of the prescription offered as part of a conditionality package' (Mosley *et al.*, 1991: 90). The significant powers of discretion accorded to the BWIs under the practice of conditionality have enabled them to extract a wide range of policy commitments from borrowing states, with conditionality enabling more intrusive reforms without giving rise to the corresponding threat of a challenge by members for breaching institutional constitutional norms or subjecting the institutions to broader international legal sanctions.

The use of conditionality in Bank and Fund arrangements has enabled the institutions to circumvent limitations to their constitutional roles and facilitated the expansion of their operations beyond what their initial founders envisaged when the institutions were established. For the IMF, this has meant a shift away from its original role as an organisation for multilateral financial discipline focused on short-term, counter-cyclical financing to that of a development agency engaged in long-term rehabilitation. IMF financing is no longer viewed as a means of ensuring international financial stability but as an end in itself. Meanwhile, conditionality has enabled the World Bank to transit from its primary function as a provider of multilateral investment funds to one incorporating a policy and regulatory role in client states.

4.4.3 Absence of external oversight

International legal commentators have suggested that the reluctance to use the norms of international law as their primary tool lies in the institutions' resistance to countries having recourse to external justiciability. The IMF and World Bank have always been opposed to outside interference in their decision-making and administrative processes and have repeatedly opposed recourse to external adjudication on disputes. External justiciability would impose corresponding obligations on the part of the Bretton Woods institutions and limit the extent to which the dominant, non-borrowing member states can exert control within these institutions.

The Bank and the Fund have always reserved for themselves the right to interpret their own constitutions and by-laws. While both institutions have respective agreements with the United Nations giving them the authority to seek an advisory opinion from the International Court of Justice (ICJ) on matters of interpretation and on legal issues arising from their operations, this procedure has never been used in the history of the two organisations (Shihata, 2000c: 222). As Shihata observes:

> [The] IFIs have never sought interpretation of their own charters from a court of law [unlike the principal and subsidiary organs of the UN] ... Decisions on interpretation in the IFIs are also not subject to appeal before the ICJ or an arbitral tribunal.
>
> (Shihata, 2000c: 222)

The doctrine of conditionality therefore operates within this framework of self-adjudication in which the Executive Boards of the Bank and the Fund operate as both the rule-makers and rule-enforcers. The practice of conditionality allows the executive directors to set preconditions for access to development financing, determine which conditions should apply to countries, and establish if a condition has been met or breached and which penalties should be meted out to the non-compliant member state. Correspondingly, this has enabled conditionality to be utilised as a mechanism for wider economic regulation of states subject to its jurisdiction.

In this manner, conditionality operates very much like transnational merchant law, in which the juridical authority for the reconfiguration of political, economic and socio-cultural life resides in a complex web of merchant custom and privately agreed codes of conduct (see Cutler, 2003).The Bank and Fund's use of 'soft law' over 'hard law' as a means of regulating their relations with borrowing member states is driven by the same objectives as the transnational merchant's use of the 'soft, porous discretionary standards and procedures' (Cutler, 2003: 23) both to regulate commercial, 'private' relations in international trade, investment and finance and to govern the activities of the transnational merchant.

In this respect, the flexibility, reduced transaction costs and lack of justiciability of non-binding codes and custom are both politically and economically expedient, notably for the stronger party in an asymmetrical bargaining relationship. As Cutler observes: 'Weaker states on the periphery of the global political economy tend to favour hard law because it provides a certain transparency, predictability, and locking-in commitments that become more difficult for stronger states to renege on' (Cutler, 2003: 23). On the other hand, parties with greater negotiating strength prefer 'soft law', which is 'easier to breach with impunity' and offers more opportunities for 'creative lawyering' and the 'shaping of legal regulation' (ibid.).

4.5 From coercion to consent

The progressive entrenchment of conditionality as a means of regulating the behaviour of borrowing member states by the IMF and World Bank (over other means of regulation) and the corresponding intensification of conditionality's role as a mechanism for international economic governance have had a significant impact on the content and application of conditionality in practice, including, and notably so, on the development of 'ownership' as a principle governing the use of conditionality.

The concept of 'ownership' and its attendant modalities, particularly under the rubric of the PRSP, significantly alters the practice of conditionality by reconstructing the modes of governance through conditionality. Although coerciveness remains a substantial component of this new regime of conditionality, the mechanics of it depend less on the threat of sanction than on the incentive of reward for good behaviour.

Operationally, this has meant a gradual shift towards new modalities of conditionality practice, notably the gradual movement from *ex-post* conditionalities – commitments based on forecasted performance – to *ex-ante* conditionalities – commitments based on actual results rather than forecasts, and the increased application of non-binding conditionalities, such as benchmarks and triggers, and the principle of 'country selectivity' underpinning their use. It also means a shift, at least for the Bank, towards 'programmatic' lending operations – financial support based on a series of individual, interlocking lending programmes – as opposed to the conventional multi-tranche, stand-alone loan. Taken together, these reforms represent a major overhaul of the modalities of conditionality, reflecting the wider reform of the disciplinary framework of development financing brought about by the PRSP framework and its attendant instruments of aid delivery.

4.5.1 *Carrots not sticks*

As discussed in Chapter 3, the impetus for the shift in the conceptual framework of development financing came from a number of internal and external sources, including the need to respond to both an internal and an external crisis of legitimacy in the international economic order. The imperative to reshape the principles which underlie the use of conditionality was critical to resolving the increasing failure of conditionality to provide the disciplinary framework for neoliberal globalisation. Specifically, the need to rehabilitate the credibility of conditionality was viewed as essential to institutionalising the policy content of conditionality and improving its regulatory efficacy.

Former World Bank staffer Daniel Morrow, one of the architects of the PRSP framework, maintains that the conditionality regime prior to the PRSP approach failed to bring about desired policy reforms because 'too often aid-recipient governments did not fully implement or did not sustain the policies and institutional reforms to which they had committed themselves' (Morrow, 2005: 2). He argues that, as many of these reforms are 'politically and institutionally complex', these reforms would not be implemented 'without sufficient ownership' of the policies by country authorities (interview: Morrow, 2005). However, Morrow, like many others, does not question the fundamental premise of the economic and institutional reforms that are to be undertaken or the power relationship that is involved in the donor–government relationship.

Morrow's views remains reflective of the institutional outlook of the BWIs on the issue of conditionality. This perspective views the debate as one not of the politics or policy content of conditionality, but rather of the efficacy of conditionality as an instrument of regulation.[32] Here, the question is less about the legitimacy of conditionality as a mode of regulation, or about the appropriateness of the policy reforms to be implemented through conditionalities, and more about improving the enforcement and implementation of such reforms.

An integral element of this new principle of 'ownership' therefore is the notion of 'policy dialogue', which Morrissey perceives as the alternative to traditional conditionality as a means of facilitating 'policy transfer' in recipient states (Morrissey, 2004: section 1). He argues that such dialogue, 'where donors engage with recipients to aim to *convince them that particular policies should be adopted*', redresses the coercive limits of conditionality as a mechanism for regulating the behaviour of client countries – 'whereas conditionality has an element of coercion, policy dialogue is firmly rooted in *persuasion*' (ibid., emphasis added).

Such an approach corresponds to the 'game theory' analysis of conditionality. If the practice of conditionality is conceived of as a game of negotiation, the outcome of which establishes the rules of engagement between the parties, then the principle of ownership may be regarded as a continuum of conditionality, as part of the rule-making process, with the balance of power tipped towards the World Bank and the IMF. The modalities of conditionality may therefore be construed as rule-making instruments that have evolved to serve the interests of the institutions by maximising their relatively stronger bargaining position. This is effected through a gradual repositioning of policy conditions as voluntary reforms undertaken by the borrowing member state in recognition of the viability of such reforms in achieving objectives such as economic growth or poverty reduction, which, in turn, are rewarded by the disbursement of concessional financing or grant aid by the Bank, Fund and other donors to assist in the reform processes. The conferment of such policy 'autonomy' creates a tautology which shifts the burden of enforcement onto the borrowing party.

With the advent of 'country ownership' as a principle governing the use of conditionality, the focus of conditionality has shifted from its previous fiduciary objective of safeguarding the use of multilateral funds to one of policing policy compliance and gatekeeping access to funds. This ensures that only the countries most willing to undertake reforms (or most desperate for financing) are rewarded. This policy of 'country selectivity' in determining countries' access to resources is a hallmark of the PRSP framework and the new architecture of aid (see Chapter 5, section 5.3). It enables donors to identify countries with economic and social development strategies that correspond to the financing priorities of donors and 'reward' them with resources for good behaviour.

The rhetoric of 'ownership' therefore serves as a powerful discursive restraining instrument on borrowing countries' behaviour. These new modalities of conditionality further remove any rights to recourse to formal Bank and Fund law in terms of regulation as the policy reform that is initiated bears no indication, formally, of being a condition of financing. 'Ownership' removes the fiduciary duty of the Bank and the Fund to ensure that the funds are disbursed to the satisfaction of the constitutional mandate. Instead, the burden of compliance and the risk of financing is placed squarely on the shoulders of the borrowing state. As former UNCTAD special coordinator for Africa Kamran Kousari observed, this approach to self-regulation enables states to 'police themselves' so that any failures in policy implementation are attributed to the state as the primary architects of the economic programme that is funded by the BWIs rather than the Bank or Fund (interview: Kousari, 2005).

It is not surprising, then, that, in the Bank's view, 'the practice of conditionality has evolved from the idea that governments must meet a set of conditions to receive Bank financing to an approach in which the Bank supports policy reform in client countries' (World Bank, 2005c: para. 17). This evolution, viewed by Morrow as a response to the 'ownership critique' of conditionality, represents a form of 'consensual conditionality' in which financing is linked 'only to conditions that have sufficiently broad support within the recipient country', or, at the very least, to a collaborative design of the reform programme undertaken by the borrowing government in exchange for financing (Morrow, 2005: 2, 5–8).

From the Bank's perspective, therefore, the shaping of conditionality in this manner is aimed at ensuring greater success in policy implementation through the removal of the element of formal coercion that characterised previous modalities of conditionality. Harrison terms this development 'post-conditionality',[33] a regime by which the disciplinary force is no longer enforced directly through disciplinary instruments but rather through a mechanism of self-imposed discipline on the part of borrowing country authorities (Harrison, 2001b: 660). Country authorities are implicated in a regime of monetarism, fiscal austerity, liberalisation, marketisation and privatisation in accordance with the principles of the IFIs without subjecting them to a contest of negotiations in the regulatory arena. These principles may be regarded as having 'made a transition from *doctrine* (openly colonizing the state terrain through the IFIs) to *ideology* (far less contested, integrated into everyday language of policy-making)' (Harrison, 2001b: 659).

This new configuration of politics brought about by the principle of 'ownership' in conditionality has not extinguished the politics of adjustment or the power relations inherent in conditions of donor dependency, but has rather resulted in a situation where external intervention is exercised not through coercive financing terms but 'through closer involvement in state institutions and the employment of incentive finance' (Harrison, 2001b: 660). The process of negotiation – 'partnership' – that characterises the relationship between donor and borrowing government under the PRSP framework creates the conditions under which the central elements of the Washington Consensus are absorbed unquestioningly by country authorities, or at least the policymaking elite within borrowing countries.

4.5.2 From tranching to front-loading

The application of 'country selectivity' to financing decisions at the IMF and World Bank has been complemented by the increasing practice of 'front-loading' conditionality. Traditionally, conditionalities have been linked to loan disbursements, with borrowing countries having to meet specific conditions prior to the release of each tranche of the loan from the Bank or the Fund. The process of 'tranching' itself represents a fundamental element of the practice of conditionality, in which each loan is sliced into segments, with the release of each tranche dependent upon compliance with pre-established policy reform conditions.[34]

The most commonly used instrument in this regard is *performance criteria* (at the Fund) or *tranche release conditions* (at the Bank). Introduced in the 1950s, the IMF's performance criteria 'specif[y] either a quantitative target to be met or a policy action to be implemented by an agreed date (or in some cases, continuously over a specified period) for the country to be able to continue to draw on the IMF's financing' (IMF, 2002b: para. 35). Similarly, for the Bank, each segment of a multi-tranche disbursement will not be released until the agreed policy reform has been executed (World Bank, 2005g: 2, para. 4; 2004d: para. 18). If these performance criteria or tranche release conditions are not met, a country must obtain a waiver on those conditions from the institutions before the disbursements can proceed. Once again, a substantial element of discretion is given to the Executive Boards as it is up to the executive directors of the institutions to determine whether a waiver can be granted or not.

IMF programmes may also be subject to *programme reviews*, the completion of which triggers disbursements. According to the Fund, programme reviews 'provide a framework for the Executive Board to assess periodically whether the IMF-supported program is broadly on track or whether modifications are necessary for achieving the program's objectives' (IMF, 2009e). Programme reviews are therefore more extensive than performance criteria – fulfilment of all performance criteria does not necessarily mean a country has continued access to Fund financing where the terms of the financing include a programme review – as it demands detailed progress assessments of policy compliance and future policy directions.[35]

Programme reviews exemplify the opaque nature of the current practice of conditionality as new conditions could be imposed *after* the signing of the financing agreement, meaning that the terms and conditions for financing could change during the course of the financing programme, and old conditions be waived or made defunct. While this maintains an element of flexibility to enable the terms and conditions to shift with prevailing economic circumstances, critics have contended that programme reviews render the process of conditionality untransparent and unaccountable to the legislatures of the borrowing countries as the conditions are not disclosed at the point of agreement.

Veteran IFI watcher Nancy Alexander is particularly concerned that with the increasing transparency of Letters of Intent through the increasing publication of the documents 'much of the meat of the LOIs ha[s] migrated to the IMF reviews, which are not in the public domain' (Alexander, 2001: para. 1). This situation may be aggravated by changes to the IMF's conditionality framework in 2009, discontinuing formal structural performance criteria in all IMF lending instruments but continuing to monitor borrowing countries' compliance with structural reform policies through programme reviews instead (IMF, 2009g). Although it is aimed at reducing the 'stigma' of countries failing to meet structural performance criteria by formally requesting waivers, this new policy does not abolish structural policy conditions per se but instead provides a new mechanism for supervising their implementation.

The problem of transparency has been compounded by the increasing use of *ex-ante* conditionality in Bank and Fund financing. Commonly implemented through 'prior actions', *ex-ante* conditionality requires recipient states to comply with a set of policy and institutional measures *before* official financing arrangements are entered into. At the World Bank and IMF, completion of prior actions is required before a financing arrangement is presented to the respective Executive Boards for approval (IMF, 2006: para. 14; World Bank, 2005d: para. 13). This means that, unlike traditional conditionalities, which have to be complied with after the financing agreement has been entered into, prior actions are only brought to the attention of the executive directors once they have been complied with. The content of prior actions is therefore not reviewed officially, and discussions on policy and institutional reforms are undertaken largely between the staff of the IFIs and country authorities.

While the Bank and the Fund insist that such prior actions may not necessarily affect approval of financing arrangements or tranche disbursements or waivers (see IMF 2002b: para. 35), prior actions are increasingly used as both a *signalling* device and a tool of *selectivity* for determining access to financing from the Bank and the Fund.[36] The former role involves establishing 'strong, difficult-to-reverse reforms' (ibid.: para. 28) at the inception of a programme to ensure that the policies for reform have a higher chance of being implemented, while the latter role demonstrates the country authorities' commitment to the reforms favoured by the Bank and the Fund.

Prior actions are compulsory for single-tranche operations from the World Bank, most importantly for access to Poverty Reduction Strategy Credits. PRSCs are examples of the Bank's programmatic lending, an approach that has been used increasingly over the past decade. This approach involves a series of single-tranche operations sequentially presented to the Bank's Executive Board, with a medium-term framework specified at the outset, including completed prior actions, monitorable progress indicators, and expected prior actions or triggers for subsequent operations (World Bank, 2009e: para. 12; 2005c: para. 19).

Approval of each PRSC will be based upon compliance with the policies set out in the country's MTEF, and prior actions for PRSCs ought to be drawn from the country's PRSP and enshrined in the core objectives of the PRSP approach, namely rooted firmly in poverty reduction (World Bank, 2005c: para. 19), but, as will be discussed in Chapter 5, this is often not the case. Prior actions are incorporated into the PRSC loan agreement as an appendix to the agreement and referred to in the preamble. For example, the preamble to the PRSC agreement between Uganda and the IDA states that financing is provided on the basis that 'the Borrower has carried out the measures and taken the actions described in schedule 2 to this Agreement to the satisfaction of the Association', with the attached schedule referring to actions contained within the country's LDP and MTEF (Republic of Uganda, 2001). A similar procedure occurs at the Fund, where 'prior actions are incorporated into and expressly identified in arrangements' (IMF, 2002b: para. 60).

Prior actions therefore do not need explicit Board review and approval, unlike conventional conditionalities, which are considered when the borrower's LOI or LDP is reviewed by the Executive Boards. The discussions on prior actions are undertaken largely between the IMF or Bank staff and the borrowing country authorities, and agreed upon without the need for Board approval. The IMF's Guidelines on Conditionality 2002 reaffirmed the original provisions of the superseded 1979 Guidelines, which stipulated that where a programme includes prior actions 'the Managing Director will keep Executive Directors informed in an appropriate manner of the progress of the discussions with the member' (IMF, 2002b: para. 11(a)). In practice, this is conducted informally through 'country matters sessions' of the Board and informal briefings (ibid.). Proponents of prior actions contend that requiring Board approval for prior actions undermines the Bank and Fund staff's ability to negotiate with country authorities and procure advantage over 'less-reform minded interest groups' (ibid.), thereby enabling the IMF to gain an upper hand in negotiations without the requisite checks and balances that exist in a Board review.

4.5.3 Increasing institutional leverage

Critics have argued that the front-loading of conditionality discussed above significantly increases 'the leverage of Management and staff vis-à-vis the governments of developing countries' (Babb and Buira, 2004: 14). The Bank, for example, states that under the PRSC approach '[t]raditional conditionality has been replaced by a *performance* framework that reflects *an understanding between the Bank and the government* on the priorities of the country's reform programs and the financing required', with the Bank requiring 'tangible evidence of progress in achieving the objectives of the medium-term program' before each PRSC operation is approved (World Bank, 2005b: para. 11, emphasis added).

This implies a high degree of negotiation between the Bank staff and country authorities prior to the entry into force of a financing agreement regarding the institutional and policy actions to be undertaken in exchange for disbursements. In particular, there is extensive focus on the country's public financial management and expenditure systems, with all PRSCs being 'underpinned by ex-ante fiduciary assessment[s]' of these systems in order to identify what the Bank perceives to be 'deficiencies', 'fiduciary risk' and 'steps needed to secure acceptable fiduciary arrangements' (World Bank, 2005b: para. 72). Countries are expected to secure changes, including legal or regulatory reforms[37] or institutional reforms,[38] before disbursements are made, blurring the line between 'actual conditionality' and 'negotiated policy actions'.

IMF staff have admitted that the use of prior actions obscures the actual number of conditionalities that may be present in a financing arrangement due to the numerous ways in which conditionality may be manifested through the use of prior actions (interview: Plant, 2004).

At the World Bank, the use of ex-ante conditionalities is compounded by the extensive use of Country Assistance Strategies and the CPIA index (see section 4.3.2) to determine access to financing. While these requirements do not constitute fiduciary conditions per se, these prerequisites provide a greater incentive for countries in need of external financing to implement the policies set by the BWIs, as access to financing is limited until the required reforms or pre-qualification criteria are complied with. Contrast this with conventional conditionality, whereby financing is agreed upon subject to compliance with certain conditions, non-compliance with which may or may not result in the suspension of disbursements, depending on the outcome of a waiver application. Once again, this concentrates more power in the hands of the institutional staff and management as countries are pressured into adhering to CPIA policy prescriptions for continued access to external financial support (Alexander, 2004: section III).[39]

Country selectivity under the new framework of conditionality thus amplifies the political and often ideological nature of aid relationships. Countries have a financial incentive to institutionalise the policy environment expected of them by the Bretton Woods institutions and to present such reforms as part of a domestic reform package undertaken voluntarily in order to demonstrate their willingness to engage with the international community on the established terms of engagement (see Chapters 2 and 5). This repositioning of traditional conditionality performs a significant restraining function at the level of the Executive Board. By placing responsibility for the design as well as the success or failure of a programme on national authorities, irrespective of the extent of Bank and Fund input, normally dissenting voices at the respective Executive Boards (notably other developing countries) may be silenced out of deference to the supposed autonomy of the country whose policies are being debated. The new framework also complicates the structures of accountability at the Bank and Fund, as well as those internal to the state (see Chapter 5). Unlike traditional conditionality, where conditions are clearly delineated as reflecting IFI interests, the movement towards *ex-ante* conditionality and 'country selectivity' blurs the distinction between internal and external interests.

4.6 Conditionality, discipline and the new biopower

The doctrine of conditionality is an integral component of development financing and nowhere more so than at the Bretton Woods institutions, where it was conceived, extensively applied and evolved. Conditionality is a mechanism that governs not only the terms of financial support accorded to borrowing member states at the IMF and World Bank, but also the relationship between the parties involved in such financing, that is, between the borrowing members and the institution, and between the borrowing members and the non-borrowing members.

The evolution of the doctrine of conditionality demonstrates that the role and nature of conditionality have departed from the original objectives of conditionality – that is, to create a regulatory instrument that was responsive to the economic and socio-political circumstances of countries which borrowed from the Bank and the Fund and respectful of the sovereignty of nations that formed the membership of the two institutions. Instead, the flexibility which characterises the practice of conditionality has accorded the Bank and Fund wide regulatory discretion vis-à-vis their borrowing members. The substantial discretionary powers delegated to the institutions have shifted the terrain of regulation from 'hard' to 'soft' law, making adjudication of disputes difficult, if not impossible. The historical evolution of conditionality as a regulatory instrument situates ownership within the continuum of conditionality.

The evolution of conditionality, in particular the movement from *ex-post* to *ex-ante* conditionalities as exemplified by the PRSP approach, may therefore be framed as the beginning of a transition from Foucault's disciplinary society to a society of control vis-à-vis the governance of borrowing member countries in relation to the World Bank and the IMF. Foucault's conception of power in society charts a historical, epochal passage from a modality of power that is disciplinary in its function of training and normalising behaviour and whose success is derived from 'the use of simple instruments: hierarchical observation, normalizing judgment, and … the examination', to a form of power in which power is immanent within the society itself and is reproduced through networks outside the traditional institutions of discipline (Foucault, 1991: 261–263).

The historical exposition of conditionality enables us to chart the passage from the disciplinary power of conditionality, in which borrowing member states submitted to a regime of rules, customs and habits in the form of performance criteria, programme reviews and waiver requests, to a regulatory framework in which such power adopts a more indeterminate and heteromorphous form by constituting itself within the body politic of the borrowing country authorities and creating the voluntary will or desire to reform through compliance with prior actions and pre-financing triggers. This power, note Best and Kellner, 'operates not through physical force or representation by law, but through the hegemony of norms, political technologies, and the shaping of the body and soul' (Best and Kellner, 1991: 49).

Traditional modalities of conditionality regulated the behaviour of borrowing countries through: (1) a system of normalisation ('discipline') – compliance with an established set of economic truisms (the Washington Consensus) and the adoption of institutional and policy reforms in pursuit of the framework laid down by the World Bank and the IMF; and (2) the 'penalty of the norm' (Foucault, 1991: 196) – the 'nonobservance' of the prescribed economic rationale of the Washington Consensus leading to censure by the community of nation states and therefore access to multilateral funds. In contrast, the new modalities of conditionality intensify what Hardt and Negri term the 'normalising apparatuses of disciplinarity' (Hardt and Negri, 2000: 23) through ensuring that borrowing countries accept the disciplinary framework of adjustment lending and the economic rationale that underpins it, but are yet regulated through their own *desire* to adopt the reform measures and internalise them under the rubric of 'country ownership'.

In this manner, the regulatory power exerted by the financing institutions through the modalities of conditionality becomes not repressive but productive, imbued with a biological power to reproduce the mechanisms of control. In the same manner that Foucault conceives of the 'indispensable element' of *biopower* in the development of capitalism in Europe through the 'controlled insertion of bodies into the machinery of production and the adjustment of the phenomena of population to economic processes' (Foucault, 1991: 263), sustaining the Washington Consensus doctrine of reform as a global project depends on the appropriation of consent and the reproduction of life in the mirror of the Consensus framework through the concept of 'country ownership'.

Conditionality in its new manifestations – and particularly as operationalised through the PRSP framework – reflects the shifting characteristics of regulatory power in global economic governance. The modalities of conditionality have evolved to reflect the increasing importance of dialogic webs of regulation in international economic governance as opposed to mechanisms of reward and coercion (Braithwaite and Drahos, 2000: 556–558). Braithwaite and Drahos' extensive survey of actors involved in the globalisation of business regulation revealed that '[a]lmost all five hundred actors interviewed' expressed 'a strong preference for playing games of global regulation through dialogue [rather] than through rewards and sanctions' as rewards and sanctions are costly in financial and diplomatic terms (ibid.: 557–558).

According to Braithwaite and Drahos, these webs of dialogue deliver high rates of compliance with globalising reforms because such dialogue:

> (1) defines issues as a problem; (2) enhances the contracting environment so that complex interdependency and issue linkage can motivate agreement and compliance; (3) constitutes normative commitments; (4) institutionalizes habits of compliance; and (5) institutionalizes informal praise and shame for defection from the regime.
>
> (Braithwaite and Drahos, 2000: 556)

Similarly, this chapter has demonstrated that the practice of conditionality has evolved to assume a more dialogic characteristic as opposed to a disciplinary role in order to maximise the effectiveness of the reforms pursued by the World Bank and the IMF and the hegemonic actors within the Bank and Fund membership. While there remains a strong and substantial element of coercion in the practice of conditionality, the new modalities of conditionality enable the internalisation of reform in ways that were not possible under the coercive attribute of traditional conditionality.

In this case, new modalities of conditionality increase the uptake of reforms pursued by traditional conditionality as the rubric of 'ownership' enables country authorities to identify with the policy architecture of the Washington Consensus reforms and reiterate their commitment to it, notwithstanding the force of financing that underpins the pressure to comply. This capture of the *biopolitics* of the borrowing state is further reinforced by the discursive function of the PRSP approach (discussed in the following chapters), which legitimises the nomenclature of partnership, ownership and participation.

The biopolitical power exercised by the international financial institutions through borrowing member states is then reified through the structural changes that are adopted by the latter under the auspices of 'ownership' as conditionality. The legitimacy of the reforms that are undertaken under the new financing instruments/adjustment operations linked to the PRSP process must be sustained not only through the capture of policy space within the borrowing member states and of the elite policymakers who negotiate on their behalf, but also through a more systemic restructuring of the socio-political fabric of the countries subject to the reforms. Chapters 5 and 6 examine how this concept of 'ownership' has been operationalised in order to re-engineer the political, economic and social institutions of borrowing member states under the PRSP framework.

Notes

1 For example, the Ugandan PRSC Agreement, dated 5 July 2001, provides in Article III, Section 3, that 'the Borrower undertakes to implement the Program with due diligence to ensure that actions and policies adopted under the Program are put into effect', with the program of actions attached in Annex 2 of the agreement (Republic of Uganda, 2001: Article III, Section 3.01(a)).

2 US negotiators at the conference had advocated that the Fund be invested with wide discretion to impose conditions on the use of Fund resources, but UK negotiators, led by economist John Maynard Keynes, argued for full automaticity in Fund financing along the lines of a rule-based international credit union. The fear was that a highly discretionary regime 'would give the United States too much control over the use of the Fund's resources' and hence impede access to funds by other countries (Woods, 2006: 25).

3 This consideration should include 'the member's records of prudence in drawing, its willingness to offer voluntary repayment when its situation permitted, and its promptness in fulfilling the obligation to transmit monetary reserves data and in discharging repurchase obligations' (IMF, 1952).

4 The revised Article I of the Articles of Agreement now states that the purposes of the IMF include giving 'confidence to members by making general resources of the Fund temporarily available to them under *adequate safeguards*, thus providing them with opportunity to correct maladjustments in their balance of payments without resorting to measures destructive of national or international prosperity' (IMF Articles of Agreement, Article I, Section (v), emphasis added).

5 The satisfaction of this criteria is usually demonstrated by a country's satisfactory implementation of an IMF programme, such as an ECF (World Bank, 2004d: para. 5, fn. 4).

6 For example, conditionalities may trigger states' adoption of principles of deregulation and liberalisation in regulatory domains such as trade or labour treaties (Braithwaite and Drahos, 2000: 525).

7 As discussed in Chapter 1, Braithwaite and Drahos examine the phenomenon of global business regulation through the interplay between the principles contested in this process of globalisation, the actors involved in this contest and the mechanisms used by various actors to universally embed pursued principles (see Chapter 1, section 1.4; also Braithwaite and Drahos, 2000: 15–33). The ability of hegemonic actors, notably powerful state actors, to weave webs of rewards and coercion is critical to the globalisation of particular regulatory norms. Development financing or 'foreign aid' is a significant and powerful instrument of reward *and* coercion, functioning both as a means of 'raising the expected value of compliance' with prescribed regulatory reforms ('reward') and as a means of reducing the expected value of non-compliance' ('coercion') (see Braithwaite and Drahos, 2000: 550–559).

8 The GRA is the principal account through which the IMF transacts with its membership. It is made up of 'a pool of currencies and reserve assets built up from members' fully paid capital subscriptions in the form of quotas' (IMF, 2001b: 19; see also Figure 3 on pp. 230–1). Members 'borrow' from the GRA under a complicated 'purchase–repurchase' mechanism, which sees members 'purchasing' the reserve assets from the IMF with its own currency and repaying the 'loan' by 'repurchasing' its own currency from the IMF with the reserve assets subject to a rate of interest (IMF, 2001b: 21). Resources in the GRA are supplemented by borrowings by the IMF from official lenders under both the General Arrangements to Borrow (GAB) and New Arrangements to Borrow (NAB), with a group of 11 industrialised and 25 industrialised and emerging market economies, respectively (ibid.: 72–73; see also Woods, 2006: 30–32).

9 See GAB and NAB, (IMF, 2001b: 21; Woods, 2006: 30–32).

10 The reserve tranche refers to funds equivalent to 25 per cent of a country's quota at the IMF. Countries wishing to draw beyond this, known as drawing in the 'upper credit tranches', can only do so via a Stand-By or Extended Arrangement (see the following discussion). Access by members to resources in the credit tranches is subjected to annual and cumulative limits which are subject to review by the IMF's Executive Board. Until 2009, countries could normally draw up to 100 per cent of their quotas annually or 300 per cent cumulatively but with the possibility that access above these limits (sometimes up to 600 per cent of quota) would be approved by the Executive Board under exceptional circumstances (IMF, 2008c: para. 17–18). In March 2009, the Executive Board approved a doubling of these limits to 200 per cent annually and 600 per cent cumulatively for non-concessional drawings (IMF, 2009f). The same decision also introduced the Flexible Credit Line, the first IMF facility with no hard cap on the amount to be drawn by eligible members (IMF, 2009g: 2).

11 These documents are supposedly 'prepared by the country authorities, with the cooperation and assistance of the Fund staff' (IMF, 2002b: para. 10) but, as discussed in earlier chapters, it is the IMF that determines the major portion of the content of the policies contained in these documents. In fact, the IMF admits that country authorities 'generally do not write the first draft of the LOI', although they may participate in designing the programme or contribute towards the redrafting of the document (IMF, 2005c: para. 79). However, the Fund does not view this as 'a source of significant concern' as this did not mean there was no policy dialogue between the IMF and the borrowing country – 'it is clear that the task of document production is less important than the central work of program design' (ibid.).

12 This confirmed the legality of the IMF's Trust Fund established in 1976 for the same purpose but originally under an implied power (see Gold, 1996: 368–369). The Trust Fund was replaced by the Structural Adjustment Facility (SAF) in 1986 and then by the ESAF Trust in 1989 and the PRGF–Exogenous Shocks Facility (ESF) Trust in 1999. In 2009, the IMF executive directors approved the replacement of the PRGF–ESF Trust with a new Poverty Reduction and Growth Trust (IMF, 2009a: para. 6).

13 The PRGT borrows from a number of sources – central banks, governments and other official institutions – to lend to eligible countries and repays the loans with market rate interest to the lenders. The difference between the rate of interest paid to lenders and the concessional interest rate of 0.25 per cent paid to the Trust by PRGT borrowers is subsidised by contributions from bilateral donors and from earnings from the IMF (IMF, 2009h: 5).

14 Nonetheless, Gold is of the opinion that, regardless of its classification, nothing in the Trust instruments for concessional financing suggests that policies prescribed within a member's programme supported by Fund financing have contractual force, 'so that no inference could be drawn that a departure from them was a breach of [a contractual] obligation' (Gold, 1996: 369). This view appears to be supported by the recent Board decision on the Guidelines on Conditionality 2002 (IMF, 2002a: para. 9, reproduced in section 4.2.1). While reaffirming that no Fund arrangements can be considered as having contractual force, the statement does not refer specifically to general resources and can therefore be assumed to encompass all forms of IMF financing, including concessional lending under the PRGT.

15 Article 102(1) of the UN Charter states: 'Every treaty and every international agreement entered into by any Member of the United Nations after the present Charter comes into force shall as soon as possible be registered with the Secretariat and published by it'.

16 Some observers, such as Degnbol-Martinussen and Engberg-Pedersen, contend that, in any case, the institutional framework for policy-based financing, including balance

of payments support, structural adjustment and budget support, remains organised along the lines of a project, which they define as 'an externally formulated intervention in the local development process' (Degnbol-Martinussen and Engberg-Pedersen, 2003: 188). This is because most policy-based programmes have 'a clear time perspective and a series of well-defined activities financed by a donor in agreement with a partner in the developing country', enabling the donor to support 'directly only those activities that are in accordance with the goals of its development and aid policy' (ibid.).

17 Although the terms and conditions are slightly different in the event of a breach (see section 4.2.2.(b)).

18 The exception was 'liberally construed' early on by an authoritative interpretation issued by the IBRD's executive directors on 20 September 1946 at the request of the US (Shihata, 2000b: 83; 2000c: 233).

19 For the IBRD, this would include 'the facilitation of investment of capital for productive purposes, the promotion of private foreign investment, and the promotion of the "long-range balanced growth of international trade and the maintenance of equilibrium in balances of payments by encouraging international investment for the development of the productive resources of members"' (Shihata, 2000a: 379; IBRD Articles of Agreement, Article I), while for the IDA these purposes would include the promotion of economic development, increasing productivity and the raising of living standards within the less-developed members of the Association and the provision of concessional financing (IDA Articles of Agreement, Article I). The Bank's practice has been to classify policy-based loans – 'which do not indicate the specific uses to which their proceeds are to be put' – as fulfilling this requirement (World Bank, 2002b: para. 5).

20 For IDA countries, it was agreed that the Bank management would seek additional guidance from IDA's executive directors if the projected share of development policy commitments exceeds 30 per cent for any future year (World Bank, 2009e: 1, fn. 2).

21 This, however, does not detract from the fact that the disciplinary impact of conditionality is as severe as that of a covenanted legal obligation, as failure to implement policy reforms could lead to a suspension of financial disbursements from the Bretton Woods institutions and, in the case of the IMF, a corresponding declaration that a country's programme is 'off track'. The repercussions of such penalties are similar, if not equivalent to, the effect a breach of a legal obligation would have on financial flows to affected countries, as many donors condition aid on satisfactory execution of a Fund and/or Bank programme of adjustment.

22 Under the par value system, all member states had to fix their exchange rates to the gold standard or to the US dollar (original Article IV of the IMF Articles of Agreement). Currencies of IMF member states were required to maintain their value and allow their currencies to fluctuate only within a narrow band (original Article IV(3)). If a member state wanted to change the par value of its currency beyond 10 per cent from its original value, it was required to consult the Fund in advance and seek its approval (original Article IV(5)).

23 For further details on the IMF's surveillance role, see IMF, 2009i.

24 Some commentators, such as former UNCTAD senior economist Yilmaz Akyüz, have argued that there has never been a sound rationale for this move into development financing as not only are these areas better covered by other agencies, such as multilateral and regional development banks, including the World Bank, but also 'it is not clear that the Fund has the necessary competence and experience in such complex issues' of structural and institutional reform (Akyüz, 2005: 18–19).

25 See further discussion of the disjuncture between PRSP policy and practice in Chapter 6, section 6.4.

26 These may include a CAS Progress Report (CAS PR), a mid-term assessment of a country's CAS and an Interim Strategy Note (ISN), an interim document pending a full CAS (see World Bank, 2009e: para. 3).

27 Each IDA member is allocated a basic resource envelope (currently SDR1.5 million or US$2.3 million a year), with special considerations being given to 'blend' countries, which may receive less than their quota due to their ability to raise financing elsewhere; and to post-conflict countries and countries facing the aftermath of natural disasters, which may require more (IDA, 2008, Annex 1: paras 5–7).

28 Gold characterises 'soft law' in the context of the IMF as an expression of 'preference for, or of abstention from, specified behavior by members. The behavior, whether it be action, or forbearance, can fall within the regulatory or the financial jurisdiction of the IMF' (Gold, 1996: 302–303).

29 Although Sgard's analysis is based on his research into the IMF's role in sovereign debt restructuring, it can nonetheless be applied analogously to the Fund's practice of conditionality in general (Sgard, 2004).

30 The authors examined a sample of IMF credits extended under SBAs and the EFF over the period from 1986 to 1998 and came to three conclusions: (1) US commercial bank interests strongly bias IMF lending so that countries with higher exposure to US debt are offered larger loans; (2) debts owed to US banks 'occupy a privileged position within the IMF' over debts owed to other G7 countries; and (3) the size of IMF loans corresponds to US foreign policy interests, with larger loans being offered 'to governments who regularly vote with the United States in the UN than to governments who vote less regularly with the US' (Oatley and Yackee, 2004: 419, 425).

31 That is, stipulating that resources made available to a member will be repaid to be reused by other members (see Buira, 2003: 3; IMF, 2001b: 144).

32 This observation is gleaned from interviews with current and former Bank and Fund staff members as well as from attendance at institutional dialogues and meetings over the research period.

33 Although the term 'post-conditionality' is problematic as current developments demonstrate a continuity with rather than a departure from the fundamental exercise of conditionality, this terminology does not detract from Harrison's analysis of the current state of conditionality in practice.

34 Mosley *et al.* noted that the practice of 'tranching' had increased since the inception of policy-based lending at the Bank, with loans being sliced into 'smaller and smaller elements' as a means of ensuring greater Bank leverage over borrowing countries (Mosley *et al.*, 1991: 45).

35 A similar review takes place at the Bank in the context of its policy-based loans but, unlike in Fund financing, review conditions are not regarded as critical to tranche disbursements.

36 The IMF's establishment of the new Flexible Credit Line is premised on the use of *ex-ante* conditionality as an instrument of selectivity, with countries assured of upfront access to IMF resources without *ex-post* conditionalities if they meet a rigorous pre-qualification criteria (IMF, 2009g: 2).

37 For example 'the enactment of laws on fiscal responsibility, financial administration, procurement and internal audit' (World Bank, 2005b: para. 72).

38 Such as 'legislative oversight functions and new budget classifications' (ibid.).

39 Alexander, who headed various Washington, DC-based NGOs, such as the Globalisation Challenge Initiative and the Citizens Network on Essential Services (CNES), was one of the first activists who highlighted the potential pitfalls of the CPIA when the Bank proposed its implementation.

Chapter 5

Reforming the nation state

PRSPs and rehabilitating the structurally adjusted state

> [T]he state remains a vital point of concentration of capitalist power, even, or especially, in today's global capitalism, and … the empire of capital depends upon a system of multiple states.
>
> (E.M. Wood, 2005: 14)

The introduction of the Poverty Reduction Strategy Paper approach as a mechanism for governing the relationship between low-income countries and the international development community has resulted in significant changes to the domestic constitutions of these countries. A retreat from the first generation adjustment reforms which sought to roll back the state, this new approach goes further than the second generation reforms by seeking to reconstitute fundamental elements of the state, resulting in the immediate (and almost uniform) reorganisation of political and bureaucratic processes across a large swathe of countries in the third world.

Chapter 4 demonstrated that the principle of 'ownership' as enshrined in the PRSP approach represents a continuation of the existing practice of 'conditionality' in which financing is exchanged for external resources. 'Ownership', as operationalised under the PRSP framework and the attendant instruments of the 'new architecture of aid', extends the disciplinary power of conventional conditionality through the capture of the body politic of the client state. The following two chapters demonstrate how this biopolitical power exercised over these countries by the Bretton Woods institutions and, by extension, the wider donor community is reinforced by the operational changes imposed upon and absorbed by client states under the PRSP approach.

Towards this end, it is argued that the reforms implemented by the PRSP framework serve two essential purposes vis-à-vis governance of these countries in the wider global economic arena: first, the PRSP framework acts as a *disciplinary* mechanism by facilitating extensive regulatory and institutional reforms in the recipient state required to entrench the policy reforms imposed through substantive conditionalities. Second, the PRSP framework performs a *legitimising* function by reconfiguring the relations in domestic policy and political circles in order to mobilise disparate voices behind the objectives of the aforementioned substantive conditionalities.

This chapter maintains that the current drive to rehabilitate the state apparatus in developing countries, through mechanisms such as the PRSP framework, stems not from the desire to transfer policy autonomy to governments in the south but from: (1) the need to co-opt recalcitrant states into submitting to the necessary regulatory and policy reforms for the conducive operation of transnational capital, *or*, in the case of 'fragile' or post-conflict states,[1] to restore basic institutional structures to pursue such reforms; and (2) the need to mitigate the dislocations associated with the pursuit of such reforms through the rehabilitation of the state's regulatory and economic oversight function, and, to a lesser extent, its function as an overseer of citizenry welfare.

These objectives are achieved via a similarly two-tiered process under the PRSP framework. The first objective is achieved through the *capture of policy space* and the internalisation of the politics of reform by the recipient states under the rubric of 'ownership' and 'partnership', the association of the policymakers and politicians that forms the disciplinary aspect of the approach. The second objective is achieved through the *capture of political space*[2] by the donor community and of political and social capital via the PRSP consultative mechanism and a focus on social sector expenditure under the rubric of 'participation' and 'poverty reduction'. The systemic imperatives of neoliberal imperialism therefore dictate the introduction of a mechanism of control – the PRSP process – and its attendant discourses of 'ownership', 'partnership', 'participation' and 'poverty reduction' as a means of legitimising and controlling the direction of policy reform and 'development' options within the states in receipt of development financing.

This chapter considers the mechanisms through which the state apparatuses of PRSP countries are reconfigured so as to enable the capture of domestic policy space by the donor community and how these modalities of state reconfiguration serve the disciplinary and legitimising function ascribed to the PRSP framework outlined above. In particular, it considers the means through which the PRSP framework facilitates the reinscription of the state's regulative capacity – through globalising development planning and standardising bureaucratic governance in PRSP countries – and examines the manner in which such reforms have served as a disciplinary, as opposed to emancipatory, function in managing PRSP countries' engagement with the international community. This discussion will then be followed up in Chapter 6, which explores how the PRSP framework subsequently reconstitutes the relationship between this reconstructed state apparatus and its political constituents so as to further entrench and legitimise its underlying disciplinary objectives.

5.1 Rehabilitation of the state

5.1.1 The good governance agenda: continuities and discontinuities

a) The state and good governance

A dominant feature of the epistemology of globalisation in the mid- and late-1990s was the hegemony of discourses on the role of the state. Notably prevalent were theories on the erosion of state autonomy and national sovereignty in the wake of the intensification of cross-border social, cultural, technological and economic relations. This epistemic movement mirrored the prevailing conceptual framework that underlied the policies pursued by the international financial community, notably the Washington Consensus approach to economic policy of the IFIs in the 1980s and the early 1990s, premised on the need to roll back the state and on the withdrawal of the state from economic activity (see Chapter 3). The subsequent retreat from the discourse of the withering state is correspondingly tied to the shift in this conceptual and operational framework.

Consequently, commentators such as Jayasuriya and Wood have sought to reconceptualise the role of the state in light of the shifting forms of governance at the global level, notably the reinscription of state regulation in the disciplinary framework of global governance. According to Jayasuriya, the current drive to re-engineer the state's institutional form and reconstruct elements of its relationship with the exterior must be placed within the context of how 'economic order is produced and reproduced in the global economy', with the maintenance of such order in today's 'emergent global economy' contingent upon the reshaping of domestic regulatory regimes[3] (Jayasuriya, 2001a: 5–6). For Wood, this present reconstruction reflects the enduring disciplinary significance of the entity of the nation state in the sustenance of what she terms the 'empire of capital', manifested today in 'the new imperialism we call globalization' (E.M. Wood, 2005: 10–14; 154–155).

The 'good governance' agenda, the predecessor of the PRSP approach, can be viewed as forming the operational backdrop to these conceptualisations. Acknowledging the failure of policies to liberalise and deregulate economic activity without corresponding state capacity to coordinate such reforms, this agenda sought to develop the legal and institutional structures necessary to facilitate policy implementation. The role of the state was redefined as primarily 'to support markets by adopting policies and providing institutions that allow free markets to work efficiently', including regulatory institutions aimed, *inter alia*, at 'achieving and maintaining stable property rights', 'maintaining good rule of law and contract enforcement', 'minimising expropriation risks … rent-seeking and corruption' and 'achieving transparent and accountable provision of public goods' (UNCTAD, 2009: v).

An important component of governance reforms was therefore the development of what Jayasuriya terms a 'new proceduralism' (Jayasuriya, 2001b: 120) – the enhancement of accountability and transparency in economic decision-making and adjudication – but at the same time reducing or eliminating the state's productive and/or redistributive role in the economy. For example, he notes that one of the concerns of the 'good governance' agenda 'has been to ensure that the process of economic deregulation and privatization does not lead to the capturing of key markets by politically connected groups and individuals' (Jayasuriya, 1999). Towards this end, the development of the rule of law under the aegis of judicial reform and the endorsement of public sector reforms, such as anti-corruption and transparency in procurement initiatives, formed the bulk of these 'second generation reforms'. In this respect, the constitutive role of law is enrolled 'to normalize a particular structure of private rights and confine regulatory interventions by the State' in order to construct acceptance around a specific mode of social and economic organisation in developing countries (see Rittich, 2006: 215–216).

Viewed from a postcolonial perspective, the 'good governance' agenda provided the 'moral and intellectual foundation' for developing and reproducing in the third world the institutions and policies of the western liberal state to enable the furtherance of economic globalisation (Anghie, 2004: 249, 253). This necessarily implied what UNCTAD terms 'an implicit dichotomy between good and bad government systems', with good governance associated with systems prevalent in developed countries and bad governance with those of poor countries (UNCTAD, 2009: v). The 'good governance' agenda thus sought to introduce the institutional framework characteristic of western governance systems into developing countries and prescribe the aforementioned specific market regulatory role for the state (ibid.).

b) PRSPs and the new governance agenda

In spite of similarities, the 'good governance' agenda is distinctly conceptually and operationally divergent from the policy and practice that underpin the PRSP approach. As Abrahamsen notes, the policies and practice of the 'good governance' project did little to reinvigorate the functions of the state that had been circumscribed by the free market reforms of the first generation structural reforms: 'The ideal "good governance state" is still a minimal state; it is just more efficient and competent in carrying out economic reforms' (Abrahamsen, 2000: 42).

These reforms therefore entailed changes around the periphery of government functions and, while they included some contentious political and judicial reform projects, were largely technical in nature, involving the restructuring of state-owned enterprises, the development and improvement of legal and judicial institutions to facilitate such restructuring, and so on. The reforms did not intrude into the core of policy decisions in the client countries, and, *more importantly*, nor were they made preconditions for financing from the World Bank, the IMF or bilateral agencies. Instead, governance reforms were largely funded by project aid and were considerably delinked from the policy-based loans of the World Bank, and, even more so, shielded from the stabilisation programmes of the IMF.

The PRSP initiative, on the other hand, adopts a more holistic and consequently more interventionist approach to the embedding of structural reforms. 'Government effectiveness' (World Bank, 2005h: para. 7) is now considered a central plank of any World Bank operation, reflecting the Bank's new conceptual approach aimed at (1) defining 'the role of the state on the basis of its capacities'

financing programmes requires a substantial degree of domestic expertise and knowledge which 'cannot be well designed primarily by an external agency [b]ecause good design requires intimate knowledge of the local setting and institutions and because implementation requires some degree of consent from the many stakeholders' (Morrow, 2005: 4). Such domestic 'ownership' is also perceived to reduce the 'transaction costs' of implementing reforms and reflects the view, as observed by Piron and Evans, 'that "ownership" is instrumentally important to the efficient use of aid' (Piron with Evans, 2004: 4).

b) The enabling state

The conceptual shift of the PRSP framework may be viewed as recognition of the importance of the role of the nation state as a nodule for capital accumulation and neoliberal globalisation, whether in pursuit of such policies as an end or as a means of achieving socio-economic development and/or 'poverty reduction'. This is due not only to the state's inherent ability to translate transnational regulation into domestic norms – for example adjustment conditionalities and international trade obligations into local law – and maintain domestic governance mechanisms to ensure the implementation of such norms (through liberalisation and privatisation measures) but also to its power to enrol nationalist ideologies to legitimise the logic of these reforms. The modern nation state, even the most fractured state, continues to exercise sole sovereign authority over its political, territorial and economic jurisdiction and commands the domestic legitimacy in support of such authority, however circumscribed this authority and legitimacy may be.

The maintenance of discipline within a state, incorporated as the state may be into the international political economy, remains dependent on the internal state apparatuses and the political and policymaking elite who administer the institutions of the state. Consequently, the biopolitical power that is exercised by the international financial institutions and the hegemon states in the international political order needs to be translated into the local setting, through what Poulantzas (relying on Foucault) calls the instruments of 'physical constraint' – the prison, the army, the police, the judiciary – and through the 'manipulation and the consumption of bodies', an order which moulds the domestic citizenry and inserts them into 'the various institutions and apparatuses' of the state (Poulantzas, 2000: 29). The state is necessary in order to install 'a uniform *national* language' and eliminate all other languages, not only for 'the creation of a national economy and market, but still more for the exercise of the State's political role' in this market economy (ibid.: 58).

For Poulantzas, the characteristic of a capitalist state is its role in atomising or individualising components of the market economy: 'the atomization of the body-politic into what are called "individuals" – that is, juridical-political persons, who are the subjects of certain freedoms' (Poulantzas, 2000: 63). Such diffusion of elements requires the existence of both a 'centralized, bureaucratized

State' to install and organise this atomisation as well as 'a representative State' to lay claim to national sovereignty and 'popular will' to hold together this fracturing of the 'people-nation' (ibid.: 63, 65).

In this manner, while the reforms of the adjustment and governance period served to instil the form of liberal politics and liberal legality in the recipient countries through privatisation and liberalisation of the domestic economy and the installation of institutions to police this individualisation, these reforms failed to instil (and, in the first instance, dismantled) the organisational structure of the state to effectively manage the discipline of the neoliberal market reforms. As Fitzpatrick notes in relation to structural adjustment conditionalities, 'these conditions, for all their seemingly anti-statist character, still call for a strong national state to enact and enforce them' (Fitzpatrick, 2001: 214).

Therefore, it can be argued that the new conceptual framework of development financing is predicated upon the need to rehabilitate the regulative (and, to a certain extent, prescriptive) function of the state, to reinvigorate both the functions of the 'national representative State'[5] (Poulantzas, 2000: 63) as well as the 'hierarchical and bureaucratic centralism' (ibid.) of the state subject to adjustment policies. At the same time, the framework does not and cannot ascribe to the state the autonomy that is associated with full-fledged articulation of national sovereignty at the risk of fracturing the existing international political economy's dependency on this unequal relationship.

Instead, this rehabilitation is mediated through the new precepts of 'ownership' and 'partnership' under the rubric of the PRSP initiative, providing the disciplinary framework to (1) create a facilitative domestic political *as well as* a bureaucratic environment for the embedding of substantive fiscal and structural reforms à la Washington Consensus and (2) replicate this environment universally across all countries subject to the reform. At the same time, the PRSP process legitimises the reforms through the capture of political consensus (and therefore resistance) in the consultative/participatory mechanisms (see Chapter 6).

In this manner, the PRSP approach serves to address a challenge that is posed by the reinstatement of the state as the locus of current globalisation trends, that is, how these states can and should be managed internally. Describing the 'political form of globalization' as not one of 'a global state but a global system of multiple local states structured in a complex relation of domination and subordination', Wood contends that the 'administrative and coercive functions' of nation states remain important local facilitators of global capital, providing 'regularity, predictability and legal order' critical to capital's operations in each locality (E.M. Wood, 2005: 141). She argues that

> because the new imperialism depends more than ever on a system of multiple states to maintain global order, *it matters more than ever what local forces govern them and how.*
>
> (E.M. Wood, 2005: 155, emphasis added)

The PRSP approach is an attempt to facilitate this 'what' – policymakers, politicians, civil society members who share in the underlying ideology of the reforms – and 'how', commitment to what Gould describes as 'a multi-tethered program of state reform' (Gould, 2005a; 2005b: 2) in return for financing. These reforms, as Gould demonstrates through his compendium of empirical studies,[6] 'both *reorganize* and *rationalize* the social relations of aid management' (ibid.: 143) and, in the process, set a precedent for future modalities of delivering aid and also for the governance of the international political economy.

5.2 Modalities of state reconfiguration

The process of restructuring the state apparatuses under the PRSP approach takes place on two fronts: (1) through the imposition of a standardised mechanism for policy discussion and formulation – the Poverty Reduction Strategy (PRS) process – and a universal blueprint for developing national development plans – the PRSP document; and (2) through efforts to centre key policymaking processes around the PRSP and to standardise bureaucratic practice according to the principles established by the PRSP approach and the attendant norms of the new architecture of aid.

The reconstituted regulative capacity of the state is subsequently strengthened by conditioning access to financing instruments on the assessment of countries' commitments to reform processes, for example through the JSAN process, *ex-ante* conditionality and new modalities of financing, such as budget support and programmatic lending (see section 5.4).

5.2.1 Globalised development modelling

The PRSP is, in effect, a universal blueprint for instituting a process for developing and designing national economic plans. According to a senior Bank economist, the Comprehensive Development Framework (see Chapters 1 and 3) and the PRSP were both born out of a recognition by key Bank staff of the contribution of investment 'in developing a long-term strategy' towards a 'successful development experience' and the systemic failure of ad-hoc, uncoordinated development financing, particularly in low-income countries (interview: Guerrero, 2004). Much of this has been in response to the fragmented nature of financial planning in PRSP-eligible countries and the duplicity of administration relating to development financing, a perennial symptom of aid dependency.

Consequently, the PRSP approach involves, in many cases, a radical overhaul of the business of government in PRSP countries. Not only do PRSP country governments have to establish new mechanisms of domestic dialogue and consultation to fulfil the procedural requirements of the PRSP initiative, but national planning strategies and priorities must also now be reframed in the language of the new PRSP discourse. As such, the PRSP 'aims to be far more than a forum about the exchange about priorities', representing, instead, the domestic manifestation of a 'globally prescribed' set of economic and social reform policies (Craig and Porter, 2003: 60).

a) Unified policy process

Most notably, the PRSP framework requires the establishment of a 'participatory process' through which the PRSP document will be formulated 'to design and to build ownership for the strategy' (World Bank and IMF, 2005a: Annex 1, para. A1). This should include, *inter alia,* participation by all segments of the government (central ministries, regional departments, parliaments and subnational governments); other 'stakeholders' (civil society groups, groups representing minority communities, the epistemic community, the private sector, trade unions, etc.); and bilateral and multilateral donors (ibid.). It must also make provisions for consultations with representatives of 'the poor' (ibid.). The objective of the PRSP approach is thus to secure a political consensus around a set of national expenditure priorities and the economic policies to achieve those priorities.

Although the World Bank and the IMF claim that the PRS process is not prescriptive, these institutions have a fairly comprehensive template for what constitutes an appropriate policymaking and policy coordination process and consultative mechanism for policy dialogue. The Bank's *PRSP Sourcebook,* for example, details how the institution expects the process to unfold at country level, including listing actors to be engaged in the participatory process and identifying how poverty reduction and growth strategies can be defined (Klugman, 2002: 5, Figure 5.1). The tension between the objective of engendering 'country ownership' of strategies for poverty reduction and economic development *and* the need to do so under a strict timeline and prescribed conditions – a key point noted by the Bank's and Fund's internal evaluations of the PRSP (see, for example, IMF, 2004a; World Bank, 2004b; World Bank and IMF, 2005b) – is clearly highlighted through this process. Not only is the overriding framework for policy dialogue predetermined, but these 'home-grown' strategies must also fit into a series of prescribed bureaucratic action plans with specified results.

A notable effort in the task of fostering 'country ownership' in PRS processes – aside from the external consultative process discussed in Chapter 6 – is the integration of 'line ministries' into the PRSP process, broadening up the scope for policy formulation for development financing priorities to include ministries other than the finance or economic planning ministries. As the BWIs note: 'Line ministries are key to successful implementation and need to be involved in PRS formulation to help identify development objectives and prepare sectoral plans to achieve them' (World Bank and IMF, 2004: para. 28).

While this can be interpreted as a positive recognition of the role played by the cross-section of government departments in the process of social and economic development, it can also be seen as a means of co-opting policymakers who may not subscribe to the reforms required as conditionalities under financing agreements as they were previously negotiated by the finance ministry and the BWIs. By ensuring that civil servants and politicians in peripheral departments are integrated into the planning processes, the BWIs will be able to ensure that they continue 'to be active by further developing implementation action plans in their respective areas of responsibility' (World Bank and IMF, 2004: para. 28).

This measure is less about counteracting the hegemony of finance ministries in client states – which arose from adjustment-era financing relationships as these ministries assumed the role of conduits for external financing and fiscal discipline (see Harrison, 2001b: 664–665) – than about ensuring compliance with the substantive policies of post-adjustment financing. As Harrison notes, in his study of what he terms the 'post-conditionality regime' (see Chapter 4, section 4.4) in Uganda and Tanzania, finance ministries and public service ministries have gained ascendancy in the post-SAP era, the former as 'powerful producers of neo-liberal orthodoxy' and the latter as 'executors of administrative reform programmes', as a result of the ongoing efforts by external donors to internalise neoliberalism and to administer public sector reforms in pursuit of this orthodoxy (Harrison, 2001b: 668). The PRSP framework extends this process by broadening political ownership of adjustment reforms, ensuring that a broad range of ministries are involved not just in the execution of policy but in the formulation of it as well.

The scope for policy formulation under the PRSP framework is, however, severely straitjacketed in line with the reformist orthodoxies which characterise this 'new architecture of aid'. While the stated objective of the PRSP initiative is country ownership and while the BWIs have repeatedly reiterated the need to tailor country strategies to country conditions, the PRSP process and policy content remain largely formulaic and prescriptive. PRSPs are expected to address key issues and follow a set template for presentation of these issues (see Klugman, 2002: 5, Figure 5.1). In preparing an assessment of a country's PRSP in the Joint Staff Advisory Note, Bank and Fund staffs are therefore guided by a country's coverage of the following 'five basic elements':

1. assessment of poverty in the country and its key determinants;
2. setting targets for poverty reduction;
3. prioritising public actions for poverty reduction;
4. establishing monitoring of poverty trends and monitoring the impact of government policies on poverty reduction;
5. description of the participatory process.

(Klugman, 2002: 4; World Bank and IMF, 2005a: Annex 1)

The uniformity of these policy interventions is then further maintained by pivoting disbursements on the PRSP through donor-coordinated financing mechanisms, such as the Multi-Donor Budget Support (MDBS) programme in Ghana and the Tanzanian Partnership Framework for Budget Support, so that different donor programmes are consolidated around the countries' PRSPs and PRSP annual progress reports (APRs) (see, for example, Government of Ghana, 2005; Thompson, 2004; also section 5.4).[7] This consolidation of aid disbursement around the PRSP as an operational instrument raises important questions not just about the drivers of policy and regulatory reform in PRSP countries but also about government accountability for public action within these countries (see Chapter 6).

b) Universal targets and indicators

In spite of rhetoric to the contrary, the strategic priorities of the PRSP must fit into the parameters established by the World Bank and the IMF. Under the PRSP approach, priorities for public expenditure and government action in relation to most social and economic policies have largely been predetermined. As will also be discussed in section 5.5, these parameters are fairly narrow and do not allow for much deviation from the standard Washington Consensus economic model, particularly in relation to structural and macroeconomic policy.

The overarching framework for government action in PRSP countries is that of engendering 'pro-poor growth' through four priority areas identified by the Bank and the Fund, as identified by the *PRSP Sourcebook* – 'macroeconomic and structural policies', 'improvements in governance', 'appropriate sectoral policies and programs' and 'realistic costing and appropriate levels of funding for major programs' (Klugman, 2002: 4, Box 1). The *PRSP Sourcebook* notes that '[e]very PRSP would be expected to provide an adequate overall treatment of each of these four areas … although [w]hat is covered within each area will … differ across countries' (ibid.: 4).

A study by UNCTAD of the PRSP approach in Africa in 2002 criticised the policy framework which underpins PRSP formulation, questioning the PRSP approach's continued endorsement of 'the very stabilization policies and structural reforms that have barely succeeded in bringing about growth and reducing poverty' and the lack of concern for these policies on poverty (UNCTAD, 2002b: 59). The report concluded that 'there is no fundamental departure' from the policies espoused under the old structural adjustment programmes underpinned by the 'Washington Consensus' approach to economic reforms designed to 'get prices right' (ibid.: 6–7). Instead, the policies of this 'post-Washington Consensus' involve an additional focus on country institutions – 'getting institutions right' (ibid.) – with a focus on strengthening domestic institutional frameworks to support the macroeconomic and structural reforms of the previous generation of adjustment. In other words, PRSPs, particularly first generation PRSPs, 'just added a social dimension to the structural adjustment programmes of the 1990s by focusing on increasing public expenditure in social sectors' (UNCTAD, 2000, 2002, cited in UNCTAD, 2008).

Although there has been evidence to suggest that the second generation of PRSPs – prepared by countries undergoing a second round under the process – has evolved to adopt slightly more pluralistic policy approaches, they still remain tightly constrained by the aid framework under which they are prepared (UNCTAD, 2008: 100–102, 106–108). The asymmetrical power dynamics between financiers and client states resulting from resource dependency has meant that the content of PRSPs can be significantly influenced by donor preferences, with aid recipient states eschewing policy approaches which, at best, may not reflect donor financing priorities and, at worst, may incur sanctions due to incompatibility with donors' strategic policies (ibid.). As UNCTAD notes, 'there have been major shifts in the practice of policy conditionality but much less shift in its content', and the 'strategic thrust' of national development strategies contained in PRSPs remains one geared towards 'liberalization and privatization within a tight fiscal and monetary policy (ibid.: 112).

The establishment of a uniform blueprint for national development strategies within these parameters thus responds less to a need to develop appropriate indigenous policies than to a need to facilitate an effective universal mechanism through which financing may be channelled and economic policy prescriptions effectively internalised. External financiers, notably the Bank and the Fund, are therefore, inadvertently or not, engaged in these countries at a much deeper structural level than ever before, directly engaging with the process of managing and directing state policies on a wide range of domestic policy issues and unifying these processes through a common framework.

5.2.2 Standardising domestic governance

Donor influence in client countries' under the PRSP framework is extended further through measures to standardise policymaking processes in PRSP countries, in particular through efforts toward aligning the PRSP process and substantive content with existing government policymaking processes and policy documents as part of a wider objective to centralise all policymaking around the PRSP and PRSP-related documents. At the heart of this exercise is the drive to streamline the local executive and establish the institutions necessary for the successful implementation of prescribed policy reforms, strengthening the capacity of the state to deliver these reforms and of financiers to maintain oversight of such policy execution.

Paradoxically, the World Bank and the IMF have viewed such 'mainstreaming' as indicators of 'country ownership' and have consistently underscored the importance of PRSP integration 'into domestic processes such as elections, the budget and prior strategies' as indicators of 'country commitment' to the PRSP process, and, consequently, to the substantive content of the economic reforms to be undertaken under this initiative (World Bank, 2004b: 12; 2007: paras 20–22). 'Ownership' of PRS principles therefore is evidenced by the integration of the PRSP approach into national decision-making and the establishment of unified strategic frameworks based on the priorities identified through the PRS process (ibid.: paras 21–22).

a) Linking fiscal support systems

The Bank, Fund and other, notably bilateral, donors argue that without adequate links to the operational aspects of public expenditure management (PEM) the PRSP document itself lacks operational relevance and this undermines efforts to allocate resources in accordance with the expenditure priorities established through the participatory consultative process. Furthermore, the objectives of the PRSP cannot be achieved if there are unrealistic fiscal projections of resources not tied to the discipline of a working macroeconomic framework.

The Medium-Term Expenditure Framework is the primary vehicle to which the World Bank and the IMF expect countries to link their PRSP policies. The idea of an MTEF was strongly mooted by the World Bank in the mid- and late-1990s, especially in low-income countries, particularly as an instrument of public expenditure management.[8] MTEFs are required for all PRSP countries seeking Poverty Reduction Strategy Credits from the World Bank and may inform the macroeconomic framework required for IMF PRGF loans. They are also considered part of the country assessment under the HIPC initiative and under the new MDRI.

Linking public policies and budgets over a medium-term period of three to four years, the MTEF provides the fiscal and budgetary discipline that the Bank and Fund believe client countries require in order to achieve the objectives of 'pro-poor growth' (World Bank, 1998: 32, quoted in Le Houerou and Taliercio, 2002: 2). Aimed at 'integrating the top-down resource envelope with the bottom-up sector programs', the MTEF attempts to align resource allocations – determined by fiscal targets, revenue estimates and expenditures – with sector programmes, underpinned by cost estimates of development projects (ibid.: 2–3).

Countries are encouraged to dialogue with external financing agencies in formulating an MTEF in order to align expenditure priorities with potential revenue from grants, loans or debt relief. As such, Craig and Porter view the MTEF as 'the national budgetary complement to the PRSPs, together providing one, comprehensive device binding together global arrangements, national intersectoral budgeting and highly localized investments that were never possible through the "national development plan" and "national account" type devices popular in the immediate post-colonial period' (Craig and Porter, 2003: 61). Thus, it can be argued that while the PRSP represents the means by which the World Bank, the IMF and other financing agencies can control client governments' strategic priorities, the MTEF provides the framework in which these strategies are operationalised and through which they intersect with global financial developments.

While harmonisation of domestic policymaking and national development planning is, in principle, a progressive step forward, the linking of PRSP-type priorities and strategies to other economic and social development planning instruments may have the impact of subverting all other national priorities to those championed under the approach. This may be viewed as a means of disciplining countries' fiscal and budgetary options by reorienting domestic expenditure priorities and policy choices towards those which fit into the institutions' prevailing economic ideology.

The Bank and the Fund, in their evaluation of PRSPs, expect countries to address the structural and sectoral policies that support the economic reforms outlined in the document and the institutional constraints on the achievement of those objectives, including, *inter alia*, the 'prioritization and sequencing of reforms', 'private sector and financial sector development' and 'key social sector policies and programs' as well as 'policies for social inclusion and equity' (World Bank and IMF, 2005b: para. D). These institutional components have gained importance in the years since the PRSP's inception. For example, the changes in the PRS architecture which were endorsed by the Executive Board in September 2004 have reiterated that, among other things, 'the PRS initiative needs to emphasize improvements in *analysis, policies, institutions, and processes* that underpin a PRSP rather than emphasizing production of papers' (ibid.: para. 2, emphasis added).

This 'mainstreaming' exercise therefore has as much, if not more, to do with the need for donors to improve domestic financial resource management as it has to do with linking poverty reduction strategies with financial aid. Aligning government processes with the principles of PRSP facilitates the opening up of government action to public (and, hence, donor) scrutiny and encourages the participation of stakeholders, including financing agencies, in the monitoring of government policy vis-à-vis public expenditure allocations.

b) Establishing institutions for public accountability

As a consequence of the drive for accountability, one of the main initiatives of the PRS approach has the been opening up of public accounts to external inspection, including by auditors from the financing agencies and reforming PEM systems in client countries. As Gould observes, under the PRSP initiative the 'core of the reform agenda comprises a radical renovation of the mechanics of public financial management' (Gould, 2005a: 2). Linking the PRSP process to the MTEF process is one means of strengthening such oversight, and enables external financing agencies to determine the size and shape of the overall resource envelope of a PRSP country and the type of policies such resources should be spent on.[9]

Another World Bank recommendation for increasing PEM surveillance is through Bank-facilitated public expenditure reviews (PERs). The PER is an extensive review of a country's expenditure framework carried out by World Bank consultants, including analysis of the procedural and substantive aspects of a country's PEM system. A PER may include a detailed analysis of a country's fiscal framework, including the constraints that may impede 'effective use of public resources', institutional reforms necessary to expedite budget allocations and measures to improve such allocations (World Bank, 2005i: 1–2). In many cases, the adoption of an MTEF has been the result of a PER (Le Houerou and Taliercio, 2002: 1).

The PER is only one of many technical assistance projects that have accompanied the PRSP initiative in PRSP countries, albeit an increasingly fundamental one. Some of these projects aim to complement the PRSP approach by assisting countries in developing the capacity for formulating PRSP projects, but many are primarily self-serving as they aim to inform donor interventions in PRSP countries and have, consequently, increased donor presence in policy formulation. For example, PRSCs are usually underpinned by the Bank's traditional economic and sector work (ESW) assessing, *inter alia*, 'public financial management systems and key social, structural and sectoral policies', utilising the PER and other economic assessments, such as the Country Financial Accountability Assessment (CFAA) and the Country Procurement Assessment (CPA), as well as the Poverty and Social Impact Assessment (PSIA) (World Bank, 2005b: para. 6). These assessments and reviews often provide the background to determining what money is allocated to a PRSC recipient country and how much. According to the Bank, 'the PRSP provides the overall framework and policy direction for Bank assistance, the ESW informs the policy dialogue that guides the design of the PRSC and helps policy makers formulate a clear agenda to achieve the country's development objectives' (ibid.).

As the standardising of bureaucratic procedures under the PRSP approach becomes commonplace, capacity building projects to 'assist' client countries in meeting these technocratic requirements are set to increase. Aside from grant aid – such as financing under the previously operational PRSP Trust Fund (PRSTF)[10] – technical assistance may also form a part of a client country's actual PRSP and such capacity building projects may be costed as part of the country's application for concessional financing from the Bank, Fund or bilateral donors. Paradoxically, countries may end up having to repay financiers for the technical assistance projects undertaken as part of their application for financing or to meet *ex-ante* conditions, such as CPIA criteria (see Chapter 4, section 4.5) for such financing.

Bank and Fund staff have admitted that many of these governance reforms and much of the ensuing technical assistance have been implemented at the insistence of the major shareholders at the institutions in return for approval of extending limited autonomy to client countries under the CDF/PRSP framework (interviews: various, 2004). It is therefore unsurprising that PRSCs and other policy loans to PRSP countries focus extensively on public sector reforms. In 2005, '[m]ore than 45 percent of all PRSC binding measures entail public sector reforms, of which upward of 64 percent specifically address weaknesses in public financial management' (World Bank, 2005b: para. 66), while a Bank review of development policy lending in 2009 indicated that the majority of policy loans (51 per cent) extended to low-income countries in the period surveyed were aimed at strengthening PEM systems (World Bank, 2009e: para. 17).

The justification for increased PEM oversight due to the shift in financing modalities is replicated in other donor organisations, such as the European Commission (EC), which expects public financial management (PFM) indicators to serve as an important criteria for the disbursements for financing under the Poverty Reduction Budget Support programme of the EC (European Commission, 2005: paras 22, 30). For some client governments, the standards are often too onerous to comply with given the lack of institutional capacity and resources available to meet these conditions, but instead of dispensing with the requirements donors have chosen to assist countries to fulfil these criteria through technical assistance. This reliance on donor-dispensed technical assistance has ironically weakened rather than strengthened country ownership, enabling donors to exercise considerable influence over the design and implementation not just of PEM/PFM systems but also of national economic planning as a whole (UNCTAD, 2008: 107).

5.3 Ownership and the principle of country selectivity

The capture of states' policymaking space under the PRSP framework is strengthened by the operational link between the principle of 'ownership' and the policy of conditionality. The PRSP approach allows donors to respond to country initiatives and provide financing only *if* and *when* countries develop strategies that are acceptable to or correspond with the aid policies of the donor community. A corollary of the establishment of the 'ownership' principle has, therefore, been the development of the concept of 'country selectivity' as a basis for financing allocations. As discussed in Chapter 4, shifts in the modalities of conditionality at the BWIs have resulted in an increase in the use of *ex-ante* conditionality over *ex-post* conditionality (see Chapter 4, section 4.5).

The practice of 'country selectivity' may be situated within this new framework of conditionality. Although this practice does not link policy reform in client countries directly with a specific instrument of financing, it does inform financing decisions at a very political level. The exercise of 'selectivity' makes a country's access to development financing contingent on the country's policy and institutional environment and rewards countries for 'good behaviour' (the adoption of policies agreeable to the financing institutions), using certain indicators of country performance to measure countries' current and future potential for reform.

5.3.1 Rewarding 'good' behaviour

The rationale for 'country selectivity', born out of the debate on aid effectiveness (see Chapter 3), is that a country's track record on policy performance should be one of 'the most robust predictors of whether reforms will be implemented' (Koeberle, 2004: 16). Consequently, a government's commitment to future reforms is judged by its voluntary implementation of policies and institutional reforms which the financing institutions, notably the World Bank and the IMF, consider appropriate to the objectives of development and economic stability.

The Bank's view is that country ownership may be bolstered by forgoing conditionalities 'involving promises of future actions and instead allocat[ing] policy-based loans on the basis of a country's track record' (World Bank, 2005c: para. 11; see also Koeberle, 2004: 17). For a client government, then, the challenge of 'country selectivity' 'is no longer reaching agreement with the Bank on a set of reform measures' but, instead, is one of 'building sufficient support for reforms' already implemented by the country (Morrow, 2004: 6).

The PRSP framework enhances this policy of selectivity by providing a universal template upon which the practice of country selectivity may be exercised. The standardised framework across all PRSP countries facilitates more efficient resource allocation on the part of the financing agencies as it enables financing institutions to determine with greater ease which countries and projects they would support. As the PRSP represents a country's national development plan, from which the donors can select the projects and areas which they would like to support, the impetus is on the country to design a strategy which maximises the financing that is to be received, adhering to the normative framework set by the financing institutions.[11]

As discussed in Chapter 4, most PRSP countries, as IDA borrowers, are already subject to some form of 'selectivity' practice under IDA's performance-based assessment framework (see Chapter 4, section 4.5). The Bank itself acknowledges that IDA's performance rating is to ensure 'that good performers get a higher share of IDA's available resources' (IDA, 2003). It is therefore no surprise that an internal Bank evaluation of the PRSP initiative found that IDA lending has increased for PRSP countries relative to non-PRSP countries and that '[a]nnual lending volumes have been less volatile to the PRSP countries than to the non-PRSP countries' (World Bank, 2004b: 38).

The modalities of financing under the PRSP initiative reflect this new approach of rewarding 'good performers', in particular the Bank's Poverty Reduction Strategy Credits. The World Bank has indicated that PRSC financing 'should remain a selective approach that is reserved for good performers with a proven track record of program implementation' (World Bank, 2005b: para. 41). Accordingly, it is no surprise that PRSC countries tend to rate quite high in their CPIA ratings, with almost all countries for which PRSCs have been approved to date falling in the top three quintiles for the CPIA ratings (ibid.: para. 20). PRSC programmes have tended to reflect the priorities of the 'selectivity' assessments, specifically the inordinate emphasis on governance. Out of 16 CPIA criteria, five are concerned with aspects of domestic governance (IDA, 2003; A. Wood, 2005: 12), areas prioritised under the PRSP framework.

The majority of PRSCs therefore focus substantially on domestic institutional development and social sector expenditure. The Bank's own statistics indicate that 80 per cent of programmes supported by PRSCs were 'overwhelmingly focused on social sector and public sector management themes' in the years

2001 to 2003 compared to similar policy-based lending in 1998–2001, in which the same sectors only made up 45 per cent of the lending (World Bank, undated: 1, para. 3). In these programmes, Bank statistics indicate that more than 45 per cent of all PRSC conditionalities 'entail public sector reforms, of which upward of 64 percent specifically address weaknesses in public financial management' (World Bank, 2005b: para. 66). Further, as mentioned on pp. 149–150, just over half of development policy loans approved for IDA countries between 2006 and 2008 were aimed at strengthening public sector governance (World Bank, 2009e: para. 17). Additionally, while the share of PRSCs as a percentage of IDA policy-based lending has increased (from 2 out of 23 in 2002 to 10 out of 23 in 2004), the overall share of policy-based lending vis-à-vis IDA lending has remained almost the same (ibid.). If the PRSC is indeed a 'reward' for 'good performers', this may indicate that weaker 'performers' stand to lose under this new framework of 'country selectivity' as more financing is geared towards PRSC-eligible countries.

'Selectivity' and institutional reform are also gaining increasing prominence in the switchover from project and programme financing towards budget support financing (see section 5.4). Here, external financing is channelled directly into the client countries' budget and, subject to a negative list of prohibited expenditures, is not ring-fenced for a particular project or set of expenditures but is usually contingent upon the adoption of key policy actions established at the outset. The effect of seemingly untied external resources injected into cash-strapped economies reverberates beyond fiscal policies and goes to the heart of political consensus. Countries have a political impetus for institutionalising the policy environment expected of them by external financiers under the 'country selectivity' approach as the resources are channelled directly into the annual budget. As the Bank noted in its PRSC stocktaking exercise: 'The PRSC is equivalent to a vote of confidence, with the Bank *trusting* countries with proven track records to allocate untied resources consistent with PRSP priorities'[12] (World Bank, 2005b: para. 17, emphasis added).

This is a relatively new phenomenon that is not confined to Bank and Fund financing. As Harrison observes, in Uganda and Tanzania:

> Individual donors select aspects of country programmes which fit with their particular development ethos … The country strategies are clearly produced by African officials with an eye to the international orthodoxies within which donors work … it is certainly the case that a country strategy which effectively taps into international orthodoxies of development and governance stands a much better chance of being funded by donors.
>
> (Harrison, 2001b: 669)

Once again, the aim of these programmes has been largely to standardise state institutions and regulatory policies across a large cross-section of countries through a governance model set by the financiers. The practice of 'country selectivity' enables these donors to assess compliance with such policies and methodologies and thus appears to be a means of disciplining countries through the reward of financing rather than administering aid based on needs. Consequently, donors do not merely 'impose conditionality' but, via funded technical assistance, also introduce 'new methodologies' for fashioning country processes (ibid.: 671). Financing tied to public administrative reform thus 'ensures that state cadres have the capacity to take on innovations in policy techniques', with donors responding favourably with financing if countries adopt programmes aligned with donor objectives (ibid.: 668–669).

5.3.2 The JSAN guidelines and biopolitical control

The amendments to the PRSP evaluation mechanism, the Joint Staff Assessment, now known as the Joint Staff Advisory Note and introduced in 2005, encourage this 'carrots not sticks' approach to structural and institutional reform in PRSP countries. Where previously the suitability of a PRSP to serve as a 'sound basis for concessional assistance' and/or debt relief was based on an assessment of the strategy by Bank and Fund staff (World Bank and IMF, undated: para. 2) and subsequently endorsed by the Executive Boards of the Bank and the Fund as such, the new JSAN guidelines dispense with this requirement.

The removal of the endorsement mechanism of the PRSP framework addresses one of the core criticisms directed at the PRSP framework, namely the tension between the requirement for institutional approval of a country-developed strategy and 'country ownership' (World Bank and IMF, 2004: para. 101). As such, in order to 'reduce the perception of Washington "signing off" on PRSPs' (ibid.), the concluding paragraph of a JSAN no longer includes the following statement:

> The staffs of the World Bank and the IMF consider that this PRSP provides a sound basis for Bank and Fund concessional assistance. The staffs recommend that the respective Executive Directors of the World Bank and the IMF reach the same conclusion.[13]
>
> (World Bank and IMF, undated: para. 2, fn. 1)

However, the move away from a direct endorsement of PRSPs may be viewed as having less to do with a recognition of the need to confer actual rather than rhetorical policy autonomy on PRSP countries than with a need to better manage the outcomes of desired reforms. The Bank and Fund, for example, in designing the new assessment guidelines, recognise that the finality of the former JSA's concluding paragraph may lead, and has led, to 'assessments that are not always as candid and as nuanced as desired' (World Bank and IMF, 2004: para. 102). In other words, cognisant of the political and operational implications of a PRSP endorsement or, more importantly, of a failure to endorse, Bank and Fund staff may have felt constrained in their criticism of country policy in the

PRSP, and this shortcoming of the JSA approach may have prevented the assessment mechanism of the PRSP from serving a more disciplinary role vis-à-vis countries.

Consequently, the new guidelines have been designed so as to shift, once again, the regulatory mechanism from one of coercion to one of voluntary compliance. The dispensation of the aforementioned concluding paragraph has correspondingly been replaced by a specific encouragement for Bank and Fund staff 'to provide *focused*, *frank* and *constructive* feedback to countries on their PRS' (World Bank and IMF, 2005b: para. 4, emphasis added). Specifically, Bank and Fund staff are to note, in particular, areas where:

a. there are significant inconsistencies between the PRS and its policy framework and the content of Bank and Fund programs that reflect existing analytic work, and/or
b. further analysis is needed in order for the PRS to provide a framework for Bank and Fund assistance.

(IMF, 2005a: para. 4)

Therefore, although a country's access to financing from the Bank and Fund (and, accordingly, other financiers) is no longer dependent on a satisfactory assessment of its PRSP, compliance with the policy and institutional requirements of the Bretton Woods institutions has, paradoxically, become more onerous. Access to financing is now dependent on whether the PRSP countries have sought to redress the weakness in country systems identified in the JSAN. The operational link between the PRSP and concessional financing now takes place at the level of the individual financing facilities, such as in the Bank's Country Assistance Strategy or the PRGF, which 'should explicitly discuss the alignment with the country's PRS, and how a country is *addressing any serious concerns that were noted in the JSAN*' (World Bank and IMF, 2005b: para. 6, emphasis added).

Accordingly, conditions for financing now include countries instituting measures to overcome what the Bank and Fund staff view as deficiencies in their poverty reduction plans or development strategies. The IMF, for instance, will only approve a new PRGF arrangement or complete a review of an existing programme 'if weaknesses in the poverty reduction strategy that are critical to Fund support have been addressed' with the Fund staff assessing such resolutions on the basis of the country's Letter of Intent and/or Memorandum of Economic and Financial Policy (IMF, 2005a: para. 11).

The PRGF Trust Instrument had also been amended to insert a new subparagraph (g) into Section II on Eligibility and Conditions for Assistance under the Trust, which provides that the PRGF trustee, the IMF, 'shall not approve a new arrangement or complete a review' unless any weaknesses in the member's I-PRSP, PRSP or APR, 'such as those identified in the Joint Advisory Note' and which 'are critical to Fund support', have been addressed (IMF, 2004b). Again, what constitutes 'weaknesses' in policy programmes in Bank and Fund terms remains questionable.

The JSAN approach consolidates the move towards the 'country selectivity' approach of development financing as financiers can now be more explicit about what they expect from countries in return for financing. In order to remove the disjuncture between the policies articulated in the PRSP and the financing documents, which belies the actual nature of the PRSP framework vis-à-vis its rhetorical objective of 'country ownership', the JSAN now enables the IFIs to close this gap by ensuring that: (1) significant inconsistencies between the PRGF programme and the country's PRSP are addressed by the country authorities *before* financing or further financing is disbursed; and (2) where there is a lack of alignment between the PRSP and the LOI or MEFP, it is for the LOI or MEFP to 'explain how the authorities intend to modify policy coordination procedures to ensure alignment with future PRS documents' (IMF, 2005a: paras 15–16).

This ensures that country authorities comply with the policy proposals set out in their PRSP documents and operationalise the reforms as opposed to producing a PRSP merely as a bureaucratic prerequisite for financing. It also ensures that the articulation of policies contrary to Bank and Fund received wisdom is viewed as a fundamental strategy 'weakness' rather than an assertion of sovereign autonomy notionally conferred by the PRSP framework.

In the case of IMF arrangements, the Fund would expect countries to maintain the austerity of a conventional stabilisation programme in their development strategies, and where there is a failure to follow the conventional Fund prescriptions, recourse to the PRSP as a 'country document' is not sufficient for accessing further Fund financing. Instead, the resolution of the 'weakness' in policy identified by the JSAN can and will be inserted as a condition of lending, as Fund conditionality can now 'be used to remedy weaknesses in the [poverty reduction] strategy as it is implemented in PRGF-supported programmes (for example, an *unrealistic macroeconomic or fiscal framework*) where correction of the weakness is critical to achievement of program objectives' (IMF, 2005a: para. 16, emphasis added).

Although JSAN guidelines state that the 'JSAN should avoid normative language in assessing the PRS as a whole and in particular avoid language that suggests the PRS document meets or falls short of overall standards' (World Bank and IMF, 2005b: para. 5), the more 'candid' nature of assessments in the JSAN enables Bank and Fund staff to openly dismiss or commend a country's policy and institutional environment as a basis for access to concessional financing. Consequently, there will be more pressure on countries to pre-empt a negative assessment by adopting policies acceptable to the Bank and the Fund. For example, Bank and Fund staff in the JSAN of the Malawian PRSP APR commend the Malawian government for its 'candid assessment of past policy slippages included in the APR' and its efforts at reining in what the staff term the 'fiscal indiscipline' of its 'expansionary fiscal policies' through the adoption of 'sustainable macroeconomic policies' supported by an IMF 'Staff Monitored Program' (IMF, 2005b: paras 4–5).

By ensuring that countries operationalise the policies set in their PRSPs, the Bank and Fund have addressed the two most pressing criticisms of the PRSP framework: first, that the operational documents of concessional financing, such as the LOI/MEFP or the LDP, do not reflect the content of the PRSP and therefore are not 'country owned'; and, second, that where such policies are articulated so as to receive financing, these policies are subsequently not implemented by the client countries as financing has already been granted based on the PRSP document. The new JSAN guidelines thus consolidate the increasing shift towards country selectivity as a means of regulating access to financing. By ensuring that the assessments are more critical, and that assessments have a direct bearing on the financial resources received by the client state, financiers can ensure that states voluntarily adopt reforms before applying for financing on that basis.

5.4 Donor interventions and the politics of partnership

Reforms under the PRSP framework significantly increase donor influence and presence in a country, facilitating increasing and deeper policy dialogue between donors and country governments. This legitimises the presence of donors in countries by encouraging the practice of 'partnership' – the intimate collaboration between country governments and bilateral and multilateral development agencies in the design of financing programmes, budgets and prioritisation of resource allocation through innovative mechanisms of development financing and new rules governing access to such financing. Conversely, therefore, the PRSP framework increases the exposure of country policy processes to external input while, at the same time, doing very little to redress the imbalances of power characterising this new 'partnership'.

Whereas previously bilateral donors might only have confined their interventions to discussion on ring-fenced development projects, the shift to more strategic mechanisms for resource allocation – via the PRSP and PRSP-related financing instruments – has enabled these donors to play a much bigger role in the shaping of country policies. By imposing a uniform strategic development template for all PRSP countries and by standardising corresponding public policy and policy processes, the PRSP initiative has enabled donors to permeate into what Abugre terms 'the heart and lungs of public policymaking in a country' (Abugre, 2005b).

5.4.1 Micro-management and diverted emphasis

The PRSP framework provides an instrument for operationalising a normative agenda of donors, ironically delimiting the policy autonomy of countries by conferring a set of established values and strategic priorities which governments have to aspire to and which they have to adopt and implement to secure external financing. While some of these reforms may be desirable – such as focusing on social welfare programmes – this effort redefines the obligations of states vis-à-vis their citizens, reducing accountability and responding instead to the strategic priorities of the donors. Consequently, the formulation of domestic strategies remains highly influenced by a reliance on official development assistance and the history of donor oversight of policies and policymaking (UNCTAD, 2008: 107).

These imperatives are reflected in the emphasis of the first generation of PRSPs on social sector expenditure, with little variation in the development of overall economic strategies for the countries. Surveys by UNCTAD and the World Bank itself have revealed that priority areas of PRSPs have focused primarily on leveraging public expenditures for social service delivery, such as in the areas of health and education, reflective of donor priorities, with little focus on non-expenditure-related policies or actions, such as investment in economic or productive sectors (UNCTAD, 2008: 99–100; World Bank, 2004b: 15). While second generation PRSPs are increasingly incorporating more diverse economic policies, the combination of weak government capacity and resource dependency has meant that donors continue to exert significant influence on the content of PRSPs and the strategic planning framework contained therein as donor financing choices remain important determinants of which aspects of PRSPs will ultimately receive funding (UNCTAD, 2008: 100–102, 112–113).

Interviews with Bank and Fund staff also reveal that the institutions are often reluctant to finance programmes which do not fit within the general parameters of Bank financial support, even if the policies do emerge from the participatory process of the PRSP approach. Instead, where there are divergences in views between the institutions and the countries concerned, the preference is for the institutions to engage in a 'policy dialogue' with governments in order to provide 'additional analysis or information' that may 'persuade governments' to shift towards policy directions recommended by institutional staff (interview: van Gelder, 2004)[14]. This account of 'policy dialogue' highlights the leverage the Bank and Fund have over policy choices in developing countries and why critics remain highly sceptical of the 'ownership' element of the PRSP approach. The close link between the choice of policy prescriptions and financial resources, along with the Bank's influential intellectual input through such 'policy dialogue', has the effect of undermining the PRSP framework's exhortations to 'country-driven' policymaking.

Both the Bank and Fund's evaluation office[15] assessments and the Bank's own stocktaking of the PRSC framework have furnished further examples where the involvement of donors in the process has undermined rather than enhanced country autonomy over policymaking. The IMF and the World Bank, in a 2005 review of PRS processes, admitted that '[w]hile the PRS approach was intended to put countries squarely in control of policy formulation, the link to the HIPC Initiative, combined with longstanding relationships between low-income countries and the Bank and the Fund based on conditionality, often emphasized *external* accountabilities rather than domestic ones' (IMF and World Bank, 2005: para. 21, emphasis added).

This review highlighted the 'drive for the "wrong" results', contending that the focus on results-oriented development strategies in PRSPs can lead to countries 'cherry-picking' policies 'where it is easier to show results (either because data are available, causality is easier to map, or because policy, institutional or capacity constraints are not as pronounced)' (IMF and World Bank, 2005: para. 102). The review also found that often policy interventions are designed to meet objectives on which international attention is focused, such as in the aforementioned social sectors as opposed to investment in productive sectors such as economic infrastructure, and that this is driven by donors' needs to justify expenditure to their domestic constituencies and to pressure groups (ibid.; see section 5.3.1). The Bank has also admitted that negotiations under the PRSC framework can be so intensive as to lead 'several governments and some donors [to] view these measures as excessively intrusive, negotiated more in line with traditional conditionality, and not reflective of government views on the pace, timing or priorities of the reform program' (World Bank, 2005b: para. 49).

External policy and institutional interventions in PRSP countries facilitated by the PRSP framework are further supported by the shift towards budget support as a financing mechanism – such as the MDBS in Ghana (linked to the Ghanaian PRSP) and the Poverty Reduction Budget Support in Tanzania (linked to the Tanzanian PRSP) – in which policy influence is exchanged in return for a more budgetary autonomy. Outwardly, budget support is viewed as promoting 'ownership' of development policies – with IFIs and donors supporting different elements of the programme – but in reality these resources are rarely untied from the expectations of donor inputs into their policy content. As a World Vision study observed, 'in terms of political influence, donors prefer direct budget support, because relatively little money can buy significant access to political decision-making' (World Vision, 2005: 47).

An evaluation of the budget support approach by the UK's Department for International Development found that where donors are willing to lend support to a country's development agenda via disbursements to the budget, consultation and influence in government policy are expected, particularly where the agenda 'cannot be fully specified' (DFID and Oxford Policy Management, 2003: 79–80). In other words, 'in supporting the budget, donors are lending their loyalty to the government's policy programme [and,] in exchange for loyalty, donors are granted a formal "voice" in policy dialogue, debate and influence' (ibid.: Box 5f). Thus, the greater the influence donors have on policy and institutional reform, the greater the financial commitment they are likely to make to the client state.

Case studies have also demonstrated the shift towards the new 'partnership' approach to development financing, and new financing modalities such as budget support have led to increasing donor demands to be represented and have a voice 'in forums where decisions regarding the utilization of aid are made' (UNCTAD, 2008: 107). This includes during negotiations over budget priorities and the establishment of performance assessment targets, which, UNCTAD argues, often 'orient the direction and pace of national development planning in the same way as policy conditionality does' (ibid.: 113). This has been compounded by the aforementioned reliance by aid recipient countries on technical assistance provided by IFIs and donors in formulating national strategies for the purposes of mobilising development finance (ibid.: 106–107; see section 5.2.2).

Nonetheless, Harrison argues that such development partnership approaches do have their flipside for the donors. Due to heavy investment of political and financial capital in states the donors and IFIs have chosen as 'exemplars'[16] and the corresponding high costs of perceived programme failure, donors, especially the BWIs, are often reluctant to insist on strict programme compliance, often ignoring or overlooking slippages in the implementation of the aforementioned reforms[17] (Harrison, 2001b: 672–673). In these countries therefore, some form of 'mutual (but still unequal) dependence' does exist between the state and the donors, with donors willing to overlook indiscretions (including instances of corruption) where such acknowledgement would disrupt the carefully constructed 'image of partnership, progress and claims of showcase status' (ibid.: 673).

5.4.2 Discipline of the bottom line

One of the defining characteristics of the PRSP approach as it has developed over the years since its inception is the framework's emphasis on developing domestic accountability for monitoring the effectiveness of concessional financing based on the standards established by the approach. The securing of domestic political consensus to facilitate this is discussed in detail in Chapter 6, but it is important to note here that the logic behind this approach towards domestic accountability follows a similar reasoning to that which underpins the shift towards 'country selectivity'. It is to ensure that client governments undertake prescribed reforms on a public platform – that is, through the establishment of concrete goals and targets and institutional mechanisms to support implementation of such objectives – to maximise compliance with such objectives.

Accordingly, the PRSP framework does not guarantee disbursements of financing by donors in the absence of the policy environment in which the donors envisage expenditure. As discussed previously, the allocation of resources is contingent upon a plethora of other processes, of which the PRS process is only one. The UK's Select Committee on International Development observed that while donors, notably DFID, have maintained that budget support 'is not a method of buying policy reform' in the sense of traditional conditionality, 'there seems to be nothing to stop donors withdrawing DBS [donor budget support] if their conditions are not met', as had occurred with Malawi and Kenya (UK Parliament, 2003: para. 31).

In Malawi, disbursements from the IMF, IDA and a group of bilateral donors providing budget support under the PRSP-linked Common Approach to Budget Support framework[18] were discontinued in 2001 after the Malawian government failed to meet the conditions of its PRGF programme due to what the IMF terms 'fiscal indiscipline', leading to a significant reduction in government revenues to fund the Malawian Poverty Reduction Strategy (MPRS)[19] (IMF, 2005b: para. 3; Krakowski, 2004: 1, 6, 9).

These developments illustrate the continued vulnerability of PRSP countries to the behaviour of donors and regulatory reform favoured by these financiers and belie the rhetoric of the PRSP approach as a country-owned process. Moreover, while the PRSP remains the document upon which negotiations for financing are notionally based, there is very little alignment between the priorities articulated in a country's PRSP and the policies that underpin financing mechanisms, such as the Poverty Reduction and Growth Facility (now the Extended Credit Facility) or financing from integrated budget support mechanisms (see section 5.4).

Importantly, it is the IMF programme which largely determines allocations from donors as it is the country's lending programme (previously the PRGF, now the ECF) or non-lending arrangement, the Policy Support Instrument, which determines its macroeconomic framework, on which there is no debate in negotiations.[20] Although PRGF conditions were theoretically supposed to be drawn from countries' PRSPs, country experience over the past five years has not borne this out. The World Bank and IMF progress reviews of the PRSP process in 2002 highlighted the 'disconnect between the macroeconomic frameworks emerging from countries' PRSPs and those used for the national budget process and reflected in the PRGF-supported Program' (IMF, 2003c: para. 8).

The IMF and the World Bank attribute this largely to the lack of 'operational detail' on programmes and policies in the PRSP itself, including lack of clear objectives or detailed benchmarks from which lending conditions could be drawn (World Bank and IMF, 2004: para. 94; interview: Harris, 2005), rather than to the political dynamics which underlie these processes. Consequently, the Fund has argued that dialogue between the institution and country authorities on alternative macroeconomic policy options 'has been limited' due to 'data and capacity constraints in many low-income countries', thereby resulting in the macroeconomic framework presented in PRSPs often being based on estimates and analysis by the authorities and Fund staff (IMF, 2003c: para. 20). At the same time, it has always been the IMF's contention that 'greater emphasis on ownership was not meant to imply the acceptance of *any* homegrown policy package' (IMF, 2004c: para. 107) but was instead aimed at creating 'greater scope for country-driven alternatives and the investigation of alternative strategies by *expanding the policy space acceptable to BWIs*' (ibid., emphasis added; see also Chapter 6).

It is unsurprising therefore that the 2004 IMF Independent Evaluation Office (IEO) evaluation of the PRSP and PRGF frameworks found that, in practice, there is only a limited opening of policy space in macroeconomic areas under the PRGF and that the Fund generally did not look to the PRSP process as 'a significant avenue for exploring macroeconomic policy alternatives' (IMF, 2004c: para. 11). Where there has been some room to manoeuvre in this restrictive macroeconomic space, the Fund is quick to insist that 'home-grown options' formulated 'without the IMF staff pushing for a particular approach' are usually only taken up in countries which the IMF considers as having 'a strong implementation record and macroeconomic stability' (ibid.: para. 11).

Therefore, for the IMF at least, the purpose of engagement with country authorities under the PRSP framework is less about facilitating policy options on macroeconomic scenarios in the PRSP and other national development plans than about bringing PRSP policy discussions within the macroeconomic frameworks advocated by the IMF. The alignment between countries' PRSPs and the macroeconomic framework of a PRGF/PSI programme is viewed not from the perspective of harmonising Fund programmes with domestic policy options but rather as an alignment of domestic strategies with those advocated by the IMF. This objective is further highlighted in the remedial element of the new JSAN, where it is expected that the 'weaknesses' in economic programme design articulated in country PRSPs are to be addressed through policy reforms in PRGF programmes (IMF, 2005a: para. 16; see section 5.3.2).

The importance of the IMF as a gatekeeper to other sources of development financing means that, for many developing countries, ceding to the IMF's policy prescriptions is *sine qua non* (see the discussion in Chapter 2, section 2.3). The IMF's signalling role has expanded with debt relief initiatives and current shifts to programmatic and budget support lending. An 'on-track' IMF programme usually either is an explicit precondition of financing (for example for IDA credits or debt relief under the HIPC and Multilateral Debt Relief Initiative) or can be used as evidence satisfying the requirement for a sound macroeconomic framework (for example for many bilateral budget support mechanisms).[21]

5.4.3 PRSPs and the aid harmonisation agenda

Aside from improving the efficacy of aid delivery and the successful implementation of policy reform, changes in the modalities of aid governance over the past decade have also been aimed at standardising aid processes across different jurisdictions, both among donors and within recipient states. The PRSP framework has been instrumental in this process of aid harmonisation. This process, linked closely to the aforementioned 'aid effectiveness' agenda, is increasingly formalised under the auspices of the OECD-sponsored Paris Declaration on Aid Effectiveness 2005, signed by over 140 developing and donor countries and development agencies.[22] Aimed ostensibly at promoting country ownership of development strategies, harmonising donor and creditor practices and establishing 'mutual accountability' for the use of aid resources, the institutional framework established by the Paris Declaration and its attendant Accra Agenda for Action (AAA) 2008 is fast becoming the umbrella body for global aid relations.

In particular, joint financing arrangements based on the Paris Declaration principles have become common instruments for coordinating budget support financing to recipient countries (Alexander, 2007: 7; Eurodad, 2008: 19–22). Under such a framework, a Memorandum of Understanding (MOU), Partnership Framework (PF) or Joint Financing Arrangement (JFA) is usually entered into between a country in receipt of budget support and its financiers, including the multilateral development banks and bilateral aid agencies (World Bank, 2005j: para. 1). The MOU, PF or JFA outlines the objectives and procedures for engagement for the group of donors and the responsibilities of the recipient government but does not constitute a legally binding document (ibid.: para. 2). However, signatories to the document are expected to establish binding financing agreements which are 'compatible with the spirit and provisions' of the arrangement (ibid.: para. 13; Annex 1, para. 4.1).

Rather than creating space for negotiation, joint financing arrangements have had the converse effect of consolidating donor priorities and subjecting recipient countries to a single model of aid delivery. Unlike traditional bilateral aid arrangements, which – while problematic in terms of increasing transaction costs – enable recipient countries to negotiate on the basis of historical ties and wider economic and political relations with each donor country and/or institution, joint financing arrangements attempt to standardise aid relations under a single umbrella of assessment and implementation. These arrangements are supposed to be based on a country's operational development strategy and usually incorporate a common Performance Assessment Framework (PAF) setting out the performance indicators necessary to gauge government performance under the arrangement (World Bank, 2005j: para. 13). In most cases, the BWIs' instruments are adopted as the default framework, such as the PRSP as an operational strategy and the PRSP's APR and the World Bank's CPIA as performance indicators.

Although the OECD DAC guidelines stipulate that a 'good framework for aid co-ordination will enable leadership by partner governments' (OECD DAC, 2003: 18), many aid recipient governments lack the capacity to negotiate on equal terms with a single donor, let alone a group of donors and official creditors. In spite of exhortations to the contrary, the new aid regime has been designed and led by a handful of western donor states in concert with the World Bank and IMF. Developing countries have had little input into the construction of the new aid framework. Moreover, claims of harmonisation have not been borne out in practice. Instead of streamlining the number of conditionalities, research by civil society groups, such as the European Network on Debt and Development (Eurodad), has demonstrated that PAFs can be a consolidation of donors' 'shopping lists', so that the PAF becomes 'the sum of all donors' wish lists', with little clarity as to how the reforms required should be implemented and assessed (Eurodad, 2008: 20).

At the same time, tying aid flows to a single framework for conditionality design, evaluation and assessment puts countries at risk of being cut off from financial transfers from multiple sources should they fail to meet critical conditions under a joint assistance strategy. Experience has demonstrated the vulnerability of client countries under this framework, in which a harmonised mechanism for delivering financing to countries has been contingent upon successful compliance with a PRGF programme and, to a lesser extent, the general policy prescriptions of the BWIs. The aforementioned Malawian experience (see section 5.4.2), for example, serves as a critical lesson to all PRSP countries on the financial imperatives of maintaining an 'on-track' IMF programme and illustrates the increasingly tight constraints that countries operate within under such an integrated approach as the PRSP framework.

The PRSP framework formalises dialogue between client countries and financiers while at the same time abolishing formal mechanisms of legitimate dissent to conditions of financing imposed through an unequal bargaining process. Hence, the increased use of the process of 'selectivity' as a means of regulating countries' access to financing means that since extensive regulatory and institutional reforms can be instituted as a result of informal leverage through policy dialogue between client countries and financing agencies without grounding or justification in terms of an explicit financing agreement, these onerous and unconstitutional obligations could, at the very least, be challenged by both the sovereign state and by its citizens.

By masking policy leverage under the rubric of 'partnership', the PRSP framework attempts to conceal the power dynamics which underlie the aid relationship rather than addressing the inherent democratic deficits which the PRSP framework claims to redress. Instead, the politics of partnerships and the 'technologies of agency' it employs subvert the concept of development financing 'as a principle of international solidarity' and put the onus on the client state to *deserve* such assistance, placing these countries in the driver's seat in managing their own 'underdevelopment wisely' (Abrahamsen, 2004: 1460).

5.5 Control and constitutional mimicry

The PRSP initiative is only the latest in a long line of interventions by the World Bank and IMF in the social, economic and political fabric of its client countries, but it is by far the most intrusive and most extensive in terms of scope and content, and the most ambitious in terms of what it aims to achieve. The reorganisation of political and policy space in PRSP countries starts from the assumption that there is an appropriate mode of *government* and an accompanying framework for appropriate *governance* in all countries which are reliant upon external financing, not only from the BWIs but also from other multilateral and bilateral donors and from debt relief initiatives. This assumption correspondingly derives from a conviction, justified or otherwise, on the part of the architects of the PRSP initiative that the 'universal', 'non-contestable' notions of transparency, accountability and legitimacy must accompany the disbursements of such financing to these countries.

Consequently, it follows that the PRSP country, the recipient of concessional financing and debt relief, must demonstrate its desire to be disciplined by a set of rules constituting the values which represent the universal normative framework for all state resource extraction, allocation and administration. The overarching prescription of growth and poverty reduction, to be achieved through means outlined in the *PRSP Sourcebook* and in the conditionalities of resource exchange between the financing institutions and the client states, must therefore be accompanied by the institutional structures which monitor and evaluate the measures undertaken and which, most importantly, generate the necessary consensus, without which the legitimacy of the project is undermined.

All this is mediated through the aegis of the state – a notion as yet undefined but which can be collectively ascertained from the multifaceted literature emanating from the BWIs as one which consists of both the bureaucratic apparatus of state power (the civil servants, the diplomats, the executive minions) and the political circuit (the executive leaders and, to a notional extent, the legislative and judicial members) – which again is deemed worthy through its submission to the discipline exerted by the financing institutions ('country selectivity').

This chapter has demonstrated that the biopolitical power exerted over client states in the shift in the modalities of conditionality regulating developing countries' access to financial resources discussed in Chapter 5 has been reified through fundamental reorganisation of state apparatuses under the operational framework of the PRSP approach. This mode of regulation maintains disciplinary control over client states via their continuing subjection to what Foucault terms the 'disciplinary penalty' – the punishment of 'nonobservence, that which does not measure up to the rule, that departs from it' (Foucault, 1991: 194) – through the marginalisation of states which do not institute the PRS participatory requirements, which fail to meet IMF programme requirements, which depart from the 'sound' economic practice and 'good' institutional performance of a functioning regulative state. At the same time, this new mode of power supervises the internalisation of the rules and 'normalizing judgment' of the discipline (the substantive conditionalities, the rationalities of structural adjustment) through a 'series of interventions and *regulatory controls*' (ibid.: 262–263) of the supervised entity – the client state.

Where the reorganisation of the state apparatuses through the globalisation of development modelling – the setting of uniform 'development' targets, the establishment of a universal policymaking process – and the homogenising of local bureaucracy serves to establish conformity with the norms of global neoliberalism and legal order it creates by excluding those who do not play by the rules, the contingency of the reforms under the 'selectivity' process begins the process of assimilating recalcitrance by binding the state to the conditions of its own subjection.

By binding the state to the underlying logic of adjustment reforms under the rubric of 'ownership' and 'partnership', the IMF, the World Bank and other hegemonic state actors with the power of financing enrol in the 'technologies of self' – subjectivising the individual state vis-à-vis the conditions of its dependence on external resources for state functions and bringing it to bind its own collective consciousness and identities to that of the external power (see Agamben, 1995: 5; Foucault, 1991: 262–263).

This is exposed in the linearity of the 'partnership' process, in which financiers are given a seat at the policymaking table of client states but never vice versa. As the World Vision report notes, 'whereas donors get involved in influencing government PRS priorities, developing country governments do not have opportunities to directly influence donor preparation of their country assistance programmes or assistance plans' (World Vision, 2005: 47). Harrison observes that it is the 'idea of an equality of participation between the IFIs and indebted states' contained within this rubric that allows the Bank (and equally the Fund and other donor agencies) 'to involve itself in a state's politics without appearing to be intervening, interfering, or imposing' (Harrison, 2001a: 542). Discipline is then exerted by subjecting such 'ownership' and 'partnership' mechanisms to the omniscient policies of macroeconomic and structural adjustment as negotiated between the state and the BWIs.

At the heart of the PRSP reforms is therefore the validation of the clientelist relationship between the north and the south and the logic of dependence and universalisation which underpins these relationships. For Badie, this relationship of dependence necessitates the constitutional and juridical imitation of the patron state by the client state (see Chapter 2) for continued access by the dependent client state to external resource mobilisation (Badie, 2000: 14–15, 28). The internalisation of the western political order in what Badie terms peripheral states is therefore driven by the need to prove, at least on the part of the political elite ('the princes of the south'), their affinity with and adherence to the norms and standards of the patron state in return for resources from the exterior.

At the same time, this relationship of dependence is reinforced by the logic of universalisation, which stakes a universalist claim of western rationality and the construction of the 'western' state. 'Developmentalism' – a conceptualisation of 'how the universal was realized within non-Western societies' (ibid.: 51) – requires the progression from authoritarianism to a Weberian rational state with the construction of a representative 'civil society' holding the state in check (see Chapter 6) and also with the requisite institutional apparatuses in place to manage this process of accountability. As Anghie argues, in relation to the 'good governance' reforms, these extensive tentacular institutional transformations 'are directed at reproducing in the Third World a set of principles and institutions which are seen as having been perfected in the West, and which the non-European world must adopt if it is to make progress and achieve stability' (Anghie, 2004: 249).

This chapter has also demonstrated the shift in the modalities of control over developing countries exerted at the level of the global governance institutions, namely the World Bank and the IMF, and bilaterally, through donor financing aligned with the PRSP framework. The operational reforms of the PRSP framework therefore are evidence of a larger shift in the modalities of power at the very high levels of inter-state governance. This power is premised on the restoration of 'agency' to the actors in the process and the contract that such 'agency' is not 'abused' by the persons on whom it is conferred. As Abrahamsen notes, 'partnerships' under these new governance arrangements, such as the PRSP framework, 'work not primarily as direct domination and imposition, but through promises of incorporation and inclusion' so that '[f]ailure to meet the agreed criteria for inclusion in partnerships (sound social and economic policies) can be cast as the ill-discipline of particular countries' (Abrahamsen, 2004: 1464).

Further legitimacy for the project of post-adjustment reforms is correspondingly gained through the nexus of the transnational policy elite – the INGOs and expatriate policy advocates from the epistemic community, for example – and the local constituencies of the BWIs and its major shareholders. The G8 countries can and will draw upon the PRSP policy of engagement and stakeholder participation as a means to justify continued foreign policy expenditure in low-income countries. Further discipline is also provided through this practice in securing political consensus and domestic accountability by subjecting state action under the restructuring process to oversight by its own citizens and a globalised network of 'policy watchdogs'. Chapter 6 elaborates upon this second mechanism of state reconfiguration and subjectivisation to achieve the *capture of political space* where this first-tier of reforms has achieved a *capture of policy space.*

Notes

1 For a definition of these states, see: http://go.worldbank.org/NEK8GNPSO0.

2 I use the term 'policy space' to denote the arena in which decision-making is conducted – through elected officials and the civil service which supports them – and 'political space' to refer to the arena of public and parliamentary bargaining where access to and allocation of resources are contested. This in no way excludes the fact that there is often overlap between the two.

3 See Chapter 1, section 1.4 for a discussion of Jayasuriya's epistemology.

4 Also gleaned from observations of statements made at Bank and Fund public dialogues and meetings during the same period. For those inside the institutions who view the PRSP approach as a positive shift in transferring back some of the policy autonomy of client countries removed by decades of structural adjustment, the frustration arises from the conditions that have been attached to new modalities of financing such as those discussed here. These individuals contend that the PRSP framework has been circumscribed by the policies of the major shareholders – notably the G7 countries – who insist on more interventionist mechanisms for regulating the new financing facilities.

5 The role of the state in this respect is discussed further in Chapter 6.

6 Gould's edited collection compiles empirical studies of PRS processes in Tanzania, Vietnam and Honduras (see Gould, 2005a).

7 The Ghanaian MDBS, for example, is a Memorandum of Understanding between the Ghanaian government and nine financiers, including the World Bank, the UK DFID, the European Union (EU) and the African Development Bank (ADB), to

establish a common framework for the assessment, development and disbursement of grant, credit and loan agreements in support of the Ghanaian Poverty Reduction Strategy Paper (Government of Ghana, 2005; Thompson, 2004).

8 A World Bank working paper in 2002 noted that the World Bank has been actively engaged in the adoption and implementation of MTEFs in developing countries, particularly in the Africa region, which accounts for over half of the MTEFs implemented in the developing world (Le Houerou and Taliercio, 2002: 1). The authors commented: 'In fact, the MTEF has become a standard item in the Bank's PEM toolkit. More and more, MTEFs are considered the *sine qua non* of good PEM' (ibid.).

9 It is interesting to note that while in most industrialised countries and many mature developing economies such independent accountability mechanisms exist within the legislative and judicial apparatuses, usually overseen by a domestic court of law exercising administrative law or judicial review of government action, the form of PEM/PFM prescribed by the Bank and Fund usually involves accountability to external institutions, notably the BWIs themselves or other external donor agencies and ratings agencies.

10 The multi-donor PRSTF (now no longer accepting applications) was aimed at supporting all in-country PRSP formulation or implementation efforts, including technical assistance for institutionalising participatory processes, improving PEM systems and poverty diagnostics, as well as establishing monitoring and evaluation systems for PRSPs. See the PRSTF website: http://go.worldbank.org/8SREFDX0N0.

11 The close relationship between a country's PRSP and its MTEF enhances the operational link between the principle of 'selectivity' and the design of the PRSP. The overarching objective of this exercise is to eventually encourage all countries to develop an MTEF linked to a PRSP which will be used as a guide to external development financiers. As such, for the development agencies which determine the size of the resource envelope of each country depending on the country allocations, the policies contained in the MTEF (and, hence, the PRSP) may influence the resources allocated.

12 Paradoxically, one of the indicators of countries' 'commitment to reform' is the undertaking of Bank policy-based loans to support such institutional reforms in the three years leading up to the PRSC programme (World Bank, 2005a: para. 19). This not only raises questions as to the objectivity of the Bank's 'selectivity' exercise, notably as to whether this may be a case of the Bank feathering its own nest vis-à-vis increasing its lending portfolio, but also reveals a great deal regarding the motivations behind the Bank's exercise of 'country selectivity'.

13 For countries under the HIPC initiative, the paragraph also states that the PRSP provides a 'sound basis for debt relief' (World Bank and IMF, undated: para. 2, fn. 1).

14 At the time of interview, Linda van Gelder was senior economist with the Bank's Poverty Reduction Group, which is responsible for managing, among other things, the PRSP process and related operations for both the IBRD and the IDA.

15 The Bank's Independent Evaluation Group (IEG) (formerly the Operations Evaluation Department) and the Fund's Independent Evaluation Office (IEO) are 'independent' only in the sense that their staff report directly to the Executive Boards of the World Bank and the IMF and are therefore outside the institution's bureaucratic hierarchy. However, although these offices have, on occasion, furnished critical reports of the Bank's and Fund's activities, their role is primarily to assess the efficacy of Bank and Fund operations rather than to critique the policy directions of the institutions. Furthermore, all reports will have been cleared by the Executive Boards prior to publication and the staff of both institutions will have had a chance to have input into the final reports.

16 In the context of the 'new architecture of aid', Uganda and Tanzania have emerged as poster children for the successes of the new strategies, especially of the PRSP approach.

17 In many respects, this is no different to the practice under the first generation reforms in which the BWIs would often overlook countries' failures to implement certain reforms under the Washington Consensus economic model if and when the countries involved were politically or geo-strategically important.

18 These were the European Commission, the UK, Sweden and Norway (Krakowski, 2004: 9).

19 PRSC credits and budget support to the Malawian government were suspended in November and December 2001 when it failed to implement the structural and macroeconomic reforms of its PRGF programme entered into in December 2000 (Government of Malawi, 2003: para. 1; Krakowski, 2004: 6, 9)· As a result, Malawi's financial situation deteriorated drastically between 2001 and 2003 as the government built up a high level of internal debt with high interest rates, and this affected Malawi's progress towards reaching Completion Point under the HIPC initiative (Government of Malawi, 2003: para. 1; Krakowski, 2004: 6). Although Malawi completed its first successful review of the PRGF programme in 2003, indicating that its macroeconomic framework was back on track, and donors resumed budget support on this basis, this was subject to a strict IMF staff-monitored programme of fiscal adjustment (Government of Malawi, 2003; IMF, 2005b: paras 3–5; IMF, 2003b).

20 See Chapter 6 for a detailed discussion on the disjuncture between the principle of participation and the reality of the IMF policy role.

21 Positive review of a country's PRGF implementation will, for example, be sufficient to 'indicate an appropriate macroeconomic position', and IMF Executive Board decisions 'will provide sufficient information for donors to take decisions' (DFID, 2005: 3). The importance of the IMF's signalling role is also demonstrated in the recent willingness of non-HIPCs, namely Nigeria, and post-PRGF countries – such as Cape Verde, Ghana, Tanzania and Uganda – to agree to the adoption of a PSI.

22 See OECD website: http://www.oecd.org/document/22/0,3343,en_2649_3236398_36074966_1_1_1_1,00.html.

Chapter 6

Redesigning the political project

Discipline and legitimation through participatory policymaking

> By defining the reduction of poverty as the over-riding framework for all public policy and expenditure, and by seeking to extend the policy consensus to include 'civil society', the current wave of post-developmentalism reveals itself as neoliberalism reconstituted in a populist mode ... The 'consultative conditionality' that has been one of the criteria for Bretton Woods assessment of any PRS is thus a hallmark of the merging trend toward populist neoliberalism.
>
> (Gould and Ojanen, 2003: 31–32)

The participatory process is the cornerstone of the Poverty Reduction Strategy Paper framework and represents the single most extensive intervention of the Bretton Woods institutions – and the wider development financing community as a whole – in client countries to date. The requirement that PRSP countries involve a wide range of stakeholders in the discussion of policy proposals put forward in their PRSPs has led to, in varying degrees, the reconfiguration of the political landscape in PRSP countries as legal and political institutions (legislatures, constitutions, regional and local governments) and relationships (between the executive and the legislature, between state and civil society) are reorganised to conform with, and respond to, the conceptual and operational dictates of the new architecture of aid.

Central to the reorganisation of social, legal and political structures under these new 'participatory' modalities of consensus and decision-making are efforts to embed specific discourses about the nature of government and governmentality and the role of the state in resource allocation and socio-economic regulation. In particular, the participatory process places an emphasis on the links between the furtherance of a liberal political and constitutional order – exemplified by the promotion of a state/civil society dichotomy, an institutionalised relationship between the two and the decoupling of the political order from the economy – and the achievement of international development targets, including PRSP indicators (see Chapter 5).

This is accompanied by the establishment of appropriate political instruments through which public consultation on government policy, including economic and social policies promulgated and supervised by external financiers, is discussed. It creates a focal point for the convergence of resistance to the financing conditionalities, establishing strict parameters within which such contentious policy discussions may be confined.

This chapter follows on from Chapter 5, which outlined how the biopolitical power exercised by the international development community over client countries is reinforced by the operational interventions of the PRSP framework. Specifically, where the preceding chapter examined how discipline is maintained through the *capture of policy space* – the internalisation of policy and institutional reform by the policymakers of PRSP states – this chapter seeks to examine how these reforms are legitimated through the *capture of political space* – the mobilisation of domestic political consensus in support of such reforms.

Thus, this chapter examines the external[1] participatory process under the PRSP framework, considering how these socio-political changes have been operationalised in order to reconstitute political and social relations in PRSP countries, locating the participatory process within the overarching effort to rehabilitate the state apparatus under the PRSP framework. The chapter considers how the PRSP framework has reshaped the internal political dynamic and state–civil society relations within the PRSP framework, establishing a mechanism which secures both political consensus and political disciplining of the PRSP state by non-state actors.

Here, it is argued that the participatory process is aimed at securing political consensus around a set of policy reforms and development strategies which have been largely predetermined by external financiers through the capture of the state's policy space under the rubric of 'ownership' and 'partnership', and at establishing formalised channels through which resistance to such policies and grievances about policy implementation may be confined and diffused. At the same time, the participatory process serves to discipline the state by establishing an oversight mechanism that incorporates domestic stakeholders into the policy and policy monitoring process.

Equally important in this analysis is a consideration of how the PRSP framework validates the structural powers at work in the global governance arena and how the discourse of 'participation' itself creates a problematic through which the substantive conditionalities of structural adjustment may continue to apply in the post-structural adjustment era. At the heart of the PRSP reforms therefore is the questionable characterisation of PRSP countries as legitimate sites of intervention for constitutional and political reform, and the assumption that existing legal and political mechanisms in these countries are inadequate to address the wider challenge of engendering development and poverty reduction established by the PRSP framework. The effects of both the rhetoric and practice of 'participation' under the PRSP approach thus reverberate beyond changes in state administrative structures to encompass critical questions of domestic constitutional reform and the re-evaluation of state–citizenry relations within PRSP countries.

6.1 The liberal political project as an antidote to state autonomy

The capture of the policymaking apparatus of sovereign states under the PRSP framework, through the reinscription of state regulative capacity via the politics of partnership and ownership discussed in Chapter 5, is reinforced and magnified by the capture of political space through the institution of the participatory process of the PRSP approach. Where the *politics of partnership and ownership* reorganise the means by which the state encounters its external constituents – the financiers and global governance institutions – the *politics of participation* reorganises the means by which the state's domestic constituents encounter the state.

6.1.1 Responding to the 'democratic deficit'

In many respects, the efforts to restructure the internal political dynamics of SAP/PRSP countries and their relationship to the external financing community respond to the geo-strategic pressures, discussed in Chapter 3, on the existing international economic order. In particular, the participatory Poverty Reduction Strategy process responds to the question of 'voice' and 'representation' in the regulatory frameworks of economic globalisation, with the domestic consultative process specifically responding to the clamour for inclusion, notably by certain transnational actors (see section 6.3.2), in the process of decision-making and norm creation.

These 'pressures for new forms of democratization of the accountability of formal regulatory rule-making' at the national and international level have resulted from the exclusion of traditional modes of political franchise in the regulation of 'post-industrial, globalized capitalism' (Picciotto, 2000: 163), notably in the institutions of global economic governance. Where the resistance to the economic policies and norms of global trade and finance targeted what Cameron and Palan term 'a "democratic deficit" between nationally based systems of political representation and transnationally organized structures of political authority' (Cameron and Palan, 2004: 139) – the World Bank, the IMF, the WTO – addressing this political marginalisation becomes pertinent to the suppression of resistance where revision of the status quo is unfeasible or unimaginable.

Picciotto speaks of a process of remodelling the '"public" sphere of politics' in the evolving nature of the state in the current globalised economy, of transforming the ways in which domestic political structures respond to the '"private" sphere of economic activity' under neoliberal globalisation (Picciotto, 2000: 158, 161–163). The fragmentation of the public sphere – the redefinition of the role of the state from one of provider to regulator[2] – and 'the emergence of new patterns of governance' therefore necessitate a 'rethinking of accountability or legitimacy' (ibid.: 163).

Viewed from this perspective, it can be argued that the PRS process reflects the organisational, if not geo-political, response of the Bretton Woods institutions and northern state financiers towards facilitating avenues through which such forms of accountability and legitimacy may be realised to a limited degree. The participatory process is thus an attempt to redress the democratic deficits of pre-existing external *as well as* internal processes of development financing, but established on terms set by the official financiers rather than developed through an endogenous process of political barter between the affected constituencies.

In this version of enabling political franchise, it is the state that is problematised, as is the case in relation to its regulative capacity under the discourse of aid effectiveness (see Chapter 5, section 5.1). The conjoined notions of 'poverty reduction' and 'participation' in the context of a national development programme posit the issue of social and economic exclusion as one primarily resulting from the lack of: (1) access to *domestic* structures of political representation and decision-making[3] through which local constituents may seek to articulate their interests in a contest over economic resources and socio-political recognition; and (2) processes and institutions of *domestic* governance which enable political accountability and fiscal transparency to ensure that the results of the aforementioned contest and recognition are respected.

While there may be access to international structures of economic governance via a circuitous route of state mediation, the overt supposition of the PRSP framework as articulated through its discourses and practice is that the nation state bears the primary responsibility for addressing the social and economic needs of its citizenry in 'partnership' with external financiers. Hence, struggles over resource allocation and modes of economic governance affecting local individuals and communities should be directed at the state apparatus through a reorganisation of political representative structures mediated by international institutions and external financiers, such as the World Bank and the IMF. Correspondingly, the participatory process is organised so as to further circumscribe the limited policy autonomy ascribed to states under the PRSP framework by subjecting the nation state and government apparatus to scrutiny by its citizens.

The reconstruction of the state in PRSP countries through the participatory process therefore aids the rehabilitation of the regulative capacity of the state at the same time as it constrains the state by subjecting it to an internal process of accountability and external scrutiny. This reconfiguration of the political space in PRSP countries legitimises the *process* of the PRSP framework, through the restructuring of social relations between state and non-state actors and external financiers, as well as conferring credibility on the substantive content of the resultant social and economic policies, even as it fails to reform the existing policy and practice of development financing.

6.1.2 Liberal legality and neocolonial representations

This reorganisation under the PRSP framework is premised upon the logic of what some scholars have termed 'liberal populism' (Harrison, 2001a) or 'populist neoliberalism' (Gould, 2005a, 2005b; Gould and Ojanen, 2003), where legitimacy is secured for the project of neoliberal globalisation through a process of engendering broad-based political support for the requisite economic reforms. For Harrison, this approach is 'liberal because of its fundamental faith in the free market' and 'populist' because, while it neglects issues of 'class and exploitation', the ideology claims to be working in the general interest of 'the ordinary citizen' (Harrison, 2001a: 537). 'Liberal populism' thus, according to Harrison, 'constitutes an attempt to provide a political language to work with neoliberalism's approach to the economy' (ibid.).

At the same time, the operationalising of constructs of domestic 'citizenship' and the confined activism of 'civil society' provide an antidote to the state rehabilitated within the parameters of the PRSP framework. In concert with the discipline exerted over PRSP states through the reconfiguration of governance discussed in Chapter 5, the positing of the state as the primary site for realising the gains of concessional financing and the participatory process as a means to influence such outcomes obscures the substance of such financing and channels political resistance to substantive financing conditionalities towards a monitorable technical process supervised by the BWIs. The a priori assumption that the policy interventions of debt relief and concessional lending operations work towards alleviating social and economic dislocations caused not by the policies themselves but by state inefficiencies and limited accountability over resource allocation creates a logic that predicates alleviation of such dislocations on a reform of state political structures.

This premise is not novel to the PRSP approach. Conceptually, as noted in previous chapters, the World Bank has shifted steadily in this direction since the early 1990s with the emergence of the 'good governance' agenda, which was concerned primarily with the creation and sustenance of liberal legalism. Here, the brokering by judicial and administrative structures of entitlements to resources – cultural or material – by citizens and corporate entities within a state was based on the premise of individual entitlements to the market economy. The 'good governance' agenda, as characterised by Sano, was 'the child of a modified liberal agenda which made concessions to the fact that efficient resource utilisation also depended on modes of governance and public involvement' in resource allocation and management (Sano, 2002: 123).

The narratives and the operational consequences which followed from the adoption of this agenda (and subsequently that of the PRSP framework) – for example administrative and legal reform projects, civil service capacity building and technical assistance – are often premised on paternalistic if not pejorative suppositions of the nature of the state in aid-dependent countries. This reflects the continuing application of the 'dynamic of difference' characterising postcolonial international relations (see Chapter 2), in which the 'aid recipient' state is juxtaposed in binary opposition to the state apparatuses in the 'donor' countries, and is consequently in need of reconstruction.

Specifically, such representations routinely delegitimise the non-western state, often characterising its political organisation as an extension of social networks riddled with patrimony and nepotism and lacking in the formalised bureaucracy which serves as the cornerstone of western public administration. Some scholars, such as Halvorsen and Michelsen, for example, conceive of an effective, operational state on the basis of the professionalisation of its civil service – 'the precondition for the public administration of the European kind giving autonomy to objective knowledge and solutions' – and its abstraction from, but social contract with, civil society (Halvorsen and Michelsen, 2002: 154). Consequently, the failure of 'governance' in the African state (the subject of their analysis) is ascribed to the lack of civil service subscription to this 'normative foundation' – constraining the exercise of state power by its agents through a universal 'trust' in the 'values' of the state as an institution – and, instead, its affiliation to enduring kinship ties and the resource transfers such networks entail (ibid.: 154–155).

This form of constitutional superiority underlies the premise of development interventions in the third world and legitimises the 'civilising mission' of the international development project discussed in Chapter 2. The construction of third world states as sites for the manifestation and reproduction of communal leadership, and not on a programme of political franchise, thus not only has validated the ad-hoc reforms of the 'good governance' era but also forms the backdrop to constructing interventions in the successor PRSP state.

In the remedial approach taken by champions of institutional governance reforms – of rehabilitating the 'misappropriating, inefficient and patrimonial State' (Sano, 2002: 123) through a reproduction of the western political order – there is an inherent belief that the socio-political structures of the state in countries targeted for such reforms must be purged of such parochialism and patrimony in order for the state to meet the socio-political and material needs of its constituents. Therefore, in the absence of an endogenous 'civil society' in the Anglo-European tradition, which developed political representation from domestic taxation, the PRSP framework attempts to enforce institutional 'participation' in policy formulation if not in political voice.

For southern activists Chavez-Malaluan and Guttal, the PRSP framework has enabled 'the manipulation of civil society' by the external financiers, with the preference for institutionalised, transnational policy advocacy-dominated consultations reflecting the fact that 'vernacular civil society formations do not fit comfortably into the conceptualisations of state, market and society' held by the BWIs and other financing institutions (Chavez-Malaluan and Guttal, 2003: 10; 2002: 7; see section 6.3.2). The parochialism of this process is reinforced by the fact that external donors view themselves as valid intermediaries between civil society and national governments, engendering what they perceive as an absence of political franchise in the aid-dependent state.

Consequently, by representing the crisis of development as a problem of a deficient state and by drawing a causal link between poverty and domestic political representation, the intrusive structural and institutional interventions of the PRSP approach are justified whilst the structural disequilibrium in international economic relations is validated. Inasmuch as the PRSP framework provides the operational apparatus to influence the strategic direction of the political elite under universalised prescriptions for development planning, the framework also provides the umbrella under which the political consensus for these strategic decisions is consolidated and legitimised. The nation state and its political apparatus are therefore reorganised under the PRSP framework to serve a purpose that both imposes discipline on the PRSP state and legitimises the forms of discipline imposed through both the discourse and practice of the participatory process.

6.2 Participation, politics and policy accountability

6.2.1 PRSPs and participatory policymaking

The Bank and the Fund expect 'participation' to take place in most stages of the PRSP process, from early analytical work and poverty diagnosis to PRSP policy formulation to monitoring PRSP implementation (see, for example, World Bank, 2001b: 7). The World Bank defines 'participation' as 'the process through which stakeholders (those affected by the outcome of reform or capable of affecting reform) influence or share control over setting priorities, making policy, allocating resources, and ensuring access to public goods and services' (World Bank, 2004, quoted in IMF and World Bank, 2005: para. 54, fn. 63).

Since the inception of the PRSP project, the focus of the participatory process has broadened from that of participation in policy formulation to encompass, increasingly, participation in monitoring the implementation of policies. The IMF and World Bank 2005 review of the PRSP approach, tellingly subtitled 'Balancing Accountabilities and Scaling up Results', reiterates that the 'PRS approach is intended to serve as a platform for balanced and mutual accountability', requiring not only 'specific operational plans to support PRS implementation and donor alignment' but also 'that aid be provided in support of the priorities set out in the PRSP in ways that reinforce, rather than detract from, domestic accountability' (IMF and World Bank, 2005: 13).

For the Bank and the Fund, the participatory process is pivotal to efforts to operationalise this 'mutual accountability framework', under which states would be made accountable to their domestic constituents as well as to external financiers for developing a coherent and relevant economic programme to address and account for public expenditure met by external financing (IMF and World Bank, 2005: 11–13). 'Participation', according to the Bank and Fund, 'can be a key factor to enable stronger accountability mechanisms' (ibid.: para. 54) through the engagement of stakeholders in the framing of 'clear development goals and targets', as well as to 'monitor implementation in order to facilitate adjustments in policies and programs' (ibid.: para. 25). The establishment of explicit development objectives and indicators for measuring success or failure via this process would not just assist in clarifying government priorities for expenditure and increase accountability for public action but also help in crystallising 'political commitment and accountability' for countries and external financiers (ibid.: para. 27).

In this manner, the PRSP framework extracts targeted public commitments from PRSP governments on public expenditure and economic development plans within PRSP-set parameters and utilises the participatory mechanism to hold governments accountable to such commitments. Instead of subjecting the state to the discipline of conventional, external mechanisms of monitoring policy compliance,[4] the PRSP framework transfers such monitoring to domestic constituents. This includes not only the PRSP country policymakers, as discussed in Chapter 5, but also interest groups and communities under the auspices of the PRS participatory process. The PRS process thus provides the operational framework through which financier countries may enrol the support of communities in implementing the substantive socio-economic reforms of financing operations.

Accordingly, the Bank views participation as a process that 'brings elements of legitimacy, accountability, and continuity to national development strategies' (World Bank, 2005k: para. 51), with the engagement of non-state actors crucial because:

> Strategy is *legitimized* as stakeholders' inputs and assessments are accounted for ... Sustained stakeholder participation and dialogue help to *ensure continuity* of strategy even in the face of political change.
>
> (World Bank, 2005k: para. 51, emphasis added)

In considering the participatory process in the JSAN, Bank and Fund staff are advised to look at the involvement of the following in the formulation of the country's PRSP: (1) government entities – central ministries, parliaments, and sub-national governments; (2) other stakeholders, including civil society groups, women's organisations, representatives of ethnic minorities, research institutes and academia, private sector, trade unions and regional representatives; (3) bilateral and multilateral 'external development partners'; and (4) representatives of 'the poor' (World Bank and IMF, 2005a: Annex 1, para. A). Staff must also describe the '[e]xtent to which the participatory process has been well integrated with existing processes of the government for policy and decision making' and state whether the PRSP is 'related to any other current government documents that set forth national or sectoral development plans and/or budgets' (ibid.).

Bank and Fund staff have been instructed by the Executive Boards not to evaluate the participatory process in their assessment of a country's PRSP (World Bank and IMF, 2005a) and have stressed that PRSP processes should 'not undermine existing institutions and processes for decision-making' (IDA, 2001b: 5). The Bank and Fund, at least rhetorically, have maintained that the participatory process should reflect 'the different experiences and political systems of countries producing PRSPs' (IMF and World Bank, 1999: para. 20) and have reiterated that donors 'need to be aware of (and not bypass) participatory and representative processes and institutions that already exist' (IMF and World Bank, 2005: 14).

6.2.2 The participation myth

In reality, the PRSP framework has been criticised for imposing an ethnocentric model of policymaking – promulgating a form of Weberian consensual politics reminiscent of the institutionalised Anglo-American democratic tradition[5] – and which favours a core of elite transnational policy advocates whose familiarity with the language of 'international development' has enabled them to permeate domestic decision-making structures with greater ease and more influence than local representatives and civil society groups.

Furthermore, the PRS process is heavily state-directed, lending credence to the argument that 'participation' in the PRS process has less to do with fostering genuine broad-based debates on resource mobilisation and allocation than with technocratising an inherently messy process of political barter to secure domestic political consensus around the framework of globalised development planning, discussed in Chapter 5, and to universalise this practice in all PRSP countries.

This reflects the conceptual legacy of the PRSP framework, discussed pp. 172–175, underpinned by the embedded neocolonial representations of PRSP states as 'underdeveloped' and the political institutions of these states as unresponsive and non-facilitative of the essential characteristics of a liberal western order in need of reform. Paradoxically, therefore, the project of participatory policymaking within the PRSP framework serves to reinforce rather than revise underlying structures of power, both in the domestic sphere and in interactions with external actors. Most vulnerable in this equation are the marginalised communities which the PRSP project sweepingly terms 'the poor', citizens of states by whom the policies of structural adjustment are felt most acutely and often most violently, but whom the process excludes (see section 6.3.2).

The PRS process can reproduce the hierarchies of power inherent not only within the dynamic of the financing relationship between the state and its external financiers but also between the state and its internal financiers and citizens. A study of the PRS processes in Malawi and Zambia concluded that the 'embedded' concept of 'national ownership' in such processes 'may act to conserve the retrogressive institutions that produced poverty in the first place', including the 'retention of clientelist politics' which limit the access of communities to structures of policymaking and accountability (Bwalya *et al.*, 2004: 4–5). Moreover, the participatory spaces engendered by the PRS process in low-income countries remain 'invited spaces' whose accompanying institutions 'are framed by those who create them and infused with power relations and cultures of interactions carried into them from other spaces' and where 'forms of overt or tacit domination' silence or deny entry to certain actors (Cornwall, 2002, and Gaventa, 2005, in Cornwall and Schattan Coelho, 2007: 11).

Critical development scholars such as Cooke, Kothari and Mohan have further challenged the precept of 'participatory development' and its operational manifestations[6] as embedded in politics of Eurocentrism and postcolonial representations of the south and as in danger of reproducing the very disempowering discourses and structures it purports to challenge (see Cooke and Kothari, 2002; Kothari, 2002; Mohan, 2002).

Kothari, for example, argues that participatory mechanisms 'can encourage a reassertion of power by dominant groups and individuals', leading to 'the reification of social norms through self-surveillance and consensus-building' (Kothari, 2002: 142). Accordingly, the power that is embedded and disbursed in the social field – the Foucauldian biopower – is reproduced in the very act of conferring 'participation', resulting in what Cohen (1985) terms programmes of 'inclusionary social control', which make it difficult for people to discern and challenge power structures (Cohen, 1985, quoted in Kothari, 2002: 143). By using the 'promise of development assistance' to bring previously excluded communities into the design of research and policymaking, Kothari contends, 'participatory development' not only 'reduces the spaces for conflict' but disempowers those who have 'the greatest reason to challenge the prevailing hierarchies and inequalities' through the 'inducement of conformity', manipulation and the representation of knowledge (ibid.).

The Bank and Fund acknowledge that competition for external resources may skew the participatory process and undermine efforts for domestic accountability as line ministries and civil society organisations 'have incentives to align their interests to donors in a bid for financial resources and to focus on donor reporting requirements' (IMF and World Bank, 2005: para. 100). Thus, the needs and interests framed by those in the 'driving seat' of the PRSP process – ministries or transnational policy advocates familiar with the language of evidentiary policymaking (see pp. 184–187) – may not necessarily reflect those of the general populace. More critically, where communities are subject to the plethora of data-mining processes, such as the Poverty and Social Impact Assessments to support the policies of the PRS process, the unequal power relations between the researchers and policymakers and the subjects inevitably reorient the outcomes of such processes.

6.3 Reconfiguring the political landscape: PRS processes in operation

The institution of the PRS process in recipient countries has led to a reconfiguration of forces, alliances and institutional dynamics within the political structures of these states. The disciplinary and legitimation function of the PRSP framework is evidenced by the impact of the PRSP framework on the socio-political and often legal constitution of PRSP countries. While it is not within the scope of this book to consider in detail the reforms brought about by the PRSP framework in individual PRSP countries, examination of empirical studies on

PRSP participatory processes,[7] including those from the BWIs, reveals general trends in support of the aforementioned arguments. The following sections consider three critical impacts of the PRSP framework, discerned from these studies, on the constitution of the state in PRSP countries.

6.3.1 The imported state[8]

In an effort to create a universalised framework for development policymaking (see Chapter 5), the PRSP framework also attempts to reorganise systems of political franchise in PRSP countries, positing a new form of politics in these countries, notwithstanding the Bank and Fund's constitutional prohibition against such political interference.[9] Although the Bank (and Fund) suggests that countries' PRSPs 'build on and provide consistency with other current government processes' and build upon existing sectoral and national strategies (Klugman, 2002: 6), countries have, more often than not, started entirely from scratch, mainly because of pressure to adhere to formal PRSP requirements and conform with 'best practice' guidelines on participation as laid down in the *PRSP Sourcebook* and elsewhere.

These shortcomings have been noted by the Bretton Woods institutions themselves. A joint IMF and World Bank evaluation of the PRSP initiative concluded that a preoccupation with formal PRSP requirements 'has often been at the expense of adaptation of the PRS process to country circumstances', as reflected in the misplaced 'emphasis on producing documents rather than improving underlying policy processes' (World Bank and IMF, 2005b: 5). Additionally, the Bank's own evaluation found that, on the whole, 'participatory activities for the PRSP were weakly linked to established domestic participatory processes, where they existed' (World Bank, 2004b: 13). The result has been that even in countries with a pre-existing consultative mechanism, the national planning document resulting from these domestic processes still needed to be adjusted to meet the standards set by the Bank and the Fund.

a) Prescriptive participation

Empirical studies of participatory processes in PRSP countries have demonstrated an uncanny similarity in the shape and content of the participatory processes undertaken in these countries, and in many cases the PRS has replaced domestic strategic planning mechanisms where they existed prior to the PRSP framework. Some Tanzanian civil society groups, for example, had questioned the need to develop a process separate from the national planning processes, such as the National Poverty Eradication Strategy formulated in 1997, at a time when the country was already developing a Tanzania Assistance Strategy with donors (Gould and Ojanen, 2005: 26).

Meanwhile, in post-conflict Cambodia, the government was in the process of formulating the second round of its legally mandated Socio-Economic Development

Program (SEDP II)[10] in 2000 when it had to shift gears and complete a PRSP as well to access financing from the Bank and Fund (Royal Government of Cambodia, 2002: 8; World Bank and IMF, 2005b: 18). The decision to launch two parallel planning processes arose largely because Bank and Fund staff were keen to ensure the 'preparation of a strategy *document* comparable in quality to first-round PRSPs from other countries' and because the staff did not believe the SEDP would 'provide a credible alternative to the PRS process and could not be retrofitted within the required time frame' (World Bank and IMF, 2005b: 22).

Even in Uganda, the poster child of the PRSP project, whose Poverty Eradication Action Plan (PEAP), developed through a wide-ranging consultative process, set the example upon which the PRSP project was modelled, had to repackage its national strategy to suit the framework set by the Bretton Woods institutions. Former coordinator of the African Forum and Network on Debt and Development (Afrodad) Barbara Kalima, for example, observed that such massaging of 'the PEAP to conform to the PRSP framework' compromised the very ownership the Bank and Fund purport to initiate under the framework (interview: Kalima, 2004).

Yet, even in countries where there have been efforts to structure a participatory policymaking process to be sustained outside the PRSP document, these processes have remained largely formulaic and prescriptive. The Bank and the Fund themselves have admitted that the frequent cases of PRSPs produced in processes 'parallel to existing planning processes' have led to a disconnect between the PRS cycle and 'domestic political cycles' and compromised 'domestic accountability' (IMF and World Bank, 2005: para. 99).

There appears to be, as there was in the case of Cambodia, a concerted effort on the part of Bank and Fund staff as well as country authorities to initiate participatory processes that conform to the prevailing institutional vision of such processes. Country authorities are encouraged to draft and adhere to 'Participation Action Plans' (PAPs) which set out a framework for designing, formulating, organising and implementing participatory policymaking à la PRSP (World Bank, 2005k: 18–26). PAPs are to focus on '[d]eveloping institutional arrangements for coordinating the PRSP process' in countries, identifying not only the stakeholders who will be engaged as part of the process but also the coordinating framework for such arrangements (ibid.: 24).

These arrangements have commonly taken the shape of a highly government-directed process involving the establishment of a centrally directed focal point for dialogue – usually in the shape of a steering committee, task force or inter-ministerial working group – chaired by a central minister or, in some cases, the prime minister or president. Consultations have generally taken place within the framework organised by this central coordinating mechanism and, more often than not, have taken the form of consultative workshops held with invited participants from civil society groups and/or other 'stakeholders' such as trade union representatives, private sector associations, and so on. Consultations may also have taken place at regional, district and local level and may or may not have been open to the public. Draft PRSPs, written in some cases by external consultants,[11] are circulated for discussion at these consultations but, as we shall consider in pp. 194–196, are not necessarily revised to take into account the input of participants.

For example, in Zambia the Ministry of Finance played a central role in the design and coordination of the PRS process and, ultimately, the PRSP document. The ministry was charged with the responsibility of coordinating the PRSP, deciding on thematic groups and selecting participants for the consultative process and developing the terms of reference (TORs) for engagement (Bwalya *et al.*, 2004: 19). It also acted as the national secretariat for the process, drafting the initial document and preparing the final plan (ibid.). The PRS process in Malawi was also dominated by the finance ministry, with the minister of finance playing a dominant role in steering the process under the aegis of a Ministerial Committee consisting of representatives from six ministries, although the chair was held by the minister of agriculture and the National Steering Committee of the process helmed by the treasury secretary (ibid.: 9).

This state-directed pattern was repeated across PRSP countries, particularly during the development of the first generation PRSPs. In Tanzania, the government established the Inter-Ministerial Technical Committee in October 1999 to chair the PRSP process, which was coordinated by the Vice-President's Office (United Republic of Tanzania, 2000: Annex 1, para. (i)) This committee was supported by a Technical Committee, comprised of officials from various ministries and coordinated by the Ministry of Finance, charged with the task of drafting the Interim-PRSP (I-PRSP) and the PRSP, as well as coordinating the PRS process, including organising zonal and national workshops and convening consultative meetings with donors and parliamentarians (ibid.).

In Ghana, the process was coordinated by the National Development Planning Commission (NDPC), a central government agency, which was appointed by the president to establish a task force for this purpose (World Bank, 2005n: para. 120). This task force was comprised mainly of consultants from academia, local think tanks or 'highly skilled Ghanaians living abroad, who left once the GPRS[12] was approved' (ibid.). The NDPC was responsible for organising the workshops and forums for collecting views on the GPRS from government ministries, civil servants, unions, civil society and private sector representatives, among others, although it was left to the Ministry of Finance to table the draft GPRS in parliament (ibid.: Box 6).

Pakistan's PRS process was similarly piloted by a National Steering Committee headed by the federal secretary of finance and coordinated by a PRSP Secretariat based at the Ministry of Finance (Government of Pakistan, 2003: 8). In Vietnam, responsibility for coordinating the process was given to the Ministry of Planning and Investment, which established an Inter-Ministerial Working Unit to organise discussions and consultations for PRSP formulation (Socialist Republic of Vietnam, 2003: 101–102). However, much of the participatory process in the Vietnam case was handled by the World Bank and INGOs and financed largely by these organisations (World Bank and IMF, 2005b: 93).

This external financial support for the process is replicated in most PRSP countries as the majority of PRSP countries lack not only the administrative capacity but, crucially, the financial resources to undertake such an ambitious project. Pakistan's PRS communication strategy – aimed essentially at disseminating information on the process – was, as another example, developed in collaboration with the UK's DFID (Government of Pakistan, 2003: 9). Meanwhile, in Malawi, the national coordinator of the PRS process within the National Steering Committee (NSC) was a Malawian national on secondment from the World Bank office in Lilongwe, although the secondment took place prior to the PRS process and the PRSP drafting team included an IMF consultant (Bwalya *et al.*, 2004: 9).

While these examples may not be necessarily representative of all PRS processes, they do highlight uncanny similarities in the operationalisation of the PRSP framework across a diverse spectrum of PRSP countries. Although there have been some changes in the development of the second generation of PRSPs – currently completed by five countries – Burkina Faso, Ghana, Nicaragua, Tanzania and Uganda (on its third PRSP) – these changes have primarily involved strengthening existing processes and aligning local consultative and participatory frameworks around what is essentially a donor-dominated process. For example, in Tanzania the participatory element of its second PRS process was improved mainly due to funding for consultations provided by external donors (the UNDP and the World Bank) but the process continued to be divorced from other crucial parallel policymaking processes, notably the country's public expenditure review and budget cycle, leading once again to a critical disjuncture between PRSP objectives and domestic decision-making (Eberlei, 2007b: 44).

b) Enforced democracy

The universalised construction of this process of participatory policymaking further undermines the PRSP project's rhetorical underpinnings of pluralism even as its architects – the Bank, the Fund and the handful of transnational policy actors (see Chapter 3) – propound its processual heterogeneity and policy autonomy. All PRSP countries have had to introduce some form of participatory process under the PRSP framework, and many have had to amend existing legislation to enable such procedural reforms to take place.

While there are exhortations to structure 'alternative institutional arrangements' (read: non-centrally directed)[13] for participation (World Bank, 2001b: 24), the overarching objective (whether intended or consequential) has been to institutionalise and standardise political engagement across the board in PRSP countries. As a result, the consultative process is structured around a stylised bureaucracy of checklists, action plans, diagnostic tools and 'workshopping'

(Shivji, cited in Gould and Ojanen, 2005: 28), creating what a World Vision report terms 'a technocratic parallel government' to service the procedural requirements of donors (World Vision, 2005: 33).

Consequently, the PRSP framework has created consultative mechanisms in countries where such participatory policymaking has never been a tradition and, in many cases, such processes have been created in haste in response to external financing needs. For example, in Bolivia the government scrabbled together the National Dialogue 2000 in late 1999 to kick-start the consultative process that would result in the Estrategia Boliviana de Reducción de la Pobreza (EBRP), the first Bolivian PRSP, in order to meet deadlines for debt relief under the HIPC II initiative. (World Bank, 2005n: 7–8). As Bolivia is highly dependent on official development financing, external donors were heavily involved in the preparation of the EBRP and continued to use existing working groups to provide analysis of the EBRP as well as drafting the EBRP (ibid.: 23). However, the law enabling public participation in the EBRP formulation, the National Dialogue Law, was only debated and passed by the Bolivian Congress in July 2001, a year after the National Dialogue ended (ibid.: 22).

According to Molenaers and Renard – whose study of the PRSP process in Bolivia highlights the disjuncture between the rhetoric of broad-based ownership and the operational realities of disenfranchisement among poorer communities – the problem lies with the attempt to transpose a participatory process that is 'based on Western experiences, where participation and the growth of civil society [have] been (more or less) an endogenous process that evolved over centuries', leaving third world states to cope with immediate and 'considerable external pressure' to 'increase the role, weight and influence' of civil society (Molenaers and Renard, 2002: 4).

Consequently, in recent years bilateral and multilateral financiers have focused substantially on developing and strengthening civil society work and participatory mechanisms in client countries. The proliferation of organisations which 'are donor-bred and fed' has consequently meant that in many PRSP countries 'the strength of organized civil society may be to some extent artificial' and unrelated to the lives of the people it represents (ibid.: 28). In a political climate where the externally driven (and externally funded) 'civil society participation' is subsequently mandated by the national government, it is unsurprising that the outcome of this 'new partnership', as observed by Gould and Ojanen, is a 'state–society relationship' that is commensurate with the model desired by the external policy community rather than local constituents (Gould and Ojanen, 2005: 46–47).

In Malawi, for instance, the Malawi Economic Justice Network (MEJN) was formed in early 2001 as an umbrella organisation of 28 member organisations, drawing upon the international links of its initiator, the Catholic Commission for Justice and Peace (CCJP), which played a key role in the Jubilee 2000 debt campaign, to emerge as a 'singularly active player in the PRSP process, largely with funding from Oxfam' (Bwalya *et al.*, 2004: 12). Although this organisation and input from civil society into policymaking were a welcome change from the previously executive-dominated process, there were concerns about the representativeness of these organisations, many of which are not membership-based (ibid.). Furthermore, the Bwalya study found that many CSOs in Malawi, as elsewhere in aid-dependent countries, 'have been started by enterprising individuals with a laudable purpose and connections to funding sources, though often without a grassroots foundation' (ibid.). This trend has been accelerated by the PRS process by virtue of governments' need to include some vestige of civil society within the participatory mechanism.

The state apparatus is thus reconstructed to formalise mechanisms which, paradoxically, do not engender accountability as 'a national process connecting citizens and the state' but rather create 'a technocratic control mechanism' (World Vision, 2005: 33) through which governments generate the political consensus necessary to legitimise substantive policies, not only for themselves, but for the credibility of external financiers, to whom they are primarily accountable in the current international political economy. As a result, in accounting to donors, the state is required to undergo a globalised process of engagement with stakeholders so that the process is framed in a language understandable and quantifiable by the assessors of the process to qualify for disbursement of funds.

6.3.2 The politics of technocratic governance and the role of transnational advocates

As demonstrated in the preceding discussion, the participatory process in the majority of PRSP countries has been highly state-directed, largely due to the executive's urgency to complete the documentation necessary to access debt relief and concessional financial resources, but also as a consequence of positive reinforcement by the Bank and Fund of the role of the executive in economic decision-making.[14] This state-directed process has had ramifications for the efficacy of the participatory process for those who view it as the forum for political engagement.

First, the link between the completion of a PRSP (and, hence, the PRS process) and financing disbursements necessitates, as discussed in the preceding sections, the confinement of the parameters of engagement in terms of procedure (the limited scope for stakeholder involvement in the process) and substance (the scope of policy discussion). Second, and equally important, a natural progression of the above limitations has resulted in the crafting of a state-directed framework that is both *depoliticised* – in the sense that it is divorced from the political bargaining process that characterises conventional resource mobilisation and allocation mechanisms – and *exclusive and divisive* – in the sense that the space for policy engagement and influence privileges a set of actors whose familiarity with the technocracy of aid and aid relationships enables them to maximise the consultative opportunities that have opened up to the exclusion of other stakeholders.

a) Transnational civil society as default policymakers

A common feature of participatory processes in PRSPs has been the engagement by the executive arm of the PRSP government of a select core of NGO participants in the institutional framework of the PRS, leading to what Gould and Ojanen have termed a 'crowding out' of national policy space for other actors (Gould and Ojanen, 2005: 34). The 'consultative imperatives of the PRS' (ibid.: 51) have compelled governments to enter into selective 'partnerships' with civil society groups, notably a core of transnational policy advocates who correspondingly draw legitimacy from their own 'partnerships' with grassroots or local groups working primarily in basic service delivery.

This engagement under the PRSP framework has taken the form of either the contracting out of the participatory aspect of the PRS process to NGOs or a coalition of NGOs, or the entry into a contract of policy participation with a select core of NGOs, usually organisations based in the capitals and usually those with strong international links, if not as subsidiaries of international NGOs. These partnerships facilitate what Gould terms 'a vision of fast-track democracy' which legitimises the technocratic partnership between the financial institutions, the government and a 'transnational corps of development professionals' (Gould and Ojanen, 2005: 33).

Chavez-Malaluan and Guttal, activists who both participated in and studied PRSP modalities in Lao PDR (People's Democratic Republic), Cambodia and Vietnam, noted that in PRSP countries as a whole '[p]articipation has by and large been limited to inviting some prominent and well-resourced NGOs to offer their perspectives on pre-prepared documents' (Chavez-Malaluan and Guttal, 2003: 9). More often than not, the NGOs invited to the table are local 'branches' of large northern-based INGOs or 'transnational private aid agencies' (Gould and Ojanen, 2005: 34) rather than smaller, local groups who are perceived as not possessing the capacity to engage in such a process (Abugre, 2000; Chavez-Malaluan and Guttal, 2003: 10).

A study by Eberlei observed:

> What is conspicuous is the particularly active role that non-governmental organisations with strong international links … play in several PRS processes. As a rule, they run their own offices in the capital, have well-trained full-time staff and at least some financial resources to participate in the PRS process … Nearly everywhere, those organisations acting on behalf of the rural population are clearly underrepresented.
>
> (Eberlei, 2005: 4)

In Vietnam, the three INGOs invited to participate in the Poverty Task Force (PTF) charged with preparing the PPA entitled *Vietnam: Attacking Poverty* in preparation for the PRS process were Oxfam, Save the Children and ActionAid, 'because of their experience with participatory assessments and their grassroots contacts in some of the provinces', in cooperation with the Swedish International Development Cooperation Agency (SIDA), who co-financed the project (Nørlund *et a.*, 2005: 90). The privileging of INGOs continued throughout the PRS process, with representatives of local NGOs invited to participate in the process 'more as personalities than as organizations' (ibid.: 92–93).

This scenario was repeated across many PRSP countries, including Tanzania, Ghana, Cambodia, Pakistan and Honduras, where INGOs played a key role in, and sometimes dominated, either PPAs or PRSP consultations,[15] although in many cases local offices of such INGOs were 'indigenised' (see Gould and Ojanen, 2005: 34–35 on Tanzania) to the extent that the staff were drawn from the local population.[16] In Tanzania, the Policy Forum for NGOs, which was established to succeed the original Tanzania Debt and Development/PRSP coalition to lobby for greater consultative space within the PRS process, contained 'an expanded presence of transnational private agencies' (ibid.).

The 2005 World Vision report recognises the difficulty in securing the 'direct participation' of communities in the PRS process – 'material problems prevent strong organisations from emerging at the local level' – and acknowledges that this has left 'the poor reliant on civil society groups to represent them' in policy discussions, even though many CSOs are ill equipped to do so because of either 'the nature of their relationship to people as clients or beneficiaries (rather than citizens)[17] or their lack of expertise within policy arenas' (World Vision, 2005: 30).

For the most part, the absence of local stakeholder participation in the processes has been attributed to the lack of 'capacity' on the part of such participants, but Chavez-Malaluan and Guttal argue that this is usually translated as meaning 'the absence of NGOs who are already familiar with, or can be taught the formal vocabulary of modern development'[18] (Chavez-Malaluan and Guttal, 2003: 10). This is compounded by the fact that the lingua franca of the PRSP process is English and participation by local groups is limited by the fact that most documentation is produced in a non-native language.

In Cambodia, Lao and Vietnam, drafts of the I-PRSPs and PRSPs were not translated into local languages until the final stages, excluding much local input into the policy formulation (Chavez-Malaluan and Guttal, 2003: 10; 2002: 5; World Bank and IMF, 2005b: 19). In Bolivia, the World Vision report found that the 'political and technical groups maintain a colonial mentality that marginalises their efforts to represent poor groups' (World Vision, 2005: 31), with lack of effective participation compounded by the fact that representatives from poor communities invited to consultations 'had to present their proposals in Spanish instead of using their native language' (ibid.: 30).

Even if language was not an issue, the specificity of terminology employed by the PRSP framework, as in other aid and financing documentation, prevents constructive engagement by groups unfamiliar with this. Chavez-Malaluan and Guttal found that in Lao PDR, Cambodia and Vietnam:

> Local populations in the three countries are not generally familiar with the technical language that dominates policy documents and have to grapple with concepts not found in their cultures. The challenge here is not simply using precise words, but contextualising alien concepts. This makes it extremely difficult for local people, including many government officials to confidently read and respond to translated policy documents.
>
> (Chavez-Malaluan and Guttal, 2002: 5)

With country authorities desperate to complete a PRSP that will secure the necessary external financing, it is not difficult to see how governments find the idea of contracting experienced policy advocates, schooled in the development*speak* of policy formulation, both expedient and alluring. At the same time, the clamour for consultative space has continued to marginalise some groups while it has empowered others. The PRS process therefore compounds an existing problem confronting southern NGOs in which INGOs are overwhelming the space for endogenous politics and civil society representation.

The Overseas Development Institute (ODI) 'Southern Voices' project recorded concerns from southern civil society groups regarding the growing influence of INGOs at the local level in the current aid architecture. Specifically, it was noted that INGOs may be 'competing unfairly with local CSOs for financial and other programming resources' and consequently 'undermining the growth and effectiveness of an independent and autonomous indigenous civil society sector' (Menocal and Rogersen, 2006: 20).

The PRS process thus reinforces rather than redresses the power dynamics inherent in international aid relationships and re-emphasises the dependency of the south on the north. Local groups are not only being excluded from the process by their own governments because of the aforementioned lack of 'capacity', but are conversely being engaged by northern-based transnational organisations to serve as 'local partners' in the PRS process and other processes of aid dialogue. This form of 'partnership' also serves to lend legitimacy to the INGOs' advocacy and lobbying campaigns, both in the domestic political structures and in the INGOs' home ground with funders and other aid agencies.[19] The instrumentalism of this process reveals how the unequal 'partnerships' between third world governments and external financiers are subsequently reproduced in relationships between civil society organisations in the north and communities in the south.

b) Fracturing of resistance

The technocratic partnerships between the state, financing institutions and transnational policy advocates are indications of the increasing influence of the BWIs and other donors in the domestic political sphere of client countries and the divisive impact the PRS process is having on the politics of resistance in PRSP countries and elsewhere. Insofar as the participatory process creates a mechanism for the entry of certain groups into the policymaking space and excludes – whether by intention or by default – other groups, the PRSP framework determines the form and content of the domestic policymaking process. In doing so, it captures a significant part of the political space in PRSP countries, thereby fracturing the potential for critique and resistance to dominant modes of engagement and policymaking.

The Bank and Fund's rationale for the existence of 'neglected stakeholders' is that they do not fit into the temporal, geographical and methodological frames of conventional policymaking (IMF and World Bank, 2005: para. 70). The 2005 review of the process attributed the problem of marginalisation to the fact that 'direct engagement of poor people' is more time-consuming than 'existing planning cycles allow', that 'empowerment of the most vulnerable members of society is fundamentally difficult' and that the 'powerlessness' of these groups and their lack of access to networks, assets and political representation lead to a failure to vocalise concerns about the 'policies and actions which will affect them' (ibid.: para. 73).

Preferring to view the participatory process itself as problematic rather than symptomatic of such marginalisation, the institutions' recommendation is to widen the use of such participatory methods in policy formulation by, for example, recommending the 'use of participatory poverty assessments for raising the visibility of poor people's views' (ibid.). However, as highlighted in section 6.2, the engagement of marginalised communities in such exercises may serve to reinforce the source of domination and disempowerment by filtering knowledge about their needs through conventional analytical frames rather than using such data to challenge existing structures and policies. Analysts of participatory approaches have argued that the underlying power dynamics of participatory development processes – either participatory policymaking or participatory research – more often than not, shape the outcomes of such processes.

Similarly, in the PRSP framework, the needs of 'the poor' and 'local communities' who have a stake in the formulation of national and international policies affecting their lives and livelihoods are filtered through the PRS process, and resistance to policies is diffused through, first, exclusion of critical voices and, second, negotiation of resistant voices. Often the canvassed perspectives of the 'poor' are mediated through the agenda 'within which their "voices" are solicited and analysed', an exercise in validation and authentication over which the respondents have 'little or no influence' (Brock *et al.*, 2001: 24). In this case, the usefulness of the participatory process is determined by its value either in framing policies which correspond to the prescribed neoliberal policies of the Washington Consensus or in legitimating the status quo. Civil society actors are often treated, not so much as equal partners in the development process, but as a means of securing legitimacy for predetermined policies.

This has been compounded by the proliferation of 'technical assistance' and 'capacity building' projects that has accompanied the inception of the PRSP framework funded by the World Bank and bilateral donors for participation in

PRS processes. The availability of financing from such sources for engagement with the PRS process has encouraged the participation of civil society groups in the PRS process and incentivised the legitimation of the framework by such groups. Concerns over the potential for conflicts of interest of CSOs engaged in the participatory process have been expressed by numerous observers and civil society actors themselves. Many CSOs are also reliant on the same multilateral and bilateral donors for non-PRS-related activities, leading to questions as to whether such financial incentives may act as a deterrent to critical voices or as a censor of dissent, particularly among grassroots organisations (interview: Kalima, 2004).

These concerns, along with the selective participatory process favouring transnational policy advocates, have created schisms within civil society groups at both national and international levels. Where previously a division had existed between service provider NGOs[20] and NGO policy advocates, now divisions are entrenched between policy advocates who engage with participatory approaches and those who do not. There have been schisms, even within the INGOs themselves, with regard to participation in the process. The conflict which arises from implementation of the participatory process has served, in many respects, to divert attention from the substantive aspects of the economic programmes associated with the PRSP framework, such as the PRGF. More resources are increasingly spent on the politics of bargaining and negotiation among CSOs on the procedural framework of participation than on critically examining the policy prescriptions accompanying the adjustment programmes the PRSPs support, often leading to the fragmentation of traditional opposition to such policies.

6.3.3 The marginalisation of indigenous politics

One of the most critical effects of the technocratising of strategic economic planning characteristic of the PRSP framework has been the increasing marginalisation of representative politics in PRSP countries. Almost all studies of PRS processes in a range of PRSP countries, including evaluations by the BWIs, have found that the participatory process has generally sidelined electoral political structures in these countries in favour of the technocratic partnerships discussed in section 6.3.2 (see, for example, World Bank, 2004b: 11; World Vision, 2005: 31). The civil society bias inherent in the discourse and practice of the PRS process, compounded by the conservative political climate and historical relationships between the executive and external financiers, in many PRSP countries has resulted in this bypassing of domestic legislatures in the participatory process.

For many countries dependent upon external financing, the close relationship between the government, notably the finance ministries and central banks, and external financing institutions, such as the World Bank and the IMF, has been historically constituted. Finance ministers liaise very closely with Bank and Fund officials in negotiations for loans and other development financing and have often traditionally acted with a great deal of discretion and a lack of accountability, as have the Bank and Fund officials. The institution of a participatory process under the PRSP framework has not redressed this imbalance and, in some instances, may have compounded this centralisation of decision-making.

a) Rubber-stamping legislatures

The constitutional realities of many PRSP countries mirror those characteristics observed by Gould and Ojanen in Tanzania in which 'formal representative democracy is weak' as a result of the 'non-political aid relationship' between the executive arm and the financing institutions and 'de facto one-party rule' (Gould and Ojanen, 2005: 54). Eberlei and Hann, for example, note that in the 28 sub-Saharan African (SSA) countries documented in their study of parliaments and the PRSP process, only in two countries – Ethiopia and Lesotho – is the primacy of parliaments over other organs of state constitutionally established, while the 'overwhelming majority' of countries had presidential systems in which the president played a dominant role in policy formulation (Eberlei and Hann, 2003: 14).

This legacy has been difficult to shift, even with the inception of a formalised participatory framework such as the PRSP. Moreover, it could be argued that the PRSP framework has conversely restricted the already limited role of parliaments by encouraging the formation of technocratic partnerships between the state, 'civil society' and external donors. Studies of participatory processes have revealed that most legislatures in PRSP countries did not enter into the process until the later stages of the PRSP formulation and were often merely rubber-stamping what had been drafted by the executive and refined in the consultative process with non-parliamentary stakeholders.

There is no formal requirement under the PRSP framework for PRSPs or PRSP-related documents to be approved by national legislatures, even though the document aims to serve as a strategic policy document through which all other budgetary decisions will be made. Most policy decisions continue to be undertaken by executive government ministries, and monitoring is conducted by 'technocratic secretariats, usually at the behest of donors', with very little input from or oversight by parliaments (World Vision, 2005: 33).

The aforementioned Eberlei and Hann research concluded that in most of the SSA PRSP countries studied, parliamentary participation has not involved institutional participation by the legislature but has been largely 'restricted to participation by individual members of parliaments in consultation sessions' (Eberlei and Hann, 2003: 9). Even this form of participation by parliamentarians has been limited. In Malawi, it was estimated that only about one-third of MPs took part in district consultations, the primary vehicle for parliamentary involvement in the country, in spite of the fact that there were upcoming parliamentary elections (Bwalya *et al.*, 2004: 14). The lack of a parliamentarian presence in local constituencies during this key period suggests a disjuncture between the PRS process and local representative politics and between the PRSP and domestic contests over resource allocation.

A World Bank study of PRSPs and Transitional Results Matrices (TRMs)[21] found that there was significant parliamentary involvement in the PRSP process in only one-quarter of 59 countries surveyed (World Bank, 2005k: iii). Only in Uganda and Ghana was there active parliamentary scrutiny[22] of the PRSP and other development plans, whereas in another 16 countries parliaments approved a PRSP or a long-term development plan or both (ibid.: 21). In 10 of these 16 countries – Burkina Faso, Djibouti, Guinea, Honduras, Lao PDR, Madagascar, Mauritania, Mozambique, Tajikistan and Timor-Leste – parliaments were constitutionally mandated 'to approve national development plans, or in the case of many francophone countries, any laws which lay out economic and social objectives' (ibid.). In 8 of the 59 countries surveyed – Burundi, Cape Verde, Ethiopia, Liberia, Mongolia, Republic of Congo, Vietnam and Yemen – national legislatures are 'constitutionally required to approve or make recommendations on socioeconomic development plans, but parliament has not yet approved the PRS or the TRM' (ibid.: 22). In most other countries, parliaments are not constitutionally required to approve the PRSP, even if some are mandated to approve other development plans.

Where there has been parliamentary participation in the PRS process, parliaments have played a limited role in the drafting and revision of the policy content of PRSPs due to limited capacity and the short legislative time-frame allocated for discussion of the PRSP and PRSP-related documents. In Ghana, parliamentarians entered into the first GPRS process in July 2001, a year after the process was officially launched, and although parliament had formed a special committee in the GPRS and workshops were held to discuss it, the report presented by the committee on the draft PRSP 'did not bring about any substantial change in the GPRS' as '[m]any parliamentarians had been unable to understand some of the technicalities and did not have the resources to elaborate an in-depth assessment' (World Bank, 2005n: 60). In Tanzania, parliamentary engagement in the PRSP process was limited to parliamentarians' participation in a PRSP seminar in June 2000, the National Assembly's perusal of a draft of the document in July 2000 and parliamentarians' participation in a consultative workshop on the first PRSP progress report in 2001 (Gould and Ojanen, 2005: 55; World Bank, 2005l: 269).

The marginalisation of parliaments in the PRSP process has not improved with the second round of PRS processes. Eberlei's analysis of the PRS review process in five countries with second generation PRSPs found that legislatures remain sidelined from the process of PRSP formulation (Eberlei, 2007b: 45). While not necessarily bypassed (with parliamentarians kept abreast of the process through related workshops and meetings), parliaments in four out of the five countries studied were not involved systematically in the discussion and production of the PRSP (ibid.).

b) Bank and Fund involvement

Over the past few years, however, the World Bank and the IMF have become increasingly aware of the importance of parliamentarians in national development planning, such as the PRSP, particularly in securing the consensus and legitimacy necessary for successful implementation of policy reforms under financing instruments. Bringing parliamentarians into the planning framework of the PRSP also facilitates greater legitimacy for policy reform required as a condition of financing under PRSP-related financing instruments, even though the policy matrices which accompany these instruments may, and often do, depart from the policies contained in the PRSPs (see section 6.4).

The biopolitical power that is exercised by the BWIs over the state apparatus in these countries through the executive arm of government (see Chapter 5) is thus extended to the legislative arena. The link between the PRSP and budgetary processes is considered crucial as most PRSP countries require parliamentary approval of budgets. By encouraging parliamentary involvement in the drafting of the policies contained in a strategic document such as the PRSP or the MTEF, the Bank and Fund hope to inject revenue realism into the process of political bargaining over resource mobilisation and public expenditure. In other words, the Bank and Fund hope that if they enable parliamentarians to participate in the formulation of national strategic plans, these electoral representatives may acquiesce to the trade-offs of policy reform contained in the financing instruments which purport to provide the funds necessary for delivering the aforementioned development strategies. As the Bank contends:

> In countries where external loans must be approved by parliament, ensuring that external financial assistance supports country development objectives would facilitate parliamentary approval.
>
> (World Bank, 2005k: 21)

Both the Bank and Fund have now established parliamentary units to facilitate dialogue between the Bank and the Fund and parliamentarians in client countries, reflecting the increasing importance the Bank and Fund ascribe to parliaments, but also reflecting the pressure that has been put on the institutions by civil society advocates vis-à-vis the need for parliamentary scrutiny of Bank and Fund activities. Although the Bank itself has been involved in work with parliamentarians over the years,[23] it has increased its activities in this area as a result of the PRSP initiative.

Once again, the objectives of such capacity building projects are questionable. The financial support for parliamentary technical assistance both increases the leverage of the BWIs vis-à-vis the governance of client countries and creates another mechanism of accountability to donors/financiers. In some ways, the capacity building programmes are little more than an exercise in securing consensus around a set of economic policies favoured by the Bank and Fund and improving fiscal and financial oversight of domestic expenditure. For example, a

Bank handbook on public communications relating to privatisation projects advises Bank staff in borrowing countries to overcome parliamentary opposition to privatisation by working with the executive to secure parliamentary sympathy with the reforms:

> To achieve timely passage of legislation on privatization, it is necessary that the government identify a key group of legislative supporters for individual transactions and that *they be nurtured* in a systematic and consistent manner. Consensus building and communication mechanisms have to be put in place early on, so that key members of the legislature are fully briefed on upcoming proposals through institutional channels, are aware of the benefits of passage and the costs of inaction, and *develop a stake* in the success of privatization.
>
> (World Bank, 2002b: 35, emphasis added)

The BWIs often view the lack of parliamentary capacity as stemming from limited access to information and/or the incompatibility of information received with enabling parliamentarians to arrive at a consensus for supporting Bank/Fund-prescribed policies, including those involving the contentious Washington Consensus-style reforms. In many countries, Bank and Fund country office staff often liaise with local civil servants and the executive in building legislative consensus around an IMF or Bank policy reform to be implemented (see, for example, Afrodad, 2004a: 20).

In addition to securing political consensus – the legitimising of Washington Consensus-style structural and macroeconomic reforms – parliaments are also deemed as necessary to the institutional framework for domestic and external accountability of donor resources as transnational civil society is. By imbuing parliamentarians with a watchdog sensibility in political circumstances where executive power has been traditionally unchecked, the institutions hope to promote parliamentary activism by supporting members of parliament in holding the government accountable for revenue expenditure.

In this manner, parliamentarians become as accountable to the donors as the executive is in terms of national development planning and implementation of economic plans. At the same time, parliamentary power is kept in check by retaining the status quo of exclusivity in the negotiations for financing between the executive and the financing institutions. In other words, as we shall see in section 6.4, while parliaments are encouraged to hold governments accountable for the implementation of loan policies, the real decision-making power for national development policies remains in the hands of the executive in partnership with the IFIs and other donors.

6.4 The globalisation of political consensus

The reorganisation of domestic institutional and political structures under the PRSP framework is couched in the terminology of 'country ownership', 'participation' and 'poverty reduction' but its operational realities belie its rhetoric for two reasons. First, both participatory formulation and civic and parliamentary oversight of the PRSP process are moot in the context of wider national development strategies and structural reform, as the PRSP serves only as a strategic policy document with no operational teeth. The participatory PRS process does little to redress the problem of accountability and transparency in domestic policymaking, particularly vis-à-vis aid and external financing relationships between the PRSP country authorities and external donors/financiers, as the substantive conditionalities of financing instruments are not openly debated or discussed.

Second, there is a clear disjuncture between the proposals contained in the PRSP document – as a national planning document – and the policy prescriptions of these financing instruments, such as the Letters of Development Policy for the Bank and Letters of Intent for the Fund. This dissonance is exacerbated by the fact that the PRSP is essentially a proposal for public expenditure and that domestic ownership of such expenditure plans is limited by a macroeconomic and structural framework imposed by the Bretton Woods institutions. Additionally, aside from serving as a processual requirement for official debt relief, the PRSP remains operationally irrelevant to negotiations for debt relief or debt restructuring, either through the BWIs or under the Paris Club. Consequently, while the PRSP framework may engender constitutional and administrative changes within countries subject to it, it does not necessarily change their legal or non-legal normative terms of engagement with the exterior.

6.4.1 PRSPs and the lack of operational relevance

In spite of the emphasis on participation and country ownership in the PRSP process, it is clear therefore that such participation occurs only within the parameters established and approved by the BWIs. While there is increasing civic and political participation in domestic policy formulation and decision-making in countries, albeit circumscribed, under the PRSP framework, much of the participation is limited to formulation of *national* planning documents, namely the PRSP and, in a few cases, other domestic planning instruments such as the budget and the Medium-Term Expenditure Framework. The negotiations for external policy documents, such as the LDPs or LOIs and the policy matrices which accompany them, remain largely closed to public and parliamentary consultation.

Studies have shown that while the PRS process has opened up some scope for political participation in PRSP countries, this has primarily been limited to the formulation of a non-binding, non-operational document such as the PRSP or under the participatory poverty assessments. The financing conditionalities which bind the government and which ultimately, when implemented through national policies, affect the livelihoods of citizens in PRSP countries are subject to neither public nor parliamentary debate and discussion.

While the Bank and the Fund have increasingly liberalised their information disclosure policies in recent years, much of the information required by parliamentarians, civil society actors and other stakeholders in the PRSP process for them to participate meaningfully in discussions and to contribute to national development planning is not disclosed, or, if disclosed, is released 'when decisions are *fait accompli*, not in draft form or prior to government agreement or World Bank or IMF Executive Board approval where such information would be useful for public debate' (Rowden and Ocaya Irama, 2004: 11).

Although draft I-PRSPs and PRSPs may be circulated to stakeholders prior to submission to the Bank and Fund, government-prepared country policy intention documents, such as LDPs, LOIs and Memoranda of Economic and Financial Policy (MEFP), are usually only made available to the public with the *consent* of the borrowing state *after* the related loan or credit has been approved by the Bank or Fund Executive Boards (see, for example, World Bank, 2002c: para. 22). Country documents – documents prepared by the Bank and Fund staff in relation to support in a particular country – are usually only available after they have been finalised by the institutions and approved by the Boards. The Bank does not release CASs for IDA countries until they have been discussed by the executive directors and finalised;[24] nor does it release Programme Documents[25] for adjustment operations until they have been approved by the Executive Board and, in the case of non-PRSC lending, until consent has been given by the borrowing state (World Bank, 2002c: paras 20– 21).

A joint report by Afrodad and Christian Aid in 2004 concluded that, outside the PRS process, there is very little scope within the formal loan cycle of the Bank or the Fund for the active participation of parliament or civil society in designing the content of development financing agreements between the state and the IFIs (Afrodad and Christian Aid, 2004: 2, 24). In two of the five countries surveyed – Mozambique and Tanzania – there is no provision, constitutionally or otherwise, for parliamentary approval of a loan agreement or for enactment of the conditions thereof (ibid.: Table 5, Figure 5). The other three countries – Malawi, Uganda and Zambia – have requirements that parliamentary approval is necessary to authorise and ratify loan agreements made between the executive and the financing institution, but the legislatures generally do not have much control over the details of the loans or the extent to which the countries are exposed to external debt (ibid.; see also Afrodad, 2004b: 13; Afrodad, 2004c: 16, 22).

Moreover, as discussed in Chapters 4 and 5, the principle of 'country selectivity', which is increasingly guiding the World Bank's disbursement of financing to client countries, requires countries to institute institutional and structural reforms *outside* the framework of a formal financing agreement between the state and the Bretton Woods institutions. Conformity with such requirements – notably prior actions and other *ex-ante* conditionality – entails that governments undertake both minor and significant institutional and policy reforms agreed upon between the country authorities and the World Bank and/or IMF staff.

These reforms, unless they involve parliamentary approval for legislative changes, are not subject to debate or discussion outside executive circles.

Furthermore, the problem of loan scrutiny may be exacerbated by the requirements of the mandatory Joint Staff Advisory Notes of PRSPs. As discussed in Chapter 5, the JSAN dispenses with the need for a 'Washington sign-off' of a country's PRSP in order for the country to qualify for concessional financing from the institutions and shifts the onus onto the country to ensure that any structural and macroeconomic weaknesses identified in the JSAN are addressed in the country authorities' LDP, LOI or MEFP (see Chapter 5, section 5.3.2). This, and the fact that financing conditionality may be used to remedy such identified 'weaknesses' in the PRSP, moves the venue for policy discussion of substantive economic policies back to the realm of the loan document. This precludes any potential for significant domestic input into the policies that will ultimately bind the countries and affect citizen and business livelihoods, as policies discussed and agreed upon in the public documentation process of the PRSP framework remain subject to substantive revision in the loan policy documents.

6.4.2 Dissonance between policies, practice and programmes

As a result of these operational realities, it is not surprising that, while theoretically policies in the financing instruments are supposed to be drawn from the countries' PRSPs, there is a disjuncture between the PRSPs and the policy matrices of the LDPs and LOIs. In particular, while the PRSP framework encourages external input into policies for revenue expenditure (read: social sector spending), the PRSP framework appears to have curtailed country autonomy over macroeconomic policy and foreclosed public discussion on this issue.

Various studies, including the OED/IEG and IEO evaluations, have indicated that there is very little scope for discussion on macroeconomic policy issues in PRSPs and almost none in PRGF policy matrices. The IEO report found that PRS processes in the eight countries surveyed[26] rarely addressed macroeconomic concerns, with the exception of public expenditure composition, and concluded that 'outside the narrow official circle' the PRS process 'has had limited impact in generating meaningful discussions' of alternative macroeconomic and macro-relevant policy options (IMF, 2004a: 50, para. 27). Moreover, there is little use of impact assessments, such as the World Bank's Poverty and Social Impact Assessments, in the formulation of macroeconomic and structural policies under PRSPs, although the PRSP initiative was designed to incorporate the use of such tools to assist countries and national stakeholders in weighing the trade-offs of various policy options and to develop alternative macroeconomic policies to that of the Washington Consensus (Rowden and Ocaya Irama, 2004: 36; see also UNCTAD, 2002b: 59).

There also appears to be little fiscal flexibility in the design of both the macroeconomic framework of PRSPs and the PRGFs by country authorities and little alignment between the macroeconomic content of PRGF programmes and

PRSPs, even though 'PRGF-supported programs are supposed to be embedded in the overall strategy for growth and poverty reduction' (IMF, 2004b: 72, para. 2). While the IEO attributed this to the fact that many of the PRGFs studied preceded the PRSPs,[27] it conceded that this practice had continued with more recent PRGFs, in which 'slightly more than half were finalized *before* the PRSP' (ibid.: para. 3). This not only raised 'doubts about the claim that the program design is guided by the PRSP' but also, as the case studies suggested, revealed 'that the reverse influence is more common', with key elements of the PRSPs' macroeconomic framework drawn from PRGF negotiations (ibid.).

The impact of adherence to the strict macroeconomic policy package of the PRGF has had the result of constraining the very autonomy over budgetary expenditure that the PRSP framework was supposed to confer on PRSP countries and their citizenry. The IMF's traditional insistence on countries' adherence to low-inflation targets and low budget deficits has led to strict caps on the countries' public expenditure (for example through ceilings in its MTEF), thereby limiting the government's capacity to spend on areas of health, education and other public services[28] (Rowden, 2004: 13). This has constrained the ability of national stakeholders to formulate policy, even if the policy space is one confined to budgetary allocations, as expenditure, even 'pro-poor' expenditure, has to be developed within the expenditure ceilings set by the IMF. Parliaments in many PRSP countries cannot increase the expenditure ceilings beyond those outlined in the countries' MTEFs.

Furthermore, as these and other studies have also revealed, there is little to distinguish between the policies enshrined in the PRSPs and PRSP-drawn financing instruments – PRSCs and the PRGF – and the policies of the old structural adjustment loans. UNCTAD's flagship annual *Least Developed Countries* reports have routinely questioned the feasibility of the PRSP project in achieving its objectives of poverty reduction when country authorities remain disciplined by the conditionalities of multilateral lending and debt relief. Instead of forwarding alternative development strategies, the UN agency found that the first generation of PRSPs have generally 'added a social dimension to the structural adjustment programmes of the 1990s by focusing on increasing public expenditure in social sectors' (UNCTAD, 2008: 100). This policy of weaving in social safety nets to offset the dislocations of conventional stabilisation and adjustment reforms at the expense of capital investment could paradoxically hinder rather than help achievement of the objectives of domestic growth and poverty reduction under the PRSP framework (UNCTAD, 2002b: 22–25).

Although there has been a slow shift towards accommodating alternative economic planning trajectories in the second generation of PRSPs – for example through a greater balance between expenditure for productive sectors and economic infrastructure and social spending – there remains little space for discussion on development policy options overall (UNCTAD, 2008: 101–102). There also remains a disjuncture between short-term macroeconomic stabilisation objectives and longer-term development goals, as well as reliance on conventional adjustment strategies of privatisation and liberalisation as major instruments for developing productive sectors in LDCs (ibid.). This means that despite increased participation from stakeholders in the process of development planning, PRSPs continue to incorporate the fiscal, monetary and structural preferences of the Bretton Woods institutions, reflective of the dependency of these countries on financial resources from these institutions.

The process of participation therefore appears to legitimise the substantive policies of the post-Washington Consensus at the same time as it disciplines country authorities. The process subjects governments to external scrutiny, ensuring that the resources are managed in a manner consistent with the objectives of the BWIs by prioritising social sector expenditure while prohibiting discussion on macroeconomics. This creates a public space for participation and subjects the state to additional scrutiny by its own domestic constituencies, and at the same time makes sure that the domestic constituency, as remapped by the BWIs, polices its own resource allocations.

6.5 Remapping the political landscape

The participatory process of the PRSP framework has significantly redrawn the political landscape in many Bank and Fund client states, and this reorganisation of domestic political institutions under the PRSP framework has fundamentally altered the manner in which the state is made accountable, not necessarily, however, to its own citizens. Specifically, the process has subjected the state to greater external scrutiny, not just of its economic policies but of its practice of governance itself, and, hence, increased its exposure to greater external remedial action, notably to the interventions of external donors seeking to mediate the development of domestic political franchise.

The conceptual underpinnings of 'participation' under the PRSP process are therefore premised on the assumption, as is that of the good governance reforms, of a dichotomy between state and civil society and the binary opposites of what each represents vis-à-vis governance and development in developing countries. At the same time, this self-assumed, self-validating 'mediating role' of external donors between 'civil society and national governments' weakens the influence of endogenous groups in national policy formulation and national accountability processes in favour of such external oversight (Chavez-Malaluan and Guttal, 2003: 10). Consequently, the PRSP framework exerts disciplinary power over country authorities by subjecting them to a paradoxical relationship of oversight and partnership with non-state actors, notably transnational civil society organisations, who translate the language of the post-Washington Consensus in both directions. The state is scrutinised yet legitimised in this exercise of consultation.

Legitimacy in this form of participation is derived in two ways. First, at the local/national level, consensus has been massaged to lend credence to the substantive policies of 'populist neoliberalism' (Gould and Ojanen, 2005) – by appropriating the space for representative democracy and replacing it with consultative-partnership politics. Second, at the metropole level of the donor/financier agencies, the practice of participation and the discourse which accompanies it provide a feedback loop to justify aid expenditure and legitimise the role of the World Bank, the IMF and other donors to the electoral constituencies who have a stake in the foreign policy budgets of the financier countries.

Further legitimacy for the project of post-adjustment reforms is correspondingly secured through the nexus of the transnational policy elite – the INGOs and expatriate policy advocates from the epistemic community, for example – and the local constituencies of the BWIs and its major shareholders. Powerful financier countries – notably the G8 – can and will draw upon the PRSP policy of engagement and stakeholder participation as a means to justify continued foreign policy expenditure in low-income countries. Further discipline is then exerted by subjecting such 'ownership' and 'partnership' mechanisms to the omniscient policies of macroeconomic and structural adjustment as negotiated between the state and the BWIs.

This reorganisation of domestic political space has been critical given the geo-strategic imperatives underpinning the introduction of the PRSP approach. As highlighted in Chapter 3, the merging strategic interests of the bloc of developing states and transnational social movements, led by a cadre of highly specialised NGO technocrats, in the late 1990s had created a powerful wave of resistance to the systemic inequities of the international economic architecture. The PRSP framework can therefore be viewed as a means of incentivising the continued participation of southern states, notably those indebted, structurally adjusted states, in the global economic order and of managing their integration into the international system. At the same time, the project fractures the resistance to such integration by reorganising the means through which the state encounters and engages with its domestic constituents and transnational actors within its territory and influence.

In this manner, the PRSP framework resonates not only with the 'civilising mission' of the pre-colonial and colonial period, but also with the technologies of colonial management which sustained this mission. For Pahuja, the colonial continuity within international economic governance today is manifested in the quelling of what Guha terms 'the prose of counter insurgency', through which popular protests to SAPs are delegitimised through the exclusion of 'the masses, or the subaltern in crucial issues of governance' (Guha, 1998, quoted in Pahuja, 2004: 171–172). The 'potential for disruption' is therefore contained in a similar way to the suppression, in anti-colonial struggles, of voices other than those of 'the indigenous elite who had largely adopted the epistemology of the coloniser' (Pahuja, 2004: 172, relying on Guha, 1998).

Taking Pahuja's analysis a step further, it is argued that the PRSP framework goes further through attempts to appropriate this 'prose of counter insurgency' for its own ends rather than dispelling it. By formalising institutions and processes through which dissent from the policies of government may be represented and where protest may be legitimised, the PRSP framework turns resistance on its head. 'Participation' in governance structures thus becomes a means of resolving the social and economic dislocations of neoliberal economic globalisation so that dissent from the economic policies of SAP financing operations is confined and diffused.

Confinement of emancipatory politics within the territorial boundaries of a nation state, and, within it, the geographical boundaries of the district and the villages, not only problematises the state – the inefficient, predatory state (see Santos, 2006: 43) – but also creates a cartography of impoverishment which localises poverty to create a disempowering counter-discourse. Reducing economic marginalisation and social inequity to the lowest territorial denominator not only distorts the magnitude of the problem; it also minimises the potential for social dislocation and political change.

Cameron and Palan, critics of New Labour's urban regeneration policies in the UK, have contended that, 'by suggesting that the local scale is the most salient and, in practice, the only scale at which social exclusion ought to be tackled, the possibilities for intervention in poverty are similarly restricted' (Cameron and Palan, 2004: 142–143). Similarly, the localisation of poverty in the PRSP process envisages the localisation of anti-poverty politics and policies, disregarding the impacts of external economic pressures.

At the same time, the process legitimises these policy interventions inasmuch as they legitimise the institutional presence of the BWIs and bilateral donors in the country. This confines not only the disruption of resistance to the current international economic order, but also the notion of politics and political franchise within the territorial bounds of the nation state, thus fracturing the global resistance to hegemonic global practices and policies of neoliberal globalisation. Whether the global powers have been successful in quelling this resistance remains to be seen; in particular, the question remains whether such technocratic solutions are sufficient to suppress the percolating 'globalisation from below' in the next round of global economic crises, an issue which is considered briefly in Chapter 7.

This chapter and Chapter 5 have demonstrated the shift in the modalities of control over developing countries exerted at the level of the global governance institutions, namely the World Bank and the IMF, and bilaterally, through donor financing aligned with the PRSP framework. The operational reforms of the PRSP framework are thus evidence of a larger shift in the modalities of power at the very high levels of inter-state governance. This power is premised on the restoration of 'agency' to the actors in the process and the contract that such 'agency' is not 'abused' by the persons on whom it is conferred. These shifts have significant implications for the construction of global polity and countries' engagement with the international economy and the international economic law which sustains it. The merging of these multiple strands will be explored as we tie the discussions together in the following concluding chapter.

Notes

1 As opposed to an 'internal' participatory process involving members and segments of the executive, which was discussed in Chapter 5 (see section 5.21).
2 By 'provider' I mean the role of the state as an economic agent in its own right, as the primary driver of economic processes and the provider of goods and services, both in a redistributive sense (public goods and services) and a facilitative sense (capital goods, technology and general goods and services). By 'regulator' I mean the role of the state as the supervisor of economic activity of other economic agents in the private sector – individuals or corporations – acting through the market, whether via direct supervision of the market economy or via the mitigation of market failures. While most states today play both roles, the overarching logic of neoliberal globalisation has been a sustained erosion of the role of the state in the former and a circumscribed role for the state in the latter.
3 As opposed to the lack of access to supranational structures of decision-making.
4 For example via traditional modes of conditionality enforcement.
5 Halvorsen and Michelsen (2002) conceive of the Anglo-American model of public administration as a 'weak State and low trust' system of political barter which is shaped by constant 'antagonism' between the state – represented by a small cadre of specialised civil servants – and civil society 'competing for influence over the public sphere' (Halvorsen and Michelsen, 2002: 151). Here, civil society, conceived of both as citizens bearing 'certain rights' and as 'representatives of the economy', is argued to 'have been shaped as collective actors in opposition to the State' (ibid.).
6 Of which the PRSP is one of many manifestations. Other approaches include 'participatory action research', gender mainstreaming and participatory poverty assessments.
7 These studies have been drawn from a variety of sources, including from the World Bank and IMF's staff and internal evaluation departments (IMF, 2004a; World Bank, 2005k, 2005l, 2005m, 2005n, 2004b; World Bank and IMF, 2005b), research institutes (Driscoll and Evans, 2004; Eberlei, 2007a, 2007b; Gould, 2005a; McGee with Norton, 2000; Molenaers and Renard, 2002) and NGO studies (World Vision, 2005).
8 The phrase is taken from the title of Badie's treatise *The Imported State: The Westernization of the Political Order* (2000). Badie's conceptual premise is elaborated upon in various parts of this book (see Chapters 2 and 7).
9 Article IV, Section 10 of the IBRD Articles of Agreement and Article V, Section 6 of the IDA Articles of Agreement provide that the 'Bank and its officers shall not interfere in the political affairs of any member; nor shall they be influenced in the decisions by the political character of the member or members concerned'. However, this prohibition remains subject to interpretation, and interventions, such as the implementation of 'governance' conditions, have been justified by successive Bank general-counsels, including the claim that political interventions may be necessary in order to achieve the Bank's overarching mandate of development and economic growth (see Dañino, 2006; Shihata, 2000a: 220–244).
10 This was supported by the Asian Development Bank (ADB) (World Bank and IMF, 2005b: 18).
11 Such as the Albanian PRSP which was written by local consultants in light of the government's limited capacity (see World Bank and IMF, 2005a: 11).
12 Ghanaian Poverty Reduction Strategy.
13 The two 'alternative' scenarios suggested by the World Bank in its chapter on participation in the *PRSP Sourcebook* remain premised on a centralised coordinating mechanism. The first is a centrally directed government process of regional dialogue involving, for instance, coordination by the local government ministry of participatory processes structured regionally or centred upon district-level consultations which are

fed back to the central government. The second alternative arrangement propounded is where the government sub-contracts the participatory process to a coalition of NGOs and engages with the coalition as a focal point for consultative dialogue. This creates its own problems of representation, as discussed further in section 6.3.2(a) (World Bank, 2001b: 24).

14 The Bank, for example, has reiterated, on several occasions, that a 'key element of PRS ownership is *a solid leadership role* guiding the PRS content', supported by some sort of institutionalised stakeholder participation (World Bank, 2005k: 16–17, emphasis added).

15 See empirical studies in Gould (2005a).

16 This does not mean, however, that such staff, mostly made up of an elite core of western-trained 'development specialists' (often with higher degrees in 'development studies' and related areas from a western university), necessarily reflect the interests of the general populace.

17 This is because, as highlighted in Chapter 3, in many aid-dependent countries the legacy of structural adjustment has meant that CSOs have taken over the role of the state as providers of essential public services, such as health, education and sanitation.

18 For example the use of vocabulary such as participation, planning, poverty reduction, sustainability, stakeholder analysis, good governance, etc. (Chavez-Malaluan and Guttal, 2003: 10).

19 Although a couple of the larger transnational groups – ActionAid USA and World Vision, for example (see Rowden and Ocaya Irama, 2004; World Vision, 2005) – have been self-reflexive in questioning their involvement and their organisational impact on the PRSP framework – other groups have been less inclined to critique the activities of the World Bank and IMF and/or unwilling to vocalise criticism against the PRSP project for fear of losing funding.

20 See Chapter 3, section 3.5 for a fuller elucidation of the role of service delivery NGOs versus policy groups vis-à-vis their participation in local policymaking.

21 TRMs are integrated planning tools which may act as precursor to PRSPs in low-income countries under stress (LICUS) (World Bank, 2005k: iii).

22 The Bank considers that there is such substantial parliamentary involvement where parliaments play a role in the formulation, implementation and revision of the PRSP and other development plans, such as the formation of a special parliamentary committee on poverty reduction in Ghana and the participation of the Ugandan parliament in PRS implementation and revision through the preparation of the annual budget and other economic planning (World Bank, 2005h: 21).

23 Such as the establishment of the Parliamentary Network on the World Bank (PNoWB), which is now an independent NGO (see PNoWB website: http://www.pnowb.org).

24 CASs for non-IDA and non-blend countries are made available only 'at the request of the country concerned' after Board discussion and finalisation (World Bank, 2002c: para. 8). However, there are proposals to revise the Bank's Disclosure Policy to enable disclosure of CASs at the same time as they are distributed to the Executive Board (World Bank, 2009g: para. 13).

25 Documents setting out a description of the programme, 'the Bank's appraisal and assessment of the feasibility of, and justification for, the program' (World Bank, 2002c: para. 19).

26 Tanzania, Mauritania, Mozambique, Guinea, Vietnam, Tajikistan, Ethiopia and Cambodia (IMF, 2004a: 51, Boxes 2–4).

27 This was a common feature in the first generation of PRGFs, whereby the Fund continued to lend to countries eligible under the former Enhanced Structural Adjustment Facility without enforcing the new procedural requirement of having completed

a PRSP or I-PRSP to ensure that countries did not have financing disrupted in the changeover (interview: Plant, 2004).

28 An ActionAid USA report contended that this strict adherence to the IMF's low-inflation targets and public expenditure ceilings can result in countries not accepting aid that is earmarked for public services even when the resources have been pledged to them (Rowden, 2004). The IMF's rationale for such budget austerity is based on the idea that the 'rapid inflow of foreign exchange associated with the increase in aid receipts can drive up the value of the recipient country's currency', increasing the price of its exports and undermining its competitiveness on the global market, an occurrence known as the 'Dutch disease' (Ooms and Schrecker, 2005: 1821; see also Rowden, 2004: 7).

Chapter 7

Consolidation and conclusion

PRSPs, transnational governance and globalised legal regimes

> [T]he tragedy for the Third World is that the mechanisms used by international law to achieve decolonization also were the mechanisms that created neocolonialism and that, furthermore, the legal structures, ideologies and jurisprudential techniques for furthering neocolonialism largely were in place before Third-World states actually attained independence.
>
> (Anghie, 2002: 627)

The Poverty Reduction Strategy Paper framework currently forms the basis for policy dialogue and aid negotiations for over 65 developing countries. While originally intended as a multi-stakeholder harmonisation instrument for external financiers with broad-based participation, the initiative has remained primarily driven by the Bretton Woods institutions, their staff and major shareholders. The PRSP framework has altered not only the nature of these countries' relationship with development financiers, but also the terms of their engagement with external economic forces.

The impact of the PRSP framework on international economic relations and, consequently, on the constitution of global economic governance and international economic law has been significant. A historical reading of the PRSP framework, its situation within a continuum of political events and policy narratives in the period immediately preceding its inception, and its contextualisation within the legacy of postcolonial economic law and economic relations enable us to ascribe to the framework an economic, geo-political and legal significance beyond its immediacy as an instrument for aid disbursement.

This book has demonstrated how the PRSP framework has changed the regulatory landscape of international development financing and how these changes have reconfigured the internal and external political dynamics of countries subject to its interventions. It has also analysed how the reorganisation of domestic drivers of countries' policymaking processes and institutions under the PRSP project have served to mediate these countries' encounter with the international financial and trade system and the international law underwriting such engagement.

This concluding chapter seeks to consolidate the findings of the book in the context of the PRSP framework's disciplinary impact on the third world states it regulates. Accordingly, I seek here to locate the PRSP project within wider shifts in the configuration of global power and examine what these changes mean in the wider context of global economic governance and international economic law. In particular, the chapter examines how the reforms of the PRSP framework may have served to foreclose the possibilities for a radical revision of asymmetries of current rules and institutions of international economic law, yet demonstrates, at the same time, how an understanding of the forms of power which underlie this circumscription may, paradoxically, serve as an opportunity to negate this foreclosure.

7.1 A new global compact

At the outset, research for this book posed two related questions: (1) does the PRSP approach to development financing constitute a departure from the existing modalities and regulatory norms of international development financing; and (2) if the PRSP approach does constitute a departure from existing modalities and norms, what are the implications of this shift for the constitution of global economic governance and international law?

It is submitted that the PRSP approach constitutes *both a departure from* and a *restatement of* existing modalities of financing and the existing legal and political framework of international development financing. This is measured against the conceptual framework of the 'new architecture of aid' on which the PRSP initiative is based as well as the policies and programmes through which this conceptual framework is operationalised; that is, through: (1) the PRSP process itself; (2) the policy instruments the PRSP underpins, such as the World Bank's Country Assistance Strategy and Medium-Term Expenditure Framework; and (3) the financing instruments the PRSP informs, such as Poverty Reduction Strategy Credits from the Bank, concessional financing from the IMF's PRGF (now replaced by facilities under the Poverty Reduction and Growth Trust) and debt relief operations under the enhanced HIPC initiative and the Multilateral Debt Relief Initiative.

An examination of these processes and instruments demonstrates that, despite rhetoric to the contrary, the new framework for regulating aid flows has not redressed the democratic deficit of previous modalities of development financing. Instead, where there has been a change in the *process* of accessing official development financing, there has been little traction on reforming the *substance* of development financing, notably the attached economic policy conditions, and these shifts in the procedural aspects of financing have correspondingly *reinforced* rather than *revised* the nature of substantive negotiations between client states and their external financiers (see Chapters 4, 5 and 6).

At the same time, the changes to the framework of aid relations and the operational policies of official development financing have impacted on the constitution of global economic governance, specifically third world engagement in the processes and outcomes of international economic relations and international economic law. This is demonstrated through an analysis of the PRSP framework's impact on the modalities of regulating state access to development financing, notably through its effect on the instrument of conditionality (see Chapter 4) and the impact of internal interventions of the PRS process on states' relationships with their external financiers (see Chapters 5 and 6).

Accordingly, this book has demonstrated that while there are significant processual shifts in the modalities of the 'new architecture of aid', the substance of this new framework for disbursing financial assistance to low-income countries remains driven by both the bureaucratic imperatives of the Bank and the Fund and, more importantly, the geo-political and economic agenda of their major shareholders. The centrality of the BWIs to the mobilisation of external resources for postcolonial states, especially since the collapse of the Bretton Woods system in the 1970s and the debt crisis of the 1980s, has served to establish them as key institutions for managing the third world's relations with the exterior (see Chapter 2), and, consequently, as pivotal institutions for managing the crisis of legitimacy in the late 1990s which precipitated the PRSP framework (see Chapter 3).

The PRSP framework, as a subset of the wider post-Washington Consensus policymaking agenda, may be viewed as a means of quelling potential insurgency in nation states in the south in the face of the global loss of faith in the neoliberal global economy and reinscribing the discipline that its predecessor framework, structural adjustment, was failing to establish in the face of mounting dissonance in the international political economy at the time (see Chapter 3). Encapsulating the post-Washington Consensus' core of 'anti-politics' by substituting 'the politics of procedure for the politics of bargaining' (Jayasuriya, 2001a: 1), PRSPs therefore represent a conceptual departure from structural adjustment programmes in three critical areas: the constituents of domestic policymaking, external political barter and the regulation of access to capital (see Chapter 3).

This is facilitated through a reorganisation of (1) the modalities of regulating states' access to international development finance and (2) the extensive reforms wrought by the PRSP framework in the internal constitution of the recipient states, with the reorganisation of such structures predicated upon the imperative to enforce compliance with a set of policy and regulatory prescriptions that sustain rather than subvert the status quo of economic globalisation and the geo-political landscape of the postcolonial period (see Chapters 4, 5 and 6). The process of universalising national economic planning – setting uniform 'development' targets and common prioritisation of public policy – and globalising bureaucratic and political structures, by establishing a template for public participatory policymaking and intra-governmental policy dialogue, creates a framework which punishes non-conformity with pre-established norms (see Chapters 5 and 6). States which fail to play by the rules are excluded, not by coercion but through evaluation of their willingness to be subjected to these 'universal' values and objectives of state–society organisation (ibid.).

This book has thus attempted to demonstrate that the conceptual and operational premise of the PRSP framework responds not only to a geo-strategic urgency to reassert the hegemony of the northern states which underwrite the rules of multilateral engagement in the face of resistance, but also to an imperative to secure legitimacy for the reformulated rules of engagement (see Chapters 2 and 3). The modalities of the regulatory discipline imposed by the PRSP framework therefore establish new modalities of control, representing the shifting manifestations of power in the new international political economy. Specifically, this book has argued that the PRSP framework exemplifies the transition from what Foucault terms a 'disciplinary society' to a 'society of control' (see Chapters 4 and 5; section 7.4).

The response of the aforementioned crisis of legitimacy is therefore not one predicated upon the revision of international economic law and the purging of its asymmetries, but one that revises state engagement with international law and the political economy which sustains it. Correspondingly, the response of the PRSP framework to the social and economic marginalisation of states and communities resulting from neoliberal globalisation underwritten by the rules of international trade and finance is not one of international redistributive justice or one of reparational justice, but one of bilateral and financial mediation *on the terms established by the hegemon states*. The pivoting of all discourse of social and economic exclusion on the issue of 'aid' and assessing the merit of countries to access such financing subverts the real and persistent causes of such marginalisation in the global economy.

In light of the analyses of the conceptual and operational framework of the PRSP, it is possible to conclude that the PRSP framework impacts upon the constitution of international law and governance by establishing a new regulatory framework that restructures fundamental relationships between actors, states and institutions in the area of development financing policy and practice. The constituents of this new regulatory mechanism are reflective of the emerging manifestations of global disciplinary power, representing both a continuation and an exacerbation of the asymmetrical sovereignty characterising postcolonial international law and international relations, and the imperial nature of the 'development project' which has so far sustained the logic of these asymmetrical relationships between the 'core' and peripheral states of the global economy.

7.2 A new regulatory project

One of the explicit objectives of the PRSP framework is the facilitation of better aid coordination and harmonisation of aid policy and practice, using the PRSP as a vehicle and process through which official financiers can pivot negotiations and programmes of support and seeking to harmonise the fragmented regulatory webs involved in the negotiation, evaluation and disbursement of official development financing. This new regime aims to globalise aid relations across different jurisdictions by institutionalising standardised systems for economic planning and public administration in aid-recipient states. This globalisation of aid relations follows on from the rapid globalisation of regulation in areas of trade and commercial finance which has taken place in the world economy over the past three decades. The PRSP framework and its attendant processes of aid harmonisation and donor coordination therefore exemplifies, inasmuch as it intensifies, the globalisation of policymaking and regulatory norm-setting characterising international law and governance today.

7.2.1 A global administrative space

This new regulatory framework deviates from pre-existing structures of global economic governance and international economic law in two fundamental respects. First, it reconfigures the internal dynamics of relationships between the states subject to regulation and the exterior, and by doing so introduces (and universalises) new norms into economic regulation through development financing. The agenda for norm-brokerage in this new configuration depends less on the establishment of coercive rules and principles for engagement and more on the discretionary application of 'voluntary' accession to the discipline. This is demonstrated, for example, in the movement away from norms to processes in global economic regulation, such as the shift away from the use of *ex-post* conditionalities in development financing agreements to a reliance on *ex-ante* conditionalities (see Chapter 4), and in the shift towards using incentives as instruments for disciplinary control (see Chapters 4 and 5).

Here, the terms of access to development financing and the rules by which states in receipt of it are governed have therefore evolved to incorporate not just the adoption of substantive conditions – that is, the economic (and, to some extent, governance) policy reforms of the accompanying adjustment or stabilisation programme – but also the implementation of processual conditions, such as the institution of consultative decision-making mechanisms, as a criterion for accessing financial resources. The construction of the relationship between the parties to the financing assumes a more globalised form, undertaken under the tutelage and management of the BWIs and facilitated by the expansion in their discretionary powers (see Chapter 4).

Correspondingly, the effect of a globalised system of policymaking, universalised across a diverse range of third world states, is the systematic insertion of domestic state structures into the larger global regulatory order, ceding not only significant internal rulemaking and norm-brokerage to the 'international community' – represented here by the administrative capacity of the BWIs – but also the related implementation and adjudication functions as well. Where previous adjustment reforms focused on the restructuring of the economy, this new aid regime is aimed at establishing the strategic and institutional structures necessary for the implementation of such economic reforms. It moves beyond the universalisation of economic policies seen during the era of the Washington Consensus, in which states were conscripted into a unified model of economic development, and moves instead into the transnationalisation of public administrative systems and administrative law and policy.

The internationalisation of these institutions under the PRSP framework is therefore contributing to the emergence of what some scholars term a 'global administrative space' – the increasing inseparability between global and national regulatory space, in which substantive and procedural norms established at the global level, supplemented by webs of unifying national regulation and global coordination, are 'penetrating deeply into domestic regulatory programs and decisions' (Kingsbury *et al.*, 2005: 25–26). In this emerging form of transnational regulation, many of the specificities and implementation of norms are determined by 'transnational administrative bodies', including international organisations such as the World Bank and the IMF, which 'perform administrative functions but are not directly subject to control by national governments or domestic legal systems' (ibid.: 16).

The emergence of this global administrative space has been facilitated by the rise of the aforementioned international organisations as well as transnational regulatory organisations.[1] The rapid proliferation of international organisations in the postwar period, accompanied by the growth and complexity of their institutional organs, has brought about significant changes in the international lawmaking process, transforming the means by which international law is generated, the nature of the actors that produce these rules, as well as the substantive content of international law itself (Alvarez, 2006: 9, 17). In particular, the rise of international organisations as lawmakers in their own right has, in some respects, displaced traditional 'positivist state consent as the basis for all international obligations', representing a shift towards '*less* consciously created sources of international legal obligation' such as institutional precedents and customary practices generated by organisational bureaucracies (ibid.: 600). These new forms of international norm production are necessarily decoupled from the vertical accountability of states to domestic stakeholders since much of the lawmaking in this sense is produced through the actions of the international civil service, dispute settlement bodies and political organs of international organisations (ibid.: 600, 630–631).

The cessation of national control over crucial aspects of norm creation, enforcement and adjudication, including dispensing with domestic ratification of externally negotiated rules, is a hallmark of the emerging global administrative plane (Kingsbury *et al.*, 2005: 25–26; Krisch and Kingsbury, 2006: 3–4). According to Kingsbury *et al.*:

> The rise of regulatory programs at the global level and their infusion into domestic counterparts means that the decisions of domestic administrators are increasingly constrained by substantive and procedural norms established at the global level; the formal need for domestic implementation thus no longer provides for meaningful independence of the domestic from the international realm.
>
> (Kingsbury *et al.*, 2005: 26)

However, the increasing enmeshment of local and global regulatory structures has differing impacts on the third world than on the industrialised states which control the international institutions forming part of this global administrative space. As Chimni has argued, the significance of this regulatory network of international institutions for third world states today is that, together, this network 'has been established or repositioned, at the initiative of the first world and together, they constitute a *nascent global state* whose function is to realize the interests of transnational capital and powerful states in the international system to the disadvantage of third world states and peoples', resulting in an 'evolving global state formation' which is '*imperial* in character' (Chimni, 2004: 1–2). The PRSP framework may thus be regarded as part of this emerging 'global state', regulated through the new technologies of power discussed in section 7.4.

7.2.2 Discursive discipline

The second characteristic of the new regulatory framework established by the PRSP framework is the significant restructuring of the discourse of development and there is evidence of a mutually reinforcing relationship between the regulatory force of the PRSP framework and its discursive power. The concepts that are problematised by the PRSP project, namely *poverty reduction*, *participation* and *national ownership*, are constituted as new areas of regulation through dynamics of power and influence that underlie the formulation of this initiative.

Thus, in addition to approaching the PRSP framework from an analysis of an institutional process, the initiative may be viewed as a textual foundation of knowledge production, with the discourse of the PRSP process and its associated regulatory instruments embedded with meanings and representations that support the constellations of power which inhabit the process. Here, Foucault's theory of discourse politics – the creation and enforcement of norms through the construction of specific discursive relationships (see Chapter 1, section 1.4) – assists us in understanding how the formation of the rules of knowledge about particular objects reproduces the relationships of power under which they emerged and under whose authority these objects were characterised and classified (Foucault, 1972: 40–47; see also Foucault 1991: 336–337).

In this respect, the implications of the PRSP project reverberate beyond the policy and institutional incorporation of resistance to encompass a much wider range of cause and effect, and include the production and dissemination of discourses on 'development' and constructions of 'poverty'. The language of the PRSP framework has important resonance in movements for social and economic justice, but equally, and somewhat conversely, it also shapes the debate about the nature of international economic relations and represents the narratives that have gained currency in the context of these relationships due to the hegemony of the actors who underwrite their emergence. This ancillary process of knowledge production has, once again, created a universal framework through which knowledge about heterogeneous cultures and socio-political and economic organisation has been collected, filtered and disseminated, establishing a frame of reference which disciplines through marginalisation and exclusion of all which fall outside these received identities.

The implications of this on the wider global regulatory structures and networks are significant. Specifically, conceptualising 'poverty reduction' as a priority policy intervention and 'ownership' as a political project forecloses negotiations on the reform of the rules of international trade and finance that facilitate the exploitative relationships underlying the impoverishment and human dislocations in PRSP countries. The emphasis on developing and fulfilling priorities established in conformity with the parameters set by the PRSP framework – and within the qualified notions of 'poverty reduction', 'participation' and 'ownership' – thus shifts the debate away from the international arena and places the burden of meeting the challenge of social and economic developmental objectives on national governments. It is the nation state – the structurally adjusted, indebted, aid-dependent state – that now bears the primary responsibility for ensuring that the communally ascribed Millennium Development Goals are met through a further programme of structural adjustment (now renamed 'development policy' operations), foreclosing debate on issues of international economic justice, redistribution and communal responsibility for the provision and protection of public goods (see section 7.3).

Once again, the logic which sustains these interventions is that of the 'dynamic of difference' discussed in Chapter 2. Prevailing discursive representations of third world states, particularly of low-income, highly indebted countries, as incapacitated states requiring assistance from the 'international' community to enable growth and development maintains the legitimacy of the BWIs in determining for these states the appropriate terms of their engagement with the international community. The states' acquiescence to such interventions reflects the asymmetrical sovereignty which characterises postcolonial international law (see Chapter 2, section 2.1).

In this manner, where the operational dimensions of this new regulatory project act as the 'mechanism of restraint' under Stephen Gill's conceptualisation of a 'new constitutionalism', the disciplinary power of the discourse associated with the PRSP project serves as a 'mechanism of incorporation' (Gill, 2000; see section 7.4). The production and dissemination of key concepts shape the debate about the nature of the international economic order and structure the terrain of knowledge on the modalities of state engagement with the international economy, impacting significantly, as we shall see in section 7.3, on third world state engagement with it and with international economic law.

7.2.3 The rise of network governance

The third and final characteristic of the regulatory project exemplified by the PRSP framework is that of the rise in network governance. Linked to the emergence of the global administrative space and the discursive nature of new forms of regulatory control discussed in the previous sections, network governance can be best described as the decentralisation of regulatory power and regulatory institutions. Here, international lawmaking and global regulatory governance are shifted away from the traditional state-to-state bargaining process under conventional international lawmaking processes – treaty production, development of binding customary rules and, increasingly, institutional precedents established by international organisations (see section 7.2.1) – and instead focus on the production and reproduction of norms, legal and non-legal, through cooperation and convergence facilitated through networks of policymakers and regulators.

Picciotto distinguishes network governance from the classical liberal state system of government in international law in terms of these respective structures of authority, with the former assuming a polyarchical character vis-à-vis the hierarchical nature of the latter (Picciotto, 2006: 2). In other words, network governance involves a decentring of legal and political authority, a movement from the command-centred, state-led international legal paradigm with clearly established legal categories and hierarchies towards more fluid systems of regulation under which different normative systems overlap and interpenetrate (ibid.: 8). Accompanying this 'destabilisation of regulatory hierarchy' is therefore the blurring of normative forms, reflected in the 'shift from formal law to quasi-legal forms of regulation in global arenas', and the fragmentation of statehood and the transference of public regulatory authority from political organs of state to autonomous technocrats, both public and private (ibid.: 11–15).

Network governance means that many of the externally driven regulatory reforms within states are occurring not as a result of formal treaty negotiation and ratification or as a consequence of 'supranationalism' – international law which has direct applicability to legal persons within their jurisdiction (notably European Community law) – but as an outcome of networking between state, quasi-state or private regulatory agencies and their counterparts abroad (Picciotto, 2006: 1–10; Raustiala, 2002: 3–6). Driven by the rise of technological innovation, expansion of domestic regulation and globalisation, network governance relies less on adherence to formalised rules and judicial enforcement mechanisms to regulate the behaviour of target actors than on other normative means, such as codes of conduct, declarations, principles and MOUs between different state and quasi-state representatives.

Networks effect regulatory change through 'persuasion' rather than 'command' (Raustiala, 2002: 51), weaving new norms into a jurisdiction via Braithwaite and Drahos' 'webs of dialogue' as opposed to 'webs of coercion' (Braithwaite and Drahos, 2000). As such, networks foster the convergence of regulatory standards or harmonisation of laws across state jurisdictions not through 'a formal, multilateral process of negotiation' but 'through a decentralized, incremental process of interaction and emulation' (Raustiala, 2002: 52). However, the propensity of networks to be dominated by powerful actors, especially 'in situations where regulatory power is asymmetric' (ibid.; 66), renders network governance susceptible to the same power dynamics inherent in conventional international law. Raustiala argues that this characteristic of network governance has led to such transgovernmental networks being increasingly key in promoting 'regulatory export' or 'the export of regulatory rules and practices from major powers to weaker states' (Raustiala, 2002: 7, 16).

The move towards principles of 'country selectivity', and attendant *ex-ante* conditionalities under the PRSP framework and the new structure of aid governance in which coalitions of civil servants from donor and recipient countries, IFI bureaucrats and transnational civil society representatives exercise collective decision-making on aspects of economic policymaking outside domestic constitutional mechanisms for policymaking and outside the traditional state-to-state bargaining process of international norm creation, heightens this global shift towards polycentric network governance. Regulatory reforms, including key changes to legislative, administrative and judicial organisation of states subject to the PRSP process, which may not be directly relevant to the disbursement of finance but are reflective of the regulatory harmonisation objectives of dominant donor states, can be inserted into a jurisdiction without the necessary complexities of the state-to-state treaty negotiation process. This, as discussed in previous chapters, necessarily complicates the channels of democratic accountability and disrupts domestic frameworks of representative government (see Picciotto, 2006: 11).

7.3 Foreclosing international reform

One of the most important consequences of the new regulatory project forwarded by the PRSP framework has been its effect in foreclosing the possibilities for a radical revision of the rules and institutions of international economic law. The PRSP project does so by reframing fundamental tenets of international cooperation and global communal responsibility. In the PRSP discourse, the challenges of meeting developmental objectives and overcoming socio-economic exclusion in the globalised, interdependent era – of both nation states and communities within them – reside in the reconstruction of the state apparatus and *not* in the stemming of the currents of neoliberal globalisation through international mechanisms and resolution of structural inequities at the global level. This is achieved by: (1) discounting the role of the 'international' in the resolution of social and economic exclusion within states, particularly developing states in the south subject to the torrents of globalised neoliberalism; and (2) rupturing communal struggles against the forces of international impoverishment calling for a revisiting and revising of the rules of the international economy through the incentive of individual engagement.

7.3.1 Problematising the state

The mode of engagement prescribed by the PRSP framework is one that transfers to the affected state *autonomy* over, but, correspondingly, *responsibility* for, state interaction with and commitment to the norms, legal or otherwise, of the international economy. The effects of the state's wilful entry into the international market and the rules which govern it are accordingly borne by the state with assistance from the 'international' community to mitigate the dislocations of structural adjustment and macroeconomic stabilisation. Hence, redistributive justice under the PRSP framework takes place in the domestic sphere, not the international, if at all.

'Poverty' in PRSP countries is less rooted in the 'international' than in the 'national', due primarily not to the lack of financial resources caused by the inequities of current rules of global trade and finance but by (1) states' incapacity to generate or absorb financial resources due to inappropriate fiscal, monetary or structural economic policy choices and (2) states' inability or disinclination to utilise resources generated in a productive and redistributive manner (see Chapter 5). The failure of structural adjustment policies in these countries, leading to social and economic dislocations, has more to do with 'policy slippages' than 'policy design' (UNCTAD, 2002b: 5).

The state is thus problematised in the context of 'poverty reduction' and 'development' – the inability to reap the benefits of globalisation or to effectively utilise the 'aid' allocated is attributed to the 'inefficient' and 'predatory' state and the incapacity of the state to organise domestic economic functions and enrol sufficient domestic political support to legitimise its strategic role in the economy. The function of the PRS process is thus to rehabilitate the state's prescriptive and regulative capacity to enable better organised strategic development planning and to institutionalise non-state (read: civil society) oversight capacity to enable greater state transparency and accountability for resources generated, accumulated and distributed (see Chapters 5 and 6).

The nation state that is reconstituted under this framework is therefore one that is facilitative of the project of global neoliberalism and northern corporatism, rehabilitated through a series of institutional interventions of the PRSP framework. Such an assignment of responsibility, predicated upon the unquestioning acceptance of the status quo of economic globalisation processes, obfuscates the role of the international community in securing economic justice for economically marginalised nation states and their impoverished constituencies.

Consequently, the focus of the PRSP framework has consistently centred upon the necessity of PRSP countries developing a coherent programme of social sector expenditures and effective public expenditure systems to meet their international development targets, without corresponding consideration of the underlying policy design of national economic strategies and the interaction between these strategies and the global economy (see Chapter 5). The onus is therefore on specific countries to prove their capacity to absorb the financing bequeathed to them by the northern states and demonstrate the institutional discipline necessary to utilise the resources (ibid.). And where there has been a shift towards a focus on developing productive economic sectors in the second generation of PRSPs, these policies have tellingly been informed by the prescriptions of the Washington Consensus (UNCTAD, 2008: 102; see Chapters 5 and 6).

Similarly, the PRSPs' role in debt relief and debt restructuring – under the enhanced HIPC initiative, the MDRI and beyond – has centred on the role of the debtor state, notably in the domestic governance of external debt and management of public financial resources derived from official development assistance, rather than on the structural causes of sovereign indebtedness. Such an approach marginalises the systemic issues of the international financial architecture and the asymmetrical regulatory norms of international finance which contribute to the problem of sovereign debt. In problematising the debtor state, the current debt architecture – under which the PRSP framework plays an important disciplinary role – discounts the culpability of creditor states in creating the national and global conditions for the build-up of debt burdens in the third world, thereby negating the right of debtor states to access reprieve from unsustainable debt servicing, even when this prevents states from fulfilling their fundamental duties to their citizens.

7.3.2 The nation state as a site of political struggle and redistribution

It follows from the problematising of the state in economic development under the PRSP approach that the national sphere has also been constituted as the primary site for any contestation over resource allocation and redistribution and the state correspondingly has been given the primary duty to discharge the social and economic challenges ascribed internationally, such as the MDGs.

The institution of a mandatory participatory policymaking process under the PRSP framework, while enabling a degree of domestic political franchise by opening up hitherto inaccessible spaces for citizenry engagement in national decision-making processes, diverts collective struggle away from the international towards the national. Discontent resulting from the social and economic dislocations of structural adjustment and integration into an uneven international trade and finance playing field by individual countries is now refocused on the individual state and not the community of nations.

The emphasis in the PRSP framework on 'priority public actions' and the linking of state economic resources to clear, targeted and accountable public expenditure may result in more transparent resource allocation, but it also places the responsibility of providing public goods on national governments. This diffuses dissent on the inequality of current global economic structures and the injustices of global policy decisions by refocusing the debate away from the resource constraints third world states face as a result of external pressures towards one centred on how states can best allocate limited resources to meet developmental challenges.

Furthermore, the access to political structures and limited possibilities for engagement in national strategic planning via participatory processes in individual countries has the effect of fracturing globalised resistance, in the form of either mass citizenry mobilisations or global civil society cooperation. By relocating the site for resource contestation from the international or the exterior to the national or the interior, the PRSP framework decentralises political mobilisation. The reconfiguration of the political space in PRSP countries legitimises the *process* of the PRSP framework, through the restructuring of social relations between state and non-state actors and external financiers, as well as conferring credibility on the substantive content of the resultant social and economic policies, even as it fails to reform the existing policy and practice of development financing or the asymmetrical rules of international economic law.

Moreover, the emphasis on 'poverty reduction' as priority governmental action subverts the principle of 'development' encompassing calls for fairer rules in the international economic order to facilitate such growth (see section 7.3.3). It does not address the asymmetries which prevent countries' attainment of fuller economic and social objectives, such as addressing the declining terms of trade for commodity-dependent states in the south as a result of continuing depreciation of prices for primary commodities, the tariff escalation rules in multilateral trade law, the intransigence of northern policies on agricultural subsidies or the crippling effects of sovereign indebtedness.

Additionally, as donor-driven participatory processes have paradoxically created a culture of upward rather than downward accountability of national governments, participants of such processes can and have been inadvertently conscripted into acting as watchdogs for the international donor community. Recipient states remain highly accountable to IFIs and donors but rarely vice versa, and donors, not domestic constituents, remain the primary consumers of financial information and government performance reviews under the new aid regime (Afrodad, 2007: 21; Nkombo, 2008: 5). This increases external oversight of government policies and expenditures but does not necessarily improve accountability for public decisions. The relationship between public authorities and domestic stakeholders and citizens, normally tested and resolved through local administrative and judicial arrangements – such as constitutional courts and judicial review procedures – acquires a different form when placed within this context of donor accountability. Consequently, while the globalisation of policymaking under the PRSP framework and the new architecture of aid conscripts countries into an emerging 'global administrative space' (see section 7.2.1), creating what some have termed 'a new level of supranational economic governance' (Bissio, 2007: para. 7), it does not establish corresponding measures for administrative or regulatory oversight of the institutions and agencies charged with ultimate budgetary and policy decision-making at that level.

7.3.3 Subverting the 'right to development'

The assignment of responsibility for addressing developmental challenges to individual nation states is not exclusive to the PRSP framework. It reflects the conceptual framework that has consistently guided official aid flows (including resources for debt relief) from northern to southern states in the postcolonial period which have sought to resist the incorporation of any language of redistribution or universal collective responsibility in the area of social and economic cooperation in bilateral and multilateral financing relationships or within the international financial architecture as a whole.

The circumscription of the role of the international community, particularly that of the northern states and northern capital, which represent the principal beneficiaries of the current international economic order, in any normative framework for international development has been a significant feature of all international negotiations in the area of trade, finance and development cooperation since the collapse of the third world movement for a New International Economic Order in the 1970s and 1980s and the gradual erosion of the UNCTAD mandate in the structural adjustment era.[2]

The refusal of western states to acknowledge collective responsibility for the condition of third world states and to accept complicity in their social and economic marginalisation from the international economic order was evidenced by the north–south split[3] in the voting patterns for the UN Declaration on the Right to Development in 1986. The Declaration, championed by the Group of 77 developing states stressed 'the collective obligation of all states to create a just and equitable international environment for the realisation of the right to development' and emphasised 'a collective duty of all states to eliminate barriers, such as unfair trade rules and the debt burden' (Nyamu-Musembi and Cornwall, 2004: 8).

The most heavily contested elements of the Declaration involved questions on the nature of the right to development, specifically the assignment of rights and duties, and the balance between the national and international characteristics of these rights and duties. For southern governments, the 'right to development' is international in character and the responsibility for realising such a right 'cannot remain at the national level', as 'globalisation, international trade, foreign domestic economic policies, foreign debt and intellectual property rights constrain national development efforts' (Piron, 2002: 18–19). The 'right to development' therefore encompasses a revision of the rules of international trade and finance to enable greater participation and control of developing countries in the global economy, including but not exclusively in the establishment of international mechanisms to implement the principles of the 1986 Declaration (ibid.). Specifically, the southern states have argued that this right 'cannot be reduced to international development assistance, nor to national eradication programmes' (ibid.).

In contrast, contemporary interpretations of the 'right to development' by northern states remain based on the 'partnership' model which underpins the PRSP framework – 'one based on shared responsibilities and mutual commitments between developed and developing countries and international organisations' (ibid.: 5). In particular, northern governments do not recognise the provisions of the 1986 Declaration as forming part of customary human rights law or forming a normative basis for their aid financing, external trade and foreign policies vis-à-vis developing states. Instead, these governments have generally interpreted the 'right to development' as a right of individuals against states, notably the right of citizens in developing countries against their own states, and not as a right exercised by states against other states. While recognising the international dimension of the 'right to development', northern governments have argued that it is states which 'have primary responsibility for the realising of the [right to development]' (ibid.: 18) and that such 'assistance is based on a moral – not legal – obligation to alleviate poverty' (Nyamu-Musembi and Cornwall, 2004: 9; Piron, 2002).[4]

Consequently, all subsequent international negotiations on social and economic cooperation have been couched in the new language of 'partnership' and 'poverty reduction', in contrast to the call for international cooperation and redistributive justice that underpinned third world calls for an NIEO. Just as the Millennium Declaration which gave birth to the MDGs focused on individual state responsibility to meet 'internationally agreed' developmental objectives, the Monterrey Consensus adopted at the 2002 UN Financing for Development (FFD) Conference focused on the responsibility of the international community to mobilise and increase the effective use of national and international financial resources to achieve these objectives (para. 3). The Monterrey Consensus declared that achieving such targets 'demands a new *partnership* between developed and developing countries', including the commitment to 'sound policies, good governance at all levels and the rule of law' (para. 4).

The PRSP framework not only provides the operational mechanism for such a partnership but also ensures that discussions on external resources and redressing countries' social and economic exclusion remain at the level of the state and at the level of individual financing arrangements with official creditors, whether on a bilateral or multilateral basis. By establishing the parameters for negotiation within a small cartel of donors and creditors, the discourse created by the PRSP approach limits the capacity of PRSP countries to form collective demands for equity at the international level. The issue of creditor co-responsibility for the debt and development crisis of the third world does not feature within the terms of this discourse of development 'partnership', and crucial questions of equity and redistribution in international law are peripheralised. The core of the PRSP framework thus reflects an effort to 'manage' world poverty rather than to resolve it.

7.4 Biopower and the new technologies of discipline

7.4.1 A biopolitical global constitution

At various junctures, this book has contended that the PRSP framework constitutes a new form of discipline of third world states in the current postcolonial period, representing both a continuation with and an extension of old mechanisms of imperial and neo-imperial control. It has been argued that this may be framed as the beginning of a transition from Foucault's disciplinary society to a society of control vis-à-vis the governance of third world states (see Chapters 1, 4 and 5). The construction of a new global regulatory framework for disciplining third world states under the aegis of the PRSP framework is evidence of the shifting modalities of power at the global level. The evolution of the disciplinary instrument of official development financing into its current state marks a wider reconfiguration of the aforementioned forms of global governance and the post-colonial juridical order which sustains it, signalling a refinement of the wider techniques of discipline and reflective of this shift (see Chapter 4; Gill, 2000: 14–15; Hardt and Negri, 2000: 22–24).

As discussed in Chapter 1, the Foucauldian conception of power rests upon its plurality of forms and its immanence in the social field. For Foucault, power is not hierarchical, dispersed, as it were, from a central institutional structure, but is something which proliferates and reproduces at the micro or capillary levels of society, which is then assumed by institutional forces (Foucault, 1994: 339–345). Hence, the study of power should involve the study of 'power relations' rather than the institutional manifestations of such power (ibid.: 343; see Chapter 1, section 1.4). Evaluation of the institutional manifestations of this power has located such power in the wider frame of power relations – between the object of power (third world states) and the authorities of power (the first world and their institutions, namely the World Bank and the IMF).

Foucault classifies the technologies through which this power is exercised within these relationships into two forms: (1) *disciplinary power* – the building blocs of the institutional exercise of power; and (2) *biopolitical power* – the regulation of the body (or body politic in the case of states) – a more sophisticated means 'around which the organisation of power over life was deployed' (Foucault, 1991: 261–262; see Chapters 1 and 4). For Hardt and Negri, the new paradigm of power in the postmodern economy of today is biopolitical in nature, 'a situation in which what is directly at stake in power is the production and reproduction of life itself' (Hardt and Negri, 2000: 22–25). The supervision of the body of the object of power 'is imbued with the mechanics of life', its supervision 'effected through an entire series of interventions and *regulatory controls: a bio-politics of the population*' (Foucault, 1991: 262).

Therefore, while the PRSP framework continues to possess the elements of the disciplinary society – the structuring of policy processes, substantive economic engagement and socio-political organisation within certain parameters of thought and practice, and 'normal' or 'deviant' behaviours therein sanctioned or prescribed by the BWIs and their major shareholding states – this new regulatory project also exercises this biopolitical control over third world states. In this new schema of power, contend Hardt and Negri, the 'mechanisms of command become ever more "democratic," the 'behaviors of social integration and exclusion proper to rule are thus increasingly interiorized within the subjects themselves' (Hardt and Negri, 2000: 23). This, as we have seen, is demonstrated through the PRSP framework's focus on 'ownership', 'partnership' and 'participation'.

The formation of the new imperialism, according to Hardt and Negri, is thus premised on the 'establishment of a global society of control' in servitude to capital and its need to realise a world market (Hardt and Negri, 2000: 332). Consequently, the essence of 'imperial administration' is therefore 'to manage this process of integration and therefore to pacify, and control the separated and segmented social forces' to short-circuit the possibilities for resistance (ibid.). Again, we have seen, from our discussion on pp. 221–222 and in the preceding chapters, how the PRSP framework serves to fracture the resistance to the asymmetries of neoliberal globalisation through the process of integration and fragmentation.

This analysis dovetails with Gill's conception of a 'new constitutionalism' in the world order. This 'new constitutionalism', featuring the politics of incorporation and co-optation, represents the 'dominant political-juridical form' of today's global political economy, the counterpart to its 'socio-economic form', which Gill terms 'disciplinary neoliberalism' – the organisation of society in accordance with the dictates of global capital (Gill, 2000: 3). Although Gill does not refer to Foucault's work on biopower, his construction of the new global constitution, like Hardt and Negri's, is also premised upon the capillary effect of power in the current world order and the shift in modalities of discipline based on the exercise of such power (see ibid.: 16–18). According to Gill, 'the crucial strategic significance of new constitutionalism is how it seeks to provide political anchorage for the power of capital in the *long term*' through the use of political and legal measures (1) to reconfigure the state apparatuses in favour of global capital, (2) to construct and extend capital markets and (3) to deal 'with the dislocations and contradictions produced by disciplinary neoliberalism' (ibid.: 3; 11–15).

The movement away from the first two mechanisms of regulatory control – applying legal and constitutional means of facilitating capital mobility and liberal capital markets – which Gill terms 'mechanisms of restraint', towards the third mechanism, termed 'mechanism of incorporation' – aimed at facilitating 'legitimation as well as compensatory measures to prevent social atomisation' resulting from the effects of neoliberal globalisation (ibid.: 15–16) – exemplifies the development of the PRSP operational apparatus. Gill argues that while the punitive mechanisms of restraint, or so-called 'locking-in' measures, insulate against the potential of regulatory revisions wrought by neoliberal globalisation, mechanisms of incorporation represent 'the consensual counterpart in that they seek to reduce the demands for other types of reform in the first place' (ibid.: 18).

Consequently, the PRSP framework represents one, albeit an important one, of the many means by which this biopolitical power is exercised over third world states. Increasingly, in other areas of regulation – from bilateral and multilateral trade rules, through the regulation of intellectual property rights, to the adoption of financial codes and standards under agreements such as the Basel Code for Banking Supervision – the modalities of power are shifting from the coercive force of disciplines to the pervasive power of biopolitics. Instead of coercive or punitive regulation, third world states internalise the rationalisation and normalisation of a particular world view and economic engagement.

7.4.2 Resistance and 'globalisation from below'

The philosophy of the aforementioned new biopolitical power, however, is inherently subversive, presenting us with opportunities to explore the possibilities for rebuilding the fractured resistance and the fragmented alliance which, in many ways, demonstrated this new biopolitical power's effectiveness by the very imperative to implement a framework such as that of the PRSPs. Foucault, for one, argued that while discourses and biological discipline are controlled by the institutional manifestations of power, they are not subservient to it and counter-discourses and bio-struggles have the potential to resist the normalised identities and create new forms of consciousness if unleashed (Foucault, 1994: 342–348; 1991: 262–267; 1972: 40–46; see also Best and Kellner, 1991: 57–58). This is because '[a]t the very heart of the power relationship, and constantly provoking it, are the recalcitrance of the will and the intransigence of freedom' (Foucault, 1994: 342), creating the potential for resistance once the mechanisms of discipline are unravelled.

Similarly, for Santos, the conventional processes of globalisation – the globalisation of hegemonic localisms (western capitalist business norms and western culture, for instance) and the localised impact of this globalism[5] – also bring with them an intensification of other relationships, notably the globalised organisation of subordinate actors in the global system (Santos, 2002: 178–180). This parallel process of what Santos and others have termed 'globalisation from below' (manifested in the aforementioned dissonance in the international political economy in the 1990s) cannot be easily extinguished, as such organisation, aimed at counteracting the 'detrimental effects of hegemonic forms of globalization', tends also to evolve 'out of the new opportunities for transnational creativity and solidarity created by the intensification of global interactions' (ibid.: 180). This form of globalisation, which Santos terms 'subaltern cosmopolitanism', enables 'subordinate nation-states, regions, classes or social groups and their allies to organize globally in defense of perceived common interests' and 'is intended to counteract the detrimental effects of hegemonic forms of globalization' (ibid.).

The opportunities to challenge the existing mode of social, economic and political organisation afforded by the opening up of policy and political spaces under the PRSP framework must therefore be located within this context. Although suffused with embedded power relations and forms of overt or tacit domination reflective of their conceptual and political origins, the spaces for invited participation – both by aid-dependent countries in international policy and lawmaking arenas and by domestic stakeholders and citizens within the national framework – may also act as what Cornwall and Schattan Coelho term 'spaces of possibility in which power takes a more productive and positive form' (Cornwall and Schattan Coelho, 2007: 11). In this manner, while the terms of engagement may be established by the dominant actors within the process, the discourse and practice of participation and partnership put forward by the PRSP approach may yet reconstruct the relationships between the respective actors within the process towards a more symmetrical interaction. Additionally, as suggested by Santos, the opportunities for global collective engagement by actors affected by the debt and development crisis of the third world may yet be realised by the globalisation of opportunities of engagement.

In uncovering the planes of conceptual rationalisation under which the principles and operational forms of the PRSP framework have emerged, it is therefore hoped that the process may unmask the dynamics of power which underpin this new regulatory force in order to shape a new resistance to the colonising force of this power. Importantly, unmasking the hegemonic unity of purpose, geo-strategic and economic, of the PRSP framework may yet lead to a unifying of the disparate and fragmented opposition – segmented through processes such as the PRSP initiative – to redraw the landscape of global and local resistance to the excesses of neoliberal globalisation, and, with hope, the landscape of the asymmetrical global economy and postcolonial international law.

7.5 Concluding remarks and directions for further research

This book has attempted to situate the emergence of a new regulatory framework for development financing – the PRSP framework – within the wider context of global governance and international law. Specifically, it has argued that this initiative has wider ramifications outside its immediate role as a mechanism for regulating state access to external financial resources and that, located within a specific temporal and geo-political context, it contributes towards foreclosing the possibilities of reforming an inherently asymmetrical system of law and governance.

Since the inception of this research, the PRSP framework has been extended to more low-income countries and has served as the centrepiece for new financing and non-financing initiatives. The PRSP framework or a similar initiative is expected to form the basis of the new United Nations financing model and it is anticipated that the Bretton Woods institutions will play a significant role in the reconfigured United Nations system, which will see greater centralisation of the UN's sustainable development functions and funding[6] (United Nations, 2006). One of the key pillars of this new UN framework would be the application of a 'results-based' funding mechanism based on national country priorities and based on '[c]ountry-led development frameworks, such as poverty reduction strategies, [which] are seen as the main vehicle to achieve internationally agreed development goals', serving as platforms for 'aligning all partners' contributions to national development priorities and provid[ing] an inclusive forum for policy dialogue' (United Nations, 2006: 12).

The proposals also call on the UN to work closely with World Bank and the IMF 'in supporting countries in their national development strategies, including Poverty Reduction Strategies and MDG Strategies', and envisage closer cooperation between the BWIs and the UN to establish common frameworks for data collection and performance monitoring (ibid.: 36). Given the extensive development of the PRSP as an operational framework for policy dialogue and as an instrument for regulating disbursement of development financing, it is likely that it will be adopted as the default mechanism for the UN system as well. There is therefore scope for further research into the new ways of operationalising the PRSPs and new PRSP-enabling instruments, and their impact on their client states and the communities within them.

Furthermore, the insertion of the PRSP framework into the UN system also demonstrates, once again, the 'forum shift'[7] in the regulatory regime pertaining not only to international development financing but also to the governance of the global economy as whole. The movement of the regulatory agenda from the UN to the BWIs signifies, again, how international regulatory arenas have been adapted to suit the interests of dominant states in the global economy. This is also demonstrated by the evolution of the content of Bank and Fund programme conditionalities, both in terms of their modalities of discipline – from *ex-post* to *ex-ante* (discussed in Chapter 4, section 4.5 and in section 7.1) – and in the content of the conditions, from structural conditionalities to the prevalence of public governance conditions.

More research is necessary to consider the impact of such a 'forum shift' and the new modalities of power on the constitution of both global economic relations and international economic law, as well as third world engagement in them. Consideration of other institutional manifestations of these new forms of power, both under the emergence of the 'global administrative space' (and the attendant proposals for global administrative law) outlined pp. 208–210 and at the national level, such as through new mechanisms of conditionality, is necessary, if not imperative, in order to consider the wider implications and impact of this new disciplinary force and the emerging modalities of power which accompany it.

Additionally, there is a need to examine the localised impact of the PRSP framework, particularly from a legal anthropological perspective. As in the context of the 'global', much of the research on the local manifestations of the PRSP framework have been in the realm of political economy or sociological disciplines. There remains a gap in scholarship examining the legal and constitutional impact and the manifestations of power relations through processual and substantive shifts in the framework of development financing at the national and local levels.

Finally, there is also scope to consider the impact of the PRSP framework and its attendant discourses on the shape and form of global and local resistance to the inequities of the current international trade and financial order. While it was beyond the scope of this book to consider in detail the effect of the project on resistance movements – whether locally or globally – or to analyse the possibilities for the future of the political coalitions which contributed to the incipient crisis of faith and catalysed the creation of the PRSPs, this does not extinguish the need for research to further our understanding of the continuing significance of the initiative in regulating global and local economic and political forces and the future of organised (and disparate) resistance to the asymmetries of the global economic order.

Notes

1 The distinction between international organisations and transnational regulatory organisations lies in their constitution – whereas international organisations are formal institutions established through treaties by states and possess international legal personality (that is, the capacity to act on the international legal plane separate from its constituent member states), transnational regulatory organisations are not established by formal treaty but nonetheless consist of government officials expert in the specific aspects of regulation that are subject to their regulation (see Alvarez, 2006: 9).

2 See discussion in Chapter 2, section 2.2, and Chapter 3, section 3.2.

3 While eight developed countries voted for the declaration, with eight others abstaining (out of a combined total of 146 votes in favour), this number was almost reversed in the subsequent resolution for a plan of action calling for a binding resolution of the debt burden, the elimination of protectionist trade policies in the north and an increase in official development financing, with 11 developed countries voting against the resolution (Nyamu-Musembi and Cornwall, 2004: 8–9).

4 According to Nyamu-Musembi and Cornwall, the UK foreign office 'specifically advised proponents of a rights-based approach within the UK's Department for International Development to exclude any reference to the [1986] declaration' (ibid.: 9).

5 Santos defines globalisation as 'the process by which a given local condition or entity succeeds in extending its reach over the globe and, by doing so, develops the capacity to designate a rival social condition or entity as local', the most important implication of this definition being that globalisation will always necessarily entail the successful globalisation of a given local rule or norm, usually of the hegemon actor (Santos, 2002: 178).

6 This new system has been recommended by a high level panel of experts convened by the United Nations to examine ways of reforming the UN. The panel recommended the establishment of a 'One UN' at country and headquarters level, merging the existing 10 UN agencies into one central programme and one central budget (United Nations, 2006: 2–3). At the national level, the 'One UN' system will consolidate all the UN's programme activities under a single umbrella, headed by a single resident coordinator and financed through a single budgetary framework (ibid.). At the headquarters, this means the establishment of a UN Sustainable Development Board 'responsible for endorsing the One UN Country Programme, allocating funding and evaluating performance against objectives agreed with the programme country (ibid.). While this is expected to streamline the currently fragmented nature of UN operations – under which different agencies operate individually and have budgetary autonomy for different operations – there are some concerns that the proposed system will centralise too much authority, resulting in the more powerful state actors in the UN system controlling the disbursement of financing (and attaching relevant conditions to the funds) from a more centralised framework. This model emulates, in many ways, the World Bank model of financing.

7 See Chapter 1, section 1.4, for a description of Braithwaite and Drahos' concept of 'forum shifting'.

Appendix

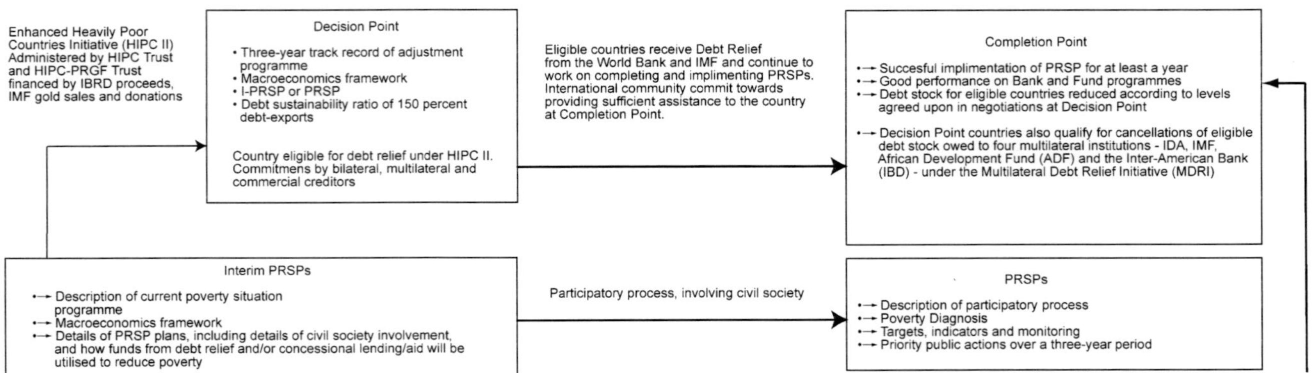
Enhanced Heavily Poor Countries Initiative (HIPC II) Administered by HIPC Trust and HIPC-PRGF Trust financed by IBRD proceeds, IMF gold sales and donations
Decision Point
• Three-year track record of adjustment programme
• Macroeconomics framework
• I-PRSP or PRSP
• Debt sustainability ratio of 150 percent debt-exports
Country eligible for debt relief under HIPC II. Commitmens by bilateral, multilateral and commercial creditors
Eligible countries receive Debt Relief from the World Bank and IMF and continue to work on completing and implimenting PRSPs. International community commit towards providing sufficient assistance to the country at Completion Point.
Completion Point
Succesful implimentation of PRSP for at least a year
Good performance on Bank and Fund programmes
Debt stock for eligible countries reduced according to levels agreed upon in negotiations at Decision Point
Decision Point countries also qualify for cancellations of eligible debt stock owed to four multilateral institutions - IDA, IMF, African Development Fund (ADF) and the Inter-American Bank (IBD) - under the Multilateral Debt Relief Initiative (MDRI)
Interim PRSPs
Description of current poverty situation programme
Macroeconomics framework
Details of PRSP plans, including details of civil society involvement, and how funds from debt relief and/or concessional lending/aid will be utilised to reduce poverty
Participatory process, involving civil society
PRSPs
Description of participatory process
Poverty Diagnosis
Targets, indicators and monitoring
Priority public actions over a three-year period

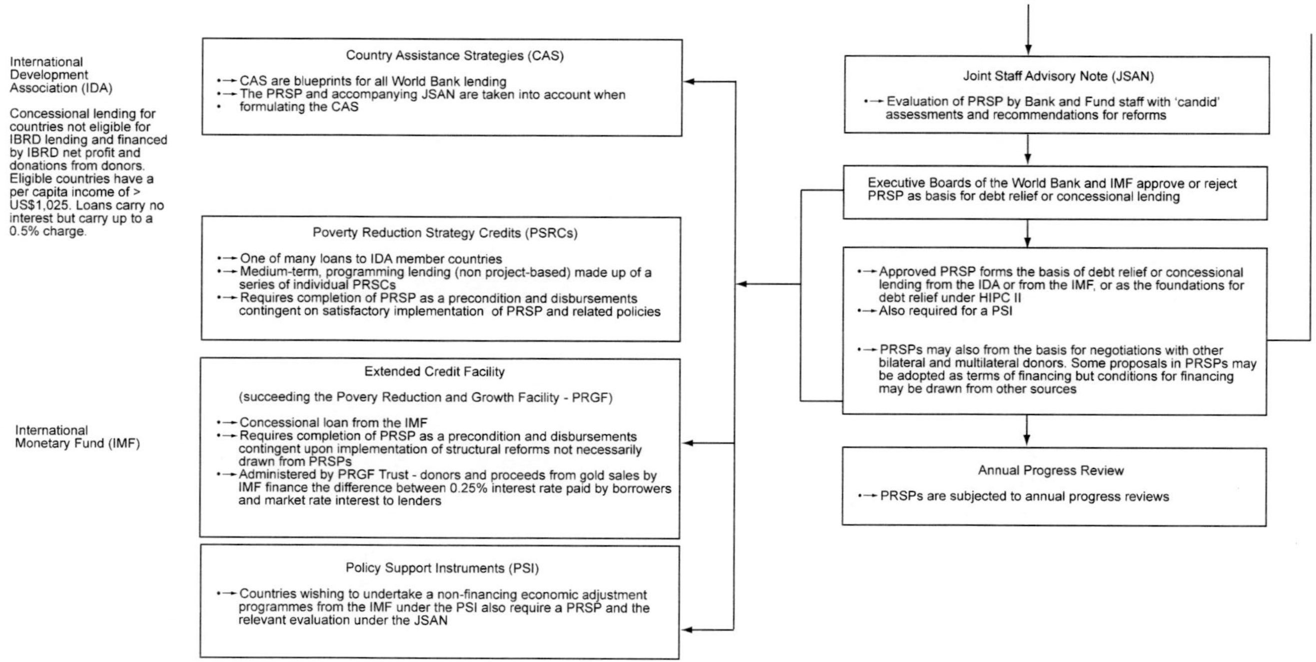

Figure 1 Relationship between the PRSP and financing instruments

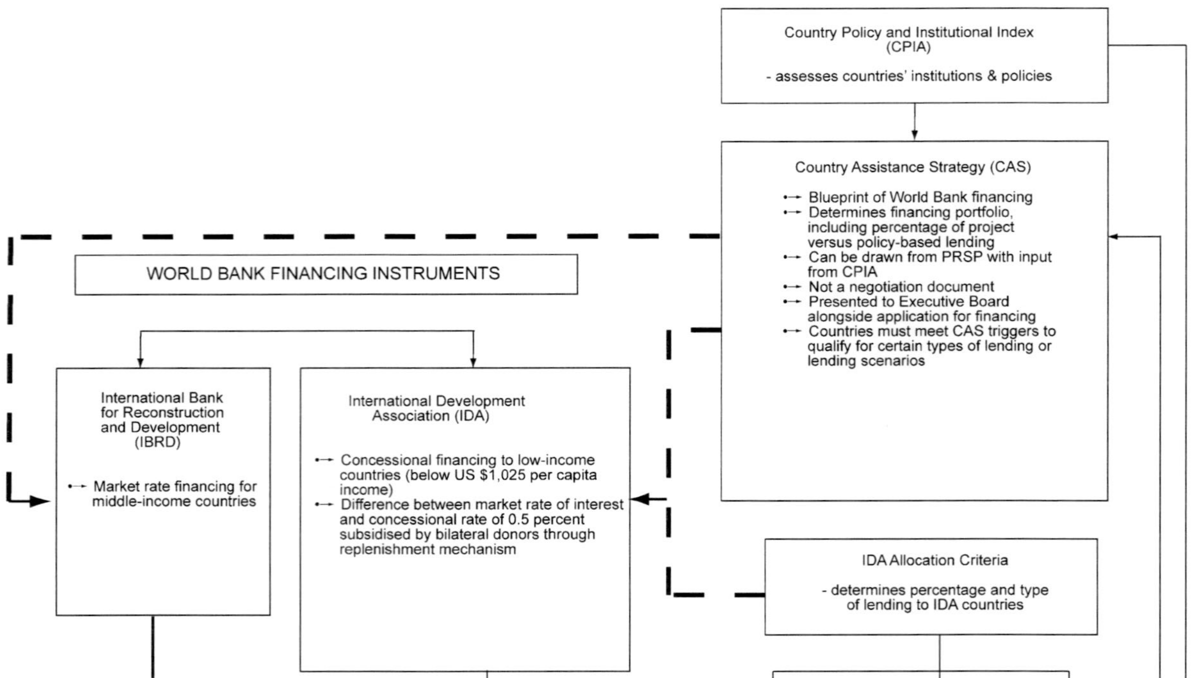

Country Policy and Institutional Index (CPIA)
- assesses countries' institutions & policies
Country Assistance Strategy (CAS)
Blueprint of World Bank financing
Determines financing portfolio, including percentage of project versus policy-based lending
Can be drawn from PRSP with input from CPIA
Not a negotiation document
Presented to Executive Board alongside application for financing
Countries must meet CAS triggers to qualify for certain types of lending or lending scenarios
WORLD BANK FINANCING INSTRUMENTS
International Bank for Reconstruction and Development (IBRD)
Market rate financing for middle-income countries
International Development Association (IDA)
Concessional financing to low-income countries (below US $1,025 per capita income)
Difference between market rate of interest and concessional rate of 0.5 percent subsidised by bilateral donors through replenishment mechanism
IDA Allocation Criteria
- determines percentage and type of lending to IDA countries

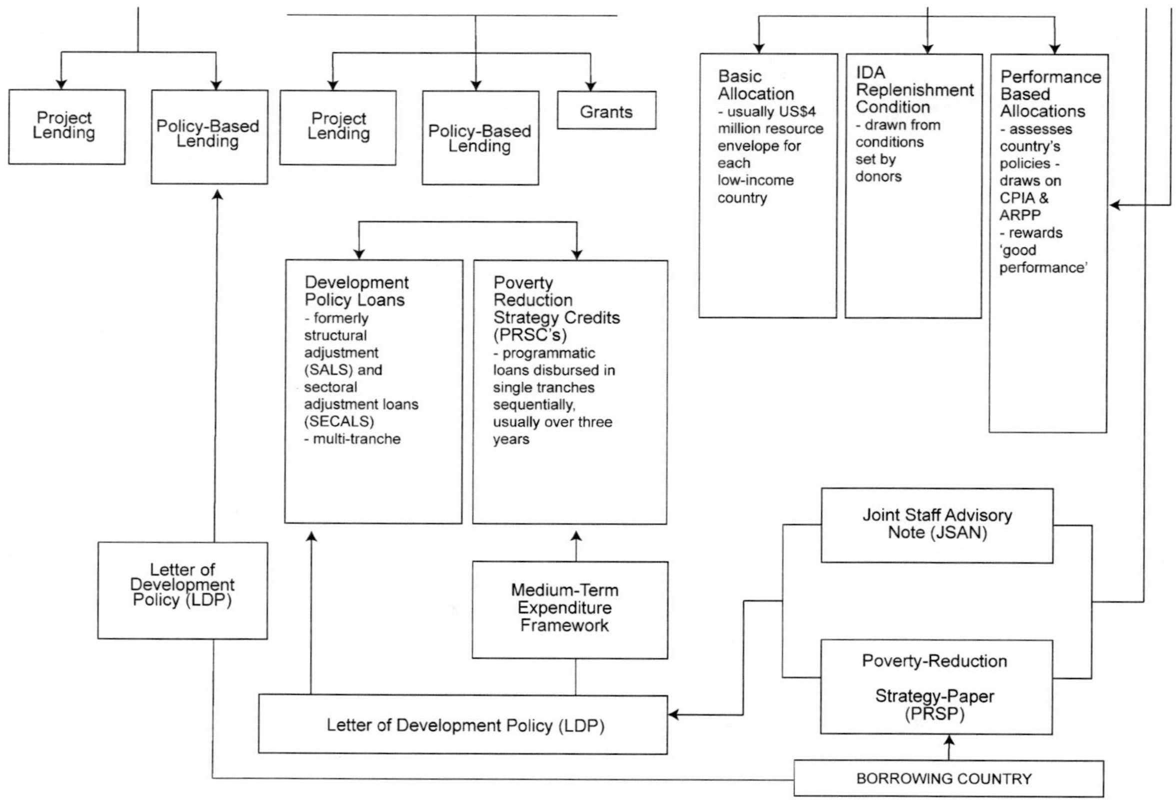

Figure 2 World Bank financing structure

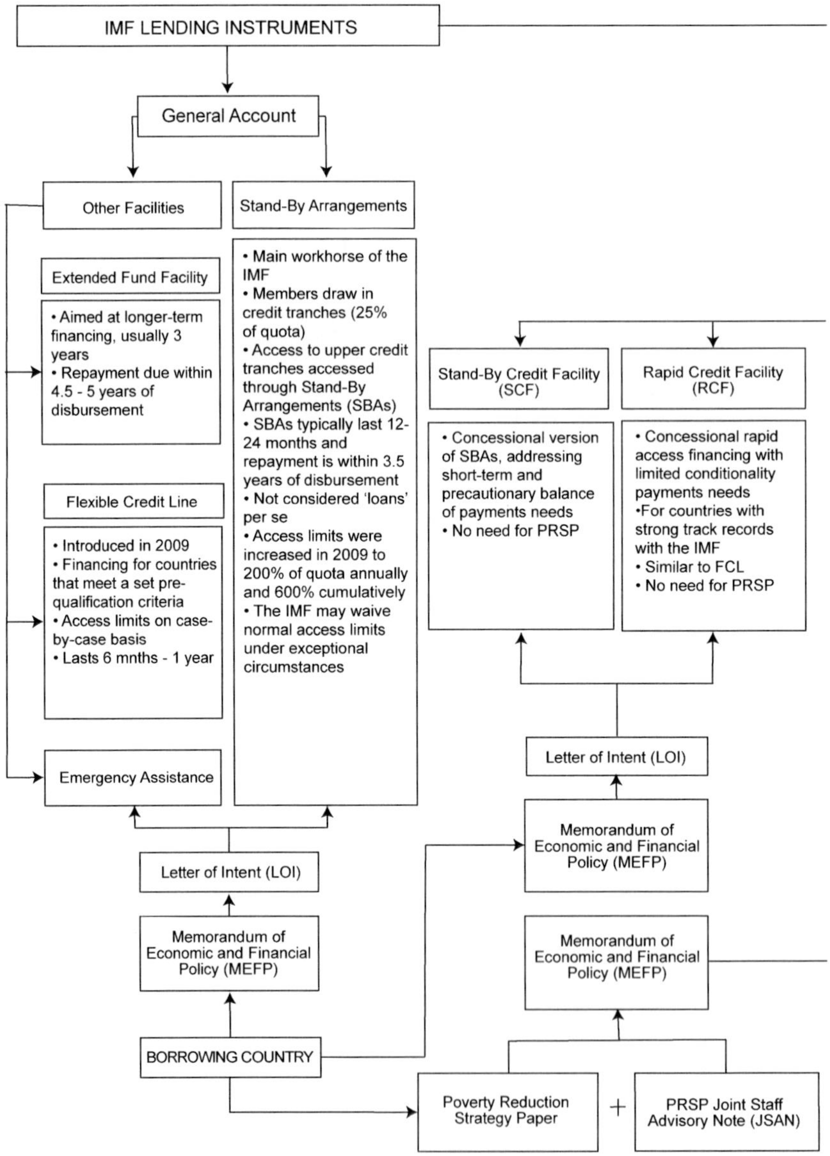

Figure 3 IMF financing structure

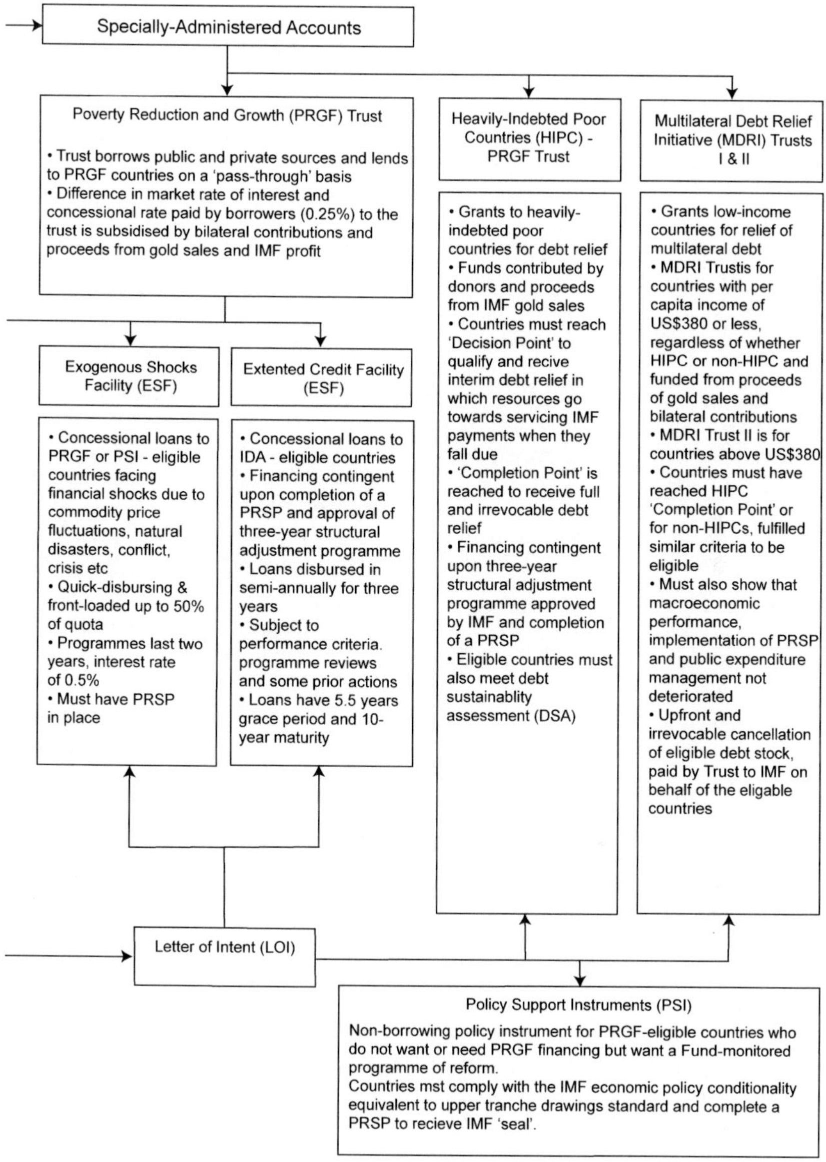
Specially-Administered Accounts
Poverty Reduction and Growth (PRGF) Trust
• Trust borrows public and private sources and lends to PRGF countries on a 'pass-through' basis
• Difference in market rate of interest and concessional rate paid by borrowers (0.25%) to the trust is subsidised by bilateral contributions and proceeds from gold sales and IMF profit
Heavily-Indebted Poor Countries (HIPC) - PRGF Trust
• Grants to heavily-indebted poor countries for debt relief
• Funds contributed by donors and proceeds from IMF gold sales
• Countries must reach 'Decision Point' to qualify and recive interim debt relief in which resources go towards servicing IMF payments when they fall due
• 'Completion Point' is reached to receive full and irrevocable debt relief
• Financing contingent upon three-year structural adjustment programme approved by IMF and completion of a PRSP
• Eligible countries must also meet debt sustainablity assessment (DSA)
Multilateral Debt Relief Initiative (MDRI) Trusts I & II
• Grants low-income countries for relief of multilateral debt
• MDRI Trustis for countries with per capita income of US$380 or less, regardless of whether HIPC or non-HIPC and funded from proceeds of gold sales and bilateral contributions
• MDRI Trust II is for countries above US$380
• Countries must have reached HIPC 'Completion Point' or for non-HIPCs, fulfilled similar criteria to be eligible
• Must also show that macroeconomic performance, implementation of PRSP and public expenditure management not deteriorated
• Upfront and irrevocable cancellation of eligible debt stock, paid by Trust to IMF on behalf of the eligable countries
Exogenous Shocks Facility (ESF)
• Concessional loans to PRGF or PSI - eligible countries facing financial shocks due to commodity price fluctuations, natural disasters, conflict, crisis etc
• Quick-disbursing & front-loaded up to 50% of quota
• Programmes last two years, interest rate of 0.5%
• Must have PRSP in place
Extented Credit Facility (ESF)
• Concessional loans to IDA - eligible countries
• Financing contingent upon completion of a PRSP and approval of three-year structural adjustment programme
• Loans disbursed in semi-annually for three years
• Subject to performance criteria. programme reviews and some prior actions
• Loans have 5.5 years grace period and 10-year maturity
Letter of Intent (LOI)
Policy Support Instruments (PSI)
Non-borrowing policy instrument for PRGF-eligible countries who do not want or need PRGF financing but want a Fund-monitored programme of reform.
Countries mst comply with the IMF economic policy conditionality equivalent to upper tranche drawings standard and complete a PRSP to recieve IMF 'seal'.

Bibliography

Abrahamsen, Rita (2004), 'The Power of Partnerships in Global Governance', *Third World Quarterly* 25 (8).

——(2000), *Disciplining Democracy: Development Discourse and Good Governance in Africa*, London and New York: Zed Books.

Abugre, Charles (2005a), Untitled presentation at the Global Civil Society Strategy Meeting on International Financial Institutions, Accra, 23–26 February.

——(2005b), 'Presentation at the Warwick Law Conference 2005', University of Warwick, Coventry, 6 May.

——(2000), 'Who Governs Low-Income Countries?', interview in *News and Notices for IMF and World Bank Watchers* 2(3), Fall, Washington, DC: Citizens Network on Essential Services (CNES).

Afrodad (2007), 'A Critical Assessment of Aid Management and Donor Harmonisation: The Case of Mozambique', Harare: Afrodad.

——(2004a), 'The Loan Contraction Process in Africa: Making Loans Work for the Poor. The Case of Tanzania', Harare: Afrodad.

——(2004b), 'The Loan Contraction Process in Africa: Making Loans Work for the Poor. The Case of Zambia', Harare: Afrodad.

——(2004c), 'The Loan Contraction Process in Africa: Making Loans Work for the Poor. The Case of Malawi', Harare: Afrodad.

——(2004d),'The Loan Contraction Process in Africa: Making Loans Work for the Poor. The Case of Uganda', Harare: Afrodad.

Afrodad and Christian Aid (2004), 'Owning the Loan: Poor Countries and the MDGs: A Christian Aid and AFRODAD Report on How National Ownership of the Loan Process Can Help Poor Countries Reach the Millennium Development Goals', April, London: Afrodad and Christian Aid.

Agamben, Giorgio (1995), *Homo Sacer: Sovereign Power and Bare Life*, trans. Daniel Heller-Roazen, Stanford: Stanford University Press.

Agarwal, Vinod K. (2000), 'Legal Aspects of Debt Negotiations', in *Negotiation of Specific Clauses of Loan Agreements*, Document No 10, Geneva: United Nations Institute for Training and Research (UNITAR).

Ahmed, Masood (2004), 'Bridging Research and Policy', paper presented at the Development Studies Association Annual Conference, 'Bridging Research and Policy', London, 6 November 2004.

Akyüz, Yilmaz (2006), 'Rectifying Capital Market Imperfections: The Continuing Rationales for Multilateral Lending', in Kaul, Inge and Conçeiào, Pedro (eds), *The New Public*

Finance: Responding to Global Challenges, New York and Oxford: UNDP and Oxford University Press.

——(2005), 'Reforming the IMF: Back to the Drawing Board', TWN Global Economy Series 7. Penang: Third World Network.

——(2004), 'The Rationale for Multilateral Lending: A Critical Assessment', Draft Paper for Discussion, 5 July, on file with author.

Alexander, Nancy (2007), 'The New Aid Model: Implications for the Aid System', mimeo, 20 September, on file with author.

——(2004), 'The World Bank as "Judge and Jury": The Country Policy and Institutional Assessment (CPIA) Rating System and the PRSP', Citizens Network on Essential Services (CNES) Briefing, 27 August, Washington, DC: CNES.

——(2003), 'The Roles of the IFIs in Decentralization and Service Delivery', Background Paper for the Ford Foundation 'Workshop on Decentralization and Service Delivery', Santiago, March.

——(2001), 'Short Comment on Conditionality', in *External Comments and Contributions on IMF Conditionality*, September, Washington, DC: IMF.

Alvarez, José E. (2006), *International Organizations as Law-makers*, Oxford: Oxford University Press.

Ambrose, Soren (2000), 'Stiglitz, Maverick World Bank Economist, Pushed Out', *Economic Justice News Online* 2(4), available at http://www.50years.org/cms/ejn/story/215.

Anghie, Antony (2004), *Imperialism, Sovereignty and the Making of International Law*, Cambridge: Cambridge University Press.

——(2002), 'Colonialism and the Birth of International Institutions: Sovereignty, Economy and the Mandate System of the League of Nations', *New York University Journal of International Law and Politics* 34(3).

——(2000), 'Time Present and Time Past: Globalization, International Financial Institutions and the Third World', *New York University Journal of International Law and Politics* 32, Winter.

Babb, Sarah and Buira, Ariel (2004), 'Mission Creep, Mission Push and Discretion in Sociological Perspective: The Case of IMF Conditionality', paper presented at the XVIII G24 Technical Group Meeting, 8–9 March, Geneva.

Badie, Betrand (2000), *The Imported State: The Westernization of the Political Order*, trans. Claudia Royal, Stanford: Stanford University Press.

Banerjee, Abhijit, Deaton, Angus, Lustig, Nora and Rogoff, Ken (2006), *An Evaluation of World Bank Research, 1998–2005*, Washington, DC: World Bank.

Best, Steven and Kellner, Douglas (1991), *Postmodern Theory: Critical Interrogations*, New York: Guildford Press.

Biel, Robert (2000), *The New Imperialism: Crisis and Contradictions in North/South Relations*, London and New York: Zed Books.

Bissio, Roberto (2007), 'Paris Declaration on Aid Effectiveness: Application of the Criteria for Periodic Evaluation of Global Development Partnerships – As Defined in Millennium Development Goal 8 – From the Right to Development Perspective: The Paris Declaration on Aid Effectiveness', Human Rights Council, 8th Session, A/HRC/8/WG.2/TF/CRP.7, 31 December 2007.

Boughton, James M. (2001), *Silent Revolution: The International Monetary Fund 1979–1989*, Washington, DC: IMF.

Braithwaite, John and Drahos, Peter (2000), *Global Business Regulation*, Cambridge: Cambridge University Press.

Bretton Woods Project (2006), 'Analysis Casts Doubt on Bank Scorecard: CPIA Numbers Made Public for First Time',

——(2000), 'Comments on Ravi Kanbur's Resignation', 11 August, available at http://www.brettonwoodsproject.org/article.shtml?cmd[126]=x-126-15489.

Brock, Karen, Cornwall, Andrea and Gaventa, John (2001), 'Power, Knowledge and Political Spaces in the Framing of Poverty Policy', Institute of Development Studies (IDS) Working Paper 143, October, Brighton: IDS.

Brown, Bartram S. (1992), *The United States and the Politicization of the World Bank: Issues of International Law and Policy*, London and New York: Kegan Paul International.

Broz, J. Lawrence and Hawes, Michael Brewster (2006), 'Congressional Politics of Financing the International Monetary Fund', *International Organization* 60 (3).

Buira, Ariel (2005), 'The Bretton Woods Institutions: Governance without Legitimacy?', in Buira, Ariel (ed.), *Reforming the Governance of the IMF and the World Bank*, London: Anthem Press.

——(2003), 'An Analysis of IMF Conditionality', paper prepared for the XVI Technical Group Meeting of the Intergovernmental Group of 24, 13–14 February, Port of Spain.

Burnside, Craig and Dollar, David (1997), 'Aid, Policies and Growth: Revisiting the Evidence', Policy Research Working Paper No. 569252, Washington, DC: World Bank.

Bwalya, Edgar, Rakner, Lise, Svåsand, Lars, Tostensen, Arne and Tsoka, Maxton (2004), 'Poverty Reduction Strategy Processes in Malawi and Zambia', Bergen: Christian Michelsen Institute.

Callaghy, Thomas M. (2003), 'The Paris Club and International Economic Governance', in Aggarwal, Vinod K. and Granville, Brigitte (eds), *Sovereign Debt: Origins, Crises and Restructuring*, London: The Royal Institute of International Affairs.

——(2001), 'Networks and Governance in Africa: Innovation in the Debt Regime', in Callaghy, Thomas, Kassimir, Ronald and Latham, Robert (eds), *Intervention and Transnationalism in Africa: Global–Local Networks of Powers*, Cambridge: Cambridge University Press.

Cameron, Angus and Palan, Ronen (2004), *The Imagined Economies of Globalization*, London, Thousand Oaks, CA and Delhi: Sage Publications.

Cammack, Paul (2001a), 'Making the Poor Work for Globalisation?', New Political Economy 6 (3).

——(2001b), 'Making Poverty Work', in Panitch, Leo and Leys, Colin (eds), A World of Contradictions: Socialist Register 2002, London: Merlin Press.

Cassen, Robert *et al.* (1986), *Does Aid Work? Report to an Intergovernmental Task Force*, Oxford: Clarendon Press.

Chang, Ha-Joon (2001), 'Commentary', in Chang, Ha-Jonn (ed.), *Joseph Stiglitz and the World Bank: The Rebel Within. Selected Speeches by Joseph Stiglitz, Former Chief Economist of the World Bank*, London: Anthem Press.

Chavez-Malaluan, Jenina Joy and Guttal, Shalmali (2003), 'Poverty Reduction Strategy Papers: A Poor Package for Poverty Reduction', January, Bangkok: Focus on the Global South.

——(2002), 'Structural Adjustment in the Name of the Poor: The PRSP Experience in the Lao PDR, Cambodia and Vietnam', January, Bangkok: Focus on the Global South.

Chimni, B. S. (2004), 'International Institutions Today: An Imperial Global State in the Making', *European Journal of International Law* 15 (1).

——(2003), 'Third World Approaches to International Law: A Manifesto', in Anghie, Antony, Chimni, B. S., Mickelson, Karin and Okafor, Obiora (eds), *The Third World and International Order: Law, Politics and Globalization*, Leiden and Boston: Martinus Nijhoff Publishers.

Chossudovsky, Michel (1997a), *The Globalization of Poverty: Impacts of IMF and World Bank Reforms*, Penang: Third World Network.

——(1997b), 'The IMF's "Social Safety Net" for the Institutional Speculator', *Third World Resurgence* 86, October.

Chowla, Peter (2008), 'IMF Governance Renovations: Fresh Paint while Foundations Rot', *Bretton Woods Update* 60, London: Bretton Woods Project.

Christiansen, Karin with Hovland, Ingie (2003), 'The PRSP Initiative: Multilateral Policy Change and the Role of Research', ODI Working Paper 216, August, London: Overseas Development Institute.

Cling, Jean-Pierre, Razafindrakoto, Mireille and Roubaud, François (eds) (2003), *New International Poverty Reduction Strategies*, London: Routledge.

Cooke, Bill and Kothari, Uma (2002), 'The Case for Participation as Tyranny', in Cooke, Bill and Kothari, Uma (eds), *Participation: The New Tyranny?*, London and New York: Zed Books.

Cornia, Giovanni Andrea, Jolly, Richard and Stewart, Frances (1987), *Adjustment with a Human Face: Protecting the Vulnerable and Promoting Growth (A Study by Unicef)*, Oxford: Clarendon Press.

Cornwall, Andrea and Schattan Coelho, Vera (2007), 'Spaces for Change? The Politics of Participation in New Democratic Arenas', in Cornwall, Andrea and Schattan Coelho, Vera (eds), *Spaces for Change? The Politics of Citizen Participation in New Democratic Arenas*, London and New York: Zed Books.

Craig, David and Porter, Doug (2006), *Development Beyond Neoliberalism? Governance, Poverty Reduction and Political Economy*, London and New York: Routledge.

——(2003), 'Poverty Reduction Strategy Papers: A New Convergence', *World Development* 31 (1).

Crush, Jonathan (1995), 'Introduction: Imaging Development', in Crush, Jonathan, *Power of Development*, London and New York: Routledge.

Cutler, Claire (2003), *Private Power and Global Authority: Transnational Merchant Law in the Global Political Economy*, Cambridge: Cambridge University Press.

Dañino, Roberto (2006), 'Legal Opinion on Human Rights and the World of the World Bank by the Senior Vice-President and General Counsel', 27 January, Washington, DC: World Bank.

Dawson, Thomas C. (2002), 'Stiglitz, the IMF and Globalization', speech to the MIT Club of Washington by IMF Director of External Relations, available at http://www.imf.org/external/np/speeches/2002/061302.htm.

Degnbol-Martinussen, John and Engberg-Pedersen, Poul (2003), *Aid: Understanding International Development Cooperation*, London and New York and Copenhagen: Zed Books and the Danish Association for International Cooperation.

DFID (2009), 'Eliminating World Poverty: Building Our Common Future', White Paper presented to Parliament by the Secretary of State for International Development, July, Cm 7656.

——(2005), 'Macroeconomic Issues Underlying Budget Support and the Signalling Role of the IMF', UK's submission to the International Monetary Fund (IMF), January, London: DFID.

——(2004), 'Poverty Reduction Budget Support', DFID Policy Paper, May, London: DFID.

DFID and Oxford Policy Management (2003), 'General Budget Support Evaluability Study, Phase 1: Synthesis Report, Volume 1', DFID Evaluation Report 643, October, London and Oxford: DFID and Oxford Policy Management.

Dollar, David and Svensson, Jakob (1998), 'What Explains the Success or Failure of Structural Adjustment Programs?', Policy Research Working Paper Series 1938, Washington, DC: World Bank.

Doty, Roxanne Lynn (1996), *Imperial Encounters*, Minneapolis and London: University of Minnesota Press.

Driscoll, Ruth and Evans, Alison (2004), 'Second Generation Poverty Reduction Strategies', paper prepared for the PRSP Monitoring and Synthesis Project, September, London: Overseas Development Institute.

Eberlei, Walter (ed.) (2007a), *Stakeholder Participation in Poverty Reduction*, INEF Report 86/2007, Duisburg: Institute for Development and Peace (INEF).

——(2007b), 'Participation in PRS Revision Process', in Eberlei, Walter (ed.), *Stakeholder Participation in Poverty Reduction*, INEF Report 86/2007, Duisburg: Institute for Development and Peace (INEF).

——(2005), 'Fighting Poverty without Empowering the Poor?', Bonn/Berlin: VENRO/GKKE.

Eberlei, Walter and Hann, Heike (2003), 'Parliaments in Sub-Saharan Africa: Actors in Poverty Reduction?', December, Eschborn: Deutsche Gesellschaft für Technische Zusammenarbeit (GTZ).

Elster, Jon (1989), *Nuts and Bolts for the Social Sciences*, Cambridge: Cambridge University Press.

Escobar, Arturo (1995), *Encountering Development: The Making and Unmaking of the Third World*, Princeton, NJ: Princeton University Press.

Eurodad (2008), 'Turning the Tables: Aid and Accountability under the Paris Framework: A Civil Society Report', Brussels: Eurodad.

European Commission (2005), 'EC Budget Support: An Innovative Approach to Conditionality', February. Brussels: European Commission.

Fitzpatrick, Peter (2001), *Modernism and the Grounds of Law*, Cambridge: Cambridge University Press.

——(1992), *The Mythology of Modern Law*, London: Routledge.

Fogarty, Edward A. (2003), 'Moving Mountains (of Debt): NGOs, the HIPC Initiatives and the Decentralization of Multilateral Debt Governance', in Aggarwal, Vinod K. and Granville, Brigitte (eds), *Sovereign Debt: Origins, Crises and Restructuring*, London: The Royal Institute of International Affairs.

Foucault, Michel (1994), *Power: Essential Works of Foucault 1954–1984, Volume 3*, ed. James D Faubion, trans. Robert Hurley and others, London: Penguin.

——(1991), *The Foucault Reader: An Introduction to Foucault's Thought*, ed. Paul Rabinow. London: Penguin.

——(1972), *The Archaeology of Knowledge and the Discourse of Language*, trans. A. M. Sheridan Smith, New York: Pantheon Books.

Fox, Jonathan A. and Brown, L. David (1998), 'Introduction', in Fox, Jonathan A. and Brown, L. David (eds), *The Struggle for Accountability: The World Bank, NGOs and Grassroots Movements*, Cambridge, MA and London: The MIT Press.

GAO (2001), 'International Monetary Fund: Efforts to Advance US Policies at the Fund', Report to Congressional Committee, GAO-01-214, January, Washington, DC: General Accounting Office (GAO).

George, Susan and Sabelli, Fabrizio (1994), *Faith and Credit: The World Bank's Secular Empire*, Boulder, CO: Westview Press.

Ghani, Ahsraf, Lockhart, Claire and Carnahan, Michael (2005), 'Closing the Sovereignty Gap: An Approach to State-Building', ODI Working Paper 153, September, London: Overseas Development Institute.

Gill, Stephen (2000), 'The Constitution of Global Capitalism', paper presented at the International Studies Association Annual Convention, Los Angeles.

Gladwell, Malcolm (2000), *The Tipping Point: How Little Things Can Make a Big Difference*, London: Abacus.

Gold, Joseph (1996), *Interpretation: The IMF and International Law*, London, the Hague and Boston: Kluwer Law International.

Gould, Erica (2003), 'Money Talks: Supplementary Financiers and the International Monetary Fund Conditionality', *International Organization* 57 (3).

Gould, Jeremy (ed.) (2005a), *The New Conditionality: Poverty Reduction Strategies: Aid and Domestic Politics*, London: Zed Books.

——(2005b), 'Poverty, Politics and States of Partnership', in Gould, Jeremy (ed.), *The New Conditionality: Poverty Reduction Strategies: Aid and Domestic Politics*, London: Zed Books.

Gould, Jeremy and Ojanen, Julia (2005), 'Tanzania: Merging in the Circle', in Gould, Jeremy (ed.), *The New Conditionality: Poverty Reduction Strategies: Aid and Domestic Politics*, London: Zed Books.

——(2003), 'Merging in the Circle: The Politics of Tanzania's Poverty Reduction Strategy', Policy Paper 2/2003, Helsinki: Institute of Development Studies, University of Helsinki.

Government of Ghana (2005), 'Harmonisation and Alignment in Ghana for Aid Effectiveness: A Common Approach for Ghana and Its Development Partners', available at http://www.aidharmonization.org/download/255652/Harmonisation.pdf.

Government of Malawi (2003), 'Malawi: Letter of Intent, Memorandum of Economic and Financial Policies, and Technical Memorandum of Understanding', 19 September, Washington, DC: IMF.

Government of Pakistan (2003),'Accelerating Economic Growth and Reducing Poverty: The Road Ahead (Poverty Reduction Strategy Paper)', December, Washington, DC: IMF.

Guttal, Shalmali (2004), 'Integrating Knowledge, Politics and Policy for Social Change', paper prepared for the UNRISD Conference on 'Social Knowledge and International Policy Making: Exploring the Linkages', 20–21 April, Geneva.

Hall, David and de la Motte, Robin (2004), *Dogmatic Development: Privatisation and Conditionalities in Six Countries*, a Public Services International Research Unit (PSIRU) Report for War on Want, London: PSIRU.

Halvorsen, Tor and Michelsen, Gunnar Guddal (2002), 'Good Governance and Public Sector Reform: The Human Rights Consequences of Structural Adjustment', in Sano, Hans-Otto and Alfredsson, Gudmunder (eds), *Human Rights and Good Governance: Building Bridges*, The Hague: Kluwer Law.

Hardt, Michael and Negri, Antonio (2000), *Empire*, Cambridge, MA and London: Harvard University Press.

Harrison, Graham (2005), 'The World Bank, Governance and Theories of Political Action in Africa', *British Journal of Politics and International Relations* 7 (2).

——(2001a), 'Administering Market Friendly Growth? Liberal Populism and the World Bank's Involvement in Administrative Reform in Sub-Saharan Africa', *Review of International Political Economy* 8 (3).

——(2001b), 'Post-Conditionality Politics and Administrative Reform: Reflections on the Cases of Uganda and Tanzania', *Development and Change* 32 (4).

Hatcher, Pascale (2006), 'The Politics of Crafting the Technocratic State: The World Bank, Governance and the End of Politics', paper presented at the Singapore Workshop on the World Bank, 18 September, Singapore.

Helleiner, G. K. (2002), 'Developing Countries in Global Economic Governance and Negotiation Processes', in Nayyar, Deepak (ed.), *Governing Globalization: Issues and Institutions*, New Delhi: Oxford University Press.

Higgott, Richard (2000), 'Contested Globalization: The Changing Context and Normative Challenges', *Review of International Studies* 26.

Hopkins, Terence K. and Wallerstein, Immanuel (1996), 'The World-System: Is There a Crisis?', in Hopkins, Terence K. and Wallerstein, Immanuel (eds), *The Age of Transition: Trajectory of the World System, 1945–2025*, London and Atlantic Highlands, NJ: Zed Books.

Hudson, Michael (2003), *Super Imperialism: The Origin and Fundamentals of US World Dominance*, London and Sterling, VA: Pluto Press.

IBRD (2009), 'Subscriptions and Voting Power of Member Countries', 30 September, Washington, DC: IBRD.

IDA (2009), 'Subscriptions and Voting Power of Member Countries', 30 September, Washington, DC: IDA.

——(2008), 'Additions to IDA Resources: Fifteenth Replenishment IDA: The Platform for Achieving Results at the Country Level', report from the Executive Directors of the International Development Association to the Board of Governors, approved by the Executive Directors of IDA on 28 February, Washington, DC: IDA.

——(2006), 'IDA'S Implementation of the Multilateral Debt Relief Initiative', 14 March, Washington, DC: IDA.

——(2003), 'Allocating IDA Funds Based on Performance: Fourth Annual Report on IDA's Country Assessment and Allocation Process', March, Washington, DC: IDA.

——(2001a), 'The IDA Deputies: An Historical Perspective', November. Washington, DC: IDA.

——(2001b), 'Poverty Reduction Strategy Papers and IDA 13', May, Washington, DC: IDA.

IMF (2009a), 'A New Architecture of Facilities for Low-Income Countries', 26 June, Washington, DC: IMF.

——(2009b), 'IMF Executive Directors and Voting Power', updated 17 December, available at http://www.imf.org/external/np/sec/memdir/eds.htm.

——(2009c), 'IMF Members' Quotas and Voting Power and IMF Board of Governors', updated 18 December, available at http://www.imf.org/external/np/sec/memdir/members.htm.

——(2009d), 'IMF Lending', A Factsheet, 9 September, available at http://www.imf.org/external/np/exr/facts/howlend.htm.

——(2009e), 'IMF Conditionality', A Factsheet, 15 September, available at http://www.imf.org/external/np/exr/facts/conditio.htm.

——(2009f), 'IMF Overhauls Non-Concessional Lending: Facilities and Conditionality', Public Information Notice (PIN) No. 09/40, 3 April.

——(2009g), 'IMF Implements Major Lending Policy Instruments,' 24 March, available at https://www.imf.org/external/np/pdr/fac/2009/pdf/032409.pdf.

——(2009h), 'Financing the Fund's Concessional Lending to Low-Income Countries', A Factsheet, 1 October, available at http://www.imf.org/external/np/exr/facts/concesslending.htm.

——(2009i), 'IMF Surveillance', A Factsheet, June, available at https://www.imf.org/external/np/exr/facts/surv.htm.

——(2008a), 'IMF Board of Governors Adopts Quota and Voice Reforms by Large Margin', Press Release No. 08/93, 29 April, available at http://www.imf.org/external/np/sec/pr/2008/pr0893.htm.

——(2008b), 'Reform of Quota and Voice in the International Monetary Fund', in *Selected Decisions and Selected Documents of the IMF*, 33rd Issue, Washington, DC: IMF, updated 2009.

——(2008c), 'Review of the Fund's Financing Role in Member Countries', 28 August, Washington, DC: IMF.

——(2007), 'Bilateral Surveillance over Members' Policies', Executive Board Decision No. 13919-(07/51), in *Selected Decisions and Selected Documents of the IMF*, 33rd Issue, Washington, DC: IMF.

——(2006), 'Operational Guidelines to IMF Staff on the 2002 Conditionality Guidelines', revised on 9 January 2009, Washington, DC: IMF.

——(2005a), 'Guidance Note for Fund Staff on the Modified Poverty Reduction Strategy Framework and the Implications for PRGF and HIPC Operations', 30 June, Washington, DC: IMF.

——(2005b), 'Malawi: Annual Progress Report: Joint Staff Advisory Note', August, IMF Country Report No, 05/279, Washington, DC: IMF.

——(2005c), 'Review of the 2002 Conditionality Guidelines', 3 March, Washington, DC: IMF.

——(2004a), *Report on the Evaluation of Poverty Reduction Strategy Papers (PRSPs) and the Poverty Reduction and Growth Facility (PRGF)*, Washington, DC: IMF.

——(2004b), 'Poverty Reduction Strategy Papers: Proposed Amendments to the Poverty Reduction and Growth Facility (PRGF) Trust and PRGF–HIPC Trust Instruments', 4 November, Washington, DC: IMF.

——(2004c), *Report on the Evaluation of Poverty Reduction Strategy Papers (PRSPs) and the Poverty Reduction and Growth Facility (PRGF)*, Washington, DC: IMF.

——(2003a), 'International Standards: Strengthening Surveillance, Domestic Institutions, and International Markets', Washington, DC: IMF.

——(2003b), 'IMF Completes In Principle First Review of Malawi's PRGF Arrangement, Approves in Principle US$9.2 Million Disbursement, and Approves US$6.6 Million in Interim Assistance under the HIPC Initiative', IMF Press Release No. 03/174, 20 October, Washington, DC: IMF.

——(2003c), 'Aligning the Poverty Reduction and Growth Facility (PRGF) and the Poverty Reduction Strategy Paper (PRSP) Approach: Issues and Options', 25 April, Washington, DC: IMF.

——(2002a), 'Guidelines on Conditionality', Executive Board Decision No. 12864 (02/102), 25 September, Washington, DC: IMF.

——(2002b), 'The Modalities of Conditionality: Further Considerations', 8 January, Washington, DC: IMF.

——(2001a), 'Conditionality in Fund-Supported Programs: Policy Issues', 16 February, Washington, DC: IMF.

——(2001b), 'Financial Organization and Operations of the IMF', Pamphlet Series No. 45, 6th edn, Washington, DC: IMF.

——(2000), 'IMF Names Masood Ahmed to Poverty Strategy Post', News Brief No. 00/7, 28 January, Washington, DC: IMF.

——(1999), 'Instrument to Establish the Poverty Reduction and Growth Facility Trust', Executive Board Decision No. 12087 (99/118), 21 October (Annex to Decision No. 8759 – (87/176) ESAF), 18 December 1987), in *Selected Decisions and Selected Documents of the International Monetary Fund*, 28th Issue, 31 December 2003, IMF: Washington, DC.

——(1998), *External Evaluation of the ESAF: Report by a Group of Independent Experts*, Washington, DC: IMF.

——(1952), 'Executive Board Decision No. 10-(51/11)', 13 February.

——(undated), 'About Country Policy Intentions', available at http://www.imf.org/external/np/loi/mempuba.htm#loi.

IMF and World Bank (2005), 'Review of the Poverty Reduction Strategy Approach: Balancing Accountabilities and Scaling up Results', 19 August, Washington, DC: IMF and World Bank.

——(1999), 'Poverty Reduction Strategy Papers: Operational Issues', 10 December, Washington, DC: IMF.

Jackson, Robert H. (1990), *Quasi-States, Sovereignty, International Relations and the Third World*, Cambridge: Cambridge University Press.

Jayasuriya, Kanishka (2001a), 'Governance, Post Washington Consensus and the New Anti Politics', Hong Kong: Southeast Asia Research Centre, Working Paper Series No. 2, April.

——(2001b), 'Globalization and the Changing Architecture of the State: The Regulatory State and the Politics of Negative Co-ordination', *Journal of European Public Policy* 8 (1).

——(1999), 'Globalization, Law and the Transformation of Sovereignty: The Emergence of Global Regulatory Governance', *Indiana Journal of Global Legal Studies* 6 (2).

Kalderimis, Daniel (2004), 'IMF Conditionality as Investment Regulation: A Theoretical Analysis', *Social and Legal Studies* 12 (1).

Kapur, Devesh (2003), 'Do as I Say Not as I Do: A Critique of G7 Proposals on Reforming the Multilateral Development Banks', G24 Discussion Paper No. 20, February, Washington, DC: G24.

——(2002), 'The Changing Anatomy of Governance of the World Bank', in Pincus, Jonathan R. and Winters, Jeffrey A. (eds), *Reinventing the World Bank*, Ithaca, NY: Cornell University Press.

Kapur, Devesh and Webb, Richard (2000), 'Governance-Related Conditionalities of the International Financial Institutions', G24 Discussion Paper Series No. 6, August, Washington, DC: G24.

Khor, Martin (2005), 'Implications of Some WTO Rules on the Realisation of the MDGs', TWN Trade and Development Series No. 25, Penang: Third World Network.

——(2001), 'A Critique of the IMF's Role and Policy Conditionality', TWN Global Economy Series No. 4, Penang: Third World Network.

——(1999a), 'The Revolt of Developing Nations', Third World Network Briefing, 6 December, available at http://www.corpwatch.org/article.php?id=330.

——(1999b), 'News from Seattle', Third World Network WTO Briefing, 4 December, available at http://www.africaaction.org/docs99/wto9912.htm.

Kingsbury, Benedict, Krisch, Nico and Stewart, Richard B. (2005), 'The Emergence of Global Administrative Law', *Law and Contemporary Problems* 68 (3 & 4).

Klugman, Jeni (2002), 'Overview', in Klugman, Jeni (ed.), *A Sourcebook for Poverty Reduction Strategies*, Washington, DC: World Bank.

Koeberle, Stefan (2004), 'Conditionality: Under What Conditions?', Background Paper for the 'Conditionality Revisited: Development Policy Forum', World Bank, Paris, 5 July, Washington, DC: World Bank.

Kothari, Uma (2002), 'Power, Knowledge and Social Control in Participatory Development', in Cooke, Bill and Kothari, Uma (eds), *Participation: The New Tyranny?* London and New York: Zed Books.

Krakowski, Michael (2004), 'Pitfalls of "Automatic Donor Co-ordination": The Malawi Experience, 2000–2004', Hamburg Institute of International Economics (HWWA) Report 242, Hamburg: HWWA.

Krisch, Nico and Kingsbury, Benedict (2006), 'Introduction: Global Governance and Global Administrative Law in the International Legal Order', *European Journal of International Law* 17 (1).

Lastra, Rosa María (2006), *Legal Foundations of International Monetary Stability*, Oxford: Oxford University Press.

Lawson, Andrew, Booth, David, Msuya, Meleki, Wangwe, Samuel and Williamson, Tim (2005), 'Does General Budget Support Work? Evidence from Tanzania', July, London and Dar Es Salaam: Overseas Development Institute and Daima Associates.

Le Houerou, Philippe and Taliercio, Robert (2002), 'Medium Term Expenditure Frameworks: From Concept to Practice, Preliminary Lessons from Africa', World Bank Africa Region Working Paper Series No. 28, February, Washington, DC: World Bank.

Lowenfeld, Andreas F. (2008), *International Economic Law*, 2nd edn, Oxford: Oxford University Press.

McGee, Rosemary and Brock, Karen (2001), 'From Poverty Assessment to Policy Change: Processes, Actors, Data', IDS Working Paper 133, July, Brighton: IDS.

McGee, Rosemary with Norton, Andy (2000), 'Participation in Poverty Reduction Strategies: A Synthesis of Experience with Participatory Approaches to Policy Design, Implementation and Monitoring', IDS Working Paper 109, Brighton: IDS.

Mallaby, Sebastian (2004), *The World's Banker: A Story of Failed States, Financial Crises, and the Wealth and Poverty of Nations*, New York: Penguin.

Mattei, Ugo and Nader, Laura (2008), *Plunder: When the Rule of Law Is Illegal*, London: Blackwell.

Mawdsley, Emma and Rigg, Jonathan (2002), 'A Survey of the World Development Reports 1: Discursive Strategies', *Progress in Development Studies* 2 (1).

Maxwell, Simon (2003), 'Heaven or Hubris: Reflections on the New "New Poverty Agenda"', *Development Policy Review* 21 (3).

Menocal, Alina Rocha and Rogerson, Andrew (2006), 'Which Way the Future of Aid? Southern Civil Society Perspectives on Current Debates on Reform to the International Aid System', ODI Working Paper 259, January, London: Overseas Development Institute.

Merry, Sally Engle (1992), 'Anthropology, Law and Transnational Processes', *Annual Review of Anthropology* 21.

Miller-Adams, Michelle (1999), *The World Bank: New Agendas in a Changing World*, London and New York: Routledge.

Mohan, Giles (2002), 'Beyond Participation: Strategies for Deeper Empowerment', in Cooke, Bill and Kothari, Uma (eds), *Participation: The New Tyranny?*, London and New York: Zed Books.

Molenaers, Nadia and Renard, Robrecht (2002), 'Strengthening Civil Society from the Outside? Donor-driven Consultation and Participation Processes in Poverty

Reduction Strategies (PRSP): The Bolivian Case', paper prepared for delivery at the 2002 Annual Meeting of the American Political Science Association, 29 August–1 September 2002, Antwerp: Institute of Development Policy and Management, University of Antwerp.

Morrissey, Oliver (2004), 'Alternatives to Conditionality in Policy-Based Lending', Discussion Paper (revised) for the 'Conditionality Revisited Development Policy Forum', World Bank, Paris, 5 July, Washington, DC: World Bank.

Morrow, Daniel (2005), 'Aid Conditionality: Deja Voodoo?', paper presented at the School of Advanced International Studies, John Hopkins University, Washington, DC, 28 March.

——(2004), 'Adjusting Conditionality: Prescriptions for Policy-Based Lending', Background Paper for the 'Conditionality Revisited: Development Policy Forum', World Bank, Paris, 5 July, Washington, DC: World Bank.

Mosley, Paul, Toye, John and Harrigan, Jane (1991), *Aid and Power: The World Bank and Policy-Based Lending, Vol 2*, London: Routledge.

Murray Li, Tania (2007), *The Will to Improve: Governmentality, Development and the Practice of Politics*, Durham, NC and London: Duke University Press.

Nkombo, Nachilala (2008), 'Development Aid and National Ownership: A Review of Critical Experiences from Africa: Milestones, Good Practices, Failures and Future Research Options', paper prepared for the 'Promoting Ownership and Reforming Conditionality: Strategic Planning Workshop', 18–20 February.

Nørlund, Irene, Tran Ngoc Ca and Nguyen Dinh Tuyen (2005), 'Vietnam: Dealing with Donors', in Gould, Jeremy (ed.), *The New Conditionality: Poverty Reduction Strategies: Aid and Domestic Politics*, London: Zed Books.

Nyagamusira, Warren and Rowden, Rick (2002), 'New Strategies, Old Loan Conditions: Do the New IMF and World Bank Loans Support Countries' Poverty Reduction Strategies: The Case of Uganda', April, Kampala and Washington, DC: Ugandan National NGO Forum and RESULTS Educational Fund.

Nyamu-Musembi, Celestine and Cornwall, Andrea (2004), 'What Is the 'Rights-Based Approach' All About? Perspectives from International Development Agencies', IDS Working Paper 234, November, Brighton: IDS.

Oatley, Thomas and Yackee, Jason (2004), 'American Interests and IMF Lending', *International Politics* 41 (3).

OECD DAC (2003), 'Harmonising Donor Practices for Effective Aid Delivery: Good Practice Papers', DAC Guidelines and Reference Series, Paris: OECD DAC.

Ooms, Gorik and Schrecker, Ted (2005), 'Expenditure Ceilings, Multilateral Financial Institutions, and the Health of Poor Populations', *The Lancet* 365, 21 May.

Otto, Dianne (1996), 'Subalternity and International Law: The Problems of Global Community and the Incommensurability of Difference', *Social and Legal Studies* 5 (3).

Pahuja, Sundhya (2005), 'The Postcoloniality of International Law', *Harvard International Law Journal* 46 (2).

——(2004), 'Global Formation: IMF Conditionality and the South as a Legal Subject', in Fitzpatrick, Peter and Tuitt, Patricia (eds), *Critical Beings: Law, Nation and the Global Subject*, Aldershot: Ashgate.

——(2000), 'Technologies of Empire: IMF Conditionality and the Reinscription of the North/South Divide', *Leiden Journal of International Law* 13 (4).

Pender, John (2001), 'From "Structural Adjustment" to "Comprehensive Development Framework": Conditionality Transformed?', *Third World Quarterly* 22 (3).

Picciotto, Sol (2006), 'Regulatory Networks and Global Governance', paper presented at the 'WG Hart Legal Workshop 2006: The Retreat of the State: Challenges to Law and Lawyers', Institute of Advanced Legal Studies, University of London, London, 27–29 June.

——(2000), 'Liberalization and Democratization: The Forum and the Hearth in the Era of Cosmopolitan Post-Industrial Capitalism', *Law and Contemporary Problems* 63 (4).

Pincus, Jonathan R. and Winters, Jeffrey A. (2002), 'Reinventing the World Bank', in Pincus, Jonathan R. and Winters, Jeffrey A. (eds), *Reinventing the World Bank*, Ithaca, NY: Cornell University Press.

Piron, Laure-Hélène (2002), 'The Right to Development: A Review of the Current State of the Debate for the Department for International Development', London: ODI.

Piron, Laure-Hélène with Evans, Alison (2004), 'Politics and the PRSP Approach: Synthesis Paper', ODI Working Paper 237, March, London: ODI.

Poulantzas, Nicos (2000), *State, Power, Socialism*, trans. Patrick Camillier, London: Verso.

Qureshi, Asif and Zigler, Andreas (2007), *International Economic Law*, 2nd edn, London: Sweet and Maxwell.

Rajagopal, Balakrishnan (2003), *International Law from Below: Development, Social Movements and Third World Resistance*, Cambridge: Cambridge: Cambridge University Press.

Raustiala, Kal (2002), 'The Architecture of International Cooperation: Transgovernmental Networks and the Future of International Law', *Virginia Journal of International Law* 43 (1).

Republic of Mauritania (1987), 'Development Credit Agreement (Structural Adjustment Credit) between the Islamic Republic of Mauritania and the International Development Association', Credit No. C1812, 26 June.

Republic of Uganda (2001), 'Development Credit Agreement (Poverty Reduction Support Credit) between the Republic of Uganda and the International Development Association', Credit No. 3510-UG, 5 July.

Rich, Bruce (2002), 'The World Bank under James Wolfensohn', in Pincus, Jonathan R. and Winters, Jeffrey A. (eds), *Reinventing the World Bank*, Ithaca, NY and London: Cornell University Press.

Rittich, Kerry (2006), 'The Future of Law and Development', in Trubek, David M. and Santos, Alvaro (eds), *The New Law and Economic Development: A Critical Appraisal*, Cambridge: Cambridge University Press.

Rowden, Rick (2004), 'Blocking Progress: How the Fight Against HIV/AIDS Is Being Undermined by the World Bank and the International Monetary Fund (IMF)', a Policy Briefing by ActionAid USA, Global AIDS Alliance, Student Global AIDS Campaign and RESULTS Educational Fund, September, Washington, DC: ActionAid etc.

——(2001), 'IMF–WB–WTO: Synthesis Report: An Overview of the Increased Coordination of the International Monetary Fund (IMF), World Bank, and the World Trade Organisation (WTO) Trade Liberalisation Measures', Second Draft Working Paper, October, Washington, DC: RESULTS Education Fund.

Rowden, Rick and Ocaya Irama, Jane (2004), 'Rethinking Participation: Questions for Civil Society about the Limits of Participation in PRSPs', an ActionAid USA/ActionAid Uganda Discussion Paper, April, Washington, DC: ActionAid USA and Uganda.

Royal Government of Cambodia (2002), 'National Poverty Reduction Strategy', 20 December, Washington, DC: IMF.

Rustomjee, Cyrus (2005), 'Improving Southern Voices in the IMF Board: Quo Vadis Shareholders?', in Carin, Barry and Woods, Angela (eds), *Accountability of the International Monetary Fund*, Ottawa, Cairo, Dhaka, Montevideo, Nairobi, New Delhi and Singapore: Ashgate and the International Development Research Centre (IDRC).

Said, Edward (2003), *Orientalism*, London: Penguin.

Sano, Hans-Otto (2002), 'Good Governance, Accountability and Human Rights', in Sano, Hans-Otto and Alfredsson, Gudmunder (eds), *Human Rights and Good Governance: Building Bridges*, The Hague: Kluwer Law.

Santos, Boaventura de Sousa (2006), 'The Heterogeneous State: and Legal Pluralism in Mozambique', *Law and Society Review* 40 (1).

——(2002), *Towards a New Legal Common Sense: Law, Globalization and Emancipation*, 2nd edn, London: Butterworths Lexis Nexis.

SAPRIN (2004), *Structural Adjustment: The SAPRI Report: The Policy Roots of Economic Crisis, Poverty and Inequality*, London, New York, Penang, Manila and Bangalore: Zed Books, Third World Network, IBON Foundation and Books for Change.

Scheurich, James L. (1997), *Research Method in the Postmodern*, London and Washington, DC: The Falmer Press.

Scholte, Jan Aart (2000), *Globalization: A Critical Introduction*, Basingstoke and London: Macmillan Press.

Sen, Amartya (2001), *Development as Freedom*, Oxford: Oxford University Press.

Sender, John (2002), 'Reassessing the Role of the World Bank in Sub-Saharan Africa', in Pincus, Jonathan R. and Winters, Jeffrey A. (eds), *Reinventing the World Bank*, Ithaca, NY: Cornell University Press.

Sgard, Jérôme (2004), 'IMF in Theory: Sovereign Debts, Judicalisation and Multilateralism', Centre d'Études Prospectives et d'Information Internationales (CEPII) Working Paper No. 2004–21, available at http://www.cepii.fr/anglaisgraph/workpap/summaries/2004/wp04–21.htm.

Shihata, Ibrahim (2000a), *The World Bank Legal Papers*, The Hague: Kluwer Law International.

——(2000b), *The World Bank in a Changing World, Volume III*, The Hague: Kluwer Law International.

——(2000c), 'The Dynamic Evolution of International Organizations: The Case of the World Bank', *Journal of the History of International Law* 2 (2).

Socialist Republic of Vietnam (2003), 'The Comprehensive Poverty Reduction and Growth Strategy', 21 November, Washington, DC: IMF.

South Centre (1996), *For a Strong and Democratic United Nations: A South Perspective on UN Reform*, Geneva: South Centre in association with the Non-Aligned Movement.

Stewart, Miranda (2003), 'Global Trajectories of Tax Reform: The Discourse of Tax Reform in Developing and Transition Countries', *Harvard International Law Journal* 44, Winter.

Stiglitz, Joseph (2002), *Globalization and Its Discontents*, London: Penguin.

——(2001), 'Participation and Development: Perspectives from the Comprehensive Development Paradigm', remarks at the International Conference on 'Democracy, Market Economy and Development', Seoul, February 1999, in Chang, Ha-Joon (ed.), *Joseph Stiglitz and the World Bank: The Rebel Within. Selected Speeches by Joseph Stiglitz, Former Chief Economist of the World Bank, with a Commentary by Ha-Joon Chang, University of Cambridge*, London: Anthem Press.

Stone, Diane and Wright, Christopher (2007), 'The Currency of Change: World Bank Lending and Learning in the Wolfensohn Era', in Stone, Diane and Wright, Christopher (eds), *The World Bank and Governance: A Decade of Reform and Reaction*, London and New York: Routledge.

Szablowski, David (2007), *Transnational Law and Local Struggles: Mining, Communities and the World Bank*, Oxford: Hart.

Tamanaha, Brian Z. (1995), 'An Analytical Map of Social Scientific Approaches to the Concept of Law', *Oxford Journal of Legal Studies* 15 (4).

Tan, Celine (2007a), 'IMF Facing Financial Crisis, Needs Revenue Overhaul', TWN Info Service on Finance and Development (Feb07/01), 8 February, available at http://www.twnside.org.sg/title2/finance/twninfofinance016.htm.

——(2007b), 'World Bank's New Initiatives in Fight for Financial Survival', TWN Info Service on Finance and Development (Oct07/03), 12 October, available at http://www.twnside.org.sg/title2/finance/twninfofinance100703.htm.

——(2006a), 'Reclaiming Development: Reasserting the Role of the UN in Finance and Economic Matters vis-à-vis the Bretton Woods Institutions', research paper submitted on behalf of the Third World Network to the 'United Nations High-Level Panel on System-Wide Coherence' civil society consultations on the reform of international financial institutions, 18–19 June.

——(2006b), 'Responsible Financing or Unwarranted Interventions: Fiduciary Obligations in Loan and Aid Contracts Between Donors, Client States and Citizens', Briefing Paper for the European Network on Debt and Development (Eurodad), March.

——(2001), 'Bank and Fund Watchers Must Watch WTO', Bretton Woods Project Briefing Paper, November, London: Bretton Woods Project.

Tarullo, Daniel K. (1985), 'Logic, Myth and the International Economic Order', *Harvard International Law Journal* 26 (2).

Thompson, Nii Moi (2004), 'A Review of the Multi-Donor Budget Support (MDBS)', 26 May, Accra: Integrated Social Development Centre (ISODEC).

Trubek, David M. and Santos, Alvaro (2006), 'Introduction: The Third Moment in Law and Development Theory and the Emergence of a New Critical Practice', in Trubek, David M. and Santos, Alvaros (eds), *The New Law and Economic Development: A Critical Appraisal*, Cambridge: Cambridge University Press.

Tucker, Vincent (1999), 'The Myth of Development', in Munck, Ronaldo and O'Hearn, Denis (eds), *Critical Development Theory: Contributions to a New Paradigm*, London and New York: Zed Books.

UK Parliament (2003), 'Select Committee on International Development, Eighth Report', London: House of Commons.

UNCTAD (2009), *The Least Developed Countries Report 2009: The State and Development Governance*, Geneva: UNCTAD.

——(2008), *The Least Developed Countries Report 2008: Growth, Poverty and the Terms of Development Partnership*, Geneva: UNCTAD.

——(2002a), *The Least Developed Countries Report 2002: Escaping the Poverty Trap*, Geneva: UNCTAD.

——(2002b), 'From Adjustment to PRSPs: What's New?', Geneva: UNCTAD.

United Nations (2007), *UN Programmes Launched to Harmonize Development Efforts, Eliminate Inefficiency*, New York: UN.

——(2006), 'Delivering as One: Report of the Secretary-General's High Level Panel', 9 November, New York: UN.

United Republic of Tanzania (2000), 'Poverty Reduction Strategy Paper', 1 October, Washington, DC: IMF.

US Congress (2000), *Report of the International Financial Institution Advisory Commission (Meltzer Commission)*, available at http://www.house.gov/jec/imf/meltzer.htm.

Van Houtven, Leo (2004), 'Rethinking IMF Governance', *Finance and Development*, September.

——(2002), 'Governance of the IMF: Decision-Making, Institutional Oversight, Transparency and Accountability', IMF Pamphlet Series No. 53, Washington, DC: IMF.

Van Waeyenberge, Elisa (2006), 'The Missing Piece: Country and Policy Institutional Assessments at the Bank', paper presented at the Singapore Workshop on the World Bank, 18 September, Singapore.

Vandermoortele, Jan (2003), 'Are MDGs Affordable?', *Development Policy Journal* 3.

Vilanova, Juan Carlos and Martin, Matthew (2001), 'The Paris Club', Publication No. 3, London: Debt Relief International.

Vreeland, Raymond (2007), *The International Monetary Fund: Politics of Conditional Lending*, Abingdon and New York: Routledge.

Wade, Robert (2001), 'Showdown at the World Bank', *New Left Review* 7.

Whaites, Alan (2002), 'Making PRSPs Work: Can Rhetoric and Reality Coincide?', in Whaites, Alan (ed.), *Masters of Their Own Development? PRSPs and the Prospects for the Poor*, Monrovia, CA: World Vision International.

Williams, David (2000), 'Aid and Sovereignty: Quasi-States and the International Financial Institutions', *Review of International Studies* 26 (4).

Williamson, John (2004), 'A Short History of the Washington Consensus', paper commissioned by Fundacion CIDOB for the 'From the Washington Consensus Towards a New Global Governance' Conference, Barcelona, 24–25 September.

——(2002), 'What Washington Means by Policy Reform', available at http://www.iie.com/publications/papers/williamson1102–2.htm; originally published in Williamson, John (ed.) (1990), *Latin American Adjustment: How Much Has Happened?* Washington, DC: Institute for International Economics.

Wilks, Alex (2000), 'The World Bank's Knowledge Roles: Dominating Development Debates', *Bretton Woods Update* 40, May, London: Bretton Woods Project.

Wood, Angela (2005), 'Demystifying "Good Governance": An Overview of World Bank Governance Reforms and Conditions', Dublin: Trocaire.

Wood, Ellen Meiksins (2005), *The Empire of Capital*, London: Verso.

Woods, Ngaire (2006), *The Globalizers: The IMF, the World Bank and Their Borrowers*, Ithaca, NY and London: Cornell University Press.

World Bank (2009a), 'International Bank for Reconstruction and Development, International Finance Corporation, International Development Association: Executive Directors and Alternates', 31 October, Washington, DC: World Bank.

——(2009b), 'Repowering the World Bank for the 21st Century: Report of the High-Level Commission on Modernisation of World Bank Group Governance', October, Washington, DC: World Bank.

——(2009c), *World Bank Annual Report 2009*, Washington, DC: World Bank.

——(2009d), 'Financial Crisis: What the World Bank Is Doing', updated 22 September, available at http://www.worldbank.org/financialcrisis/bankinitiatives.htm.

——(2009e), '2009 Development Policy Lending Retrospective: Flexibility, Customization, and Results', 27 October, Washington, DC: World Bank.

——(2009f), 'Country Assistance Strategies: Retrospective and Future Directions', 1 September, Washington, DC: World Bank.

——(2009g), 'Toward Greater Transparency through Access to Information: The World Bank's Disclosure Policy', 10 December, Washington, DC: World Bank.

——(2007), 'Results-Based National Development Strategies: Assessments and Challenges Ahead', December, Washington, DC: World Bank.

——(2005a), *World Bank Annual Report 2005*, Washington, DC: World Bank.

——(2005b), 'Poverty Reduction Strategy Credits: A Stocktaking', 24 June, Washington, DC: World Bank.

——(2005c), 'Review of World Bank Conditionality: Issues Note', 24 January, Washington, DC: World Bank.

——(2005d), 'Review of World Bank Conditionality: Legal Aspects of Conditionality in Policy-Based Lending', 29 June, Washington, DC: World Bank.

——(2005e), 'Country Assistance Strategies', Bank Procedure (BP) 2.11, June, Washington, DC: World Bank.

——(2005f), 'Fourteenth Replenishment of IDA Resources Finalized: Largest Funding Increase in Two Decades, But More Resources Needed', available at http://go.worldbank.org/GUI8PV9IM0.

——(2005g), 'Review of World Bank Conditionality: Recent Trends and Practices', 30 June, Washington, DC: World Bank.

——(2005h), 'Review of World Bank Conditionality: Content of Conditionality in World Bank Policy-Based Operations: Public Sector Governance, Privatization, User Fees and Trade', 30 June, Washington, DC: World Bank.

——(2005i), 'Linking the PRSP to the Budget: How PERs Can Help the Example of Madagascar', Washington, DC: World Bank.

——(2005j), 'Good Practice Note for Development Policy Lending: Budget Support Groups and Joint Financing Arrangements', June, Washington, DC: World Bank.

——(2005k), *Enabling Capacity to Achieve Results, Volume I: Overview, 2005 CDF Progress Report*, Washington, DC: World Bank.

——(2005l), *Enabling Capacity to Achieve Results, Volume II: Country Profiles, 2005 CDF Progress Report*, Washington, DC: World Bank.

——(2005m), *An Operational Approach for Assessing Country Ownership of Poverty Reduction Strategies, Volume I*, Washington, DC: World Bank.

——(2005n), *An Operational Approach for Assessing Country Ownership of Poverty Reduction Strategies, Volume II: Country Case Studies Bolivia, Ghana, Kyrgyz Republic, Senegal*, Washington, DC: World Bank.

——(2004a), 'Eligibility of Expenditures in World Bank Lending: A New Policy Framework', 26 March, Washington, DC: World Bank.

——(2004b), *The Poverty Reduction Strategy Initiative: An Independent Evaluation of the World Bank's Support through 2003*, Washington, DC: World Bank.

——(2004c), 'Development Policy Lending Replaces Adjustment Lending', 10 August, Washington, DC: World Bank.

——(2004d), 'Operational Policy 8.60: Development Policy Lending', August, Washington, DC: World Bank.

——(2004e), 'Country Policy and Institutional Assessment: An External Panel Review', report of a panel of external experts convened to review the methodology and process of the World Bank's Country Policy and Institutional Assessment, 5 April, Washington, DC: World Bank.

——(2004f), 'Country Policy and Institutional Assessments: 2004 Assessment Questionnaire', 6 December, Washington, DC: World Bank.

——(2003a), *Toward Country-Led Development: A Multi-Partner Evaluation of the Comprehensive Development Framework Synthesis Report*, Washington, DC: World Bank.

——(2003b), 'Operational Policy 3.10: Financial Terms and Conditions of IBRD Loans, IBRD Hedging Products, and IDA Credits', January, Washington, DC: World Bank.

——(2002a), 'From Adjustment Lending to Development Policy Support Lending: Key Issues in the Update of World Bank Policy', Policy Paper, 6 June, Washington, DC: World Bank.

——(2002b), 'Public Communication Programs for Privatization Project: A Toolkit for World Bank Task Team Leaders and Clients', available at http://siteresources.worldbank.org/EXTDEVCOMMENG/Resources/wbtoolkitbook3602.pdf.

——(2002c), 'From Adjustment Lending to Development Policy Support Lending: Key Issues in the Update of World Bank Policy', Policy Paper, 6 June. Washington, DC: World Bank.

——(2001a), 'Lending Operations: Choice of Borrower and Contractual Agreements', Operational Policy OP 7.00, February, revised August 2004. Washington, DC: World Bank.

——(2001b), 'Organizing Participatory Processes in the PRSP', Draft for Comments, available at http://siteresources.worldbank.org/INTPCENG/1143240-1116506251485/20508873/Organizing+Partcipatory+Processes.pdf.

——(undated), 'Interim Guidelines for Poverty Reduction Support Credits', available at http://wbln0018.worldbank.org/html/eswwebsite.nsf/PRSC/Guidelines+PRSC?OpenDocument.

World Bank and IMF (2005a), 'Guidelines for World Bank and IMF Staffs for Joint Staff Advisory Notes (JSAN) for Poverty Reduction Strategy Papers', Washington, DC: World Bank and IMF.

——(2005b), *The Poverty Reduction Strategy Initiative: Findings from 10 Country Case Studies of the World Bank and IMF Support*, Washington, DC: World Bank Operations and Evaluation Department (OED) and IMF Independent Evaluation Office (IEO).

——(2004), 'Poverty Reduction Strategy Papers: Progress in Implementation', 20 September, Washington, DC: World Bank and IMF.

——(1999), 'Heavily Indebted Poor Countries Initiative (HIPC) and Enhanced Poverty Focus of IDA and IMF Concessional Programs', Joint Statement by Co-Chairmen of the Joint Meeting of the Interim and Development Committees of the World Bank and the IMF, 26 September, Washington, DC: World Bank and IMF.

——(undated) 'Guidelines for Joint Staff Assessment of a Poverty Reduction Strategy Paper', Washington, DC: World Bank and IMF, available at http://poverty.worldbank.org/files/jsa%20guidelines.pdf.

World Vision (2005), 'Poverty Reduction: Are the Strategies Working? Towards Mutual Responsibility and Accountability: Can the New Poverty Reduction Strategies Engage the Poor?', ed. Tembo Fletcher, June, London: World Vision UK in partnership with World Vision Zambia and World Vision Bolivia.

Zukin, Sharon and DiMaggio, Paul (eds) (1990), *Structures of Capital: The Social Organisation of the Economy*, Cambridge: Cambridge University Press.

Documents

World Bank and IMF legal documents

International Bank for Reconstruction and Development (IBRD) Articles of Agreement
International Development Association (IDA) Articles of Agreement
International Monetary Fund (IMF) Articles of Agreement

IBRD General Conditions for Loans, 1 July 2005 (amended 12 February 2008)
IDA General Conditions for Credits and Grants, 1 July 2005

UN documents

Charter of Economic Rights and Duties of States, General Assembly Resolution 3281 (XXIX), 12 December 1974.

Declaration on the Right to Development, General Assembly Resolution 41/128, 4 December 1986.

Monterrey Consensus of the International Conference on Financing for Development ('Monterrey Consensus') 2002, Report of the International Conference on Financing for Development, Monterrey, Mexico,18–22 March 2002.

Cited interviews

(Designations of persons at time of interview.)

Nancy Alexander, Director, Citizens Network on Essential Services, 30 April 2004, Washington, DC.

Pablo Guerrero, Advisor to the Vice-President, Operations Policy and Country Services, World Bank, 26 April 2004, Washington, DC.

Elliot Harris, Advisor, Policy Development and Review Department, IMF, 22 April 2005, Washington, DC.

Barbara Kalima, Director/Coordinator, African Forum and Network on Debt and Development (Afrodad), 24 April 2004, Washington, DC.

Ravi Kanbur, 23 November 2004, University of Warwick, Coventry.

Kamran Kousari, Special Coordinator for Africa, Division on Globalization and Development Strategies, UNCTAD, 25 February 2005, Accra.

Daniel Morrow, Consultant, World Bank, 14 April 2005, Washington, DC.

Mark Plant, Assistant Director, Policy Development and Review Department, IMF, 4 May 2004 and April 2005, Washington, DC.

Linda van Gelder, Senior Economist, Poverty Reduction Group, World Bank, 28 April 2004, Washington, DC.

Alan Whaites, Director, World Vision International, 15 April 2004, Milton Keynes.

Abberra Zerabruk, Senior Counsel, and Sheila Braka, Legal Counsel, World Bank, 27 April 2004, Washington, DC.

Index

Abrahamsen, Rita 137, 166
Abugre, Charles 85
accountability: Bretton Woods institutions 171–78, 184, 190, 193–94, 198, 216; conditionalities 127; Country Financial Accountability Assessment 149; country selectivity 159; decision-making 4–5; democratic deficit 171; institutions of state 148–50, 165; legislatures 193; Medium-Term Expenditure Framework 148; norms, production of 209; participation 171–78, 184, 190, 193–94, 198; policy 171–78, 184, 190, 193–94, 198; politics 175–78; priorities 215; public expenditure management 148–50; regulatory reform 213; universality 163
Accra Agenda for Action (AAA) 161–62
ActionAid 85–86
actors, principles and mechanisms, relationship between 9–12
adjustment conditionalities 46–48, 62
administrative space 208–12, 216
advocacy 2, 69, 76–77, 184–89
agency 4–5, 66, 166, 200
Ahmed, Masood 69, 72
Alexander, Nancy 124
Anghie, Antony 8, 24, 27, 30, 165
anti-globalisation protests 1–2, 78
Asian financial crisis 2, 74
asymmetries 24–37, 50–51, 211
automaticity of finance 103–5
autonomy 24–25, 95, 156–57, 171–75, 182

Badie, Betrand 26, 30, 50–51, 165
balance of payments 100, 103, 111
bargaining power, inequality of 96, 121, 156, 163, 165, 177–78
benchmarks 97, 120
Best, Steven 128
Biel, Robert 63
bilateralism 34–35
biopolitics 140, 153–56, 161, 196, 218–21
biopower 127–29, 139–40, 164, 170, 192, 218–22
Bolivia 183, 186
Braithwaite, John 9–12, 14–16, 102, 129, 212
Bretton Woods institutions 7, 31–51: accountability 171–78, 184, 190, 193–94, 198, 216; asymmetries governance 32–35, 52, 81; autonomy 24–30; bargaining power, inequality of 96, 121, 156, 163, 165, 177–78; bilateralism 34–35; biopolitical control 140, 153; biopower 182; cartelisation of development funding 33; centralisation 85; civil society 77, 173–74, 179–89, 192–95, 198–99, 215–16; coercion of indebtedness 48–50; colonial encounter, legacies of 31–33; compensating losses 44–50; Comprehensive Development Framework (CDF) 74–75; conceptual framework of PRSP, response to 72–75; concessional windows 34; containment and crisis 86–88; crisis financing 44, 48–49; crisis of Bretton Woods system 44–45, 111, 206; debt 34–36, 44, 48–50, 206; debt crisis of 1980s 206; debt relief mechanisms 34–36; decision-making structures 31–34, 81–84, 119, 169, 177, 184; democratic deficit 171; development agencies, as 38; difference, dynamic of 37–41; disbursement of development

financing 67–68; discipline 63–64, 110; economy, financing the post-colonial 41–45; effectiveness of aid 69–71; engagement, management of terms of 41–50; forum shifting 36; fragmentation of states 83, 85; franchise, reorganizing the 179; global compact, PRSPs as a 205–7; globalisation 24–25, 31–36, 51–52, 62; governance 24–25, 31–37, 51–52, 62, 137–38, 165–66, 170–74, 184–89, 200; government departments 143–44; growth, catalysing 42–43; Heavily Indebted Poor Countries Initiative (HIPC) 34–35; independence 35; indigenous politics, marginalisation of 192–93; International Development Association 34–35; international law 1–3, 24–25, 31–36, 51–52, 62; internationalisation of decision-making 82–84; Joint Staff Advisory Notes (JSAN) guidelines 153; knowledge production and dissemination 37–41, 51–52; low-income countries 32–33; marginalisation of post-colonial states 31–33, 192–93; mission creep 34; monopolising the forum 35–36; Multilateral Debt Relief Initiative (MDRI) 34–35; New International Economic Order 36; normalcy, narratives of 31; operationalisation of PRSPs 81, 194–96; oversight 5, 40, 100, 118–20, 150, 192–94; ownership 94–95; participation 169–200; partnership 74–75, 135, 141, 156–63, 185, 187, 217–18; policing the financial system 39–41; policymaking 70–72, 143–45, 165, 169–200; postcolonialism 23–37, 50–52, 62; problematising poverty 37–38; protests 76–77; public sector reforms 85; quota reviews 33–34; regulation 207–13; rehabilitation of the state 134–66; Relationship Agreements 36; representation structure 32; sustainable development 222; UNCTAD, marginalisation of 36; United Nations 31, 33–36, 222–23; United States 33, 34; universalisation 51, 145–46; voting power 32–34, 81; Washington Consensus 61, 63–68, 74–75 *see also* conditionalities; International Monetary Fund (IMF); structural adjustment policies (SAPs); World Bank

Brock, Karen 15, 63, 68

Brown, Gordon 74

Brown, L David 77

Broz, J Lawrence 117

budget support 145, 158–60, 162

Burkina Faso 182, 191

Burnside, Craig 70–71

Callaghy, Thomas M 49, 68, 76

Cambodia 179–80, 185–87

Cameron, Angus 171, 200

campaigns for debt relief 75–78

capacity building 149, 188–89

capital 29, 43, 135, 140–42, 206

capture of policy space 135, 138, 150, 170

capture of political space 135, 170, 171

cartelisation 33, 49

Cassen, Robert 67

categories of law 17

Chang, Ha-Joon 74

Charter of Rights and Duties of States (UN) 62

Chavez-Malaluan, Jenina Joy 174, 185–87

Chimni, BS 8, 46–47, 210

Christiansen, Karin 80

citizenship 173

civil service 83–84, 144, 173–74, 181, 213

civil society: advocates 2, 69; Bretton Woods institutions 77, 173–76, 179–89, 192–95, 198–99, 215–16; conflicts of interest 189; decision-making 213; difference, dynamics of 173; participatory policymaking 4, 173–76, 179–89, 192–95, 198–99, 215–16; partnerships 185; rehabilitation of state apparatus 173; specialist NGOs 69; transnational civil society as default policymakers 185–87; universalisation 165

civilisation 27, 28, 39–40, 50, 174, 199

codes and standards 220–21

coercion 17, 48–50, 102, 120–29, 221

Cohen, Stanley 178

Cold War 63

collective responsibility 216–18

colonialism *see* postcolonialism

Common Approach to Budget Support framework 160

compensating losses 44–50, 62

Comprehensive Development Framework (CDF) 4, 74–75, 142
concessional financing 105–6, 111–12, 164
conditionalities 94–129: accountability 127; adjustment conditionalities 46–48, 62; automaticity of finance 103–5; balance of payments 100, 103, 111; bargaining power, inequality in 96, 121; benchmarks 97, 120; biopolitical control 154–56; biopower 127–29, 139, 164; capture of policymaking space 150; coercion and consent 120–29; compensating losses 46–49, 62; concessional financing 105–6, 111–12, 164; conditions for financing 96–98; constitutional limitations, circumventing 107–10; contract 95, 96, 99, 102–3, 106, 109–10; control 116–17; Country Assistance Strategies (CAS) 97, 108, 113–14, 126; country selectivity 150–56; creditworthiness 99; debt default 96, 99; decision-making 208; deconstruction of conditionality 102–10; default regulatory instrument, conditionality as 102–10; development policy loans 100–101, 106, 114; discipline 95–96, 110, 112, 116, 118, 120, 122, 127–29, 134, 139, 164; discretion 102, 112, 116–17; due diligence 96, 101, 109; economic coercion 102; economic governance 102, 110–20; enforcement 141; entitlement 105; *ex ante* conditionalities 120, 124, 126, 127, 142, 208, 213, 223; *ex post* conditionalities 120, 127, 150, 208, 223; external oversight, absence of 118–20; fiduciary objectives 96, 99, 104, 106, 117–18, 122; foreign policy 117; front-loading, from tranching to 123–25, 126; game theory 121; GATT 47; General Resources Account (GRA) 103–6; globalisation 120–21; good behaviour, rewarding 150–53; governance 95, 102, 110–20, 128–29, 138, 152–53, 213; government departments 144; guidelines 99–100, 125; harmonisation 162–63; individual processes of negotiation 116; institutions of state 121–27, 126, 152–53, 164; International Court of Justice's opinions on operations of Bretton Woods institutions 119; International Development Association 107–10, 113–15; International Monetary Fund 49, 95–106, 109–20, 123–26; Joint Staff Advisory Notes (JSAN) guidelines 154–56; Letter of Development Policy (LDP) 109, 125; Letter of Intent (LOI) 104, 124; liberalisation 46, 146; loan agreements 107–10, 125; Medium-Term Expenditure Framework (MTEF) 109, 125, 156; Memorandum of Economic and Financial Policy (MEFP) 104–5; mission creep 117–18; modalities of conditionality 95, 99, 120–21, 129; negotiation 121–23, 125, 160; network governance, rise of 213; new architecture of aid 94, 134; non-compliance, sanctions for 96, 98, 101, 103–4, 109–10, 153; norms 47, 96, 101–2; oversight, absence of external 118–20; ownership 94–129; par value system, collapse of 112; participatory policymaking 74–75, 170, 194; partnership 74–75, 156–57; performance criteria 97, 101, 104–5, 123–24; phased drawings 104–5; policy conditionalities 46, 71, 95–102, 105–9, 113–18, 121–29, 135, 146, 150; postcolonial economies, control over 95; post-conditionality 122; Poverty Reduction Strategy Credits 125–26; prior actions 97, 124–25; private commercial interests, influence of 47–48; privatization 146; programme conditionalities 96, 97–98, 109–10; programme reviews 97, 123–24; public sector reform 151–53; regulation 102–10, 122, 206; rehabilitation of the state 142; reserve tranche, borrowing beyond the 104–5; resistance 170; resource dependency, governance through 113–15; reviews of programmes 97, 123–24; selectivity, principle of country 150–56, 195–96; soft law 106, 116, 119–20, 127; stages, disbursements made in 101; standby arrangements 103–5; state sovereignty 98, 127; structural adjustment policies 46–47; tariff rates, reduction or elimination of 47; templates 151; tranche release conditions 97, 110, 123; tranching, front-loading and 123–25; transparency 124; treaties 107; triggers

97, 120; trust funds and concessional financing 105–6; United Kingdom 98; United States 98, 117; variation in terms 124; Washington Consensus 123, 127–29; weaknesses in poverty reduction strategy 154; World Bank 95–97, 100–102, 106–20, 126; World Trade Organization 47
conflicts of interests 189
constitutions 107–10, 163–69, 170, 206, 218–21
consultation 75, 180–83
contract 3–5, 95–96, 99, 102–3, 106, 109–10
control 14, 66, 153–56, 161–66, 196, 207, 219–20
Cooke, Bill 8, 178
coordination 207–8
Cornia, Giovanni Andrea 70
Cornwall, Andrea 68, 221–22
corporations, replacement of government with 85
corporatism 214
Country Assistance Strategies (CAS) 3–4, 97, 108, 113–14, 126, 154, 205
Country Financial Accountability Assessment (CFAA) 149
country ownership 4–5, 94–129: biopolitics 153; biopower 127–29, 139; budget support 156–57; capture of policymaking space 150; coercion and consent 120–27; conditionalities 94–129; country selectivity 150–56; decision-making, integration of PRSP into 146–47; deconstruction of conditionality 95–102; default regulatory instrument, conditionality as 102–10; development financing 25, 79; discipline 95, 127–29, 134, 139; economic reform 138–40; Enhanced Structural Adjustment Facility 71; governance 95, 110–20; internalisation of politics of reform 136; Joint Staff Advisory Notes (JSAN) guidelines 153; Letter of Development Policy 156; mainstreaming 146–47; Medium-Term Expenditure Framework 156; modalities of conditionality 95, 99, 120–21, 129; negotiations 211; new architecture of aid 94, 134; objectives of conditionality 95; Paris Declaration on Aid Effectiveness 161; participation 66, 171, 177, 180, 193–94; partnership 157, 160; policy 81, 88, 95, 121, 143–44, 171, 177, 180, 193–94; politics 123; postcolonial economies, control over 95; priorities 211; rehabilitation of the state 125, 138–41, 150–56; Washington Consensus 128–29; World Bank 139
Country Policy and Institutional Assessment (CPIA) 114–15
Country Procurement Assessment (CPA) 149
country selectivity 124–25, 150–56, 159, 164, 213
Craig, David 147
creditworthiness 99
crisis financing and financial crises 2, 44–45, 48–49, 65, 74, 78
critical postmodernism 15–16
Crush, Jonathan 15
culture 7–8, 26, 28, 73
customary human rights 217–18
Cutler, Claire 52, 119–20

de la Motte, Robin 66–67
debt 1–2: alternative sources of finance, ability to obtain 49–50; Bretton Woods institutions 34–36, 44, 48–50, 206; cartelisation 49; coercion of indebtedness 48–50; compensating losses 44, 48–50; conditionalities 96, 99; crisis of 1980s 206; culpability of creditor states 215; default 96, 99; Heavily Indebted Poor Countries Initiative (HIPC) 205, 215; Jubilee 2000 75–76; lobbying 2; Multilateral Debt Relief Initiative (MDRI) 3, 34–35; non-governmental organisations 75–76, 79–80; Paris Club 4; preferred creditors, BWIs as 48; public opinion 75–76; relief, campaigns for 75–76
decentralisation 85, 212, 216
decision-making: accountability 4–5; Bretton Woods institutions 31–34, 81–84, 119, 169, 177, 184; civil servants 213; civil society 213; conditionalities 209; fragmentation of states 82–84; internationalisation of decision-making 82–84; International Monetary Fund 119; marginalisation 82, 84; ownership 146–47; participatory policymaking 169, 177,

184; structures 31–34, 81; World Bank 119
definition of development financing xiv
Degnbol-Martinussen, John 96
democracy, definition of 182–83
democratic deficit 163, 171–72, 205
dependency 113–15, 165
development modelling 142–45, 164
Development Policy Loan (DPL) 66
difference, dynamics of 26–27, 30, 87, 173, 211
disbursement of development finance 66–68
discipline: biopower 170, 219, 221; bottom line, discipline of the 159–61; Bretton Woods institutions 63–64, 110; capture of policy space 170; conditionalities 95–96, 110, 112, 116, 118, 120, 122, 127–29, 139, 164; control 207; discourse, discipline of 14–16; discursive discipline 210–11; governance 52, 136; International Monetary Fund 110, 112; legitimacy 86; nation states 140; neoliberalism 220; new architecture of aid 94, 134; new technologies 218–22; non-compliance, sanctions for 164; ownership 95, 127–29, 134, 139; participatory policymaking 87, 170, 173, 178, 198; partnership 159–61; postcolonial international law 52; power 16–17; regulation 210–11; rehabilitation of the state 141; structural adjustment policies 61, 62–64, 82; Washington Consensus 206; World Bank 110
discourse politics 210
discretion 102, 112, 116–17
Dollar, David 70–71
Doty, Roxanne Lynn 37, 50
Drahos, Peter 9–12, 14–16, 102, 129, 212
due diligence 96, 101, 109

Eberlei, Walter 185, 190–91
economic and sector work (ESW) 149
economic coercion 102
economic exclusion 70, 218
economic liberalism 63
economic nationalism 63
effectiveness of aid 5, 69–71, 148–51, 159–62, 172, 214, 218
Elster, Jon 10
endorsement of PRSPs 153–54
engagement, management of terms of 41–50
Engberg-Pedersen, Poul 96
Enhanced Structural Adjustment Facility (ESAF) 34–35, 65, 71
epistemic communities 68–72
Escobar, Arturo 15, 28
Ethiopia 190
ethnocentricism 177
Eurocentrism 178
European Commission 150
ex ante conditionalities 120, 124, 126, 127, 208, 213, 223
ex post conditionalities 120, 127, 150, 208, 223
examplar states 159
Extended Credit Facility (ECF) (IMF) 3
Extended Fund Facility (EFF) (IMF) 44

fear of exit and entry 79–80
fiduciary objectives 96, 99, 104, 106, 117–18, 122
finance ministries 144, 189–90
financial crises and crisis financing 2, 44–45, 48–49, 65, 74, 78
fiscal support systems, linking with 147–48
Fitzpatrick, Peter 26, 141
Flexible Credit Line (FCL) (IMF) 44
Fogarty, Edward A 76
foreign policy 63, 73, 117, 166, 199
forum shifting 11–12, 36, 223
Foucault, Michel 9, 12–15, 127, 164, 178, 207, 210, 219–21
Fox, Jonathan A 77
franchise, reorganizing the 179, 215–16
front-loading 123–25, 126
functions of law 17–18

game theory 121
GATT 47
Gaventa, John 68
General Resources Account (GRA) 103–6
Ghana 145, 158, 181, 182, 186, 191
Gill, Stephen 211, 220
globalisation 31–36: actors, principles and mechanisms, relationship between 9–12; administrative space 208–12, 216; below, globalisation from 221–22; biopolitical global constitutions 218–21; Bretton Woods institutions 24–25, 31–36, 51–52, 62; conditionalities

120–21; critical postmodernism 16; dependency 113–15; development modelling 142–45, 164; economic order 12; empire of capitalism 137; forum shifting 11–12; governance 10–14, 135–37, 205–6; historical context of PRSPs 60; inequality 61; institutions of state 208–10; legitimacy 173; nation states 140; neoliberalism 52, 61–62, 140, 173, 214, 220; participatory policymaking 193–98; policymaking 193–98, 208–9, 216; political consensus 193–98; postcolonialism 206; power 12–14; principles and norms 10–11; regulatory globalisation 10–12, 220; rehabilitation of the state 141, 142–45, 164; resistance 221–22; structural adjustment policies 61–62; structural Marxism 16; Washington Consensus 1, 64–65
Gold, Joseph 103, 112
good behaviour, rewarding 150–53
Gore, Al 72–73
Gould, Erica 117
Gould, Jeremy 86, 142, 148, 183, 185, 190
governance 30–37: asymmetrical governance 33–34, 36–37, 52, 81; Bretton Woods institutions 24–25, 31–37, 51–52, 62, 137–38, 165–66, 170–74, 184–89, 200; capture of policy space 138; civil service ascription, lack of 174; conditionalities 95, 102, 110–20, 128–29, 138, 152–53, 213; continuities and discontinuities 135–38; discipline 136; economic deregulation 136; economic governance 102, 110–20; fiscal support systems, linking 147–48; fragmentation of states 86; globalisation 10–14, 135–37, 205–6; good governance 135–38, 173–74; improvements 145; institutional reform 174; international economic law 206; international economic relations 205–6; network governance, rise of 211–13; new proceduralism 136; participation 170–74, 184–89, 200; policymaking 138, 146, 170–74, 184–89, 200; postcolonialism 137; privatization 136; public sector reform 136–37, 149–50; rehabilitation of the state 135–38, 146–50, 163; rule of law 136–37; standardising domestic governance 146–50; state and good governance 135–37; technical assistance 149; technocratic governance, politics of 184–89; Washington Consensus 136, 138; World Bank 137–38
government departments: departments 143–44, 176, 181–82, 189–90; erosion of government 84–85; finance ministries 144, 189–90; participatory policymaking 143–44, 176, 181–82, 189–90
Guttal, Shalmali 40, 174, 185–87

Hall, David 66–67
Halvorsen, Tor 174
Hann, Heike 190
Hardt, Michael 219–20
harmonisation 161–63, 207–8
Harrigan, Jane 66
Harrison, Graham 84, 122, 144, 152, 159, 165, 173
Hatcher, Pascale 73
Hawes, Michael Brewster 117
Heavily Indebted Poor Countries Initiative (HIPC) 1, 3, 34–35, 68, 75–76,
hegemony 87, 44
Higgott, Richard 61, 64, 78
historical context of PRSPs 60
Honduras 186, 191
Hopkins, Terence K 29
Hovland, Ingie 80
hybridisation 68–69

IMF *see* International Monetary Fund (IMF)
imperialism 219–20 *see also* postcolonialism
imported state 179–84
incapacitated states, developing countries as 211
Independent Evaluation Office (IEO) (IMF) 160–61
indigenous politics, marginalisation of 189–93
individuals, atomization of body politic into 140–41
information, access to 193, 195
institutions *see also* Bretton Woods institutions; state institutions

International Court of Justice's opinions on operations of Bretton Woods institutions 119
International Development Association (IDA) 34–35, 107–10, 113–15
international economic law 1–9
international economic order 12, 60–88, 211, 216–17
international economic relations 28–29, 204–6, 210–11
International Finance Corporation (IFC) 43
international law 1–10, 23–52, 207, 209, 212
international legal order 48–50, 79–80
International Monetary Fund (IMF) 2–3, 7–8: ad hoc bailouts 44; Articles of Agreement 98–100, 105, 110–13; Asian financial crisis 74; automaticity of finance 103–5; compensating loss 44, 48–49; concessional financing 111–12; conditionalities 49, 95–106, 109–20, 123–26; creditworthiness 99; crisis financing 44, 48–49; culture 7–8; debt 48–49; decision-making 119; discipline 110, 112; Extended Credit Facility 3; Extended Fund Facility 44; Flexible Credit Line 44; foreign policy 117; General Resources Account 103–6; global governance 23–24; Independent Evaluation Office 160–61; international law 7, 23–24; knowledge production 37–41; Medium-Term Expenditure Framework 147; moral hazard 44; non-governmental organisations, lobbying by 70; organisational structure 7–8; overdraft facility 44; Paris Club 49; participation 66; policy conditionalities 99–100; policymaking 70, 143–45; postcolonial international law 23–24; prior action 125–26; programme reviews 123–24; Rapid Credit Facility 3; rescheduling 49; stabilisation programmes 2, 74; standby arrangements 3, 44; surveillance work 39–40; United Kingdom 98; United States 98; Washington Consensus 63–65; World Bank 98 *see also* Bretton Woods institutions; structural adjustment policies (SAPs)
international non-governmental organisations (INGOs) 1–2, 85–86, 185–87, 199
international organisations 209 *see also* non-governmental organisations (NGOs)

Jackson, Robert H 30
Jayasuriya, Kanishka 11, 12, 83, 136, 138
Joint Staff Advisory Notes (JSAN) guidelines and biopolitical control 4, 142, 153–56, 161, 196
Jolly, Richard 70
Jubilee 2000 1–2, 75–76, 183–84

Kalderimis, Daniel 101–2, 105
Kalima, Barbara 180
Kanbur, Ravi 72
Kellner, Douglas 128
Kenya 159
Kingsbury, Benedict 209
knowledge production and dissemination 16, 37–41, 51–52, 59, 210
Kothari, Uma 8, 178

Lao PDR 185–87, 191
language 140, 186
Lastra, Rosa Maria 7
legal pluralism 16–18
legislatures 190–93, 195
legitimacy: competing agendas for change 68–80; crisis of legitimacy 60–88; discipline 86; epistemic coalition, rise of the 69–72; functions of law 17–18; institutional response to conceptual framework for PRSPs 72–75; international economic order 60–88; neoliberal globalisation 173; non-governmental organisations 76–78, 86; non-Western state, delegitimising the 173–74; participation 66, 171–76, 178, 198–200; participatory policymaking 171–76, 178, 198–200; populist neoliberalism 198–99; rehabilitation of the state 166; structural adjustment programmes (SAPs) 61–66, 72, 86; universality 163; Washington Consensus 61, 63–68
Lesotho 190
Letter of Development Policy (LDP) 109, 125

Letters of Intent (LOI) 104, 124, 155
Li, Murray 13
liberal legality 172–75
liberal populism 171–72
liberalisation 46, 141, 146, 198
loan agreements 107–10, 125
lobbying 2, 70
losses, Bretton Woods institutions and compensating 44–50, 62
Lowenfeld, Andreas F 7
low-income countries, definition of xv–xvi

macroeconomics 145, 160–61
mainstreaming 146–48
Malawi 155–56, 159–60, 163, 177, 181–84, 190, 195
Malaysia 78
marginalisation of states 31–33, 36, 177, 188–93, 207, 210–11
Marxism 16
Mattei, Ugo 30
McGee, Rosemary 15
Medium-Term Expenditure Framework (MTEF) 109, 125, 147–50, 156, 194–95, 205
Meltzer Commission 73
Memorandum of Economic and Financial Policy (MEFP) 104–5
mercatocracy 52
Merry, Sally Engle 17
Michelsen, Gunnar Guddal 174
micro-management 156–59
Millennium Development Goals (MDGs) 4, 211, 215, 218, 222
Miller-Adams, Michelle 87
mission creep 34, 117–18
Mohan, Giles 178
Molenaers, Nadia 183
Monterrey Consensus 218
moral hazard 44
Morrissey, Oliver 121
Morrow, Daniel 121, 122
Mosley, Paul 66, 70, 99, 100, 116–18
Mozambique 195
Multi-Donor Budget Support (MDBS) programme 145
Multilateral Agreement on Investment (MAI), campaigns against 77–78
Multilateral Debt Relief Initiative (MDRI) 3, 34–35
Multilateral Investment Guarantee Agency (MIGA) 43
Musveni, Yoweri 74–75

Nader, Laura 30
nation states: autonomy 24–25, 171–75; biopolitical power 140; capital accumulation 140, 141–42; collective responsibility 216–17; conditionalities, enforcement of 141; constitutions, reform of 206; democratic deficit 171–72; discipline 140; economic plans, PRSPs as blueprint for 142; fragmentation 82–86; globalisation 140; good governance 135–37; imported state 179–84; individuals, atomization of body politic into 140–41; language 140; legitimacy 173–74; marginalisation 31–33, 36, 177, 188–93, 207, 210–11; neoliberal globalisation 140; non-Western states, delegitimising 173–74; participation 87–88; physical constraints, instruments of 140; political struggle, as site of 215–16; politics, confinement of emancipatory 200; problematising the state 213–15; recognition of statehood 28; reconstruction 87–88, 213; redistribution, as site of 215–16; reform 134–66; rehabilitation 125, 134–66, 170, 173; reorganisation 171–72, 175, 206; state sovereignty 140–41; Western state 165; Westphalian model 52 *see also* state institutions:
national economic plans, PRSPs as blueprint for 142–45
nationalism 62–63
negotiations 4, 116, 121–23, 125, 160, 211
Negri, Antonio 219–20
neocolonial representations 172–75
neoliberalism 52, 61–62, 85, 140, 173, 198–99, 214, 220
network governance, rise of 211–13
new architecture of aid 3, 30, 36, 49, 60–61, 66–68, 134, 152, 205–6, 216
new constitutionalism 220
new imperialism 219–20
New International Economic Order (NIEO) 36, 62, 217, 218
new proceduralism 136
Nicaragua 182

non-compliance, sanctions for 96, 98, 101, 103–4, 109–10, 153
non-discrimination 24
non-governmental organisations (NGOs): advocacy 76–77; civil society 2, 69; consultation 75; debt relief 75–76, 79–80; fragmentation of states 85–86; geo-strategic interests 75–80; government, replacement of 85–86; international non-governmental organisations 1–2, 85–86, 185–87, 199; legitimacy 86, 166; lobbying 2; Multilateral Agreement on Investment (MAI), campaigns against 77–78; new non-state actors 76–78; participatory policymaking 185–89, 199; policymaking 70; political influence 1–2; specialists 69; Structural Adjustment Participatory Review International Network (SAPRIN) 77; structural adjustment policies 77–78; World Bank 73, 77
normalcy, myth of 28–29
norms 10–11, 17–18, 28, 47, 96, 101–2, 209–10

Oatley, Thomas 117
objects of development, developing countries as 82
OECD Development Assistance Committee (DAC) xiv–xv
Ojanen, Julia 86, 183, 185–86, 190
operation of PRSPs 81, 87, 194–96, 205–6
Other 26–27, 37
overdraft facilities 44
oversight 5, 40, 100, 118–20, 150, 192–94
ownership *see* country ownership
Oxfam International 75, 76, 80, 85–86

Pahuja, Sundhya 8, 78–79, 199–200
Pakistan 181–82, 186
Palan, Ronen 171, 200
Paris Club 4, 67–68, 76
Paris Declaration on Aid Effectiveness 161–62
participation 4, 81, 87: agency, PRSPs and 66; centralisation of control 66; development financing 74–75; epistemic communities 70; international legal order 46–50; International Monetary Fund 66; legitimacy 66; management 45–50; Medium-Term Expenditure Framework 194–95; ownership of development programmes 66; Policy Framework Paper 66; policymaking 87–88, 143; poor, representatives of the 143; postcolonial economic order 45–50; PRSP framework 143; reconstruction of the state 87–88; rehabilitation of the state 135; Washington Consensus 66; World Bank 66 *see also* participatory policymaking
participatory policymaking 143, 169–200: accountability 171–73, 175–78, 184, 190, 193–94, 198; agency, restoration of 200; bargaining power, inequality of 177–78; biopower 178, 192; Bretton Woods institutions 169–200; capacity building 188–89; capture of policy space 170; capture of political space 170, 171; civil service, professionalisation of 174; civil society 4, 173–76, 179–89, 192–95, 198–99, 215–16; civilisation 174, 199; commitments 176; conditionalities 74–75, 170, 194; constitutional reform 170; consultation 180–83; decision-making 169, 177, 184; definition of participation 175; democracy, enforcement of 182–84; democratic deficit 171–72; discipline 87, 170, 173, 178, 198; ethnocentricism 177; Eurocentrism 178; external process 170–200; finance ministries 189–90; franchise, reorganizing the 179, 215–16; globalisation of political consensus 193–98; governance 170, 171, 173–74, 184–89, 200; government departments 143–44, 176, 181–82, 189–90; imported state 179–84; indigenous politics, marginalisation of 189–93; information, access to 193, 195; international law 207; international non-governmental organisations 185–87, 199; language 186; legislatures 190–93, 195; legitimacy 171–76, 178, 198–200; liberal legality 172–75; liberalisation 198; marginalised communities 177, 188, 189–93; monitoring implementation of policies 175–76;

myth of participation 177–78; neocolonial representations 172–75; non-governmental organisations 185–89, 199; ownership 171, 177, 180, 193–94; Participation Action Plans (PAPs) 180; partnerships 185, 187; pluralism 182; policies, practice and programmes, dissonance between 196–98; policy accountability 175–78; policy autonomy 171–75, 182; politics 1 69–200; postcolonial representations 178; Poverty and Social Impact Assessments 178; power relations, inequality of 177–78; prescriptive participation 179–82; privatisation 198; PRS process 178–93; PRSP framework 169–200; rehabilitation of state apparatus 170, 173; relevance, lack of operational 194–96; reorganisation 171–75; representatives of the poor 176; resistance, fracturing of 187–89, 215–16; rubber-stamping legislatures 190–91; socio-political changes 170; stakeholders 176, 180–81, 186, 188, 198–99; state autonomy 171–75; technical assistance 188–89, 192; technocratic governance, politics of 184–89; transnational advocates, role of 184–89; transnational civil society as default policymakers 185–87; transparency 194; universalisation 182; Washington Consensus 188, 193, 198

partnership 74–75, 135, 141, 156–63, 185, 187, 217–18

performance 97, 101, 104–5, 114–15, 123–24, 162, 216

phased drawings of finance 104–5

physical constraint, instruments of 140

Picciotto, Sol 171, 212

pluralism 16–18, 182

policy: accountability 171–78, 184, 190, 193–94, 198; autonomy 95, 171–75, 182; capture of policy space 135, 138, 150, 170; change 71–72; conditionalities 46, 71, 95–102, 105–9, 113–18, 121–29, 135, 146, 150; Country Policy and Institutional Assessment 114–15; design 214; Development Policy Loan (DPL) 66; dialogue 67, 121; Enhanced Structural Adjustment Facility 71; epistemic communities 69–72; harmonisation 207–8; implementation, monitoring 175–76; Joint Staff Advisory Notes (JSAN) guidelines 154–56, 161, 196; operational policy 100–101; ownership 81, 88, 95, 121, 143–44, 171, 177, 180, 193–94; Policy Framework Papers 56, 61; poverty 15, 70; reform conditionalities 101–2, 106–7, 117–18, 121–29, 135, 150; regulation 101–2, 122; sectoral policies 145; state sovereignty 68–69; structural adjustment policies 70–72, 82–83, 87–88, 214; unified policy process 143–45; Washington Consensus 214; weaknesses 154–56, 161, 196; World Bank 70, 73–74, 143–45 *see also* participatory policymaking; policy-based lending; policymaking

policy-based lending: Bretton Woods institutions 42; conditionalities 46, 100–102, 106–7, 114, 117–18, 121–29, 150; definition xvi; project financing xvi, 66–67; structural adjustment policies (SAPs) 82–83; Washington Consensus 63

policymaking: autonomy, lack of 156–57; Bretton Woods institutions 70–72, 143–45, 165, 169–200; civil society 185–87; epistemic communities 69–70; five basic elements, coverage of 144–45; globalisation 208–9, 216; governance 138, 146, 170–74, 184–89, 200; government departments, participation of 143–44; institutions of state 72; International Monetary Fund 70, 143–45; Multi-Donor Budget Support (MDBS) programme 145; non-government organisations, lobbying by 70; ownership 88, 143–44; structural adjustment policies (SAPs), limitations of 70, 87–88; templates 143–45; transnational civil society 185–87; World Bank 70, 143–45 *see also* participatory policymaking

politics: accountability 175–78; autonomy 171–75; biopolitics 140, 153–56, 161, 196, 218–21; biopower 219, 221; capture of political space 135, 170, 171; conditionalities 114–15, 123, 126; confinement of emancipatory politics 200; consensus, globalisation of political 193–98; currency of change 74–75;

discourse politics 210; exclusion from politics 70; franchise, reorganizing the 179; globalisation of political consensus 193–98; indigenous politics, marginalisation of 189–93; liberal political project 171–75; marginalisation of indigenous politics 189–93; non-governmental organisations 1–2; ownership 123; participatory policymaking 169–93; partnership 156–63; reconfiguring the political landscape 178–93, 216; remapping the political landscape 198–200; resistance, fracturing of 187–89, 215–16; socio-political changes 170; state sovereignty 68–69; struggle, nation states as site of 215–16; technocratic governance 184–89
populist neoliberalism 198–99
Porter, Doug 147
postcolonialism: asymmetrical relations 26, 27–30, 50–51; asymmetrical sovereignty 24–25, 211; Bretton Woods institutions 23–37, 50–52, 62; civilisation 27, 28, 50; conditionalities 95; continuities and consolidation of postcolonial law 50–52; cultural difference 26; development financing 23, 60; discipline 52; dynamics of difference 26–27, 30; economy, control over 95; economy, financing the postcolonial 41–45; globalisation 23–52, 206; governance 23–52, 137; historical context of PRSPs 60; institutions of state 27; international law 23–52; International Monetary Fund 23–24; legacies of colonialism 31–33; non-discrimination 24; Other 26–27; ownership 95; postcoloniality of international law 25–27; representations 178; reproducing colonial asymmetries through post-colonial law 27–30; self-determination 24; state sovereignty 24, 26–27; subjects and objects of international law 26; technologies 27; universalisation 26–27; Westphalian model 52; World Bank 23–24
postmodernism 16
Poulantzas, Nicos 140–41
Poverty and Social Impact Assessments (PSIA) 149, 178
Poverty Eradication Action Plan (PEAP) 75
Poverty Reduction and Growth Facility (PRGF) 65, 154–55, 205
Poverty Reduction and Growth Trust (PRGT) 3
Poverty Reduction Budget Support (PRBS) programme 150
Poverty Reduction Strategy Credits (PRSCs) 3, 125–26, 151–52, 205
Poverty Reduction Strategy (PRS) process 4–5, 142, 178–93
power: bargaining power, inequality of 96, 121, 156, 163, 165, 177–78; biopower 127–29, 139–40, 164, 192, 218–22; discipline 16–17; globalisation 12–14; management of possibilities 13; network governance, rise of 212–13; postcolonial relations 60; Poverty Reduction Strategy Papers (PRSP) 12–16; power relations 12–13; regulatory patterns 12–14; representational power 14–16; structural adjustment policies 87
preferred creditors, Bretton Woods institutions as 48
prior actions 97, 124–26
priorities 145–48, 157, 211, 215–16
private entities: influence 47–48; International Finance Corporation 43; replacement of government 85
privatization 136, 141, 146, 193, 198
problematising poverty 37–38
process of accessing finance 204
programme: conditionalities 96, 97–98, 109–10, 123–24; policies, practices and programmes, dissonance between 196–98; reviews 97, 123–24
project financing 66–67
protests 76–77
public expenditure management (PEM) 147–50
public expenditure reviews (PERs) 148–49
public opinion 75–76
public sector reform 85, 136–37, 149–53

Qureshi, Asif 7

Rajagopal, Balakrishnan 8
Rapid Credit Facility (RCF) (IMF) 3
Raustiala, Kal 213
Reagan, Ronald 63

recognition of statehood 28
reconstruction of state 87–88, 171–75, 213
redistributive justice 214
reform 67–68: accountability 213; conditionalities 101–2, 106–7, 117–18, 121–29, 135, 150; constitutional reform 170, 206; embedded economic reforms 138–40; foreclosing international reform 213–18; institutions of state 4–5, 35, 121, 126, 135, 148, 150–53, 174; internal constitutions of nation states 206; internalisation of politics of reform 135; nation states 134–66; ownership 135; participatory policymaking 170; policy 101–2, 106–7, 117–18, 121–29, 135, 150; procedural reform 3; public sector 85, 136–37, 149–53; regulation 213; Washington Consensus 138–40
regulation 10–14, 17, 87, 101–10, 138–42, 205–13, 220–21
rehabilitation of the state in developing countries 125, 134–66, 170, 173
Renard, Robrecht 183
representational power 14–16
reserve tranche, borrowing beyond the 104–5
resistance 77–79, 87, 170, 187–89, 215–16, 221–24
restraint, mechanisms of 211, 220
reviews 71, 148–49, 216
Rich, Bruce 73
right to development, UN declaration on 216–18
rubber-stamping legislatures 190–91
rule of law 30, 136–37
Rustomjee, Cyrus 81

Said, Edward 37
sanctions for non-compliance 96, 98, 101, 103–4, 109–10, 153
Sano, Hans-Otto 173
Santos, Boaventura de Sousa 221–22
Save the Children 85–86
Schattan Coelho, Vera 221–22
Scheurich, James L 13
Seattle meeting 1999 2, 78
self-determination 24
Sgard, Jerome 116–17
Shihata, Ibrahim 107–8, 119
social contract, PRSPs as new 3–5
social exclusion 70, 213, 218
social services 157
socio-political changes 170
soft law 17, 106, 116, 119–20, 127
sovereignty *see* state sovereignty
stabilisation programmes 2, 74
stakeholders 176, 180–81, 186, 188, 198–99
standby arrangements 3, 44, 103–5
state fragmentation 82–86
state institutions: accountability 148–50, 165; administrative space 209–10; categories of law 17; conditionalities 121, 126–27, 152–53, 164; Country Policy and Institutional Assessment 114–15; development financing 7; epistemic community 72; globalisation 27, 208–10; governance 27; Joint Staff Advisory Note (JSAN) guidelines 153; legitimacy 72–75; partnership 159; policing individualisation 141; policymaking 72; postcolonial international law 27; postwar legal order, foundation of 27; process, PRSPs as institutional process 16; reform 4–5, 35, 121, 126, 135, 148, 150–53, 174; rehabilitation of the state 135, 141; standard systems, institutionalization of 207–8; technologies, development and implementation of new 27; Western state 165; Wolfensohn legacy 72–74 *see also* Bretton Woods institutions; particular institutions
state sovereignty 23–27, 30, 40–41, 68–69, 83, 98, 127, 141, 211
states *see* nation states; state institutions
Stewart, Miranda 47, 70
Stiglitz, Joseph 73–74, 78
Structural Adjustment Participatory Review International Network (SAPRIN) 77
structural adjustment policies (SAPs): autonomy, circumscription of 25; Charter of Economic Rights and Duties of States (UN) 62; conditionalities 46–47, 70; debt repayments 64; decentralisation 85; Declaration and Program of Action of New International Order 62; design 83; development financing 61–64; difference, dynamics of 87; discipline 61, 62–64, 82; economic growth 64; economic liberalism 63; economic

rationalism 69; Enhanced Structural Adjustment Facility 71; epistemic communities 69, 71–72; fragmentation of states 82–85; globalisation 61–62; government, erosion of 84–85; International Monetary Fund 1, 63–64; legitimacy 61–64, 72, 86; limitations 61–64, 70, 87–88; nationalism 62; neoliberalism 61–62, 85; New International Economic Order 62; non-governmental organisations 77–78; policy 70–72, 82–83, 87–88, 214; power 87; public sector reform 85; state fragmentation 82; Structural Adjustment Participatory Review International Network (SAPRIN) 77; universal targets and indicators 145; Washington Consensus 65–66; World Bank 1, 63–64
structural Marxism 15–16
subaltern cosmopolitanism 221
substance of accessing finance 205
surveillance work 39–40
sustainable development 222
Svensson, Jakob 70–71
Szablowski, David 17

Tanzania 144–45, 152, 158, 179, 181–82, 186, 190–91, 195
targets 145–46, 159, 164
tariff rates, reduction or elimination of 47
Tarullo, Daniel K 28–29, 30
tax reform 47
technical assistance 149, 159, 188–89, 192
technologies: biopower 218–22; discipline 218–22; governance 27, 184–89; new technologies, development and implementation of new 27; postcolonial international law 27
technologies of self 165
Thatcher, Margaret 63
Toye, John 66
tranche release conditions 97, 110, 223
tranching, front-loading and 123–24
transparency 124, 163, 194, 215
triggers 97, 120
trusts 3, 105–6, 154–55

Uganda 74–75, 80, 125, 144, 152, 180, 182, 191, 195
UN Charter 24
UN Development Agency, marginalisation of 36
United Kingdom 74–75, 98, 156
United Nations (UN) 31, 35–36, 62, 216–18, 222–23
United States 33–34, 72–73, 98, 117
universalisation 26–27, 51, 66–68, 145–46, 163–65, 182, 208–9

Vietnam 181–82, 185–87, 191
voting power in Bretton Woods institutions 32–34, 81
vulnerability due to class, gender or race 70

Wallerstein, Immanuel 29
Washington Consensus: Bretton Woods institutions 61, 63–68, 74–75; conditionalities 123, 127–29; crisis lending 65; discipline 206; economic reform 138–40; Enhanced Structural Adjustment Facility (ESAF) 65, 71; fragmentation of states 82; globalisation 1, 64–65; governance 136, 138; legitimacy 61, 63–68; ownership 128–29; participation 66, 188, 193, 198; policy-based finance 63; policy design 214; policymaking 188, 193, 198; Poverty Reduction and Growth Facility (PRGF) 65, 205; regulative capacity of the state, reinventing the 138–40; rehabilitation of the state 138–40, 141; structural adjustment policies (SAPs) 65–66; universal framework for disbursement 66–68; universal targets and indicators 145; universalisation of state policies 208–9; World Bank 63, 73–74
Weber, Max 165, 177
Western state, construction of the 165
Westphalian model 52
Wolfensohn, James 70–74, 77
Wood, Angela 136, 141–42
World Bank 2–8: agendas, appropriation of outside 87; civil society 77; compensating loss 48; conditionalities 95–97, 100–102, 106–20, 126; cooptation of outside elements 87; Country Assistance Strategy 113–14, 205; culture 7–8, 73; decision-making 110; definition xiv; development financing 65–66, 70–71; Development Policy Loan (DPL) 66; economic and sector work (ESW) 149; governance 23–24, 137–38; IBRD Articles of

Agreement 43; integrated development model 73; International Finance Corporation 43; international law 7; lobbying 70; Medium-Term Expenditure Framework 147, 205; Meltzer Commission 73; Multilateral Investment Guarantee Agency 43; non-governmental organizations 70, 73, 77; Operational Policy 65–66, 100–101; organisational structure 7–8; ownership 139; participation 87–88; policy 70, 73–74, 143–45; political currency of change 74–75; postcolonial international law 23–24; Poverty Reduction Strategy Credits (PRSC) 3; prior actions 125; private capital flows, loans supportive of 43; public expenditure reviews 148–49; special circumstances exception 107–8; structural adjustment policies 63–64, 73; United Kingdom election 1997 74; United States 72–73; Washington Consensus 63, 73–74; Wolfensohn legacy 70–74, 77 *see also* Bretton Woods institutions
World Trade Organization (WTO) 2, 47, 77–78
World Vision 85–86, 186

Yackee, Jason 117

Zambia 177, 181
Zigler, Andreas 7

Taylor & Francis

eBooks

FOR LIBRARIES

ORDER YOUR **FREE 30 DAY** INSTITUTIONAL TRIAL TODAY!

Over 22,000 eBook titles in the Humanities, Social Sciences, STM and Law from some of the world's leading imprints.

Choose from a range of subject packages or create your own!

Benefits for you

- Free MARC records
- COUNTER-compliant usage statistics
- Flexible purchase and pricing options

Benefits for your user

- Off-site, anytime access via Athens or referring URL
- Print or copy pages or chapters
- Full content search
- Bookmark, highlight and annotate text
- Access to thousands of pages of quality research at the click of a button

For more information, pricing enquiries or to order a free trial, contact your local online sales team.

UK and Rest of World: **online.sales@tandf.co.uk**

US, Canada and Latin America: **e-reference@taylorandfrancis.com**

www.ebooksubscriptions.com

ALPSP Award for BEST eBOOK PUBLISHER 2009 Finalist

Taylor & Francis eBooks
Taylor & Francis Group

A flexible and dynamic resource for teaching, learning and research.